Royal Renegades

Also by Linda Porter

Crown of Thistles:
The Fatal Inheritance of Mary Queen of Scots

Mary Tudor:
The First Queen

Katherine the Queen:
The Remarkable Life of Katherine Parr

LINDA PORTER

Royal Renegades

*The Children of Charles I and the
English Civil Wars*

MACMILLAN

First published 2016 by Macmillan
an imprint of Pan Macmillan
20 New Wharf Road, London N1 9RR
Associated companies throughout the world
www.panmacmillan.com

ISBN 978-1-4472-6754-6

1 3 5 7 9 8 6 4 2

A CIP catalogue record for this book is available from the British Library.

Map artwork by ML Design
Typeset by Ellipsis Digital Limited, Glasgow
Printed and bound by CPI Group (UK) Ltd, Croydon, CR0 4YY

Visit **www.panmacmillan.com** to read more about all our books
and to buy them. You will also find features, author interviews and
news of any author events, and you can sign up for e-newsletters
so that you're always first to hear about our new releases.

For Emma and Phil

Contents

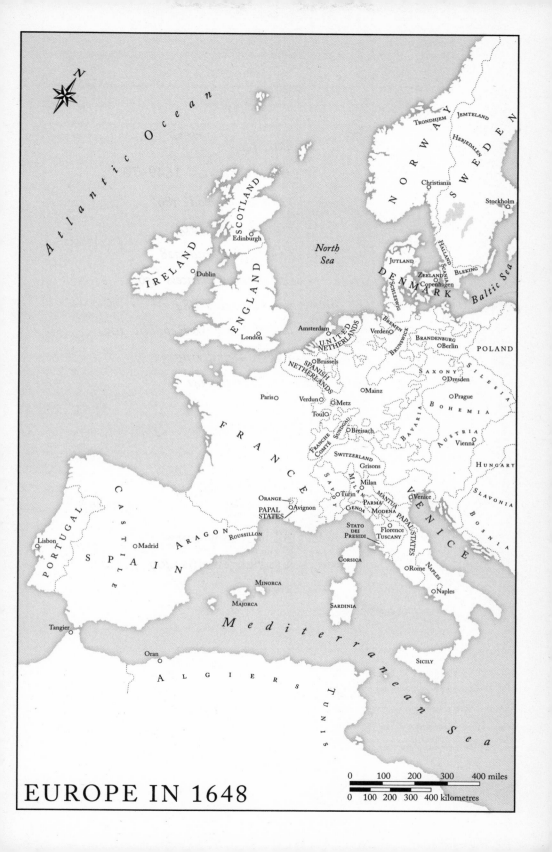

EUROPE IN 1648

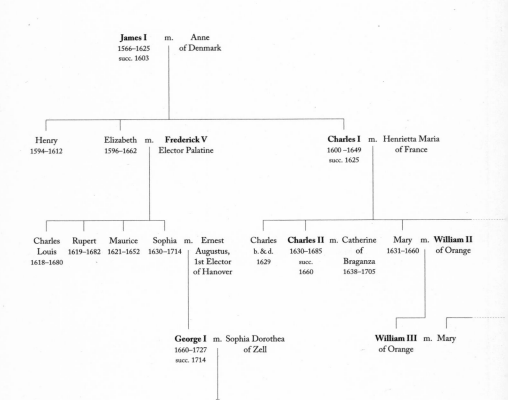

James I m. Anne
1566–1625   of Denmark
succ. 1603

Henry   Elizabeth m. Frederick V   Charles I m. Henrietta Maria
1594–1612   1596–1662   Elector Palatine   1600–1649   of France
                                                                     succ. 1625

Charles   Rupert   Maurice   Sophia m. Ernest   Charles   Charles II m. Catherine   Mary   m. William II
Louis   1619–1682   1621–1652   1630–1714   Augustus,   b. & d.   1630–1685   of   1631–1660   of Orange
1618–1680   1st Elector   1629   succ.   Braganza
                                              of Hanover   1660   1638–1705

George I m. Sophia Dorothea   William III m. Mary
1660–1727   of Zell   of Orange
succ. 1714

House of Stuart

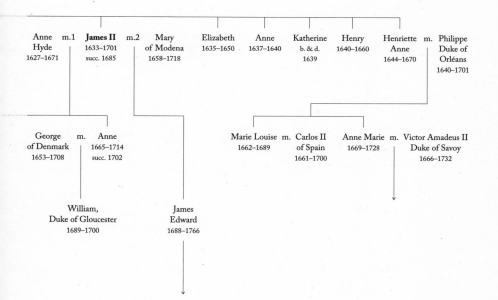

Anne Hyde 1627–1671 m.1 **James II** 1633–1701 succ. 1685 m.2 Mary of Modena 1658–1718 | Elizabeth 1635–1650 | Anne 1637–1640 | Katherine b. & d. 1639 | Henry 1640–1660 | Henriette Anne 1644–1670 m. Philippe Duke of Orléans 1640–1701

George of Denmark 1653–1708 m. Anne 1665–1714 succ. 1702 | Marie Louise 1662–1689 m. Carlos II of Spain 1661–1700 | Anne Marie 1669–1728 m. Victor Amadeus II Duke of Savoy 1666–1732

William, Duke of Gloucester 1689–1700 | James Edward 1688–1766

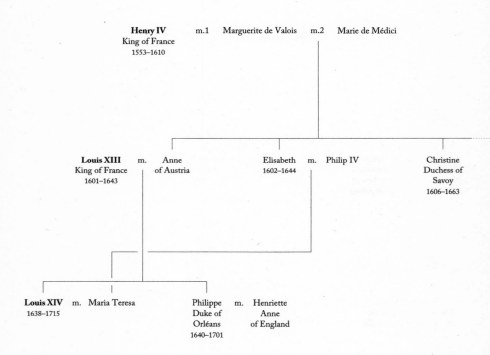

Henry IV   m.1   Marguerite de Valois   m.2   Marie de Médici
King of France
1553–1610

Louis XIII   m.   Anne   Elisabeth   m.   Philip IV   Christine
King of France   of Austria   1602–1644   Duchess of
1601–1643   Savoy
                                                                                   1606–1663

Louis XIV   m.   Maria Teresa   Philippe   m.   Henriette
1638–1715   Duke of   Anne
                                        Orléans   of England
                                        1640–1701

House of Bourbon

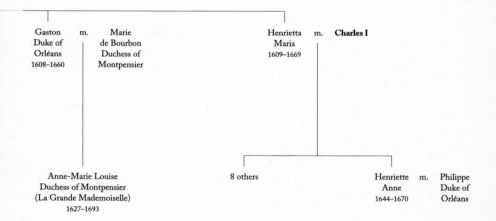

Gaston
Duke of
Orléans
1608–1660

m.

Marie
de Bourbon
Duchess of
Montpensier

Henrietta
Maria
1609–1669

m.

Charles I

Anne-Marie Louise
Duchess of Montpensier
(La Grande Mademoiselle)
1627–1693

8 others

Henriette
Anne
1644–1670

m.

Philippe
Duke of
Orléans

Prologue

Dover, 13 June 1625

He was looking at her feet. She was not quite as short as reports had led him to expect. Could she be wearing heels? French women were renowned for their attention to appearance and detail. They were far less restricted than their counterparts at the stifling Spanish court, where he had gone, in person, to seek his first bride. And this girl was no bashful infanta. The self-possessed teenager who stood before him followed his gaze, speaking up for herself immediately. 'Sire,' she said, raising the hem of her dress, 'I stand upon mine own feet. I have no help by art. Thus high am I, and neither higher nor lower.' Her forthrightness was in contrast to her opening words to him, the carefully considered proprieties of international diplomacy and wifely duty. She had come to this country 'to be used and commanded by you',[1] she assured him. Little did she know that he was far from confident himself.

How could he be? The twenty-five-year-old monarch always known to his father as 'Baby Charles', the boy who could not walk until he was four because of rickets, who had become the unexpected heir when his gifted elder brother died so suddenly of typhoid, had served a long apprenticeship under the watchful gaze of his clever but unfathomable father, James, the sixth Scottish king to bear that name but the first of England. Now, after just three months on the throne, kingship was as new to this spare, short young man (he was only five feet four inches tall) as the role of queen consort was to this even more diminutive girl of fifteen. Yet the excitement and nervousness that he had felt when he left Canterbury that morning to meet his bride for the first time was alleviated by her winsome mixture of assertion and submission. He took her aside into a private apartment, away from the gaze of their courtiers, so that they could have some time alone together before facing the world as a couple.

There the stress and unfamiliarity of her situation suddenly unnerved her. She confided that she was afraid she would make mistakes and asked him not to be angry with her if she gave offence unintentionally. Acknowledging that her youth and ignorance of English customs might cause difficulties, she asked that he would advise and correct her himself, rather than put her through the humiliation of being upbraided by an intermediary. The king was charmed. He reassured her that she had not 'fallen into the hands of strangers'. God had sent her to be his wife.

The little queen had heard that before, from the priests and nuns who had instructed her in Paris and, most recently, from her ailing mother when they parted at Amiens in northern France. Marie de Médici, the French queen mother, exhorted her youngest daughter, in a letter she was to keep with her, never to forget that 'you are a daughter of the Church' and to pray daily for her husband's conversion to Catholicism. The king of England saw God's intentions differently. But for now he embraced her warmly and, her confidence restored, they emerged together so that she could introduce her attendants and followers. There were many of them, for Henriette-Marie de Bourbon had arrived with a retinue worthy of her past as a French princess and her future as queen of England, the wife of Charles Stuart. She would lose the French version of her name quickly, discovering that one of the many disquieting things about her new situation was that no one, including her husband, could take her name seriously. He wanted

her to be known as Queen Mary but she has come down to us as
Henrietta Maria, one of England's most notorious queens consort.

The precedents were not encouraging. The last French queen
consort of England had been Margaret of Anjou, Shakespeare's
'she-wolf of France', whose desperate attempts to hold the Lan-
castrian throne for her mentally ill husband, Henry VI, had caused
his Yorkist opponents to characterize her as an unnatural terma-
gant during the Wars of the Roses. Commentators in 1625 stayed
politely quiet on this point, but there was no escaping the controversy caused by Henrietta Maria's religion. The marriage of a
Catholic princess to a Protestant monarch was unprecedented in
Europe. Pope Urban VIII, whose dispensation was needed, saw in
the proposed match the opportunity to alleviate the condition of
English Catholics, viewed as an oppressed minority by the papacy.
Hopes were even raised of the more distant possibility of restoring
England to the old faith. The stipulations of the marriage treaty,
signed in Paris on 10 November 1624, meant that the princess
brought with her a dowry of 800,000 crowns, which was most
welcome, and strict commitments regarding her religious rights
and those of her children and household, which were not. Suspen-
sion of the penal laws against Catholics was agreed but, given
parliamentary opposition, was never, in reality, going to happen.
Furthermore, the English had given help over many years to the
Huguenots, the French Protestants. The possibility of friction was
real even before Henrietta set foot in her new country.

She did, though, definitely want to be queen of England and
she had grown impatient during the protracted diplomatic negotiations, despite the charm and encouragement of James Hay, earl
of Carlisle, the able Scot sent to talk terms with the chief minister
of France, Cardinal Richelieu. Whatever the challenges, Henrietta
wanted and expected a crown. In this she was very much her
parents' daughter. Not that she had known her father, Henry IV
of France, the Protestant king of Navarre who had been heir to
the throne as the Valois line faded. He had brought to an end the
vicious blood-letting of half a century of religious warfare in

France in the wonderfully pragmatic declaration that Paris was 'well worth a Mass'. One of France's most flamboyant and capable kings, his strong hold on the country was brutally ended by the knife of his assassin, François Ravaillac, a deranged former monk who got into his carriage on the afternoon of 14 May 1610, stabbing him twice. The king, who is said to have had premonitions of disaster, but was probably just suffering the cares of state, did not survive.

So the regency of a shocked country passed to his wife, the Italian Queen Marie de Médici, daughter of a famous and still very wealthy house. Despite the fact that she had borne him three sons and two daughters, the couple were seldom on good terms, passing long periods when they would not speak to one another. Henry was twice Marie's age, hopelessly given to philandering (there was a growing brood of illegitimate children by various mistresses) and though he was initially pleased by her blonde buxomness and penchant for flashing diamonds, her looks were already on the wrong side of ample when they married. By the time her last child, Henrietta Maria, was born in November 1609, Marie had long since become, in her husband's mind, a fat and fretting irritant who was always badgering him about his mistresses and the fact that, ten years after their marriage, she was still uncrowned. Henry IV publicly acknowledged that he found her boring. Yet he finally gave in about the coronation, and Marie was crowned at the abbey of Saint-Denis, north of Paris, the day before his murder. Despite her constant moaning, it can hardly have been the outcome she had wished for so soon after her day of triumph. Terrified and confused, the royal children spent the night of 14 May under armed guard in the Louvre.

Their mother obtained the regency on behalf of her son while the rest of Henry's family, including his illegitimate offspring, grew up together, mostly at Saint-Germain-en-Laye, with occasional visits to the other splendid palaces for state occasions. However, over-reliance on Italian favourites and poor political judgement, as well as growing estrangement from the young

Louis XIII, saw Marie overthrown in 1617. She left in disgrace for the castle of Blois in the Loire, taking Henrietta Maria with her. It would be several years before they returned and Marie agreed, reluctantly, to share power on her son's behalf with the new rising star, Cardinal Richelieu.

Henrietta Maria looked much more like her father than her mother but his death so early in her life meant that Marie de Médici would have the greater influence on her. A Catholic who liked ritual and devotion, the dowager queen made sure that religious instruction was a central part of her daughter's life. Her spiritual education was supervised by the Carmelite nuns of the convent in the Faubourg Saint-Jacques. It would have lifelong associations for the Bourbon princess. But so, too, did her mother's love of building, of patronizing artists,[2] of jewels, theatre, music and dance. The girl who arrived in the hastily refurbished suite of rooms made ready for her in midsummer 1625 had become accustomed to sumptuous surroundings and lavish entertainments. The French courtiers accompanying her were consequently sniffy about Dover castle and it was, in truth, still more of a fortress than a palace, but Charles had inspected the work there himself to make sure it was fit for a queen of England.

She, however, was very clear in her French identity as a Bourbon princess, reinforced by the most splendid of weddings in Nôtre Dame on 8 May 1625. Charles was not present at this ceremony, for reasons of both religion and state. The duke of Chevreuse stood in for him as Henrietta, flanked by her brothers, Louis XIII and Gaston, duke of Orléans, entered the cathedral. It was a brilliant spectacle, attended by all the princes of the blood and their wives. At its centre, Henrietta, dressed in a robe of cloth of gold and silver embroidered with the French national flower, the lily, sparkled in diamonds and precious stones, much as her husband's grandmother, Mary Queen of Scots, had done when she married the dauphin Francis more than sixty years earlier. The various phases of the ceremonial took many hours, a test of endurance to which Henrietta rose superbly. Feasting and festivities followed until, on 24 May, George Villiers, duke of Buckingham, favourite of the old king James and now of his son, arrived to take the bride back to her new kingdom. The French court did not like his demeanour, and his embarrassing flirtation with Anne of Austria, Louis XIII's wife, threatened to dent Anglo–French relations severely at what should have been a time of mutual rejoicing.

Detained at the French coast for several days by adverse weather, Henrietta finally set sail on 22 June. Then the crossing, in marked contrast to later voyages she made across the Channel, was calm and Dover was reached in seven hours. Shortly after she set foot on English soil, the rain began to fall. It had not stopped when Charles arrived the next morning, eager to meet his bride.

Whether she could adapt to the demands of becoming an English queen was not yet clear but her French-speaking husband seemed kind, even if he was a heretic and presided over an inferior court. It was just as well he spoke her language, as Henrietta's education had not included English, or much of any linguistic or academic study beyond reading and writing. Aside from these early, encouraging exchanges, she could only rely on the reports she had received in France from Charles's ambassadors to form an opinion of him. She already knew there would be much to learn.

The reaction of Charles I to this tiny girl with her dark curls and the frankness of youth was, initially, one of relief. But it was later reported that, as the royal couple prepared to leave for Canterbury, an unseemly squabble took place over who should accompany the queen in the royal coach. In one version, Madame de Saint-Georges, the heavily pregnant childhood friend of Henrietta and the chief lady of her bedchamber, elbowed her way past Buckingham's sister to take what she saw as her rightful place by her mistress's side. This was not the case, and the dispute was subsequently embroidered by French diplomats who disliked the duke of Buckingham.[3] Whatever her private feelings, the queen did not challenge English court etiquette and rode in the carriage with her husband and the Buckingham ladies.

After a reception in the Great Hall of St Augustine's Abbey in Canterbury, the king and queen were prepared by their attendants for the wedding night. Henrietta's upbringing could scarcely have prepared her for the physical side of marriage, though the duchess of Chevreuse had perhaps given her some idea of what to expect beforehand. We know little of Charles's previous sexual experience but with the dashing Buckingham as a constant companion he can hardly have been ignorant. When he arrived in Henrietta's bedchamber he dismissed the servants and bolted all seven locks on the door. The next morning he seemed in good spirits, though Henrietta, who apparently found the experience uncomfortable, was more subdued.

When the couple arrived in London, to an enthusiastic greeting from the citizens despite the prevalence of the plague, he took Henrietta to the palace of Whitehall. It was not the Louvre, though it was hardly spartan. There she found herself on view to the great and the good of her new country for the first time. An observer 'perceived her to be a most absolute delicate lady . . . much enlivened by her radiant and sparkling black eye.' And he noted that she treated her servants and women in a manner that was 'sweet and humble', as well as 'mild and gracious'. In fact, the greatest pity was 'that she wanted the knowledge of the true religion'.[4] Thus was the queen's Catholicism marked out as a source of regret from the outset. But for the king, this was only one of many difficulties which would ensue and it was not the most personally galling. Charles I soon had cause to wish that his wife would extend her sweetness and humility to include him. Instead, he was to find that his wife's determination to stand on her own feet and to maintain the observance of the religion in which she had been raised was a potent, disruptive force, which would have a major impact on their relationship, their family and the politics of England.

Part One

'Gather ye rosebuds while ye may'

ROBERT HERRICK

1625–40

CHAPTER ONE

Trouble and Strife

*'Thank God she is so careful of herself that I have no need to
use other authority than that of love.'*

Charles I to Marie de Médici, 29 May 1630

CHARLES I'S LETTER TO HIS mother-in-law alludes to the
serious difficulties which beset the marriage in its early years.
These were not just the result of a clash of very different personalities but rather of national and international pressures that
threatened to destabilize the relationship and the interference of
individuals, both English and French, who made matters worse.
The king was a reticent man but in his private life, as in his
approach to government, he was very sensitive that his authority
should not be undermined. Nine years older than Henrietta
Maria, Charles's patience with his young wife's defence of her
beliefs, and her dependence on the French household who exercised a suffocating influence over her, was short-lived. But he
was partly to blame for the distance that soon grew between the
royal couple, as affairs of state and the need to recall parliament
distracted him. Meanwhile, his favourite, George Villiers, duke of
Buckingham, manoeuvred to minimize any influence the queen
might begin to have over Charles and tried to foist ladies of his
family on her as attendants. Moved from one royal palace to
another to avoid the plague that would not go away, Henrietta felt

confused and overlooked. The English seemed to have no intention of introducing greater toleration of Catholics and relations
between France and England deteriorated in the face of English
support for the Huguenots, the French Protestants besieged in
La Rochelle by the forces of Henrietta's brother, Louis XIII.

The queen, for her part, made little attempt to adjust to her
situation. Filled with the warnings of those around her that
England was a hostile country full of heretics, she retreated into
her French identity, relying for succour on the *piété dévote* of the
Catholicism in which she had been raised and the priests and con-
fessors who continually exhorted her to hold firm in her beliefs,
while not giving an inch to the customs of the country of which
she was now queen. After twelve months in England, she still
could not speak a word of its language. Her refusal to attend her
husband's coronation in February 1626, or to be crowned herself
by a Protestant archbishop, was not merely an insult to her husband but to the English people as a whole, and one that they never
forgot. Yet Cardinal Richelieu, the brilliant politician who con-
trolled the French government, was not pleased with this situation.
A coronation confirmed a queen's position and the legitimacy of
her children. This defiant Bourbon princess was the first queen
consort in English history to refuse to be crowned. Given these
difficulties, the suggestions of the French ambassador that Henrietta might be crowned by a Catholic minister outside Westminster
Abbey were not just unacceptable, but pathetic.

Charles had other, more intensely personal reasons for resenting the influence of his wife's religious advisers. Their insistence
that she abstain from sexual relations on the numerous saints' days
and religious festivals of the Catholic calendar frustrated a man
who clearly needed physical intimacy and who was also anxious
for an heir. Perhaps he did not work as hard as he might have
done in the first, fraught year of their relationship to forge a
strong bond between them but Henrietta Maria's attitude seemed
to strike at the heart of his authority, both as husband and ruler.
He could not stomach her contradictions of him in public, often

over inconsequential things such as whether it was raining or not. This kind of pettiness amazed and confused the young queen but it was naive of her to assume that it would go unremarked. To her credit, she tried to make amends and there were periods when the quarrelling ceased as the couple strove to move forward together with more understanding and tolerance. Nor was Henrietta invisible at court. The recriminations between the newlyweds were eagerly reported by the French at the time and especially by Henrietta's ill-natured and self-serving chamberlain, the count of Tillières, but they overlook the fact that the queen, however much threatened by the pre-eminence of Buckingham and distressed by her husband's attempts to replace her French ladies with English ones, had begun to create a role for herself by the time of her first Christmas in England, when she had only just celebrated her sixteenth birthday. Always fond of masques and theatricals, which were an established part of English as well as French court life, only a few months after her marriage the young queen began her involvement in what was to become a notable feature of the years of her husband's personal rule. During the winter of 1625–6 she prepared a French *pastorale*, a simple musical play evoking rural life. The scenery and costumes were designed by the famous theatre designer and architect Inigo Jones and the production was presented by the queen and her ladies at the end of February 1626. In her first eighteen months in England she also presented three masques. Evidently not all of her time was consumed by quarrelling with her husband. These theatricals were well received by Italian commentators, though the more radical English Protestants were dismayed at the idea of a queen acting on the stage.[1] Clearly, Charles did not disapprove of all of his wife's activities.

Yet neither he nor Henrietta seemed able to sustain a more tranquil approach to one another as the first anniversary of their wedding drew near. One of their worst rows took place in bed, when they were discussing appointments to the lands the queen had been given as part of her marriage settlement. She wished to make her own nominations but Charles clearly did not trust her to make appropriate choices. Henrietta bridled. 'Then she bade me plainly take my lands to myself; for, if she had no power to put in whom she would in those places, she would have neither lands nor houses of me; but bade me give her what I thought fit in pension.' Shocked by this impertinence, Charles added: 'I bade her remember to whom she spoke.' After she had said her piece, the king blamed her French household for encouraging her disaffection. He would, he said, 'put them to rights'.[2] It was a threat that the queen failed to take seriously. She was, however, greatly troubled by the reports of her bad behaviour that were finding their way back to her mother in France.

The king was deeply disturbed by his wife's failure to adapt to her role as queen of England. She seemed unable to find a place for him in her heart and those around her were encouraging her to behave like a French exile at his court. He particularly blamed Madame de Saint-Georges – 'Mamie', as Henrietta always affectionately referred to her childhood friend – and the bishop of Mende, the most senior ecclesiastical figure in the queen's retinue. Mende was a young aristocrat on the make, who had hoped he would be the person to crown Henrietta as queen of England. Despite the diplomatic sensitivities inherent in making an enemy of him – Mende had strong personal connections to Cardinal Richelieu – Charles was ever more determined to break his hold over Henrietta.

Perhaps the king had never sufficiently acknowledged his wife's youth or fully appreciated the difficulties her Catholicism would bring. Chapels had been set up for the private worship of the queen and her entourage in all the royal palaces and although some were well appointed, others were initially rather makeshift affairs, which increased the resentment of the queen's priests. Exactly one year after Henrietta's arrival, Charles's patience with his wife's entourage had reached breaking point. When he chose to act decisively, he was not a man to do things by half measures. He felt his marriage was on the rocks. On 12 July 1626 he poured out the bile of a year's resentment in a letter to Buckingham,

whose own role in the difficulties of the couple's relationship may
have been overstated, but who had undoubtedly wanted to ensure
that Henrietta did not come between him and Charles.

> Thus having had so long patience with the disturbance of
> that which should be one of my greatest contentments, I can
> no longer suffer those, that I know to be the cause and
> fomenters of these humours, to be about my wife any longer
> . . . Therefore you shall tell my brother, the French King, as
> likewise his mother, that this being an action of so much
> necessity, I doubt not but he will be satisfied with it; espe-
> cially as he hath done the like himself, not staying until he
> had so much reason.

This was a reference to Louis XIII's dismissal of his wife Anne
of Austria's Spanish servants, an action which caused temporary
uproar in the French court, though the course of the two marriages would turn out very differently.

Anne of Austria's dismay was nothing to that of her sister-in-
law. Summoned to hear the king's decision about the fate of her
household, Henrietta impolitically declined, pleading that she had
a toothache and needed to stay in her apartments at St James's
Palace. The king would no longer be deterred by prevarication and
disobedience. He went to the queen's lodgings with several councillors and while he broke the news to his wife in private, the rest
of her French household were gathered together by his secretary,
Edward Conway, and told they must leave. They did not go
quietly. Gathering angrily in the courtyard below, they watched
as the distraught and appalled queen struggled with her husband
at the window. In her fury, Henrietta hit the panes of glass so hard
that they shattered and her hands bled. Restrained by Charles (the
nearest he ever came to offering her physical violence), Henrietta
wept and shook uncontrollably. But it was to no avail. Protesting
volubly, her attendants were removed to Somerset House. Still
they would not leave of their own accord, claiming they had been
unpaid for several months and had no money for the journey.

Their apparent devotion to their mistress did not stop some of them from pilfering items from her trousseau, very little of which was left after their eventual departure. In early August, infuriated by their refusal to depart, Charles ordered Buckingham, by then returned from his diplomatic mission to France, to 'send all the French away tomorrow out of the town. If you can, by fair means (but stick not long in disputing), otherwise force them away; driving them away like so many wild beasts, until you have shipped them; and so the devil go with them!'[3]

Henrietta's initial reaction to the forcible removal of her French household was a flood of tears and a refusal to eat. At this, the very nadir of her marriage, she began at last to understand its significance. She was wedded to Charles and must remain that way; it was not some unpleasant episode from which she would emerge triumphant, with all the expectations she had brought with her from France vindicated. Her husband had high standards but he did not yet know how to love her. Too many others had come between them and their mutual obstinacy made matters worse. The queen wrote in desperation to her mother: 'Consider that I am your daughter and the most afflicted there be in the world. If you do not take pity on me, I am in despair.'[4] Yet however much she may have contemplated the end of her marriage and hoped that her mother would wave a magic wand to return her to the happier days of her childhood at Saint-Germain-en-Laye, Henrietta Maria was England's queen. There was no going back.

In reality, she was less isolated than has sometimes been supposed. She had been left with more than a dozen French attendants in her chamber and a considerable number of lesser servants, including her tailor and kitchen staff. Nor did the expulsion of the majority of her household bring about a rupture with France. Charles and his advisers had gauged France's reaction correctly; Louis XIII could hardly criticize an action that he himself had taken in his own marriage and Henrietta's diplomatic significance was not lost on either country, surviving even the war of 1627–9, when the English supported French Protestant rebels in the west of France. Henrietta continued her involvement in court entertainments and though there was an eventual thaw in relations with her husband, the relationship was still bumpy. A year after the French household had been booted out of England, Charles wrote to Buckingham: 'I cannot omit to tell you that my wife and I were never better together; she upon this action of yours [a reference to Buckingham landing on the Isle of Rhè, opposite La Rochelle] showing herself so loving to me, by her discretion on all occasions, that it makes us all wonder and esteem her.'[5] Henrietta's discretion was not entirely uniform, however, and neither was her husband's tact. She returned to the question of appointments to her lands one more time, perhaps hoping that submitting to Charles in other matters might have strengthened her hand in this connection. It had not. When she pointed out that Queen Anna, Charles's mother, was allowed to nominate her own officers, Charles was dismissive. His mother, he said, was 'a different sort of woman'. When Henrietta tartly pointed out that there was, indeed, a difference between a Bourbon princess and a Danish one, Charles reminded her coldly that she was the youngest of Henry IV's daughters and had only brought a simple dowry with her. She was therefore not of much account.

The arrival of a new ambassador from France, the experienced and eminently diplomatic Marshal de Bassompierre, in September 1627, seems to have helped both husband and wife approach their relationship in a more mature fashion. The king was struggling with recalcitrant parliaments and their increasing insistence that, if he wanted more money for his foreign policy he must accept what he viewed as a reduction in the royal prerogative, a clash of wills they never satisfactorily resolved. Meanwhile, the hostility to Buckingham and his unsuccessful overseas ventures, which were both costly and humiliating, grew. Against this contentious backdrop, Henrietta began to learn English. She also accepted the Villiers women into her court circle and looked for new friends among the women of the English nobility. The chief of these was

Lucy Hay, countess of Carlisle, the wife of the man who had negotiated her marriage. The countess was a Percy by birth, a family with a long tradition of opposition to the English Crown, but she was ambitious, witty, intelligent and attractive. For a while she was Buckingham's mistress, and he may have viewed her as a means of extending his influence over Henrietta, while Lucy and her husband were eager to ingratiate themselves with a young and insecure queen. Henrietta Maria and the countess had little in common, but in the same way that her husband was reliant on the racy duke of Buckingham, Henrietta, for many years (despite the occasional falling out), was close to the vibrant and self-serving Lucy, who is credited with introducing her to make-up.[6]

Thus matters improved in the royal marriage but both parties were still subject to outside influences and they spent considerable periods apart. Marie de Médici fretted about the distractions of the English court, pleading with her daughter to 'continue your exercises of piety, and do not listen to those who wish to divert you from them, under the pretext of gaiety. Their counsel is pernicious and will bring to you terrible miseries . . .'[7] Charles's political difficulties, meanwhile, showed no sign of abating and Buckingham's defeat at La Rochelle exacerbated popular resentment against a man who was consistently regarded as recklessly ambitious. And all this while, Charles was acutely aware that there was no child of his marriage. His heir remained his beloved sister, Elizabeth of Bohemia, herself an exile and victim of the Thirty Years' War in Europe, a conflict that showed no sign of easing and into which Charles, like his father, was reluctant to be drawn.

Henrietta Maria's life was changed by the thrust of a dagger into Buckingham's body in August 1628. His assassin was a discontented soldier, John Felton, whose grievances over lack of advancement and the arrears of his pay appear to have tipped him over the edge into temporary insanity. Whatever Felton's true motives, the cheap dagger he had bought was well aimed. As the duke prepared to leave the Greyhound Inn, where he was staying in Portsmouth, Felton stabbed him through the left breast.

Mortally wounded, there was nothing anyone could do to save Buckingham. He had been preparing to ride to meet the king, who was staying nearby, but he never arrived. Utterly broken by the unexpected tidings of the violent death of his closest confidant and friend, Charles fell on his bed weeping. Despite the extremity of his grief, he held a crisis meeting with his privy councillors at a very late hour. The next day, however, he passed alone.

Buckingham was unpopular with most of his contemporaries and has generally been given short shrift by historians. He was certainly a divisive figure and the fact that his military career was unsuccessful has tended to colour judgements of him. Yet while he seems to have gloried in his prominent status, playing up to his reputation as a larger-than-life figure who was profligate with money and with women, a corrupt man who abused the king's confidence, he was also committed to the Protestant cause and was, for the most part, a competent naval administrator.[8] Though he was clearly one of a number of impediments during the early years of the royal marriage, his role in the difficulties has been given undue influence by hostile French commentators.

When she learned of the news, Henrietta Maria was a hundred miles away at Wellingborough in Northamptonshire. It was dramatically conveyed to her in a letter from Lord Carleton, who described 'the screechings, tears and distractions' of the duchess of Buckingham at seeing the blood of her husband gushing from him.[9] Profoundly shocked, Henrietta acted with a tact and compassion that she had not previously exhibited. Her first thought was to comfort her own ladies-in-waiting, many of whom had connections to Buckingham, and her husband was most gratified when he learned of this. Then she hastened to support him. Charles was moved by her devotion, realizing at last that he could learn to love her for what she was, a lively, affectionate young woman who could brighten his existence, with whom he could share his innermost thoughts and in whose company he could relax. Thereafter, they became inseparable. Once the funeral was over, Charles was able to concentrate fully, for the first time in three years, on his wife. They left London and travelled in the country, hunting at Hampton Court and visiting friends. Charles did not neglect the business of government; indeed, he began to involve his wife more frequently in the wider sphere of politics, including consulting her on political appointments. Their affection for one another deepened into an abiding devotion. It was to be one of the closest marriages in English royal history and Charles embraced the chivalric aspect of his love for the queen in November 1628, riding in the joust to celebrate his wife's nineteenth birthday. By Christmas, Henrietta Maria was pregnant. She had become, and would always remain, his 'dear heart'.

CHAPTER TWO

A Loving Family

'On Saturday last ... the queen happily gave birth to a prince, about midday, and so the king sees his desires fulfilled and the succession established.'

The Venetian ambassador to the Doge, 7 June 1630

HENRIETTA MARIA'S FIRST pregnancy ended in the premature birth of a son in May 1629. It was apparent from the first that the child would not live and he was hastily baptized with his father's name, dying only two hours after he had come into the world. The royal couple were clearly distressed by this setback – the queen referred to it in a letter to her mother as 'my misfortune' – but also confident enough in their newly cemented relationship to hope for a better outcome in the future. Some Protestants, however, angry at the king's dissolution of yet another parliament in March 1629 and the proclamation that followed, which began with the ominous assertion that 'princes are not bound to give account of their actions', rejoiced at the Catholic queen's loss.

The disorderly scenes that accompanied the rejection of the House of Commons' Petition of Right and her husband's determination that he would now rule without parliament seem not to have affected the queen's health. Indeed, opposition to Charles made it all the more necessary to continue trying for an heir. Henrietta recovered well and during the autumn her craving for mussels signalled to the world that she was expecting again. Fearful that her daughter's liking for energetic exercise might have brought about the previous premature delivery, Marie de Médici sent a sedan chair, 'a beautiful chaise', described by Henrietta as 'handsomer than I deserve. Had I even no wish to go out in a chaise, that would make me go . . . I hope God will grant me the favour to go to the end of my term, and as to what depends upon me, I will take all possible care of myself.[1] The French queen mother's thoughtful gift was also acknowledged by Charles, who told her that his happiness depended on Henrietta's safe delivery, signing himself 'your very affectionate son-in-law and servant'. On 29 May in St James's Palace, at about noon, his optimism and Henrietta's fortitude were rewarded with the birth of another son. And it was clear from the outset that this one would live.

He was a large, swarthy child (the queen later called him her 'black boy'), a Bourbon rather than a Stuart in appearance, contented to the point of laziness, a trait he would never entirely lose. The baby was named Charles, like his dead elder brother, and christened in the Chapel Royal, in a ceremony where everyone wore white satin with crimson embroidery, a costume that harked back to the marriage of King James IV of Scotland and Margaret Tudor in 1503. The child's godfather was his uncle, Louis XIII of France, and his godmother was Marie de Médici, who, with characteristic extravagance, sent him diamonds. As the Corporation of London had also presented him with a gold cup worth £1,000 he was far wealthier as a newborn than he would be as an exile in his twenties. Though protocol required that neither of his parents was present at the ceremony, he was surrounded by the nobility of Great Britain and was later styled as prince of the same, though he was always known as the Prince of Wales. In fact, he was the first heir to the throne of England to be born in that country since 1537. It was as fine a start in life as could have been wished by his parents and Charles was determined to ensure that Henrietta continued to have the best of everything. Between 1629 and 1636 the furnishings in her bedchamber and the royal nursery nearby were replaced three times, at a cost of over £7,000, most of which was spent on sumptuous bed curtains and other textiles.[2]

Henrietta Maria wrote to her old friend, Mamie Saint-Georges, not forgotten despite the trauma of her removal to France four years earlier, with a charming and good-humoured description of the infant's progress: 'If my son knew how to talk, I think he would send you his compliments: he is so fat and so tall, that he is taken for a year old, and he is only four months: his teeth are already beginning to come: I will send you his portrait as soon as he is a little fairer, for at present he is so dark that I am ashamed of him.'[3] Yet the greater part of the letter concerned Henrietta's urgent requirement for more French petticoats and said nothing at all about her husband or the state of the country. The following year she wrote again to Mamie about her son, in less than flattering terms about his appearance: 'He is so ugly that I am ashamed of him, but his size and fatness supply the want of beauty. I wish you could see the gentleman, for he has no ordinary mien [expression]; he is so serious in all that he does, that I cannot help fancying him far wiser than myself.' Young Charles's solemnity and chubbiness were not her only preoccupations in 1631, for she also confided to Mamie Saint-Georges, 'I think I am on the increase again.'

Her suspicions were well founded. Eighteen months after the arrival of their first child, the royal couple were again parents, this time of a girl, Mary, the Princess Royal, born on 4 November 1631. The little princess was not as healthy as her strapping brother, however, and there were fears that she might not survive, resulting in a hasty and low-key christening by Archbishop Laud. 'Some apprehension there was at first,' it was reported, 'of danger in the child, whereof his majesty made a pious use, and caused her forthwith to be baptized by the name of Mary, without other solemnity than the rights of the Church.' The doubts surrounding the new princess's health were short-lived. She and Henrietta were soon said to be in perfect health, 'so nothing is wanting to make this joy entire, both to his majesty and the entire kingdom'.[4]

Other children followed regularly over the next nine years. James, duke of York, the second son, a fair, blue-eyed child and his mother's favourite, was born in November 1633. James's arrival was greeted with a christening ceremony that befitted his rank and role as the additional heir, coming close to that of Prince Charles in its solemnity and pomp. A procession of heralds, London aldermen, judges, knights of the Privy Council and various viscounts, barons and earls were in attendance, led by the great court figures of the queen's chamberlain, the earl of Dorset (whose wife was appointed lady governess to the royal nursery), the earl of Lindsey and the lord chamberlain, the earl of Pembroke. These were names mostly from the old noble families of Tudor times and their continuing influence represented a conscious effort on the part of Charles I to maintain links with the Elizabethan age, which seemed to him to represent the ideal of a relationship between monarchy, aristocracy and common people. Prince James, whose Catholicism would become a bugbear to his elder brother many years later, began life with godparents of unimpeachable Protestantism, the Dutch prince of Orange and the prince palatine, son of Charles I's sister, Elizabeth of Bohemia, herself James's godmother. Elizabeth, countess of Kent, carried the baby, a role which would have pleased her grandmother, the famous Bess of Hardwick. As a statement of the enduring importance of the nobility, the christening of Prince James made a powerful impact.

The royal family continued to grow. James was followed two years later by Elizabeth, then by Anne in 1637. The queen made an excellent recovery after the birth of her third daughter, as the countess of Leicester reported to her husband in March 1637: 'The queen is the best in her childbed that ever I saw. The king dines and sups with her and sits by her the greatest part of the day. The little princess shall be privately christened by her brother and sister.'[5] This picture of the devotion of the royal couple is all the more touching in the context of Princess Anne's sadly short life. Their next child, Katherine, born in 1639, died shortly after birth but Prince Henry, duke of Gloucester, who came into the world as troubles were mounting for his parents in 1640, was a healthy boy. The youngest child of Charles I and Henrietta Maria was born during the Civil Wars, in 1644, and baptized as Henrietta. History, however, knows her as Henriette Anne, or by her eldest brother's fond nickname, Minette.

Like all royal children, the world of this brood of little Stuarts was both privileged and rarefied. Each had a staff of their own immediate servants and Charles became particularly fond of his nurse, Christabella Wyndham, an affection which would be revived during his time in the West Country during the Civil Wars, when Mrs Wyndham was living with her husband in Somerset. Many aspects of the children's lives, including tutors, were shared, as was accommodation. For some years, before Prince Charles's household was enlarged and his governor appointed, the children all lived together. During the winter their residence was St James's Palace, a magnificent Tudor edifice built by Henry VIII, according to a sixteenth-century Spanish diplomat, as a home for his own children. Its interior decoration was exuberant: 'Painted and gilded fleur-de-lys, sunbursts, white harts, daggers, portcullises and the famous thornbush from which Henry VII had plucked his crown on Bosworth Field' were among its riot of visual display.[6] Summers were frequently passed at Richmond, which was farther out of London and considered healthier. Nor were the Stuart children without playmates. Brought up with them were the two sons of the assassinated duke of Buckingham, the second duke, named George, after his father, and his younger brother, Lord Francis Villiers. The king believed that he owed his friend the education of these handsome, lively boys within his own family and the duchess, who had married again and converted to Catholicism, was not allowed to keep them with her when she moved to Ireland with her second husband.

There would also be visits to Whitehall and to Hampton Court when the court moved there for recreation, or to escape the diseases of the warmer months. Charles and Henrietta Maria were, in comparison with earlier monarchs, affectionate and attentive parents, but it is easy to sentimentalize their relationship with their children. This was not a modern family, living under one roof. The king and queen had their own roles to play in national life and they viewed their offspring within the wider context of these obligations and expectations. Still, they came to visit regularly, walking with them in the orchards of St James's and inspecting their educational progress. The elder children were brought to court on state occasions to learn what was expected of them in such circumstances. Despite his distant public persona, Charles I was always at his most relaxed with his wife and family. Though he had not enjoyed the more carefree upbringing of Henrietta, he seems to have demonstrated greater outward affection towards his children than she did. A small man himself, he kept a record of their heights as they grew, on an oaken staff at the palace of Oaklands. They were always delighted to see him, rushing to greet him, for example, when he returned from Scotland in 1638.

Yet Charles I was as much dynast as affectionate father and he was determined to use his children in the demonstration of his majesty and power. The paintings of them which he commissioned are an abiding reminder of his taste and interest in art and also of his understanding of how it could be used to reinforce the image of Stuart kingship. He was not entirely pleased with some of the paintings of his family, which he thought depicted too much of their childish appeal and not enough of the dignity of the Stuart royal house. A modern eye is, of course, charmed by the portraits for precisely the reasons that the king had reservations about them. Yet the earliest painting of Charles and Henrietta with the Prince of Wales combines many of the elements that the monarch valued. He and his queen are fashionably but not ostentatiously dressed, she sitting and he standing at either end of a velvet-covered bed, with Prince Charles uncomfortably perched next to his mother, looking as if he might be about to tip over. But while the viewer is, at first, drawn to the slightly comical two-year-old, in his baby cap and apron (the style for all aristocratic boys under four years of age), it soon becomes apparent that the crown lying in the centre of the bed is intended as a potent symbol of the monarchy and the promise of the child's future.

A series of paintings by van Dyck charts the growth of the royal family, culminating in the group portrait of the children painted in 1637 in which they are almost upstaged by a huge dog at the centre, on whose head Prince Charles rests a commanding hand. Mary and James stand respectfully to one side and Elizabeth holds the baby Princess Anne, whose chubbiness belies her eventual ill health. This picture hung over the king's breakfast table at Whitehall, while the queen displayed another van Dyck, of her three eldest children, at Greenwich. Her attachment to this portrait survived the vicissitudes of the Civil Wars and was hanging in her French house at Colombes when she died. Throughout the 1630s, van Dyck was also painting Henrietta Maria, showing her development as a confident consort. There is a kind of tranquillity about her at this time that depicts a real contentment. No wonder she described herself as the happiest of women.

At St James's Palace, the life of the Stuart children followed an established routine. English royalty had a tradition of rising early, with the notable exception of Elizabeth I, who always slept badly and was not a morning person. Helped to dress by their attendants, the youngsters began the day with a service of prayer followed by a substantial breakfast of mutton, chicken and bread washed down with ale. Lessons and physical exercise made up the rest of the morning and early afternoon, until they met together for dinner, the main meal of the day, at three o'clock. Here there was plenty of choice. The fare they were offered could include game, meat and fish with desserts of tarts and custards and sometimes sweetmeats such as marzipan. The food was accompanied by wine from Italy. English water was still of doubtful purity in the seventeenth century and no one would have considered it as a beverage to accompany food. The last meal of the day was supper, a lighter version of dinner, and then the younger children were put to bed. The older ones, however, were sometimes invited to sup at Whitehall with their parents, so that they could learn court etiquette.

Charles I was a stickler for protocol. At this time, when he was ruling without parliament, he needed the support of his nobility – the elaborate ritual of the christenings of his two sons bore witness to this – and he made considerable efforts to enhance its role by reviving chivalric customs and restoring its 'ancient lustre', which many believed had been tarnished by the louche court of his father, James, and the profligate award of new titles.[7] The king was keen to ensure that his children knew how to behave in public, whether at audiences with visiting diplomats or at an evening's entertainment at Whitehall. Though they were no doubt impressed by the grandeur of these occasions, the formality placed demands on the children, and particularly on the apparently greedy Prince Charles, who did not share his parents' abstemious appetites. Nor could four-year-old Princess Mary be persuaded to sit still for her portrait, as her embarrassed mother reported to the child's aunt, the duchess of Savoy, in 1635.[8]

There were, however, compensations and not just the plentiful supply of dolls, lead soldiers and other toys enjoyed at playtime. One of the most important facets of court culture in the 1630s was the masque. Charles I and Henrietta were both enthusiastic patrons and participants in these lavish spectacles, encouraging their children to take part as they grew old enough. The masques were a key feature of the winter season, providing light and colour at an otherwise gloomy time of year. It became a custom for the king and queen to create a masque for each other in which they would both act – a further indication of their mutual affection, as well as a vehicle for Charles, a monarch who loved the visual arts, to use this idealized world to reinforce his image. And for Henrietta Maria, brought up in the theatre of the French court, involvement in all aspects of the production was a stimulating alternative to the demands of frequent pregnancies. In January 1631, Charles produced a piece called *Love's Triumph* at the Banqueting House at Whitehall. He played the hero and his wife the

Queen of Love. Her role was to rid the court of the gods of all disorder and vice and to reinstate honour and virtue. This was a theme that Charles wished to impress on his aristocracy and, indeed, the country as a whole. He saw it as the duty of a monarch and the lynchpin of his kingship. The following month, Henrietta and her ladies, including Lucy Hay, delighted their audience in their green, gold and silver costumes for the masque *Chloridia*, in which the queen played a nymph who became a goddess through the love of Zephyrus, the west wind. By the age of six, Prince Charles himself, resplendent in blue and crimson taffeta, was being cast in the leading role of the curiously named *Prince Britomart* for yet another production, this time at Windsor. Set in a distant time of Romans and Druids in Britain, the play was acted out by Charles and the Villiers boys who danced, sang and recited verses.

These masques have been regarded as frivolous and costly extravagances on the part of a royal couple who were seriously out of touch with the growing climate of resentment in the British Isles against the king's personal rule and the measures he took to obtain finance without parliament. But such a retrospective judgement overlooks the symbolic importance which Charles I attached to these entertainments and their place in his vision of kingship. As he rehearsed for one of these extravaganzas in 1637, he described himself as the 'happiest king in Christendom'. Happiness is not an emotion one tends to associate with Charles I but, in the 1630s, with his lively and supportive wife and their family, he believed that the culture of the court bound the nobility to him and would safeguard his throne. For his children, secure in their privileged lifestyle, such entertainments reinforced their royal identity, providing an exciting alternative to their normal routine. These were halcyon days.

Until the Prince of Wales was seven, the overall responsibility for his welfare and that of his siblings lay with the countess of Dorset. Born Mary Curzon, she was the daughter of a Derbyshire family who had married Edward Sackville, fourth earl of Dorset, in 1612. It was customary for ladies in charge of royal children to be of mature years – Lady Dorset was in her forties when appointed, and a mother herself – but she had not been the first choice for the job. Instead, she took the post originally intended for Jane Ker, countess of Roxburghe, a member of the Scottish aristocracy with a long-standing connection to the Stuart court and a favourite of Charles I's mother. But Lady Roxburghe was Catholic and the king did not consider her a fit governess for his sons. Lady Dorset was deemed a suitable replacement. Though Henrietta Maria's marriage treaty had stipulated that she should have the responsibility for her children's upbringing in their early years, Charles would not honour these terms and, by 1630, the queen was not inclined to dispute with him on this point. And as the education of their daughters was held to be of less national significance, Lady Roxburghe was soon to find employment as the head of Princess Mary's household. Her influence on the princess's religion cannot have been great, for Mary remained a Protestant throughout her life, despite later maternal pressure. As Lady Dorset's family was also partly Catholic, her appointment seems to have been acceptable to the queen. In fact, both the countess and her husband were pro-French and loyal supporters of Henrietta Maria and of the Stuart dynasty.

The task of being governess to the royal children was far from a sinecure. It called for organizational and financial management skills as well as tact. An appropriate moral climate was to be maintained and there were always concerns about illnesses. Lady Dorset was no spendthrift and like lady governesses before her she found herself juggling the requirements of appropriately luxurious accessories for the children (a cradle of crimson damask with gold and silver fringe and 'six pair of fine Holland sheets') with staff shortages, such as when she asked Sir Thomas Wentworth, the lord deputy of Ireland, if one of the duke of York's servants could be spared from going to Ireland because the duke had so few people to wait on him.[9] The possibility that one of the children might fall seriously ill or even die was a constant concern and the fact that the queen had a habit of rushing to her children under such circumstances cannot have made Lady Dorset's life any easier. In fact, the first letter that Henrietta Maria wrote to Prince Charles was occasioned by a nasty bout of illness that had struck the seven-year-old. His refusal to take his medicine caused the queen concern: 'Charles,' she wrote, 'I am sore that I must begin my first letter by chiding you, because I hear that you will not take physic. I hope it was only for this day and that tomorrow you will do it, for if you will not I must come to you and make you take it, for it is for your health.'[10]

By the summer of 1638, the prince was no longer Lady Dorset's charge. Like heirs to the throne before him, he was moved to a separate establishment under a male governor, while his brother and sisters remained at St James's Palace. The new head of his household was William Cavendish, earl, and later duke, of Newcastle-upon-Tyne. Though their time together was to be cut short by external events, the earl of Newcastle had considerable influence over the future Charles II.

This northern aristocrat was then aged about forty-five and was a long-serving courtier, having been one of Prince Henry's companions before the untimely death of James I's elder son. Talented and ambitious, he was born in the Elizabethan age and it has been said that he, like Charles I, espoused the values of this earlier period: 'Newcastle's "Elizabethanism" was at the core of a carefully constructed identity. It provided a set of standards and aspirations that he sought to live his life by, but, at the same time, it also underpinned a calculated pitch for political preferment.'[11] Newcastle was blessed with many of the necessary attributes of a courtier. He was an outstanding horseman, fencer and jouster and an accomplished writer of plays and verse, counting Ben Jonson among his friends. Two of his plays were performed by the King's Men at the Blackfriars theatre between 1639 and 1641, so he evidently found time to continue his literary career while supervising the Prince of Wales. Yet, despite being a court 'insider', he was not of the old nobility; Buckingham had proposed him for a title shortly before his assassination in 1628. His ambition did not endear him to everybody and he had made no secret of his desire to be the prince's governor. In pursuit of this goal, he endured some anxious moments, writing to his first wife in 1636: 'I find a great deal of venom against me, but both the king and the queen hath used me very graciously . . . they say that absolutely no other shall be for the prince . . .'[12]

Newcastle got his wish, as befits the descendant of a tenacious family. Like the countess of Kent, he was also a grandchild of Bess of Hardwick. But it certainly cost him, for in the execution of his office he spent the extraordinary sum of £40,000. Being governor gave him overall direction of the preparation of Prince Charles for the throne, though the appointment of Brian Duppa, bishop of Chichester, as the chief tutor to the prince and the duke of York was suggested by Duppa's patron, Archbishop William Laud. Duppa met with no opposition from Newcastle, who respected his scholarship and moral qualities. The boy's equestrian training Newcastle undertook himself. 'Too much contemplation spoils action,' he wrote in a letter of advice to the prince. It was apparently taken to heart, for neither as boy nor man did Charles II put much store on study, despite having the philosopher Thomas Hobbes as his tutor while in exile.[13] One piece of Newcastle's wisdom, however, proved both accurate and prophetic. It was, his governor noted, unwise to place too much emphasis on religion, 'for one may be a good man, but a bad King'.[14] This was not a distinction that the young prince's father ever understood.

Charles had moved away from his siblings but he still shared some of his lessons with James and family events continued to play an important part in his life as he rode with his governor and sat in the schoolroom. In the mid-1630s he had met his cousins, Charles Louis and Rupert, the sons of his exiled aunt, Elizabeth of Bohemia, and though it is often supposed that he was impressed by these older, rather dashing boys, there is little evidence to suggest how he reacted to them. Being an exile, as Charles would learn only too well, was far from romantic. And if the predicament of the palatine princes was not sufficient to alert the royal children to the vagaries of power politics, the arrival of their grandmother, Marie de Médici, in autumn 1638 certainly left an impression, both on them and a deeply sceptical English public.

It was a dubious distinction of this troublesome lady that she caused problems wherever she went. The rapprochement with Louis XIII of the 1620s had always been uneasy and in the struggle with Richelieu for influence over her son, Marie was simply not a clever enough politician to win. Her pro-Spanish machinations angered the chief minister of France while the staunchly Catholic queen mother abhorred the fact that the cardinal still allowed Huguenots freedom of worship, despite defeating them militarily. She grew increasingly impatient and her clumsy attempts to overthrow Richelieu culminated in the disaster of the so-called Day of the Dupes, in November 1630, after which she was exiled from the French court for a second time and confined to the chateau of Compiègne. The following year she fled to the Spanish Netherlands, living in Brussels and making what amounted to a state visit to The Hague in 1638, shortly after the inception of the new Dutch republic, which, despite the Calvinism of many of its leaders, was pleased to be able to welcome the disgraced mother of Louis XIII. Yet however warm the reception in Holland, it was never going to be a suitable place for Marie to reside. So her thoughts turned, in the same year, to her daughter in England and she decided to move to join Henrietta Maria, whom she had not seen for thirteen years.

Marie was fond of her children but a shortage of funds probably played as much a part in her desire to come to England as maternal yearning. Charles I was not keen to play host to his mother-in-law but he eventually accepted her arrival with dignity, ensuring that she had an appropriate reception at Harwich, after a miserable voyage across the North Sea, and going himself to Chelmsford in Essex to escort her to St James's Palace, where the pregnant Henrietta and the rest of the family were waiting for her. When the carriage carrying Marie and her son-in-law arrived, the four eldest royal children witnessed an emotional reunion between their mother and grandmother while the king privately wondered how he was to meet the cost of providing for Marie and her surprisingly large entourage. His anxieties, given that he was himself having to find increasingly arcane and unpopular means of raising money during his personal rule, were well founded. Marie de Médici was an expense he could ill afford. He was also concerned about her influence over her daughter in matters of religion. Charles I's religious policies were, if anything, even more disliked than his financial ones, and the tide of anti-Catholicism was growing. Increasingly, Puritan rhetoric was aimed at Henrietta Maria and the king did not need his mother-in-law to aggravate the situation.

What the royal children made of Marie is harder to say. They were not her only grandchildren; her daughters had families of their own in Spain and Italy and her younger son, Gaston, duke of Orléans, was an indulgent father to his daughter Anne, the supremely self-confident cousin not yet encountered by the little Stuarts. And just a month before Marie arrived in England, Anne of Austria had, at last, given birth to an heir to the French throne, the future Louis XIV, a child Marie would never see. Marie had her own apartments at St James's and, according to Henrietta, her health improved after her arrival in England. 'I found her at first a little changed,' she wrote to her sister in Italy, 'but it was just the hardship of the voyage. She is now looking well again, and has given me a second lease of life by being able to see her and serve her again.'[15]

Henrietta's happiness at her mother's arrival was soon tempered with sadness. At the beginning of January 1639, she gave birth to a fourth daughter, Katherine, who only lived a few hours. The grief-stricken queen was ill after the delivery but recovered well and was pregnant again by the autumn. The following summer, in July, she bore a third son, Henry, duke of Gloucester, who was born at Oatlands Palace in Surrey, a favourite residence of the queen. It was an easy delivery and the child showed every sign of health. It has been said that he was named for his mother and maternal grandfather, Henry IV of France, but it seems equally possible that Charles I was remembering his own brother and acknowledging the importance of Henry as an English regal name.

Welcome as this new prince was, the year 1640 ended with a tragic loss for the royal family. Just before Christmas, Princess Anne died. Her demise was not entirely unexpected, as her health had been poor throughout her short life. Van Dyck flattered to deceive in his family portrait, where his depiction of the infant in her sister Elizabeth's arms suggests a bonny baby. Anne suffered from recurring respiratory problems, probably tuberculosis. This disease, so prevalent at the time, had been the scourge of the Tudors but was less common among the Stuarts. Though aware that Anne was often ill, the suddenness of her death, at which neither parent was present, distressed Charles and Henrietta. The little princess's deathbed scene was described by the Victorian writer Mary Anne Everett Green in a manner almost as maudlin as the death of Little Nell in Dickens' *The Old Curiosity Shop*. 'Her health, from early infancy, was extremely delicate; a constant feverish cough showed a tendency to disease of the lungs, and before she had completed her fourth year, consumption terminated her existence.' The child's fortitude in the face of death was remarkable. Her attendants gently reminded her that she should say her prayers as the end approached and the exhausted child did her best. 'I am not able to say my long prayer [the Lord's Prayer],' she told them, 'but I will say my short one: Lighten mine eyes, oh Lord, lest I sleep the sleep of death.' 'This done,' added Mrs Green, 'the little lamb gave up the ghost.' An autopsy report remarked '. . . it is easy to judge that this princess could not be long lived and that a great part of her life (under the good pleasure of God) has been at least as much owing to art as to nature.'[16]

Henry's birth and Anne's death symbolized the uncertainties facing the Stuart royal family in the year 1640. While the rhythm of their daily lives, of the schoolroom, of riding lessons, public

occasion and private pastime continued, there were strong undercurrents of discontent flowing all around them, in the three
kingdoms that their father had tried to govern as an absolute
monarch, imposing his will on a realm that was increasingly frac-
tured by religious differences and constitutional debate about his
methods of government. As yet, this meant little to his five
surviving offspring but there were subtle hints that an observant
child could have noticed. Their parents were ageing and less
relaxed. Henrietta, worn thin by the demands of childbearing,
was beginning to lose the bloom and vivacity of her youth. Her
devotion to her husband was unwavering but the king himself
was beset by difficulties and the grey was starting to come in his
beard. Prince Henry, the newest addition to the Stuart line, slept
peacefully in his cradle but he would never really know his father,
or experience the light-hearted childhood of his siblings. The
world around them all was changing and they would be as severely
affected by it as the humblest of their father's subjects.

Part Two

Storm Clouds
1640–42

CHAPTER THREE

The King at Bay

'There was never a king that had a more great and weighty cause to call his people together than myself. I will not trouble you with the particulars . . .'

Charles I gives an early indication of his attitude
to parliament after eleven years of personal rule

'My grandfather left you four kingdoms and I am afraid your majesty will leave me never a one.'

The Prince of Wales to Charles I,
as reported to Archbishop Laud, May 1640

IT WAS, PERHAPS, IRONIC that Charles I's difficulties should have begun in Scotland, the land of his birth. The king was, however, a stranger to his northern realm. He had left at the age of three and a half and begun his reign as a distant monarch. Scotland felt his absence but he was oblivious to the damage this could cause. It was a very different country from England and its much smaller population (about 750,000 at the start of the seventeenth century to England's nearly five million) was divided both linguistically and geographically between the Gaelic-speaking Highlands where clan organization held sway and the Anglo-Scots-speaking Lowlands. The divisions should not, however, be oversimplified. Some of the Highland clans were Catholic while others were staunchly Protestant, and kinship remained an important aspect of Scottish society regardless of where one lived. The power of the largest landowners and leading aristocratic families, though challenged by Charles I and his father, had not seriously diminished and they could still command a great deal of local support from the Scottish populace, particularly if an extension of the royal prerogative could be represented as a general threat to Scotland as a whole. Higher taxation, recession and resentment of interference from London were factors that bound many Scots together. However, some leading members of the Scottish nobility had found their way south to serve at court and enjoy the perquisites that came with office. Charles had deliberately forged marriages between them and English aristocrats, notably that of his cousin, James Stuart, duke of Lennox, to Buckingham's daughter, Mary Villiers. Many others were not so readily tempted, clinging vigorously to their Scottish identity and their Scottish lands. Other Scots felt differently altogether. It is estimated that, in the period 1603 to 1638, as many as 100,000 Scots, propelled by economic hardship, emigrated either to Northern Ireland, where their presence in Ulster would have long-term repercussions, or to Europe.

Although a Stuart, Charles I had little feel for the country or its people, and still less appreciation of the difficulties that would ensue when he tried, in 1637, to force the introduction of a new prayer book and a largely Anglican religious organization on the Scots.[1] Yet there were early signs, if he had cared to read them, of the opposition that he would likely face. When, after eight years on the throne, he belatedly travelled to Edinburgh for his coronation in the summer of 1633, he initially met with a warm welcome from the inhabitants of the city, curious to see their monarch. But, with that unique ability to cause offence that characterized much of the king's public dealings with his subjects, things did not go well thereafter. The choice of Edinburgh was unusual – Scottish kings were traditionally crowned at Scone, near Perth – but it was the form of the ceremony itself that rankled with the Scots. The abbey kirk of Holyrood was elaborately decorated with a communion table that looked suspiciously like an altar, and there were candles and a crucifix. The sober supporters of the Scottish Kirk disdained anything that looked like Romish trappings and they were even more disquieted when Charles made an ostentatious display of kneeling ceremoniously before he ascended the coronation dais. The service itself, in which six fully robed Scottish bishops participated, was conducted using the English *Book of Common Prayer* and even one of the king's staunchest Scottish supporters noted that the coronation had 'bred great fear of inbringing of popery'.[2]

Despite this affront to the sensibilities of the Scottish Kirk, several more years were to pass before concerted opposition to the religious policies of Charles I resulted in full-scale rebellion. The flashpoint came in the summer of 1637. Secure in his vision of a uniform, centralized polity, a kind of Caroline imperialism which embraced Church and state in each of the three kingdoms, the king was unlikely to have paid much heed to warnings, even if these had been forthcoming. His advisers in Scotland chose not to risk royal displeasure by suggesting that the introduction of the prayer book was unwise and so Charles proceeded without any anticipation of widespread opposition. Impatient for action, he instructed the bishop of Edinburgh to issue an edict on 16 July 1637 ordering the use of the new liturgy in all the city's churches the following week.

The riot in St Giles's Cathedral that marked the introduction of this unwelcome imposition has passed into legend. Although five more years would go by before civil war broke out in England, it might be argued that it was the women of the Edinburgh congregation who first raised their weapons – in this case, the stools on which they sat – in anger. Jenny Geddes, the supposed leader of this civil disobedience, probably never existed, but it is certain that 'all the common people, especially the women' led the disorder which ensued when the dean of St Giles opened the new prayer book to read the collects. Shouting that popery was being brought in, the women aimed their stools at the dean and at the bishop of Edinburgh. Eventually the troublemakers were thrown

out but the trouble spread to the streets and the earl of Roxburghe's coach was attacked when he left the cathedral, resulting
in a sword fight between his retainers and the protestors in which
the nobleman himself was compelled to take part. But the real
humiliation of this extraordinary day was reserved for the hapless
bishop of Edinburgh himself, of whom it was said that he had
never before 'got such a laxative purgation'.[3]

Despite the impression that might have been given at the
time, this was no spontaneous outburst from the lower orders. It
had been several months in the planning and the women were
Presbyterians from the Edinburgh mercantile community, not
serving wenches from the local taverns. They were deeply opposed
to the changes the king sought to impose, as were their menfolk.
So, too, were important figures in the Protestant aristocracy,
including the earl of Loudoun and Lord Balmerino. Perhaps they
hoped one riotous assembly would be enough to stop the king and
Laud in their tracks. If so, they were to be disappointed. Fearing
that the example of the Scots might lead to a similar response
from Protestant radicals (known as Puritans) in England, Laud
counselled the king to stand firm.[4] As it was not in Charles's
nature to back down in the face of such turbulence, the archbishop
need not have worried about the royal response. Charles was
determined that his authority must not be questioned and
announced that further opposition to the prayer book in Scotland
would be viewed as treasonous. Thus the die was cast.

In a confused and threatening atmosphere, the Scottish Privy
Council abandoned Edinburgh in the autumn of 1637. By the
beginning of 1638 an ad hoc government had been set up in
defiance of the king. Aware as this new government was of the
precariousness of the situation, it was decided to engage the active
support of all Scots by forming a band of mutual association, to
which all adult males in Scotland could subscribe. So was born the
National Covenant, the most revolutionary document of its time
and one which would have a profound effect on Charles I, his
children and the entire British Isles.

Published on 28 February 1638, the Covenant was the work of the Presbyterian clergyman Alexander Henderson and a twenty-seven-year-old lawyer, Archibald Johnston of Warriston, destined to become an important figure in Scottish politics, especially through his writings. From the same Edinburgh mercantile background as the stool-throwing matrons, he was deeply religious, a fine draftsman and propagandist, and utterly convinced that God had called him, unworthy as he was, to the defence of religion in Scotland. In his diary, the night after the Covenant was first subscribed, he wrote of Scotland as a 'new Israel', in language reminiscent of the later beliefs of the Independents of Cromwell's army.

What, then, did the Covenant actually say? It does not make easy reading but contained within its convoluted wording was a new definition of the relationship between the Crown and the subject wherein loyalty was only to be given to a 'Covenanted king' who had sworn to uphold the 'true religion'. In the case of Scotland, this meant Presbyterianism. There was no direct mention of episcopacy but this was implicit in the Covenant's challenge to the royal prerogative, at least in the way Charles I had attempted to enforce his vision of uniformity in religion and state on the Scots.[5] The Covenant made clear that Charles was expected to defend the Kirk and to govern according to the laws. If he failed to do so, then resistance was not just permitted but a moral obligation. No one, wrote Henderson and Johnston, should 'fear the foul aspersions of rebellion'. Their aim was to 'maintain the true worship of God, the majesty of our King and the peace of the kingdom'. Charles I would have recognized these goals as his own, though he intended to realize them in fundamentally different ways.

The 'new Israel' was not so easily to be achieved as the king's opponents hoped. The Covenant certainly heightened national consciousness in Scotland and attracted a great deal of support, except in the traditionally Catholic Highlands and the conservative towns of Aberdeen and St Andrews. But support for it was not universal – less than half the Scottish nobility subscribed to it – and it progressively became a tool for those who wished to coerce and threaten as much as those who sought to achieve national unity. The most optimistic of the Covenanters, however, saw it not just as an instrument to promote a godly Scotland but as a force that might transform the whole of Britain. This possibility was not lost on the king and his supporters or on his increasingly vocal opponents in England. As Laud wrote the following year, 'It is much to be feared this Scottish violence will make some unfitting impression upon both this church and state.'[6]

The king's response to the crisis in Scotland foreshadowed his approach to the greater upheavals which were to follow in his three kingdoms. He took this challenge to his authority personally: 'I will rather die,' he wrote to the marquess of Hamilton in June 1638, 'than yield to those impertinent and damnable demands (as you rightly call them), for it is all one, as to yield [is] to be no king in a very short space of time.'[7] Then he played for time, hoping, as he would continue to do until shortly before his death, to divide those who opposed him. He used Hamilton, the leading Scottish nobleman and a more competent politician than has often been supposed, to deal with the Covenanters. The king would not come north himself. Hamilton offered, in the king's name, a number of concessions, including withdrawal of the much-hated prayer book and a new Covenant of Charles's own. This deceived no one and in early December 1638 the Glasgow Assembly of the Scottish Kirk rejected the king's religious settlement, abolishing episcopacy for good measure. Meanwhile, the Covenanting movement had taken a number of steps towards the centralization of Scottish government and the creation of a standing army. It was also strengthened by the support of Archibald Campbell, earl of Argyll, a Presbyterian but also the head of one of the most powerful Highland clans. Faced with this growing threat, Charles had no alternative but to try to re-establish his authority in Scotland by force. The repercussions of his ultimately unsuccessful attempts would engulf England and Ireland and lead to civil war.

*

THE COVENANTERS were better prepared to fight in the summer of 1639 than the king but the first Bishops' War, as the Scottish conflicts came to be known, ended without bloodshed when Charles I agreed to treat with the Scottish commissioners at Berwick in June. His decision not to risk battle, when he had a substantial (though largely untrained) force, the support of his northern aristocracy and could, furthermore, tap into the long-standing English antipathy against the Scots, has been called one of the greatest mistakes of his life. It was also uncharacteristic for the ruler, who, whatever his shortcomings, was not lacking in courage. He seems to have been unnerved by reports that the Scots had a massive force of 45,000 to his own of about 15,000. This was untrue but it brought him hastily to the negotiating table. Here he debated energetically with the Scottish commissioners, asserting that he was determined 'to clear myself of that notorious slander that I shut my ears to the just complaints of the people of Scotland'. The Scots felt otherwise but it is interesting to note Charles's sensitivity on this point and his appreciation of how it had damaged his image. The outcome of discussions was that the Covenanters would disband their army and the king would call an assembly of the Kirk and a parliament in Scotland with powers to legislate on all matters religious and civil. The problem was that neither side trusted the other so the treaty was soon a dead letter. The king knew almost immediately that Berwick had solved nothing and he prepared to fight again the following year. But before he could do so, he needed an injection of money that could not be supplied by the various inventive measures he had used to support his rule in England for the previous eleven years since he had dissolved parliament in 1629. He had no recourse now but to recall it.

The year 1640 was characterized by increasing apprehension and ferment in England. It was a year of dashed and raised hopes, aristocratic plotting, parliamentary defiance and military ignominy. The heightened sense of tension can be seen in the fears allegedly expressed by the ten-year-old Prince of Wales, quoted at the start of this chapter. The report is said to have come from the prince's household but though it found its way into Laud's papers, we do not know whether the younger Charles ever actually uttered such doubts to his father.[8] The thought that those around him might be encouraging such ideas was disturbing enough.

The king's problems began in April with the summoning of the Short Parliament. Here was a golden opportunity to strengthen the position of the Crown, gain access to money to fund a further campaign against the Scots and unite the English in support of the Stuart dynasty. The failure of the king and his advisers to achieve a successful outcome during the first meeting of parliament in eleven years was the result of blinkered thinking and an inability to offer even the smallest crumb of compromise. He could have had money, loyalty and an invaluable propaganda victory if he had been willing to make concessions but such an approach was alien to Charles's view of kingship. A number of his advisers, including his secretary, Windebank, and Thomas Wentworth, who had arrived back from his spell as lord deputy of Ireland in the autumn of 1639 and had recently been ennobled as earl of Strafford, urged the king to proceed firmly. A second and more serious military confrontation with the Scots seemed unavoidable. Now was not the time, in their view, to listen to a host of demands that might go to the heart of how England was ruled. Windebank believed this was the House of Commons' last chance to demonstrate unswerving loyalty and if it failed to do so, then the outcome would be ominous, with the king falling back on 'extraordinary means, rather than, by the peevishness of some few factious spirits, to suffer his state and government to be lost'.[9]

The tone of Charles I's dealings with the Short Parliament, which first met on 13 April 1640, was set in the condescending opening address of the lord keeper, Lord Finch, who enlarged on the king's all-too brief opening lines. The essence was that the king needed money to subdue the treacherous Scots and he would deal with grievances at a later point. This was no basis for co-operation and the debates of the Commons over the next three weeks would centre on their financial and religious complaints. Alarmed that he was not getting anywhere with the MPs, Charles took his case directly to the House of Lords on 24 April where, despite the misgivings of some peers, his request for the granting of financial support without strings was agreed. The king was particularly peeved that the Lower House did not seem to trust him which, indeed, it did not, especially after he had tried to pre-empt its authority. By the beginning of May, Charles was fast losing patience. Belatedly, he tried to negotiate, offering to give up the hated ship money for a hefty grant of subsidies.[10] But by that time Charles's opponents were gaining the upper hand and could use parliamentary procedure to scupper this last-ditch attempt at reaching a workable way forward. Left with, as he saw it, no alternative, Charles resorted to his behaviour of the 1620s: he dissolved the Short Parliament on 5 May 1640. He needed another way to rule, to restore order and to defeat the Scots.

It was Strafford, 'Black Tom Tyrant', the strong man of Ireland, where the parliament had already been prevailed upon to vote money for the king, who urged firmness in the Privy Council meeting that took place on the evening of the Short Parliament's dissolution, saying:

> Go on with a vigorous war as you first designed, loosed and absolved from all rules of government, being reduced to extreme necessities. Everything is to be done that power must admit . . . they refusing you are acquitted towards God and man. You have an army in Ireland you may employ here to reduce this kingdom. [I am] confident as anything under heaven Scotland shall not hold out five months. One summer well employed will do it. Venture all I had, I would carry it or lose it.[11]

These were the words of a hard, blunt Yorkshireman and they would take him, the following year, to the scaffold.

*

THE DISSOLUTION of the Short Parliament heightened tensions in London and around the royal family, even as Henrietta Maria was preparing to give birth to her eighth child, Prince Henry. The queen's popularity had plummeted and she was again viewed as a Catholic import with a dangerous influence over English politics. The origins of this increasing tide of invective lay in the late 1630s, in the shifts of European politics and in the queen's own behaviour. She had never forgotten that a crucial part of her mission to England was to protect Catholics and uphold Catholicism. As the decade of the 1630s progressed, observers feared that her influence, like her confidence, was growing. A new chapel, designed by Inigo Jones, was finally completed at her chief London residence, Somerset House, in December 1635. The festivities surrounding its dedication lasted three days and alarmed Protestant commentators, especially as the king himself was present for some of the time. Ever conscious of her Bourbon heritage, the queen had actually been willing to support an anti-Spanish policy that appealed to English Protestants at court, in return for concessions to Catholics. The arrival of papal agents in London in the mid-1630s thrilled Henrietta but alarmed the king's opponents. George Conn, the Scot who represented the Vatican in London, set up his own chapel in Long Acre and it became the focus of a Catholic revival. Close to the queen, Conn proselytized at court and may even have hoped to convert Charles I. His expectations were entirely unfounded in this respect. Charles was devoted to his wife but emphatically not to her religion.

Contemporary observers, seeing the queen's growing public commitment to Catholicism and noting that it had become fashionable at court, where several of her ladies converted in 1637–8, were not so sure. 'Our great women fall away every day,' lamented one commentator. The most notable of these was Anne Boteler,

countess of Newport, whose own husband was so incensed by her
conversion that he urged the king to ensure that the laws against
Catholics were properly enforced and even suggested that the
queen's chapel at Somerset House be closed to English Catholics.[12] The return of the duchess of Chevreuse, an inveterate
troublemaker, heightened tensions when she took Princess Mary
to Mass with her, and the arrival of Marie de Médici, renowned
for her hatred of Protestants, only fuelled the flames. Yet Henrietta Maria, firm in her convictions and consistently underestimating the force of public opinion in an age in which printed
broadsides and news-sheets were becoming much more common,
ploughed on with her crusade. Her actions made it all the more
easy for the Scots and their English supporters to justify their
defiance as a necessary protection of the Protestant religion. As
the situation in Scotland deteriorated and the king's need for
money became more urgent, the queen solicited financial aid from
Catholics and also, secretly, from the Pope. This was done without
her husband's approval. The money she garnered made little difference – it would barely have supported the army for a week –
but her passionate Catholicism had done more damage to herself
and the court than she could possibly have imagined. Within
a few days of the dismissal of the Short Parliament there was
widespread unrest in London. Apprentices and sailors rioted in
Whitehall, shouting abuse at the queen. Scratched on the window
of the king's antechamber were the words 'God save the King,
confound the Queen and her children.'[13]

The king and his advisers, under threat of a Scottish military
invasion, looked for other backers, preparing to take Spanish gold
if no other source of finance could be found. To a country where
the fear of papist conspiracy was deeply embedded, this looked
like the most heinous of developments. Aristocratic critics of the
king, including leading peers such as the earls of Northumberland,
Warwick, Bedford and Essex, met secretly to clarify their plans
and to establish secret communications with the Scots. By late
June they were engaged with their Scottish 'friends' in planning

an invasion of the north of England, with the ultimate aim of forcing the king to recall parliament in the face of such a full-blown crisis. Such a course was clearly treasonable but they proceeded nevertheless.[14] Fearful for the queen in the last stages of her pregnancy and alarmed by the vociferous criticisms of her, Charles moved Henrietta to Oatlands for the birth of Prince Henry, on 8 July. His joy in the arrival of a third son was short-lived. On 17 August, the Scots invaded England.

The defeat of Charles I in the second Bishops' War was a military and political disaster. At Newburn near Newcastle-up-on-Tyne on 29 August 1640 the forces of the Scottish general Alexander Leslie, occupying a superior position on high ground, routed the English and inflicted the greatest Scottish defeat on an English army for 300 years. They then occupied Newcastle and waited for the king, who had left London for York, to come to terms with them. Losing control of Newcastle, the hub of England's coal supply, meant that London could be cut off from winter fuel unless an accommodation was reached with the Scottish rebels. Seizing the initiative, the disaffected nobles in London presented the king with the Twelve Peers' Petition, which tied together various grievances such as the conduct of the war against the Scots, fear over the use of Strafford's Irish army in England and the spread of popery to try to put the case for a recall of parliament. The king's response was to call a great council of peers (the first since Mary Tudor's reign) to meet him at York in September to discuss how best to deal with the crisis of his affairs. In this turmoil, his thoughts were still very much with his wife and family left behind in London. Their protection was uppermost in his mind when he ordered the earl of Salisbury to make sure that the gentlemen pensioners, normally assigned to him, be appropriately armed and prepared as 'a strong guard . . . ready upon all occasions for the defence and safety of our dearest consort the Queen, and our royal children, kingdom and city of London.'[15]

Despite the machinations of the disaffected lords like Bedford and Holland, the majority of the peers were not opposed to the king in the autumn of 1640. But many of them were very concerned about the state of the country. Weeks before the Scottish invasion, the elderly earl of Dorset, Henrietta Maria's lord chamberlain and husband of the royal children's governess, wrote in anguish to his friend the earl of Salisbury, a man who was teetering on the brink of support for Charles I's aristocratic critics:

> I do assure you the King is confident you will not be against him nor in person or purse contribute aught to his destruction. Self-preservation is to be allowed to all the world and so much your Lordship must pay unto yourself but let no passion or evil counsel transport you beyond it . . . for no doubt there are too many hot-headed people both here and at London that advise and persuade desperate ways . . . the day of doom in my opinion approaches and if the wisdom and temper of some above mediate not an accommodation speedily, one day of battle will decide under what power or person we must all hereafter breathe.[16]

Dorset's statements look like hyperbole in retrospect and his prayer that one day of battle might settle matters was a forlorn hope given what was to follow. Yet he was a thoughtful man, and a faithful but not unquestioning supporter of the king. Over the coming years, he clung to the desire, which he shared with many of his background, that there could be a compromise between the king and parliament. Though the earl's enemies would have been amused by the papal ambassador's reference to him as 'il conte de Dormat', he defended Henrietta Maria's reputation with determination in the House of Lords in 1640–1, helping to prevent the threat of impeachment. Given the queen's scheming, she scarcely deserved his loyalty.[17]

The meeting at York revealed both Charles I's isolation and his unfailing optimism that he could still overcome the Scottish rebellion. 'For so long as the Scotch army remains in England,' he told the peers, 'I think no man will counsel me to disband mine:

for that would be an unspeakable loss to all this part of the kingdom by subjecting them to the greedy appetite of the rebels,
besides the unspeakable dishonour that would thereby fall upon
the nation.' Having done his best to uphold and foster aristocratic
concepts of honour during the previous decade, Charles was
clearly appealing to what he viewed as perhaps the nobility's most
fundamental belief, but while the majority of those present had
an inherent respect for kingship they felt that Charles was being
unrealistic. A committee was nominated to negotiate with the
Scots at Ripon during October 1640. These discussions, however,
had wider implications. They were to be finalized in London with
the input of the English parliament, whose financial support was
vital if the king were, as agreed, to meet the costs of the occupying
Scottish army in northern England. Even more humiliating
was the abandonment of all the religious changes thrust upon
Scotland since 1637. Thus his northern kingdom's defiance was
transformed into a wider crisis. Charles I's authority in the
autumn of 1640 lay in ruins.

When the new parliament, summoned for 3 November, was
opened, there was an articulate group of men in the Commons
prepared to take up the groundswell of popular agitation and an
influential, determined group of aristocrats in the House of Lords
ready to challenge the king. This does not mean that any of his
opponents in England were seriously considering deposing him,
though the Scots might have felt differently. Sir Benjamin Rudyard, in a speech to the House of Commons, spoke for many when
he castigated both Puritan extremists and Catholic plotters,
noting, 'Religion has been for a long time and still is the great
design on this kingdom.' But his loyalty to Charles I was unshaken:

> The King likewise is reduced to great straits, wherein it were
> undutifulness beyond inhumanity to take advantage of him
> . . . His Majesty has clearly and freely put himself into the
> hands of this parliament and I presume there is not a man in
> this House but feels himself advanced in so high a trust. But

if he prosper no better in our hands than he has done in theirs who have hitherto had the handling of his affairs, we shall forever make ourselves unworthy of so gracious a confidence.[18]

The Long Parliament, as it is known to history, sat for thirteen years, through war, regicide and republic. Its members were often at odds, sometimes vehemently so, but in the autumn of 1640 they were optimistic of a better future for their country. And Rudyard was right: religion was for them a burning issue. In the first week of the session, a petition was presented for the release from prison of the savagely punished Puritan writer John Lilburne, a victim of the Court of Star Chamber. The MP who presented the petition was an obscure country gentleman of the middling sort from East Anglia. His name was Oliver Cromwell.

*

IT HAS BEEN SAID that Henrietta Maria influenced the king to summon parliament again. In mid-September the earl of Hertford reported that the queen had told him that a parliament was 'the only way'.[19] Her motives for this advice are unclear but she shared, and even encouraged, Charles's natural predisposition to divide his critics. Henrietta had recovered quickly from the birth of Prince Henry but she and Charles had been apart during his unsuccessful campaign in the north of England. When they met again at Theobalds Palace in Hertfordshire much had changed. Her instinct was always to defend her husband and her children, an admirable aim, but not one which she embraced with any real political understanding. Still underestimating her unpopularity and the relentless war that would be waged against her in the theatre of public opinion, she was unable to help the king capitalize on his advantages. Charles I's intransigence and his inability to reach out to the populace at large would cost him dear. He was good at missing opportunities, such as his failure to process through the streets of London to the opening of parliament on

3 November. This was a great state occasion and, properly managed, could have reinforced the king's image and the panoply of
royal majesty. Instead, Charles chose to go downriver by barge.

Yet the tide was by no means entirely flowing against him and
in the first months of the New Year, it seemed that real progress
might be made. Feeling against the Scots, and the expense of their
occupation of northern England, was growing. The House of
Commons was divided over the abolition of episcopacy, fearing
undue Scottish influence in English affairs. In January, Charles
made a conciliatory speech in which he promised to take the
Church of England back to 'the purest times of Queen Elizabeth's
days' – evoking the spirit of Good Queen Bess was always a
shrewd move – give up (by implication, at least) illegal ways of
raising revenue without parliamentary approval and allow parliament to meet once every three years, a more 'democratic' concession than the arrangement for fixed five-year terms that is
currently law in the United Kingdom. By early March 1641 it
seemed that the king was building a solid body of support and had
regained the initiative. He was to lose it very soon through a series
of misjudgements and an underlying inflexibility entirely typical
of the man.

During the spring and summer of 1641 Charles I's attention
was focussed on those to whom he was closest: his chief adviser,
Strafford, his wife, Henrietta Maria, and his elder daughter, Princess Mary. He would also involve Prince Charles, disastrously,
in the unfolding drama and cause Prince James to question his
resolve. Suddenly, just when it seemed he might be able to move
forward more effectively, he contrived to make his own position,
and that of those dearest to him, infinitely more difficult.

Strafford stayed in Yorkshire for a time after the Scots' victory,
aware of his deep unpopularity in London. When he did return,
summoned by the king (a reckless move in itself), on 11 November 1640, he was accused of high treason, arrested and committed
to the Tower of London two weeks later. It took till 22 March for
the charges against him to be formalized and his trial in the

House of Lords to begin. Since Strafford had shown uncondi-
tional loyalty to Charles I the charge of high treason had to be
formulated in a way that accused him of subverting the legal order
of the state and the body politic. Many of the charges related to
his time in Ireland, where he had certainly governed in an arbi-
trary fashion, but so had many of his predecessors in the office of
lord deputy. It was not easy to make these accusations stick in
England. Eventually, the only charge that mattered was that he
had intended, in his advice to the king and Privy Council on the
night of the dissolution of the Short Parliament, that his Irish
army could be used to subdue 'this kingdom'. But which kingdom?
Strafford asserted that he had meant Scotland and other councillors either conveniently could not remember what they thought
he intended or avowed that they had believed him to be, indeed,
talking about Scotland. The sole witness against him was Sir
Harry Vane, who had taken notes at the meeting. Strafford, a
superb orator, could, and did, challenge the charges, effectively
demolishing the case against him.

Frustrated, the House of Commons moved on 10 April 1641
to bring an act of attainder against Strafford. This allowed for the
earl to be found guilty of treason and condemned to death, by
legislation, without a further hearing. Things had come to this
pass through the king's intransigence. He could have disbanded
the much-feared Irish army. He could have dismissed Strafford
from his service, thus defusing some of the venom against him.
But he seems to have wanted Strafford to stand trial as a matter
of honour, viewing the attack on the earl as an indirect attack
on the entire basis of the Stuart monarchy. He assured the beleaguered Strafford: 'Upon the word of a king, you shall not suffer
in life, honour or fortune.' So why, then, did he fatally compromise
what little chance was left for his 'faithful and able servant' by
failing to stop the shenanigans of his wife and her closest advisers
in what have become known as the Army Plots?

The king had already agreed to a scheme whereby a petition
was to be introduced into the House of Commons by Prince

Charles's master of the horse, Henry Percy, putting army pay on
a regular footing in an attempt to fund the expensive royal force
still camped in the north. This was a controversial move extremely
unlikely to endear the king to his critics in the House of Commons, but far more serious was the idea conjured up, with the
queen's approval and encouragement, by two of her closest counsellors, Sir Henry Jermyn (who had converted to Catholicism)
and the poet laureate Sir John Suckling. They proposed to bring
the army south and try to free Strafford. It became apparent in
early April 1641 that neither of these schemes, which the king
considered might be stronger if brought together, would succeed.
But the royal couple were not yet ready to give up and on 3 May
one hundred specially recruited mercenaries attempted to storm
the Tower of London, where Strafford was held. The threat was
defused by the House of Lords, who sent the earl of Newport
to defend the Tower and a deputation to persuade the king to
abandon such a direct attack against parliament. There was, as it
happened, little appetite in the army to pursue what was, in effect,
a coup against the legislative body of England. Charles might
have been less inclined to consider an action which presaged his
overall attitude to opponents in the years of civil war that were to
follow, namely that the end justified the means, had he listened
less to the queen. Though there has always been dispute about the
extent of Henrietta Maria's influence on her husband, at this key
juncture, with a man's life at stake, it seems to have been considerable. As Charles I's most recent biographer has remarked:

> She was an inveterate plotter who loathed the House of
> Commons and had little respect for the constitutional
> restraints that were recognised by most of the politicians
> around Charles . . . in the past she had had relatively little
> impact on politics because of her husband's capacity to
> separate his decision-making from his personal affections.
> But by early 1641 this was changing, as she herself became
> an issue because of the attention directed to popish plotting
> and Catholic courtiers.[20]

While one might question whether Henrietta Maria was already an inveterate plotter in 1641 she certainly became so afterwards. Nor can it be denied that she could exert a kind of emotional blackmail over Charles. The king loved her and his alarm for her safety and that of their children was genuine. Henrietta could and did exercise a kind of emotional blackmail by threatening to leave the country if he could not face down his opponents and protect her. Her contempt for the underlying principles of English government is not entirely explained by her being French and ignorant of the constitutional repercussions of her views. They were simply at odds with anyone who did not believe, as Charles I did, in the divine right of kings.

None of this intriguing helped Strafford. The earl went to his death with great bravery on the morning of 12 May 1641 on Tower Hill. The king had not been able to save him in the end. Fearful for the safety of his family, Charles tried one last, desperate move. But even in this he was to be humiliated. His last request, that to reprieve Strafford would be 'an unspeakable contentment to me', was delivered in person by Prince Charles to the House of Lords. The letter was returned unopened and the prince sent away. On hearing that Charles had signed the act of attainder against him Strafford is supposed to have remarked, 'Put not your trust in princes.' Their father's inability to impose himself and to save a faithful servant left a powerful imprint on the memories of both Prince Charles and Prince James. The Prince of Wales had sat under a canopy of state on a dais throughout Strafford's trial, a visual reminder of the solemnity of the occasion – and of royal impotency in the face of an obdurate parliament. He and his brother may not have been aware of the London mob rioting outside the queen's apartments or that their father was so frightened for their safety that he considered removing to Portsmouth. And all the while, the court had been celebrating the marriage of their sister, Princess Mary, to Prince William of Orange.

*

THE JUXTAPOSITION of the marriage of Mary Stuart into the House of Orange and the trial of Strafford may seem inauspicious but for Charles I it had suddenly become a key element of his foreign policy. As his domestic situation deteriorated, he looked for Protestant allies in Europe. The idea of such a match had been mooted in the late 1630s, when the initiative came from the Dutch. Fearful of the effect on trade of a possible dynastic alliance between the Stuarts and Philip IV of Spain, the Dutch opened discussions on a treaty to circumvent this eventuality. Initially, Charles would only offer Princess Elizabeth as a spouse for Prince William, anticipating, as did Henrietta Maria, that Mary would make a grander union in Spain. Like his father, Charles I wanted to reap the rewards of dividing his children's marriages between Catholic and Protestant countries in Europe, as the last decade of the Thirty Years' War played itself out. The marriage between Elizabeth and William had been agreed by all the parties concerned but when a Dutch delegation arrived in England early in 1641 they were surprised, and pleased, to be offered the king's elder daughter, Mary. Charles's authority in Britain had become more fragile and as the rumours of a popish plot whirled through London the sealing of a higher profile alliance with the United Provinces seemed more attractive. He was also mindful of the fact that his elder sister, Elizabeth of Bohemia, was a long-term exile at The Hague and that she might be helped by such a marriage. Moreover, it could go a considerable way towards appeasing public opinion at home while potentially providing Charles with finance and military resources offered by William's father, Frederick Henry. Unwilling to be drawn into the English king's domestic troubles, the Dutch balked at a wider political alliance. Charles did, however, ensure a clause in the marriage treaty that Mary was to remain in England until she was twelve years old, when she would legally be of age to agree formally to her marriage. It is possible that the king and queen both hoped that, by that time, their situation would have improved and Mary could abjure the

Dutch marriage, leaving her free to wed the heir to the Spanish throne.

It is true that the nine-year-old bride was far from thrilled with the prospect of becoming a princess of Orange. Being thrust forward as a replacement for her younger sister piqued her pride, of which she already had plenty. Portraits of Mary in early childhood and her mother's remarks about her wilfulness suggest that she was already something of a little madam with strong views of her own. The Catholicism of her mother and of her governess, the countess of Roxburghe, made no impact on her. She was already, and would always remain, very much her father's daughter, distant, unadaptable and convinced of her own superiority. A Dutch princeling seemed unworthy of a Stuart princess.

Nevertheless, there were many safeguards for her welfare in the terms of the marriage treaty. She was to be allowed to worship according to the rites of the Church of England rather than the stricter Calvinism of Dutch Protestantism. All her English servants were to accompany her when she moved to The Hague and any replacements, as the years passed, were to be English, not Dutch. The expenses of Mary's household were to be paid by her husband and she was to receive an additional £1,500 in living expenses. Should William pre-decease her, she would receive £10,000 a year and be given two residences. Thus safeguarded, Mary awaited the arrival of her bridegroom, while attending Strafford's trial with her parents. Whether she followed much of what was going on, finding it harrowing, tedious or merely regarding it as a duty that went with her rank, is impossible to say.

Prince William arrived with a fleet of twenty vessels under the command of the Dutch Admiral van Tromp, accompanied by an entourage of 250 people, at Gravesend on 19 April 1641. There he was allowed time to recover from a very stormy crossing of the North Sea before his entry to London amid tight security. He went first to Whitehall to meet Charles and Henrietta Maria, where his gifts of diamonds and pearls worth £23,000 were happily received by the cash-strapped king. Mary was at Somerset

House suffering from a heavy cold and he did not see her until the next day. Settled into the earl of Arundel's residence on the Strand, the boy passed the time until the actual day of his wedding in preparing for the ceremony, dining with his future in-laws, and getting to know Mary and her brothers.

William was a good-looking and well-educated boy of fifteen who realized that he had been fortunate to make a marriage better than he might have expected. Whatever the difficulties faced by Charles I and the disaffection of the noisier elements of London's populace, civil war did not appear to be an imminent danger. Mary got over her cold and reacted positively to his attentions – indeed, the two children seem to have taken at least a reasonable liking to one another at this early stage. Their marriage took place on 2 May in the Chapel Royal of Whitehall Palace, where the bishop of Ely officiated at a simple ceremony scarcely different from the liturgy used today by the Church of England. Mary, wearing a silver gown, was led in by her brothers and attended by sixteen young ladies of the nobility. Charles gave his daughter away and Henrietta Maria, Marie de Médici and Princess Elizabeth watched from a private gallery. Afterwards, there was a mid-afternoon wedding dinner and in the evening a mock consummation of the marriage, when William, wearing a robe of blue and green satin, was escorted into the marital bedchamber by Charles I and lay at a discreet distance from Mary, who was modestly wrapped up in a sheet. The young couple kissed several times, before William got up to go to his own chamber.

The wedding portrait painted by van Dyck, showing two serious young people splendidly attired, presents a picture of a handsome but uncertain couple. William wrote several days later to his parents: 'Although we were at first very solemn towards each other, now we feel more at ease; I find her to be more beautiful than the painting. I love her very much and I believe that she loves me too.'[21] Despite trying to persuade Charles to give his permission for Mary to return with him to The Hague, William left alone at the end of the month. They would not be apart for long.

Civil War

STRAFFORD'S WAS NOT THE only unnatural death in London
during the anxious spring and summer of 1641. Disease hit the
city hard. Many, both great and small, were carried away by the
particularly vicious conjunction of two epidemics. An outbreak of
smallpox claimed the life of Francis Russell, earl of Bedford, one
of the leading aristocratic critics of the king, before Strafford
himself even went to the scaffold. Then, as the hotter, unhealthy
airs of summer crept over the capital, so too came a serious outbreak of the plague, a centuries-old scourge that regularly saw
the departure to the countryside of those, like the royal family,
who could afford to leave and had other residences to inhabit.
Ordinary citizens had to take their chances and many died, as the
outbreak continued into the autumn.[1]

As the summer progressed, both the king and queen were

laying plans to move – though in quite different directions and not just because of the dangers of pestilence. Strafford's execution brought a temporary respite for Charles I in his quarrels with the English parliament and he felt confident enough, by July, to prepare to go back to Scotland, with the aim of seeking help in that country that might benefit him in his dealings with England. The Scots had grown weary of the inconvenience and expense of occupying northern England and cracks were starting to appear in the Covenanting movement. Charles hoped to exploit these and break the relationship between his disaffected nobles in England and their Scottish supporters. He arrived in Edinburgh on 14 August and stayed there till mid-November. His wife, meanwhile, remained in southern England. From August onwards, when her mother, alarmed by the rising tide of anti-Catholicism, left England, the queen felt increasingly vulnerable.[2]

Given her strength of character, it is easy to be dismissive of Henrietta Maria's fears in the summer of 1641. She was undoubtedly highly strung and given to hyperbole, writing to her sister Christine in August 1641: 'Please pardon me because I haven't written to you often. I must tell you that the sudden change in my fortunes has made me mad. From the highest degree of happiness I have fallen into unimaginable sorrows of all kinds.' She went on to add that it was not just herself who was suffering, but Catholics in general and the royal family's own loyal servants at court who were being removed from them. 'I am,' she said, 'kept here like a prisoner and not even allowed to accompany the king to Scotland.'[3] There was, alas, nothing that the duchess of Savoy could do to help her younger sister beyond providing a sympathetic ear. Christine's own situation was, if anything, worse than Henrietta's in 1641. She had been a widow for three years and was beset by difficulties as the regent for her colourfully named son, François-Hyacinthe. The duchy of Savoy was caught up in the seemingly endless wars that afflicted the Italian peninsula and Christine found herself at loggerheads with her two brothers-in-law and her late husband's father, who were not keen to give this strong-willed and capable French princess any real authority. Henrietta later claimed that Christine 'would have helped me powerfully with money and troops, if her father-in-law had left her a rank conspicuous enough and free from his magnates, and free from the miseries to which the poor princess was reduced'.[4] These were very big 'if's and they demonstrate Henrietta's tenuous grasp of political reality in continental Europe as well as in the British Isles. For her, politics were always refracted through an intensely personal prism. Yet neither she nor Christine were to find any material assistance from France, the land of their birth, despite the arrival of two sons to their brother, Louis XIII, in 1638 and 1640 after nearly a quarter of a century of marriage to Anne of Austria. The ill-suited French royal couple never got on from the moment Anne arrived in France. She suffered four miscarriages early on but had not conceived for sixteen years. Months passed with the king and queen scarcely seeing each other so the births of the dauphin Louis, destined to be the greatest king of the seventeenth century, and his brother, Philippe, surprised the French court and the entire country. These boys would play an important part in the lives of the Prince of Wales and his youngest, as yet unborn, sister.

Meanwhile, Queen Henrietta Maria's fears for her safety were very real and the constraints lately placed on her by parliament seemed to her frighteningly restrictive. Guards had been appointed for the queen and her sons, to report on her activities and prevent those deemed unsuitable from coming anywhere near her. Desperate to escape, the queen tried to convince her enemies in both Houses of Parliament that she was ill and must be allowed to leave the country. She claimed to be suffering from the effects of 'discontents of mind and false rumours and libels spread concerning her'.

The queen's pleas fell on deaf ears, despite a committee of both Houses having been established to assess her request. There were fears that the real object of the journey was to sell off Crown assets and to link up with Catholics on the continent. So Henrietta did not get her way. Instead, she and the royal children were moved out of London for the summer to Oatlands, where Prince Henry had been born the previous year.

This palace was a country residence initially acquired and extended by Henry VIII for use while hunting to the south-west of London (which was considered the best area in the south-east of England for the chase) in the late 1530s. Though not comparable with the huge palaces in London it was no modest rural retreat, but a splendid mansion in its own right, with three adjoining quadrangular courtyards. A gateway by Inigo Jones was added in the early seventeenth century and Oatlands had a prominent prospect tower, giving wide views over the countryside. Today the site it occupied is a housing estate in Weybridge, Surrey, and little remains of the original palace but a brick gateway.[5]

Henrietta's summer in Surrey with her family was far from idyllic. Separated from her husband, without her confessor, the elderly Scottish priest, Robert Philip,[6] and supposedly removed from the influence of ill-intentioned Catholics, she was nevertheless very much in contact with events, writing frequently to Edward Nicholas, who was then acting as the king's secretary while awaiting his formal appointment, about matters of state.[7] Sadly for Nicholas, this was the beginning of a fraught relationship with the queen. He questioned her advice and he never had her confidence. Though loyal to the king, he would spend his entire exile during the Civil Wars at loggerheads with Henrietta and those around her, living in the Netherlands rather than Paris. Theirs might simply have been one of those relationships that got off to a difficult start in trying circumstances, but Henrietta probably never forgave Nicholas for suggesting to the king that her Capuchin friars should be removed.

She has been called a Lady Macbeth figure for what is perceived as her increasing influence on her husband and it is probably true that she would have seen her family's fortunes inextricably connected with the fundamentals of government and religion that her husband espoused. But though Henrietta Maria was always very free with her opinions and exhortations, Charles

I did not follow her counsels willy-nilly. Unsurprisingly, the less he did so, the more strident the queen became. The effect of her stance on her children is hard to assess because she makes no reference to them in her surviving letters from this time. But whether she cared to acknowledge it or not, there were already significant changes in the life of her eldest son, whose future upbringing was now a matter for parliament as much as it was for his parents.

*

NEWCASTLE HAD been removed from the post of governor to the Prince of Wales shortly after Strafford's execution, having been deemed as untrustworthy in the role by the king's opponents, who were suspicious of his devotion to Henrietta Maria. His replacement, William Seymour, marquess of Hertford, was a supporter of the monarchy, which probably made him acceptable to the king, but he had disliked many elements of the personal rule of the 1630s and was less personally identified with the royal family than his predecessor. Indeed, he was something of an outsider at court. Aged fifty-four in 1641, William Seymour was rather more than the elderly dimwit that is sometimes depicted. He had an interesting pedigree and a colourful past. This grandson of the unfortunate Lady Catherine Grey, sister to the Nine Days Queen, Jane, had Tudor blood. As far as the Stuart dynasty was concerned, Hertford probably came a little too close to them in his first, illicit marriage to Lady Arbella Stuart, a distant cousin who, like him, had a claim to the English throne. History seemed to be repeating itself in the swift and severe response of James I, whose reaction to this union was very similar to that of Elizabeth I to Catherine Grey's secret marriage. Both parties were imprisoned and though they managed to escape, Arbella was recaptured and confined to the Tower of London, where she died in 1615. Her husband fled abroad and did not return till after her death.

The scandal, however, left him under a cloud for many years and though he entered politics, he was not very active. His second marriage, to Lady Frances Devereux, sister of the third earl of Essex, put him in the ranks of Buckingham's opponents. For many years, he consciously avoided the court, a reminder that not all grandees were ambitious for political influence or office. The marquess enjoyed country life and he did not need the perquisites of official appointments, preferring to live quietly on his Wiltshire estates. A graduate of Magdalen College, Oxford, Seymour was described by Clarendon in his *The History of the Rebellion* as 'a man of very good parts, and conversant in books in both Latin and Greek languages, and of a clear courage . . . he was so wholly given up to a country life, where he lived in splendour, that he had an aversion, even an unaptness, for business.'[8]

So why, then, did a man dismissed by one historian as 'bookish and lazy' (a somewhat ungenerous interpretation of Clarendon's description)[9] agree to take on what he must surely have realized, by the summer of 1641, was likely to be a delicate appointment? The answer seems to be that Hertford genuinely believed in monarchy, as did a number of the king's aristocratic opponents, and that he was committed to the rule of law. Perhaps he hoped eventually to influence the young Prince Charles towards a more constitutionally based, less rigid, type of government. Time was not on his side if that were the case. Instead, he found himself caught between the increasing animosity between parliament and the Crown, responsible less for the guidance of the Princes Charles and James (who was also in his care) than for their personal safety. As early as August 1641, some MPs were doubtful that Hertford was the man they wanted in charge of the Prince of Wales, though the suggestion that two additional governors be appointed was not pursued.

In early November, as the political situation grew more tense, Hertford received orders from both Houses of Parliament that the prince should be removed from his mother to live at Richmond, where Hertford himself was based. The marquess's reception when he arrived to convey this instruction was evidently frosty. It was reported that he had stayed at Oatlands all day, 'but, in regard there was no lodging there for him, the marquess returned to Richmond'. The earl of Holland, Henry Rich, an inveterate ladies' man who had been a lover of the duchess of Chevreuse, was selected as a more acceptable bearer of bad news. A controversial intriguer who made enemies as easily as he charmed women (he would change sides from parliament to the royalists and back again during the Civil Wars), Holland was not to be so easily deterred. When he waited upon the queen 'he presented her with the reasons of both Houses, why they desired the Prince should reside at Richmond'. The Prince had, Holland told her, '. . . lost much opportunity in improving himself in his learning and study by being at Oatlands'. He went on to fire a warning shot about religion. Of course, he said, parliament did not think Her Majesty 'would intimate anything unto him concerning her religion, yet there were many about her which might prepare him with those impressions in his religion, which might sit upon him many years after'. Finally, there were concerns for the Prince of Wales's safety: 'in this time so full of danger (for we hear of new treasons every day)' it was advisable 'that the Prince might be more secure.' Holland went on to reassure the queen that parliament did not intend that she should never see her son at all – he might come when she was 'desirous to see him' – but that he should reside at Richmond. Otherwise, he said, Hertford could not 'take that charge that was required by the Parliament, nor be answerable for such servants as were about him'.

Henrietta knew well what lay behind this polite language. She and her servants were suspect. Her eldest son was being removed from her control. Of course, she thanked parliament for their care of her son and claimed that she had never intended his residence at Oatlands to be permanent: 'The occasion wherefore Her Majesty sent for him, was to celebrate the birthday of one of his sisters but that the Prince should be presently sent back to Richmond.' This was something of a lame excuse, since the birthday of Princess Mary was on 4 November and could scarcely have explained the Prince of Wales's presence at Oatlands since the summer. Henrietta concluded with the pointed remark that she was confident that when the king returned from Scotland, parliament 'will express the like care both of the king's honour and safety'.[10] The queen was a woman who liked to have the last word. But the removal of her eldest son was a significant blow. The reasons for parliament's concern had far less to do with the prince's education than they did with the general air of disquiet and dread. On 23 October a rebellion broke out in Ireland which would push the English kingdom ever closer to civil war.

*

IN TRUTH, the king's difficulties were mounting before the first reports of an uprising in Ulster came across the Irish Sea. After a promising start, when he had appeared to be working well with the parliament in Edinburgh, he had disastrously lost the initiative in Scotland. While, on the surface, the effect of his presence seemed to be beneficial, offering hope that he might still be able to use Scotland as a trump card in his dealings with English opponents, the reality was different. At the beginning of October, Edinburgh was the scene of secret meetings as a conspiracy some weeks in the planning moved closer to realization. This attempted coup was aimed at breaking the back of the Covenanter movement and, in so doing, to cut its ties to the dissidents in London. The plan was to remove Argyll and Hamilton, whose closeness to the king during the Bishops' Wars had been eroded by a rapprochement with Argyll, as well as the earl of Lanark, Hamilton's brother. This attack on three leading members of the aristocracy was bold and might have succeeded, had not some elements of the Scottish army, who were to be involved in the arrest and probable murder of the three men, revealed details to General Leslie, their commander-in-chief. Leslie warned Hamilton and Argyll, who hesitated briefly over what to do, perhaps not initially crediting that the king could have been complicit in an attempt to have them assassinated. When the danger of their position sank in, they fled to Hamilton's strongly defended home at Falkirk.

Charles had been careful to ensure that he was not directly implicated in the detail of the plot but that he knew of it and supported it seems beyond doubt. Even as his quarry was escaping, a tearful king addressed the Scottish parliament to inform them of his distress at 'the incident', a studied understatement of what had nearly come to pass. The phrase stuck, and his unsuccessful coup has been known as such ever since. Yet the implications were not lost on those surrounding the king. Endymion Porter, his groom of the bedchamber, wrote that these events had 'put everything into a worse condition than we found it . . . we can look forward to nothing but a general confusion.' The news from Scotland certainly shocked the king's opponents in the English parliament, who were alarmed not just for its implications for the constitutional gains made in the summer, but also for their own safety. A major row broke out over parliament's right to veto ministerial appointments. But still the king's supporters believed that they could gain the upper hand in England. Everything was to be thrown into confusion by news received on 31 October which prompted an emergency meeting of the English Privy Council. A weary and begrimed messenger arrived that afternoon, bearing the shattering news that a major revolt had broken out in Ireland.

The gruesome details of massacres perpetrated by rabid Catholics on innocent Protestants, men, women and children, have coloured responses to the Irish rebellion ever since. Published in the many news-sheets and pamphlets of the time were stories which reveal that press sensationalism has a long and dishonourable history. Communities put to the sword, mass drownings, the rape of women in front of their husbands, children roasted alive over spits . . . there seemed no end to the depravity of the Irish Catholic population. Almost none of this was true, but it was believed by many in England, who saw in these reports further evidence that their suspicions of Catholicism and its practitioners were correct. Yet while the rebellion in Ireland caught the English by surprise, it had been a long time coming. Resentment of the 'plantation' of English and Scottish settlers, especially in Ulster under James I, had led to widespread, festering discontent among the 'Old Irish' families, who were dispossessed of their lands, their grievances ignored by the king. The origins of the revolt lay in a sense of deep-seated alienation and a feeling that discrimination against Catholics was growing. But the pleas for greater toleration, for the king to recognize the inequitable nature of their situation, had fallen on deaf ears. What had begun as an uprising with limited aims soon spiralled out of control. Losing Ireland seemed a very real prospect, horrific to king and parliament alike.

As parliament prepared to raise an army of 8,000 men to suppress rebellion in Ireland (an initiative that, by precedent, should have been the king's) concerns began to be raised about the involvement of the queen. Henrietta's situation was not helped by the fact that the Irish rebels called themselves the 'Queen's Army'. Small wonder, then, that the Prince of Wales was removed from her influence two days after the news of the revolt reached London. But still her husband remained in Edinburgh, trying to salvage something from the wreck of 'the incident'. On 22 November, parliament presented him with its summation of all that was wrong with his government of England in the form of a Grand Remonstrance. It did not make comfortable reading for the king but he was far from cowed. His return to London on 25 November took the form of a ceremonial state entry into the city, suggested by the royalist-leaning aldermen and lord mayor, who believed that a boost to monarchical magnificence would reinforce Charles's tottering authority and give the capital some much-needed cheer at a difficult time.

Charles I did not like public occasions but he had been heartened to be reunited with his family at Theobalds, the Hertfordshire palace that he greatly enjoyed, as had his father. He was well aware of the need to impress his subjects visually and not just with words, though those were important. State entries were all about symbolism. Encouraged by Henrietta, he agreed to participate in a spectacle that was also intended to demonstrate the loyalty of counsellors whose allegiance was wavering, including the earl of Holland and, improbably, Hamilton himself, who participated as master of the horse a mere six weeks after the king had tried to have him silenced. But perhaps the most unnerving aspect of this state entry to the uninvited (not a single member of the House of Commons was included and the disaffected peers stayed away) was the implied threat of military force.

The procession formed at Hoxton to the east of the city, with Prince Charles riding before his governor, Hertford, who bore the sword of state and was followed by the king himself, riding a 'steed . . . with a stately saddle embroidered with gold and silver [thread]'. Immediately after Charles I came a coach carrying the queen, the duke of York and Princess Mary, as well as the king's nephew, the elector palatine. The people, it was said, received them 'with loud and joyful acclamations, crying out God bless and long live King Charles and Queen Mary and their majesties recip- rocally and heartily blessed and thanked the people with great expressions of joy'.[11] At two in the afternoon, a banquet was held at the Guildhall, where the king and queen and their family dined in pomp and solemnity, just as they had in the happier days of the preceding decade. Yet the day was not the triumph the organizers had hoped. The mixed messages of moderate reform and military intimidation were not lost on the nervous population of London or on those parliamentarians excluded from proceedings on 25 November 1641. And although they did not know it, the children of Charles I would never again gather with their parents in such glittering circumstances.

*

LONDON REMAINED volatile throughout December, despite the king's confidence that he might have seen off the worst that his critics could throw at him. Charles believed that he had won over the 'better sort' of Londoner and he was careful to demon- strate that he was appointing moderate counsellors. He held more frequent meetings of the Privy Council, nominated a number of

Calvinist bishops and passed Christmas at Whitehall. Yet the mood of the capital was inexorably turning against him. On 21 December elections to the Common Council of the City of London produced a major setback for the king's cause, as the moderate royalism of the lord mayor was replaced by the appointment of a majority on the City's Common Council whose sympathies lay clearly with parliament and who held radical Puritan beliefs. Not only did this strengthen the position of the king's enemies but it also meant that control of the Trained Bands, the city's militia, passed into their hands. At a time when the king appeared to be gathering his own armed forces to use against disaffected citizens in London, this was a significant development. The very next day Charles made the first of two major blunders that would cost him dearly, when he tried to replace the lieutenant of the Tower of London, Sir William Balfour, with Colonel Thomas Lunsford, a soldier of dubious reputation who was only one of such a number swilling about in London after the disbandment of the northern army. Believing that this singularly ill-chosen appointment presaged a possible coup, the Commons voted to have Lunsford removed. Amidst all this uncertainty, renewed calls for the abolition of episcopacy led to rioting over several days around parliament and an assault on the organ and altar at Westminster Abbey on 28 December.

Yet even this might not, in itself, have led to an irretrievable breakdown of trust between the king and his parliament. There had been riots before, he had armed men to suppress them (even if their presence was contentious) and progress had been made on how to deal with the Irish rebellion. On the first day of 1642, Charles I issued a proclamation condemning the rebels, saying that unless they laid down their arms they would be met by 'the powerful succours of our good subjects of England and Scotland', who would fall upon them 'with fire and sword'.[12] This was a somewhat different reaction from that with which Charles had first greeted the news from Ireland back in October, when he remarked to Nicholas: 'This may hinder some of these follies in

England.' But the one thing he could no longer hinder was the effect of anti-Catholic dread and its impact on his wife.

Fearful that the wrath of the House of Commons would lead to the impeachment of the queen, Charles made one of his greatest errors of judgement. On 4 January 1642, at about three in the afternoon, he left Whitehall Palace with his nephew, the elector palatine (but neither of his sons) by coach, to make the short journey to Westminster Hall. Accompanying him was an armed force of between three and four hundred men. While most of these waited outside, nearly one hundred of them entered the House of Commons chamber with the king, to the astonishment of those present. He had come to arrest five members – Pym, Hampden, Strode, Holles and Haselrig – and also had a warrant for the arrest of one peer, Lord Mandeville. But no monarch had ever before entered the House and Charles was well aware that he was not just breaching privilege, but making history. The members saw the slight figure of the king occupying the Speaker's chair, surrounded by men with cocked pistols and drawn swords, while the Speaker, William Lenthall, knelt at his feet. When Charles spoke, he acknowledged the gravity of the step he had taken: 'Gentlemen,' he said, with considerable understatement, 'I am sorry to have this occasion to come unto you.' Turning to the Speaker, he asked that the five members be handed over to him. Lenthall, though conscious that he was addressing his king, was not intimidated. 'I have,' he said, 'neither eyes to see, nor tongue to speak in this place but as this House is pleased to direct me, whose servant I am here.' In that crystal-clear expression of parliamentary privilege and the polite but defiant words of a man whom he himself had appointed, Charles knew that he had gambled and lost. Looking around, he remarked, 'I do not see any of them – I think I should know them.' The comment often attributed to him, 'I see the birds are flown', does not appear in the *House of Commons Journal*.[13]

The five members had already fled, hiding first in the nearby Court of King's Bench. They had only barely got away, forewarned by a lookout from the French embassy, who was watching the king's progress from Whitehall and who alerted Nathaniel Fiennes, the son of one of Charles's leading aristocratic opponents, Lord Saye and Sele. But the presence of armed men threatening the House of Commons was an image that stayed in many minds during the years to come. For the king, encouraged by the queen who was desperate for him to take decisive action, had miscalculated disastrously.[14] Perhaps he might have had the five members murdered in their beds, just as he could, several months earlier, have authorized the assassination of his Scottish enemies. Charles lacked this killer instinct when it came to individuals, though he would be less precious about spilling the blood of soldiers in warfare over the next six years. One thing, however, was now unavoidable. The royal couple could not stay in London, where their safety was under the gravest threat.

They left on 10 January, amidst secrecy and fear, taking their three eldest children with them. Fleeing first downriver by barge to Hampton Court, they arrived without any warning and their apartments were not ready for them. The family passed the first night huddled in the same bed in one room. But in the confusion, Elizabeth and Henry were left behind in London, their fate now beyond the control of the parents who had failed so miserably to protect them.

Two days later the king and queen arrived at Windsor, a safe distance from the disturbances of London but still close enough for the king to communicate with parliament. On 11 February he moved even closer, back to Greenwich. But this appearance of accommodation with his opponents was an illusion. The full extent of the king's resentment was made clear in interview with the Dutch ambassador, the baron van Heenvliet, when Charles listed all the concessions he had made and despaired that, in respect of the bishops, he was going back on his coronation oath. 'You see,' he concluded, 'how far their intentions go.'[15] But he was desperate to buy sufficient time to get Henrietta out of the country, before parliament, suspicious of the queen's motives, stepped in to prevent it. The ostensible reason for the departure was to convey Princess Mary to William of Orange, so that she could acclimatize to her new country and be prepared for her role as the consort of the heir to the House of Orange-Nassau. Heenvliet, a man who would play a significant role in Princess Mary's future, had come to London to discuss the arrangements that would be necessary to receive mother and daughter, but his emphasis on the princess, rather than the queen, evidently annoyed Henrietta. As he assured Charles that the greatest possible care would be taken of Mary, the queen grew impatient. 'You have not said anything about me. I am going too, you know,' she broke in.[16] A move which had seemed only a possibility after the May wedding of the children had now become, as far as the royal family was concerned, an imperative. It would ensure Henrietta's personal security while allowing her an opportunity to gain assistance for the king. This they hoped to achieve by pawning her jewels. There was considerable suspicion that she would take a treasure trove of valuables with her, but nothing, in the end, was done to prevent her. Husband and wife seem both to have accepted that the constitutional and religious struggles of the last two years would now be played out in armed confrontation and Charles, having surrendered control of London to his opponents, needed to ensure that he gave them some hope that this could be avoided.

By agreeing to a bill which excluded bishops from the House of Lords, Charles was able to appease his wife's anxieties that he would allow the country's militia to come under parliamentary control. As soon as he received news of her arrival in the Netherlands, Charles would move north to Yorkshire, a region that it was believed would be much more sympathetic to his cause than the rebellious capital and south-east. The first part of this strategy was put in place when the king and queen and Mary arrived in Dover on 16 February. They were obliged to wait a week until the winds changed, allowing Henrietta and her daughter to take ship. They were to board the *Lion*, accompanied by Buckingham's sister, the countess of Denbigh, his daughter, the duchess of Richmond, and Mary's governess, Lady Roxburghe. Lord Goring and Lord Arundel, committed supporters of the queen, went with her, as well as a sizeable contingent of servants and Henrietta's favourite dog. Van Tromp, who had escorted Prince William when he came to wed Mary, was despatched, this time with fifteen vessels, to protect and support the royal party across the North Sea.

Charles parted from his wife and daughter amid scenes of high emotion. Both he and Henrietta were in tears as she exhorted him to stand firm and follow the plan they had devised for suppressing his opponents. Mary, a forlorn ten-year-old leaving everything that she knew, clung miserably to her father. Eventually, she and her mother hugged him one last time and went on board. As their vessel left the harbour and put out to sea, Charles rode along the clifftops, waving his hat until their sail grew small on the horizon. It is, perhaps, the archetypal gesture of the romantic cavalier.[17] His wife returned to him the following year but he never saw Mary, the proud, reticent child who so strongly resembled him in character and appearance, again.

*

AFTER A STORMY crossing, which culminated in the second vessel springing a leak and sinking, taking the queen's chapel ornaments and most of Goring's belongings with it, the queen and princess arrived on the shores of Mary's new home. Prince William was waiting to greet them and, after some time for recovery, he took them on to the town of Brill, where Mary was introduced to her father-in-law, Prince Frederick Henry. This youngest son of William the Silent, the patriotic Dutch leader who had spearheaded the revolt of the Netherlands against Spanish rule in the latter part of the sixteenth century, was then in his late fifties and must have seemed to Mary Stuart more of a grandfather figure than a replacement for her own father. His portrait in the Bodleian Library's collection shows a man with a florid but good-humoured face and he certainly set out to be as kind and welcoming as possible to the young bride. He had been head of the House of

Orange since the death of his half-brother in 1625. Frederick Henry was half French but the fact that his mother, Louise de Coligny, was the daughter of a prominent French Protestant leader murdered in the St Bartholomew's Eve Massacre of 1571 was not something that his guest, Henrietta Maria, would have found entirely comfortable. As stadtholder of five key Dutch provinces and commander-in-chief of the Dutch army and navy, Frederick Henry's political and military roles were important, but he did not hold sovereign power over Dutch government.[18] His main concern throughout his tenure of office had been to defend the interests of the republic against the Spanish, who still ruled the southern part of the Low Countries. The marriage of his son to the king of England's elder daughter was flattering on a personal level but also somewhat problematic, given the evident difficulties of Charles I. Though there were variations among the different provinces, Holland, in particular, had a strongly Calvinist and powerful local government, whose natural sympathies lay with opponents of the House of Stuart. Frederick Henry knew from the moment of Henrietta Maria's arrival that he would need to tread carefully. In reality, he probably wished that Mary had arrived without her mother.

The princess soon discovered that the warmth of her father-in-law's greeting would not be matched by that of his wife. Frederick Henry was over forty when he married and might have stayed a bachelor if his brother, who had no legitimate children, had not threatened to disinherit him if he did not marry and produce legitimate offspring of his own. Galvanized by this stark representation of his prospects, Frederick obeyed and offered his hand to the attractive but penurious Amalia van Solms, a lady-in-waiting to Elizabeth of Bohemia, Charles I's elder sister, already an exile in The Hague. The daughter of minor German aristocrats, Amalia swiftly accepted her suitor's hand, despite an age gap of nearly twenty years. Astute and fiercely ambitious, the new princess soon entered into a headlong rivalry with her erstwhile mistress, trying to outdo her in lavish dress, jewellery, court entertainments and commissioning of portraits. Dissatisfied with her depiction by Rembrandt, Amalia commissioned van Honthorst to paint her in exactly the same pose as a portrait he had earlier produced of Elizabeth, even wearing the same accessories.

Such unseemly proud defiance did not augur well for Amalia's relationship with her little daughter-in-law, whose developing personality was, unhappily, all too similar. There seems to have been friction almost from the outset, when Mary had a tantrum within weeks of arriving in her new home. Despite the fact that she had four daughters of her own by this time, Amalia never exhibited the slightest understanding or sympathy for a child who had left the country of her birth in dismal circumstances, and who was alarmed by the crisis in which her father found himself, as well as homesick and confused. She would not give precedence to her daughter-in-law, whatever etiquette dictated. It was the beginning of a spiteful relationship that would last the rest of Mary's life.

The reception from Elizabeth of Bohemia, as might have been expected, was very different. This Stuart princess, once regarded as a great beauty, was still a striking-looking woman at the age of forty-six. The events of a troubled life had taken her far from the early childhood days in Scotland and the cultured court of her parents in England, after her father inherited the throne of the Tudors. Married at sixteen to the elector palatine, Frederick V, Elizabeth was one of the most prominent victims of the Thirty Years' War. This protracted struggle between the Catholic and Protestant powers of Europe, the last of the continent's great religious wars, brought about the loss not just of the Crown of Bohemia, which Elizabeth and her husband had unwisely accepted, but also their flight from his hereditary lands in Germany. The couple had, in truth, allowed ambition to overcome common sense and they were to pay heavily for it. Elizabeth's life in exile in the Dutch republic might have killed the spirit of a lesser woman. A resident there for over twenty years, she lost her eldest son in a boating accident in 1629 and his father, a melancholy figure whom his lively wife had supported and loved throughout their tribulations, died unexpectedly three years later. Apart from an offer from her brother that she could return to England in the 1630s, there had been no help from Charles I. Like his father, he was not keen to get involved in a European war and there was no way he could restore his sister and her family to the palatinate without becoming embroiled in the wider conflict. Elizabeth did not give up hope of changing his mind, sending her son Charles Louis to the English court. The boy's uncle was quite happy to use him as a symbol of his own dynasty and authority, while carefully refusing to commit himself to his nephew's cause.

Henrietta Maria met Elizabeth of Bohemia for the first time on the road to The Hague, within a few days of her arrival in the Netherlands. The contrast between the two women could scarcely have been more marked. Both were queens, but one was a staunch Protestant and the other was a devout Catholic. Elizabeth was tall (at nearly six foot her stature was reminiscent of that of her grandmother, Mary Queen of Scots) and she towered over Henrietta. She was still handsome, whereas the queen of England had lost all her youthful bloom. This was mercilessly noted by Elizabeth's youngest daughter, Sophia, the future electress of Hanover and mother of George I of England, who recorded her first impressions of her aunt in her memoirs.

> The fine portraits of van Dyck had given me such an idea of the beauty of all English ladies that I was surprised to find the Queen (so beautiful in her pictures) a little woman with long, lean arms, crooked shoulders and teeth protruding from her mouth like guns from a fort. Still, after careful inspection, I found she had beautiful eyes, a well-shaped nose and an admirable complexion. She did me the honour to say that she thought me rather like Mademoiselle her daughter. So pleased was I, that from that time forward I considered her quite handsome.[19]

Accompanied by her husband, mother, father-in-law, aunt and several of her cousins, Mary then made her official entry into The Hague, to be greeted by '. . . the principal citizens [who] marched out, fully armed, to meet them; bells rang, fireworks were discharged and eighty pieces of cannon, placed in the court of the old palace, fired a triple salute.'[20] The princess's impressions of her reception went unrecorded but she may have shared the reactions of one English commentator present, who described the overall response of the Dutch to the English queen and her daughter as 'more royal than hearty'.

In England she was not forgotten. The Prince of Wales wrote to her early in March 1642, telling her that he missed her and revealing some of the anxiety of a twelve-year-old boy about the circumstances that had led to their separation:

> Methinks, although I cannot enjoy that former happiness which I was wont, in the fruition of your society, being barred those joys by the parting waves, yet I cannot so forget the kindness I owe unto so dear a sister, as not to write, also expecting the like salutation from you . . . I could heartily and with a fervent devotion wish your return, were it not to lessen your delights in your royal spouse, your husband, the Prince of Orange, who, as I conceived by his last letter, was as joyful in your presence as we are sad and in mourning for your absence.
>
> My father is very much disconsolate and troubled, partly for my royal mother's and your absence and partly for the disturbances of this kingdom.
>
> Dear sister, we are, as much as we may, merry and more than we would sad, in respect we cannot alter the present distempers of these troublesome times. My father's resolution is now for York, where he intends to reside, to see the event or sequel to these bad, unpropitious beginnings . . . Thus, much desiring your comfortable answer to these sad lines, I rest, your loving brother.[21]

Charles I did indeed move north in the spring of 1642. The troubles of the previous year had allowed the formation of a royalist party around the king and the growing belief among supporters of the monarch and parliament alike that the dispute was too deep-seated to be resolved peacefully. While Henrietta set about her task of supplying him with men and arms from the continent, Charles began his own search. Taking the Prince of Wales with him, he arrived in York on 19 March. But he had misjudged the mood of the north. His welcome there was muted and he cut an increasingly forlorn figure. All the pomp and ceremony of his court at Whitehall lay in what now seemed a distant past. By the end of the month he had only thirty-nine gentlemen and seventeen personal guards attending him. Meanwhile, Henrietta bombarded him with advice and exhortation from across the North Sea.

She was, quite naturally, concerned about her children. In one of her earliest letters from The Hague she told her husband: 'Thank God Charles is with you . . . send to fetch James as soon as ever you can.' For, however improbably, the king had allowed the duke of York to return to London to join his younger brother and sister at St James's Palace. This singular miscalculation seems to have been the result of uncertainty brought about by circumstances rather than a desire to placate parliament's anxieties about his intentions for his children. When he did command the marquess of Hertford to send James to him, parliament ordered the marquess to keep the child with him in London. But Hertford disobeyed, as he had ignored an instruction in February that the Prince of Wales should not leave Hampton Court. Showing considerable resolve, the marquess personally delivered the young duke to his father on Easter Monday 1642. James's arrival in York was greeted with bonfires, while his delighted father made the eight-and-a-half-year-old duke a Knight of the Garter. This triumph, however, did not last long.

At the beginning of April, Charles was considering the idea, if he could get enough military support in the north, of leading a force across to Ireland. Its ostensible aim was to quell the rebellion there but his opponents quite rightly suspected that such a force might be used against them in England. Parliament was thoroughly alarmed at such a prospect but it continued to observe the courtesies, expressing the fear that the king would be risking his life if he followed such a course. Charles's immediate objective, however, was the arsenal at Hull. Henrietta was obsessed by its importance, referring to it almost every third word in the letters she sent him. Not that the king needed reminding of how vital it was. Ireland was just a pipe dream without its contents, and, more crucially, he was concerned that the magazine at Hull should not fall into the hands of his enemies. Parliament was equally determined that the king should not gain control of it. Caught between the two was the city's governor, Sir John Hotham. Charles was certain that Hotham would not deny him entry when he arrived outside the gates on 23 April. In fact, he was so confident of success that he decided to give Prince James his first taste of power and responsibility when he sent the boy and his cousin, the elector palatine, still trailing in his uncle's wake, to parley with Hotham before the king himself arrived. James and his party were admitted through Hull's Beverley Gate. They did not get out so easily.

The arrival of the prince, presumably intended to arouse sympathy and loyalty, put the governor in an unenviable position. The mayor and city dignitaries of Hull might have been loyal to the king but Hotham was answerable to parliament for the disposition of the garrison. He sat James and Charles Louis down to dinner and then locked and barred the gates of Hull behind them. When Charles I arrived demanding entry, he was refused. And, if this insult were not enough, his second son and his nephew were trapped in a city he had thought would capitulate easily. The soldiers of the garrison foiled the intentions of the lord mayor to throw the keys to the fortress down to the king and prepared to defend the ramparts from attack. The king did not, however, have enough men at his disposal to mount any kind of assault. Faced with the stark choice of attacking a superior force or giving in, he abandoned his attempt to secure Hull's arms. Instead, he was forced to parley over two days to negotiate his son's release. This was a tense time, as the members of the duke of York's party were released one by one.

In later years, James looked back on this incident with the certainty of hindsight. He was convinced that firmer, swifter action by his father could have brought about the surrender of the Hull garrison and spared them both the ignominy that impressed itself so strongly on the mind of a small child. Whether he believed from that moment that diplomacy was never an option in dealing with opponents is probably to read too much into his later memories of the event.[22] He had been disastrously used and was, after all, not yet nine years old. The incident was traumatic – his personal safety appeared to be threatened and the respect due to his father denied – but his view of politics and war could not yet have been fixed.

As spring gave way to summer, affairs in England drifted falteringly towards military confrontation. Parliament did not relish the idea of waging war on Charles I. A majority of the House of Lords and a small but significant minority, about two-fifths, of the House of Commons, left Westminster to support the king. At local level, the prospect of a conflict that would divide families and destroy livelihoods caused great concern. Many hoped that they could remain neutral but these hopes were soon to be dashed. The stakes were raised in early June when, following repeated demands from the king that parliament's objectives be clearly and fully set out, the Nineteen Propositions were issued.[23] To Charles, these proposals seemed draconian. Had he agreed, he would have lost control of the judiciary, the Church of England, the appointment of his counsellors and the marriage and education of his children. Buoyed by the defection of many moderate peers and several key constitutional royalists from the Commons, Charles was in no mood to give up everything that he held dear. The Nineteen Propositions were, in his view, a call to anarchy that would destroy

England. A lively bout of pamphlet warfare followed as both sides sought to bring their arguments to a wider audience.

During the summer, the Prince of Wales and the duke of York accompanied their father as he roamed through the north of England, the Welsh Borders and the Midlands searching for men and arms. Parliament, meanwhile, was raising regiments with considerable success, and had appointed an aristocrat, the earl of Essex, son of the rebel earl executed by Elizabeth I, to lead them. On 22 August, the king was at Nottingham with only a modest force to support him. But he had had enough of indecision. In the heartland of England, on a gloomy day, his sons watched as the royal standard was raised over Nottingham Castle to demonstrate that he would fight for his vision of Stuart kingship. The flag soon blew down in the wind and the rain.

Part Three

A Family Destroyed

1642–49

CHAPTER FIVE

Reunions and Partings

'We have no home.'

Charles I's reply to his sons' enquiry about
when they would be returning home

THE SAME MONTH THAT the king raised his standard at Nottingham the princes were joined by two of their cousins from the Rhineland, Prince Rupert and his brother, Prince Maurice. Despite the fact that both were young (Rupert not yet twenty-three and Maurice two years his junior) they already had plenty of experience in military matters and brought with them a sizeable number of professional soldiers and military experts recruited in the Dutch republic. Charles I was delighted by the arrival of his nephews. His own efforts at recruitment had finally borne fruit and by late September 1642, when he left Nottingham, he had an army of about 14,000 men, roughly the equal of the parliamentary forces, which were under the command of the earl of Essex. The king's cavalry contingent and the number of experienced officers in his service gave him a slight advantage over his foes.

But the king was also pleased for family reasons. He put great store on dynasty and his sister's sons were his own flesh and blood. They had grown up partly dependent on his financial support (though Elizabeth of Bohemia would have liked this to be larger), in the difficult circumstances of exile, but their spirits were undimmed. Handsome, dashing and energetic, they were a breath of fresh air at the outset of the conflict. Full of optimism, Charles I appointed Rupert as general of the horse, a cavalry command that was, in theory, subject to the overall direction of the king's commander-in-chief, Robert Bertie, earl of Lindsay, and to the council of war. Yet, with the capacity for confusion that was so characteristic of his approach to political as well as military matters, Charles also gave Rupert authority to act as he saw fit, which effectively undermined Lindsay before a shot was fired. This was a dangerous licence to give to someone described by Henrietta Maria, in one of her more balanced judgements, as 'very young and self-willed'. The queen came to resent Rupert's influence and his place in her husband's affections but her caution at this stage was not entirely misplaced.

Charles I wished to acknowledge publicly his regard for his nephew even before Rupert joined him. By nominating the prince as a Knight of the Garter at the same time as the young duke of York, he established a bond between them. They were both younger sons who could expect to follow the military life. The Garter King of Arms later wrote to Rupert: 'And that His Majesty's affection to you might be the more emphatically expressed, he elected your Highness a companion of the Order in the company of his own son, both to manifest thereby the intimateness of affection to your Highness, as well as to shew Prince James in his tender years a glorious pattern for his princely imitation of valour and martial achievements.'[1] How much of a contrast James must have noticed between Rupert and his cousin's elder brother, the much more cautious Charles Louis, who had shared his humiliation at Hull. But Charles Louis was already out of the country. He had suffered enough of being paraded around by Charles I and did not share the commitment of his siblings to the royalist cause. Indeed, he could scarcely afford to, since parliament was now the source of the funding he needed if he was ever to reclaim his birth right in the palatinate.[2] Neither had he ever forgiven his uncle for marrying Princess Mary to William of Orange, when he believed he had himself been promised her hand.

Rupert, though, cut a very different figure. Splendidly dressed and superbly athletic, he was one of those men who seemed born to sit impressively astride a horse. Almost three years as a prisoner of the Austrians, from 1639 to 1641, failed to diminish his spirit. He simply did not believe in lost causes. His effect on royalist morale, especially among the younger men, was quickly apparent. Rupert was the leader they all wished to follow. His personal bravery, knowledge of the latest military techniques from northern Europe, his determination to succeed, all were inspiring. Within weeks of his arrival, the king's cavalry numbered 2,500 men. Its position at the heart of the royalist forces was firmly established. Rupert's weaknesses were yet to be discovered. His fierce temper and poor judgement of character, his impatience and the unpleasant habit of blaming failures on subordinates would make him a divisive figure in the royalist cause, even as parliamentary propagandists cast him as a German freebooter who had betrayed Protestantism. To his supporters he was an impossibly glamorous, charismatic figure. His detractors saw only a predatory and treacherous interloper on English soil. Certainly his reputation was quickly established at the first major battle of the Civil Wars, where both his young cousins were present.

*

THE TWO ARMIES that faced each other across the Vale of the Red Horse in Warwickshire, about a dozen miles north-west of Banbury, on the night of 22 October 1642 had only just become aware of their proximity. The captain-general of the parliamentary force, the earl of Essex, was expecting to find the royalists somewhere in the area. His task was to ensure that the king did not advance any closer in the direction of London but he did not have a precise idea of the whereabouts of Charles I's men till that evening. The king, learning from his rearguard that they had encountered Essex's scouts, was, at first, surprised to learn how close the rebels were. He then halted, recalled units which had gone on ahead towards Banbury, and gave the order for a rendezvous the next day, atop the steep escarpment of Edgehill, a prominent local feature which has given the ensuing battle its name. On the morning of 23 October, the king and his council of war could see the parliamentary forces massing on the plain below. The two armies were pretty evenly matched – about 15,000 men each, though Essex may have had a slightly larger number than the king. Both sides were ready to fight. There was a belief that one decisive battle would settle the dispute between king and parliament. Many conflicts begin with such vain hopes.

The royalist high command was split at the outset, when Prince Rupert and the earl of Lindsay disagreed angrily about the form of battle itself. Lindsay resigned and was replaced by another Scottish aristocrat, Patrick Ruthven, earl of Forth. It must, however, have been apparent to all the royalist commanders that Rupert's counsel was the one his uncle was the most likely to follow. And of his bravery and experience as a cavalry general there could be little doubt. His stock was especially high following a skirmish at Powick Bridge near Worcester a month earlier, in which he had prevented a parliamentary force from intercepting a valuable consignment of bullion and plate donated to the king's cause by the reliably royalist University of Oxford. The courage of Rupert's cavalry was not in doubt but, as events were to prove, their discipline and ability to think clearly was less convincing. They were, though, a much more formidable force at this early stage of the wars than their parliamentary counterparts. Overall, the difference in the two armies, which would become apparent during the course of the battle itself, lay in the professionalism of the king's troops and the inexperience of the better-equipped but poorly-trained men under Essex.

Charles I did not intend to lead his men in person into the fight. The last king of England to do so had been Richard III a century and a half earlier and his fate was an object lesson, hardened soldier though he was. The medieval notion of a monarch leading from the front had died in the British Isles with Richard at Bosworth and James IV of Scotland at Flodden. Van Dyck might have painted Charles I in armour astride a magnificent horse, but the animal looks more confident than the king. Charles had no experience as a soldier and was sensible enough to realize that his presence would help morale but that his direct participation might spell disaster. This caution did not extend to keeping his sons away from the battlefield, however. Their presence was understandable as they would stand witness to Charles's attempts to preserve his dynasty, though there was, inevitably, an element of danger. No one seems to have anticipated a serious threat to their safety.

Both sides received encouragement from their commanders. The text of a speech said to have been given by the king before the battle was subsequently published as part of the ongoing effort to influence public opinion but though there was a long tradition of monarchs using rousing oratory before battle, so magnificently dramatized by Shakespeare in *King Henry V*, Charles could not have delivered the words attributed to him within the hearing of his entire army. Instead, he rode the length of the royalist line, accompanied by his senior officers and his two sons, speaking to 'every brigade of Horse and to all the Tertias of Foot', encouraging them to do their duty, with 'great Courage and Cheerfulness'[3]. The published speech reveals his adherence to the beliefs that never left him: that he greatly regretted the descent into civil war, that he was answerable only to God, that his honour and reputation meant more to him than anything, and that he had done nothing wrong.

> Friends and soldiers, I look upon you with joy, to behold so great an army as ever King of England had in these latter times, standing with high and full resolutions to defend your King, the Parliament, and all my loyal subjects . . . but I attribute all this unto God, and the justness of my cause; He that

have made us a king will protect us. We have marched so long in hope to meet no enemies, we knowing none at whose hands we deserve such opposition, nor can our sun shining through the clouds of malignant envy, suffer such an obscurity, but that some influence of my regal authority, derived from God, whose substitute and supreme Governor I am, hath begotten in you a confidence in my intentions. But matters are now not to be declared by words but by swords . . . Now therefore know, my resolution is to try the doubtful chance of war, which with much grief I must stand to, and endure the hazard; I deem not the effusion of blood, but since heaven hath so decreed that so much preparation hath been made, we must needs accept of this present occasion and opportunity of gaining an honourable victory, and some addition of glory to our crown, since reputation is that which doth gild over the richest gold and shall be ever the endeavour of our whole reign.[4]

In contrast, Essex's orders were entirely those of a soldier, without appeal to high-flown concepts. 'I shall,' he wrote, 'desire all and every officer to endeavour by love and affable carriage to command his soldiers, since what is done for fear is done unwillingly and what is unwillingly attempted can never prosper.' And his last point was emphatically made. He specified that 'you avoid cruelty, for it is my desire rather to save the lives of thousands, than to kill one, so that it may be done without prejudice.'[5]

It was early afternoon before the first moves of the battle began. The royalist army had descended from Edgehill during the morning and was now deployed along a front of almost two miles, roughly parallel to the opposing force. As was customary, the exchanges began with artillery fire which largely failed to hit anything but picked up momentum when Rupert and the right wing of the royalist cavalry descended on the left wing of parliament's cavalry, standing stock-still as they had been ordered, and broke them in their first charge.[6] This opened the way for the other royalist cavalry units to make a sustained assault on both wings of

Essex's forces and overwhelm his cavalry. One of his infantry brigades also collapsed. In less than an hour of battle being joined, it appeared to the royalists that Essex was on the brink of defeat.

Yet the earl, for all his caution and natural pessimism, had not given up hope. He was a man for whom life had been one long succession of humiliation and loss. A perennial outsider, his father, the favourite of Elizabeth I's dotage, had died on the block when he was a child of ten. His mother deserted him within a year and he was left penniless and alone. Though the favour of James I brought him back to court, he simply did not fit in. A serious bout of smallpox left him badly scarred, two wives cuckolded him and he was disliked by Charles I. During his time as a soldier in the early 1620s, fighting depressing, inconclusive campaigns in the service of Protestantism in the Low Countries and the Rhineland during the Thirty Years' War, he came to believe that war was futile and solved nothing. His orders before Edgehill are a revealing illustration of this view, which had not changed in twenty years. Even his attempts at happiness as a provincial aristocrat came to nothing. By 1640 he was permanently embittered – and a natural opponent of a king he personally despised. When the call to command its forces came from parliament in the summer of 1642 he willingly agreed, setting about the necessary organization with firmness and vigour. As he left to command in the field in early September, he was cheered by an enthusiastic London crowd. It was the high point of his life. But at Edgehill, only six weeks after he had raised his own standard, it looked as though his ill-disciplined army might be swept away.

The confidence of his foes was misplaced. The centre of Essex's infantry held and he had called up reserves of musketeers as well as regrouping his remaining cavalry units. Nor was it just the parliamentary forces who were lacking in discipline. The royalist cavalry had made a serious mistake. Exhilarated by their initial success, they pushed on, leaving the battlefield altogether in pursuit of the fleeing parliamentarian horsemen, intending to inflict as many casualties as they could and also taking the

opportunity of pillaging their opponents' baggage train and supplies left behind the lines near the village of Kineton. During this
onslaught, they were said by the parliamentarians to have indis-
criminately killed men, women and boys. Whether this accusation
was true or not, one thing was certain: they had left their infantry
without any cavalry support and at the mercy of parliament's
musketeers, who now proceeded to engage the royalist foot at
close quarters. Meanwhile, Essex had regrouped his remaining
cavalry, his own Lifeguards, and Sir William Balfour's five troops
of horse and was able to do considerable damage to the centre
and left of the royalist infantry brigades. The earl of Lindsay was
mortally wounded, dying a prisoner of the parliamentarians the
next day, and the king's standard-bearer, Sir Edmund Verney, was
killed. The royal standard, temporarily captured by Essex's men,
was subsequently recovered by a late rally of returning royalist
cavalry, who also rescued some of their captured officers. Sunset
brought an end to a battle which had lasted between four and five
hours, with both sides exhausted and no clear-cut victory. By that
time, the two young princes had already left the field.

As the royalist infantry came under sustained assault, the king
decided to rally his troops in person. At the same time, he gave
orders for his sons to be escorted away from the fighting. James II
recalled his father's concern:

Judging it not fit to expose the Prince [of Wales] and the
Duke of York to some danger, he ordered the Duke of
Richmond to carry them out of the battle and conduct them
to the top of the hill; who excusing himself from that
employment, the King laid the same command on the Earl
of Dorset, who answered him with an oath that he would
not be thought a coward for the sake of any King's sons in
Christendom and therefore humbly desired his Majesty to
commit that charge to some other man. Thereupon the King
laid an absolute command on Sir William Howard, with his
pensioners, who were about fifty, to go off with them.[7]

Given the reported reluctance of two of Charles I's key supporters to ensure the safety of his sons, it is hardly surprising that the situation impressed itself on the mind of a nine-year-old boy. Their desire to avoid charges of cowardice overrode any concern for the wellbeing of two children perhaps unwisely exposed to the horrors of war by their father. But then Charles I had never seen bloodshed on the battlefield himself before.

Many years later, towards the end of his reign, Charles II received an account from the royal physician, Sir John Hinton, of his narrow escape at Edgehill, in which he described what happened when the king's foot retreated:

> . . . your Majestie was unhappily left behind in a large field, at which time I had the honour to attend upon your person, and seeing the sudden and quick march of the enemy towards you, I did with all earnestness, most humbly, but at last somewhat rudely, importune your Highness to avoid this present and apparent danger of being killed or taken prisoner, for their horse was by this time come up within half musket shot in full body, at which your Highness was pleased to tell me, you feared them not, and drawing a pistol out of one of your holsters, and spanning it, resolved to charge them, but I did prevail with your Highness to quit the place . . . in some haste, but one of their troopers being excellently mounted, broke his rank, and coming full career towards your Highness, I received his charge, and having spent a pistol or two on each other, I dismounted him in the closing, but being armed *cap-à-pie*, I could do no execution upon him with my sword, at which instant, one Mr Mathews, a Gentleman Pensioner, rides in and with a poleaxe immediately decides the business, and then overtaking your Highness, you got safe to the Royal Army, and without this Providence you had undoubtedly miscarried at that time . . .[8]

Hinton was seventy-six at the time his memoirs were published, but, despite awkward punctuation and changes of tense, he managed to convey with particular immediacy the peril of the situation in which the two princes found themselves. Charles's exuberant response shows his youth and sense of drama but his peril, as Hinton well knew, had been real. Capturing the king's sons would have given parliament an early advantage of inestimable importance and might have changed the course of the Civil Wars. All of the royal children except for Mary would have fallen into the hands of the king's opponents, weakening his position and raising the real possibility that if he did not come to terms, he could easily be deposed and replaced by a more tractable successor.

As nightfall closed in on the fields below Edgehill, the king and his sons had escaped but the outcome of the first set-piece battle of what was to become an increasingly bloody conflict was indecisive. Parliament's troopers remained in the field, cold and uncertain, with their dead and injured comrades all around them. Some had not eaten for two days. Most of them got what sleep they could on the ground, where the fighting had come to a halt as the light faded. Though some of the royalist army fell back to the slopes of Edgehill, a significant number of them also remained on the field, within musket distance of their exhausted foes.[9] Estimates of the dead and wounded vary considerably. Local villagers, who were almost all supporters of the parliamentary cause, reported that they had buried just under a thousand dead on the battlefield. This tallies with James II's assessment that no more than 1,500 men were killed. Some near-contemporary sources claim a much higher death toll but this seems unlikely.[10] The injured may have numbered several thousand. Many soldiers from the parliamentary army were cared for by local villagers in south Warwickshire, who later claimed reimbursement for the expense they had incurred. Royalist injured probably fared less well, being taken back to Oxford, where overcrowding made already unsanitary conditions worse and an outbreak of typhus added to the miseries of the army.

Essex had turned the real prospect of defeat into what is

generally described as a draw, though the royalist side claimed victory. Charles wrote to his eldest son's former governor, the marquess of Newcastle, then in command of the royalist army in the north of England, of 'the defeat that the rebels have received'. In truth, he held a clear advantage, for Essex had retired to Warwick, leaving the road to London open. Urged by Rupert to launch a cavalry attack on the capital with all possible speed, Charles hesitated, not without reason as the London militia outnumbered his horse by more than two to one and he was understandably reluctant to divide his forces, leaving his infantry without cavalry support. He had seen what happened under such circumstances. This delay allowed Essex to regroup and reach London ahead of him. A brutal fight at Brentford on 12 November left many parliamentary soldiers drowned in the Thames but the next day Essex was waiting at Turnham Green, to the west of London. There his large army, some 24,000 strong, was involved in a stand-off with the king's much smaller force. Just before dusk, Charles I decided there was no point in staying any longer and withdrew his forces along the Thames Valley, eventually returning to Oxford, where he prepared to pass the winter.

The first campaigning season of the wars was over. But the absence of a clear result at Edgehill had serious implications. Hopes of a swift resolution to the conflict evaporated. Ordinary people had taken sides and while many would change as the conflict progressed it was now evident that the war would not go away. Writing two and a half centuries later, Rudyard Kipling surely captured something of the emotions that had swirled in the breasts of the men who faced each other at Edgehill:

> But there is no change as we meet at last
> On the brow-head or the plain
> And the raw astonished ranks stand fast
> To slay or to be slain
> By the men they knew in the kindly past
> That shall never come again.[11]

Prince Charles and Prince James spent Christmas at Oxford with their father. The kindly past would not come again for them, either, but they did not know this as they eagerly anticipated the return of their mother.

*

HENRIETTA MARIA landed at Bridlington in Yorkshire on 22 February 1643, after a much delayed departure from the Dutch republic. In truth, she had outstayed a welcome that had always been lukewarm. Her Catholicism posed problems in a Protestant country and the fact that she was so obviously trying to raise money for the royalist cause offended the sensibilities of the influential politicians of the province of Holland. Initially, she found her task frustrating. The money men were deterred as much by the sheer value of the items she was trying to pawn as by the underlying diplomatic sensitivities, and they were aware that if hostilities broke out between the English king and his parliament there was a risk that they would get nothing back.[12] Between March and May 1642, she made little progress. Sometimes, the situation got the better of her normally indomitable spirit but she kept this from Charles I. It was to her childhood confidante, Mamie Saint-Georges, that she poured out her anguish: 'Pray to God for me, for be assured there is not a more wretched creature in this world than I, separated from the king my lord, from my children, out of my country and without hope of returning there, except at imminent peril, abandoned by all the world, unless God assist me . . .'[13] Gradually, however, she was gathering money and munitions, though several consignments that she shipped back to England were intercepted by parliament. It was not till early September that a substantial amount of arms and money arrived, with Princes Rupert and Maurice, at Newcastle. Further frustration followed when the province of Holland issued an embargo on the export of arms to England. The queen managed to circumvent this serious restriction with the aid of Frederick Henry of Orange, who provided men instead of arms. But this was all he could do and Henrietta had realized early on that his help was always going to be limited.

Throughout this period, the queen never ceased to encourage and advise her husband. She had views about everything that touched his Crown, his authority and his relations with his opponents. Invariably, she sought to bolster his determination, counselling against any kind of accommodation. Her tone was seldom less than hectoring and sometimes condescending. 'The winds,' she told him in July 1642, 'have been so contrary, over which I have as little power as you have over the parliament.'[14] She had not, however, forgotten her younger children, imploring Charles I in June 1642 to 'send and fetch away the children who are at London; for if affairs get to an extremity they are not well to be there'. Her anxiety would turn out to be entirely justified but Charles failed to act. Elizabeth and Henry remained in London, effectively hostages before even the formal outbreak of hostilities. But by the beginning of 1643, with Charles I and the royalist army secure in Oxford and parliament apparently hesitating about the further conduct of the war, their mother felt that she could safely return to England. The Dutch were anxious for her to leave, regarding her as an interloper who had abused their hospitality. Her first attempt to depart was thwarted by towering seas that forced her back to the Dutch coast; she had to make a second parting from Princess Mary, who had been deeply distressed by saying goodbye the first time.[15]

Lady Roxburghe, Mary's governess, had already returned to England and her young charge was now faced with the prospect of growing up without the support of those she had known and loved, in a very different environment, aware of the difficulties that beset her family but unable, until she was much older, to aid them in any way. No English princess had been married abroad so young since the Middle Ages. Even Margaret Tudor, sent north as the bride of James IV of Scotland in 1503, was thirteen years old at the time of her wedding and though the Tudor princess had gone to a court much smaller than that of her father, Henry VII, she was to become a queen. Mary's title as princess of Orange was much less impressive, a fact of which the child was only too well aware. Her substantial English entourage could, though, provide reassurance and continuity. John Durie, a learned Scottish preacher committed to reconciling the various strands of Protestantism in one unified Church, took up the post of chaplain and tutor to Mary in the spring of 1642. He was much travelled in Europe, had studied at Leiden University and spoke Dutch, German and French. Durie was nearly fifty years old when he became Mary's chaplain and remained with her for three years, eventually taking up a long-delayed invitation to sit on the Westminster assembly of divines, a body set up to examine reform of the Church of England. The nature of Durie's relationship with Mary is unclear but may, perhaps, be indirectly deduced by her lifelong commitment to Protestantism. It was the one aspect of her life in the Dutch republic that she had in common with her adopted country.

The court of a child, particularly an unhappy one, was ripe for in-fighting and favouritism. Lady Roxburghe's replacement, Katherine Stanhope, was resented by Mary on her appointment and had to endure a public scene as the princess bade a tearful farewell to the governess who had been with her since her birth. But Lady Stanhope, whose second husband was the Dutch baron van Heenvliet, the man who had helped negotiate Mary's marriage, was an extremely clever woman, albeit one with a slightly racy past.[16] A mother of three children of her own and stepmother of three others, she and her husband quickly saw the advantages that might ensue from her appointment. Though pregnant at the time she took up the role, she soon established herself as an indispensable confidante of the highly strung little princess and would remain so for the rest of her life. Aware of the princess's reliance on her old governess, Heenvliet wrote to Lady Roxburghe, reassuring her that he and his wife would do all they could for Mary and would strive to ensure that she was as happy as possible in her marriage.[17] And if Mary needed family support, she could rely on her aunt, Elizabeth of Bohemia, who kept an affectionate eye on her niece.

Henrietta Maria did not allow herself to dwell on her daughter's situation. It was enough, for the present, that escorting Mary to the Netherlands had provided cover for her underlying aim of bolstering the royalist war effort, and thus, eventually, she had succeeded in making a difference. From Bridlington she soon moved to York but she was in no hurry for the reunion that her sons and husband so desired. Under the protection of the marquess of Newcastle, she thoroughly enjoyed her time in the north. Henrietta liked being the centre of attention and styled herself 'Generalissima' as she continued her politicking and raising of supplies. The spring and summer of 1643 were optimistic times for the royalist campaign and the successes that she enjoyed, the sheer relief of being active and playing a commanding role, went to the queen's head. She thought the soldiers loved her. Though Charles wanted her to join him at Oxford with all possible speed, she did not move south until 4 June. Even then, she took a route on the last stage of her journey which was counter to the one decided by her husband, when she failed to wait for Prince Rupert's escort at Walsall.

Prince Charles and Prince James finally saw their mother again, after a gap of eighteen months, in the vale of Kineton below Edgehill, on 13 July 1643. It was a symbolic site, since the royalists still believed that they had won the battle there the previous autumn. The king and queen then rode back to Oxford, which they entered to public acclaim with bells pealing. Henrietta took up residence in Merton College, in apartments that were privately accessible on foot from Charles I's lodgings at Christ Church. In these ancient surroundings, the royal couple attempted to reproduce something of the atmosphere of happier days, when their splendid court at Whitehall had been the centre of culture and pleasant amusements. This was always something of an illusion. Oxford was not London and the supporters of the Crown packed into its much smaller area brought with them illness and poverty, even as Prince Rupert, Sir Ralph Hopton and other royalist commanders seemed to have shored up the king's hold on the north and the west of England and two of the king's chief opponents of two years previously, the earls of Holland and Bedford, defected from the parliamentary cause. But matters were not so clear-cut as the royalist successes of the summer of 1643 suggested. Charles I had already lost an opportunity for a peaceful solution, rejecting a settlement that was less prescriptive than the Nineteen Propositions on 20 May. And then, at the end of September, shortly after another major but inconclusive battle near Newbury in Berkshire, the beleaguered English parliament accepted the Solemn League and Covenant with Scotland.

This agreement, in the form of a religious and military alliance between the English parliament and the Scots, changed the dimension of the war. Its trigger was over the sea in Ireland. Charles I had moved to end the Irish rebellion by offering a truce to the Catholics, enabling him to bring back at least 10,000 men to support the royalist cause, an alarming development for the English parliament but one that also caused unease in Scotland. In return for their soldiers to boost parliament's forces, however, the Scots drove a hard bargain. What they wanted was no less than a union of Scotland and England. They envisaged a godly nation but it was to be in their image: a country where the Puritanism commonly referred to as Presbyterianism was the state religion and where other forms of Protestant worship were discouraged. No toleration of any sort would be extended to Catholics. Hammered out in Edinburgh, the Solemn League and Covenant was couched in language thought to be acceptable to inhabitants of both England and Scotland and was notably respectful to the king:

Having before our eyes the glory of God . . . the honour and happiness of the King's majesty and his posterity and the true public liberty, safety and peace of the kingdoms, wherein everyone's private condition is included; and calling to mind the treacherous and bloody plots, conspiracies, attempts and practices of the enemies of God against the true religion . . . and how much their rage, power and presumption are of late and at this time increased and exercised . . . we have . . . resolved and determined to enter into a mutual and solemn league and covenant.[18]

But the English delegation under Sir Henry Vane, mindful of disagreement about reform of the Church at home, managed to get the wording of the agreement altered to say that reform would be undertaken 'according to the word of God', thus leaving considerable room for manoeuvre. A growing number of Englishmen disliked the rigidity of the Scottish religious system and were uneasy about the role of the state in religion. These Independents, as they became known, were to grow in prominence and influence in the parliamentarian army during the coming years.

The hope that a cessation of hostilities in Ireland would greatly aid the royalist war effort proved unfounded. Troops did return but their impact was negligible. Many were Protestants whose natural inclination was to support parliament. There were numerous defections as well as desertions and those who fought in the north in the winter of 1643–4 had a bad time of it. But for parliament, the agreement with the Scots brought obvious advantages. In January 1644 a large Scottish army crossed the river Tweed and moved slowly south. As Rupert campaigned energetically, but not always successfully, in the south and west during the spring, the marquess of Newcastle was losing the north for the king. Harried by Lord Fairfax and his son Thomas, who would become parliament's leading general, the royalists were routed at Selby and retired to York, where Newcastle, with a force of 4,500 men, was besieged by the Scots, the Yorkshire forces of the Fairfaxes and the Eastern Association under the earl of Manchester, numbering in total some 30,000 men. His prospects looked grim. And then, following a recruiting drive and several minor engagements in the north-west, Prince Rupert arrived on the last day of

June at Knaresborough, intending to lift the siege of York. What followed forty-eight hours later was the largest battle ever fought on English soil.

Aware of Rupert's advance, the parliamentarian forces withdrew to the west of the city, to an area of heathland known as Marston Moor, and waited. The prince entered York unopposed on 1 July. He had relieved it without a shot being fired but he was not content with that. Despite the fact that his men were weary and he was outnumbered by a good 10,000 men, he decided to engage the 'rebels' the next day, whatever the misgivings of Newcastle and the marquess's officers.

Rupert's decision to fight has been the object of much discussion. Did he misinterpret the tortuously worded orders of his uncle about the peril of York and its potential loss? The king, harried in the Midlands by Essex and Waller, was downhearted and desperate to maintain his hold on the north of England. He wrote to Rupert on 14 June:

> But now I must give you the true state of my affairs which, if their condition be such as enforces me to make more peremptory commands than I would willingly do, you must not take it ill. If York be lost I shall esteem my crown little less, unless supported by your sudden march to me and a miraculous conquest in the south before the effects of their northern power can be found here. But if York be relieved and you beat the rebels' army of both kingdoms which are before it, then, but otherwise not, I may possibly make a shift (upon the defensive) to spin out time until you come to assist.[19]

It has been suggested that two of the king's advisers, Wilmot and Digby, influenced the wording of this letter, leaving Rupert with the strong impression that his uncle expected him to give battle. There may well have been disagreements in the royalist high command about encouraging the prince to take such a course. Lord Culpepper is said to have told the king, on learning that the letter had been sent, 'Why, then, before God you are undone, for upon this peremptory order he will fight, whatever comes on't.'[20] In fact, the king's situation had improved by the end of the month of June and he was able to pursue Essex's forces into the West Country. But Rupert did not know this as he prepared to face his foes on Marston Moor.

The fighting that rolled over this open landscape of arable fields and slightly rising ground that midsummer's evening changed the course of the war. There had been a heavy, thundery downpour just before battle was joined at about seven o'clock, as the men waited amidst the rye and barley. By nine o'clock, with the light fading, it was all over. Cromwell's cavalry, the Ironsides, inflicted heavy losses on their royalist counterparts on the west of the battlefield but Fairfax was not so fortunate on the parliamentarian east, where both cavalry and infantry were soon in trouble and word of a defeat began to spread. This was, however, premature. Better disciplined by far than they had been at Edgehill and benefitting from their numerical advantage, parliamentarian officers knew the importance of staying on the field and not heading off in pursuit. The royalist cavalry under Goring did not have the same restraint and were not there to defend the rest of the royalist army when it came under a second wave of attack. As darkness began to fall, the combined armies of parliament and the Scots had won a major and clear-cut victory and Cromwell's reputation as a cavalry commander was established. Rupert escaped after hiding, it is said, in a field of beans.

These small details are a reminder of the human cost of the war. It was not just the 4,000 royalist dead and 1,500 captured at Marston Moor who suffered.[21] Local agriculture was wasted by the movements of armies and their requirements to be fed. At a time when England was still an agricultural economy, the disruption and the hardship it caused had a widespread impact, even on those who did not really support either side.

There was much bravery in every encounter. Fairfax was wounded on the field at Marston Moor and still managed to lead his cavalry unit across royalist lines to rejoin Cromwell while Newcastle's own infantry fought to the last man. But there was also gut-wrenching fear in the face of death which often caused those who could to flee. Romantic notions of gallant Cavaliers and grim-faced Roundheads are the stuff of fiction. Reality was much messier and more painful as the battle-hardened Scottish soldier, Sir John Meldrum, who fought for parliament, knew only too well. Though largely successful in the campaigns of 1644, the siege of Scarborough Castle the following year saw him fall from a clifftop, get shot through the testicles and finally die an agonizing death after receiving a bullet in the stomach. But though Scarborough Castle held out for the royalists, the north was effectively lost after Marston Moor.[22]

From Evesham in Worcestershire two days after Marston Moor (but before he knew of Rupert's defeat) Charles I wrote to 'the Lords and Commons of parliament assembled at Westminster' with a further offer of negotiation:

> We being deeply sensible of the miseries and calamities of this our kingdom, and of the grievous sufferings of our poor subjects, do most earnestly desire that some expedient may be found out, which, by the blessing of God, may prevent the further effusion of blood, and restore the nation to peace, from the earnest and constant endeavouring of which, as no discouragement given us on the contrary part shall make us cease, so no success of ours shall ever divert us.[23]

Yet just over a week later, when he learned of Marston Moor, he decided to turn his Oxford army west, to pursue the earl of Essex. This shifting of the theatre of war may have been inevitable after what had happened in the north, but he was probably also hoping to rescue Henrietta Maria, who was already in the West Country and had recently given birth to their ninth child.

*

THE QUEEN SPENT only nine months in Oxford. There she had heard Mass in the chapel of Merton College, enjoyed musical performances and pastoral plays, while presiding over an increasingly fractious court. Her influence over Charles was considerable and may have helped smooth relationships between Prince Rupert and those who disagreed with his approach to the war, men like her own supporters, Digby and Jermyn. But though she had views on everything, the king did not let her interfere in matters such as the peace negotiations or the running of the rival parliament he set up at Oxford. This does not seem to have troubled Henrietta greatly; there were still many areas in which she could get involved. The pact between Scotland and the English parliamentarians convinced her that Ireland was more important than ever as a source of support for the royalist cause and she also continued to believe that plotting could change the course of the war. Coming to terms with rebels was always anathema to a woman who saw the opposition to her husband as a personal insult that could never be forgiven. She always took the view that people should be played off against one another to the advantage of her cause; that concessions could be offered that might easily be withdrawn or not honoured once she and her husband had achieved their aims. The stigma of being a 'popish plotter' clung to the queen as closely as did the impeachment for high treason that had been passed by parliament in London in June 1643. This meant that her life was at risk if she were ever to fall into the hands of the enemy.

For some months, none of this deterred her. As well as the possibility of succour from Ireland, she actively sought money from her homeland, and began to lay the ground for a possible match for the Prince of Wales with her niece, Anne de Montpensier, the only daughter of her brother, Gaston d'Orléans. The death of Louis XIII in the spring of 1643 weakened her influence in France, though this had never been great. The throne passed to her five-year-old nephew, Louis XIV, while power now resided with his mother, Anne of Austria, as regent, and her increasingly influential adviser, the Italian-born Cardinal Mazarin. Mazarin had no intention of becoming involved on either side in England's troubles and the Montpensier marriage was, for the time being, shelved. Undaunted, Henrietta Maria tried for a marriage alliance between Prince Charles and one of the daughters of Frederick Henry of Orange. This, too, got nowhere. Many Dutch politicians believed that one Stuart marriage was quite enough. So there was, as yet, to be no bride for the fourteen-year-old heir to the English throne.

While his mother was trying her hand at diplomacy, the prince and his brother continued their education with Bishop Duppa, though Oxford then had more of the air of a garrison town than a seat of learning. As the marquess of Hertford was involved full-time in the war effort (and was quarrelling with Prince Rupert) a new governor was appointed for Charles in 1644. Thomas Howard, earl of Berkshire, had been put forward for the post in 1641 so was not a surprise choice. Though a gentleman of considerable personal courage, he left no discernible influence on his charge. Little information about the king's two eldest sons survives from this period, save for a couple of anecdotes that suggest a mixture of boredom, vindictiveness and high spirits. Prince Charles is said to have laughed at some ladies during a sermon, incurring the wrath of his father, who smacked him over the head with a cane, and also to have given his opinion that a captured parliamentarian officer should be summarily hanged before the king could question him or offer mercy.[24] Though one should not read too much into the alleged comments of a fourteen-year-old boy, the views expressed are consistent with his merciless pursuit, after the Restoration, of those who had condemned his father.

At the beginning of 1644, Henrietta Maria had more to concern her than the misbehaviour of the Prince of Wales. She realized that there was to be an addition to the royal family and all the signs were that the pregnancy would not be easy. At thirty-four she was no older than many ladies who survived multiple childbirths in the seventeenth century, but Henrietta was

unwell and Oxford was not the safest or healthiest place to antici-
pate her confinement. No amount of pleasant amusements amid
the dreaming spires could disguise the fact that the state of the
city was deplorable. Overcrowded and diseased, a fifth of its population would die during the war years. Violence was commonplace among the shifting population of soldiers and courtiers,
often at war with one another.[25] The queen's decision to leave was
prompted, however, not just by the dangers to her health posed by
the conditions in Oxford but also because the 1644 campaigning
season began early and the parliamentary forces of the Eastern
Association, under the earl of Manchester, had the city in their
sights. In such circumstances, with parliamentarian propaganda
growing ever fiercer against her, it seemed too perilous to stay. On
17 April the king and her sons accompanied Henrietta Maria
as far as Abingdon in Oxfordshire, where they took an emotional
farewell of her. The queen was seven months pregnant and
wracked with a severe cough. The brief period of reunion with her
husband was over and though both hoped that this parting would
be temporary the future seemed to her full of uncertainty and
dread.

*

ESCORTED BY Henry Jermyn, the queen's party headed west,
making first for Bath. Henrietta's original intention had been to
give birth in Bristol but with a strong parliamentary force under
Essex pursuing her, it was decided to press on to Exeter. Parliament had agreed to the request that a member of her household
be given safe conduct to London to source a supply of 'childbed
linens' and these formed part of the convoy that went with her.[26]
She sent some of the carts carrying her things back to Oxford on
21 April. A week later she was in Bridgwater in Somerset but her
health was so bad that she told her husband it scarcely permitted
her to write. Once she was established in Exeter, at the beginning
of May, the queen felt safer. But she was still so desperately unwell
that she wrote to the king's physician, Sir Theodore de Mayerne,

urgently requesting his presence: 'My indisposition does not permit me to write much to beg you to come . . . but my disease will invite you more strongly, I hope, than many lines would do.' Thoroughly alarmed, the king wrote himself to his doctor: 'Mayerne, for the love of me, go to my wife.' Parliament agreed safe conducts for Mayerne and his fellow doctor, Matthew Lister, to go to attend on the queen in her confinement.[27] A French midwife, Madame Peronne, who had assisted the queen during the birth of a number of her older children, was sent across by Anne of Austria, who also supplied a layette for the baby. Anne's own road to childbirth and motherhood had been exceptionally fraught and she felt for her dead husband's sister.

Wracked by pain and still coughing badly, Henrietta wrote to her husband a touching letter just a few days before she was delivered:

> My dear heart,
>
> I have so few opportunities of writing that I will not lose this, which will, I believe, be the last before I am brought to bed (since I am now more than fifteen days in my ninth month) and perhaps it will be the last letter you will ever receive from me. The weak state in which I am, caused by the cruel pains I have suffered since I left you, which have been too severe to be experienced or understood by any but those who have suffered them, makes me believe that it is time to think of another world. If it be so, the will of God be done! . . . Let it not trouble you, I beg. You know well that from my last confinement, I have reason to fear and also to hope. By preparing for the worst, we are never taken by surprise and good fortune appears so much the better. Adieu, my dear heart. I hope before I leave you, to see you once again in the position in which you ought to be . . .[28]

Queen Henrietta Maria gave birth to a daughter in Bedford House, the handsome residence of Exeter's governor, Sir John Berkeley, on 16 June 1644. It was a difficult delivery but the baby

appeared healthy. She was called Henrietta, after her mother, and
eventually she would be known by the names Henriette Anne, the
change of spelling explained by the country she eventually grew
up in and the second name being added in honour of the French
queen regent. But romantic novelists know her as Minette, the
nickname her brother, the future Charles II, gave her when he was
an exile in Paris.[29]

Following the explicit orders of the king, the child was christened on 21 July according to the rites of the Church of England
in Exeter Cathedral. A new font was made for the ceremony and
a canopy of state erected for this latest Stuart princess. But it was
a small group that gathered round the font to witness the dean
of Exeter, Dr Lawrence Burnell, officiate. Henrietta's sponsors
were Sir John Berkeley, Lady Poulett and Lady Anne Dalkeith
(later countess of Morton), a member of the Villiers family who
had married into the Scottish aristocracy. This resourceful and
redoubtable lady was appointed as Henrietta's governess and would
play a crucial role in her young life. This was fortunate for the
little princess, since her mother had already fled from England
a week before her baptism, landing near Brest in Brittany on
16 July.

The birth itself did nothing to relieve the queen's precarious
health. She wrote about it in graphic terms to her husband:

> Since I left you at Oxford, the disease that I began to feel
> there has constantly increased, but with attacks so violent as
> no one ever felt before. I bore it patiently, in hopes of being
> cured by my accouchement; but instead of finding relief, my
> disease has increased and is so insupportable, that if it were
> not that we ought not to wish for death, it would be too
> much longed for, by the most wretched creature in the world
> . . . You will perhaps know the particulars of my disease; it is
> always a seizure of paralysis in the legs and all over the body;
> but it seems to me that my bowels and stomach weighed over
> a hundred pounds, and as though I was so tightly squeezed

in the region of the heart, that I was suffocating; and at times
I am like a person poisoned.

To compound this agony, she had lost feeling in one of her
arms and the sight of one eye.[30]

Over such a long distance of time it is impossible to be certain
about the cause of Henrietta Maria's affliction. She may have had
multiple conditions, exacerbated by pregnancy and the puerperal
fever that lay in wait for women of all classes after delivery.
Mayerne himself diagnosed 'hysteria', though this was a common
term used to describe almost anything to do with the female
reproductive system in an age ignorant of gynaecological science.[31]
Other possibilities that have been suggested include rheumatic
fever and tuberculosis, though if it were the latter, she lived with
it for another twenty-five years. Both the plague and typhus had
been common in Oxford, so Henrietta's system, already under
stress by separation from her husband and the fear of what might
happen to her if she fell into parliamentary hands, had withstood
the rigours of a ninth pregnancy better than she realized in the
summer of 1644.

She was convinced, though, that time was running out. Essex's
army was closing in. Her request for a safe conduct to Bath was
denied on the grounds that it was a ruse to relieve Exeter. A cal-
lous response, perhaps, but one dictated by the realities of war.
Essex had been accused before, and would be again, of not pushing home his advantage but he knew better than to let the French
papist queen, the woman who represented everything that he and
his men had fought against for two bloody years, be accorded any
generosity. Whether he actually wanted to capture her is another
matter. In the end, it did not come to that. Henrietta got away.
Only a fortnight after giving birth, she fled in disguise from Exeter,
accompanied only by the ever-faithful Sir John Hinton, whose
medical expertise was vital, given the queen's poor state of health,
a lady-in-waiting and her confessor, Father Philip. Remaining
in hiding for two days in a rough hut, while the parliamentarian

infantry noisily searched for her nearby, she moved on to a rendezvous with Henry Jermyn, her dwarf Jeffrey Hudson and her beloved spaniel. Together this unlikely group made for the Cornish coast. At Falmouth, Henrietta's party found a small Dutch fleet waiting to convey her across the Channel. But even then, she was not out of danger. Pursued by vessels loyal to parliament, the queen's party had to endure coming under fire and being hit before a storm drove them away from the protection of a French fleet near Dieppe, down the coast to Brest. There, exhausted, feverish and severely depressed, Henrietta finally came ashore in her native land nearly twenty years after she had left it to become the bride of Charles I.

The king, who entered Exeter on 21 July with the Prince of Wales, was distraught at his failure to rescue his wife and bitter at those who had, in his view, ruined her reputation through calumnies and naked hatred:

> Although I have much cause to be troubled by my wife's departure from me and out of my dominions, yet not her absence so much as the scandal of that necessity which drives her away doth afflict me, that she should be compelled by my own subjects and those pretending to be Protestants to withdraw for her safety . . . [Her] merits would have served her for a protection among savage Indians, while their rudeness and barbarity knows not so perfectly to hate all virtues as some men's subtlety doth, among whom I yet think few are so malicious as to hate her for herself. The fault is that she is my wife.[32]

The king's response was understandable but too simplistic. His opponents did, indeed, hate Henrietta Maria for what she represented and many of them, of course, either did not know her at all or scarcely knew her, at a personal level. Yet she had never sought their love or approbation. She was no Elizabeth I. That popularity and the affection of one's subjects needed to be earned was a concept she never comprehended.

Princess Henrietta was ill in the first weeks of her life. She suffered convulsions but was devotedly nursed by Lady Dalkeith. When her father visited her for the first time it is said that he was reduced to tears by the vulnerability of this tiny infant and the loss of her mother. He returned in September to see the child again, having won a notable victory against his enemies at Lostwithiel in Cornwall. During his week in Exeter he made provision for his youngest child's future, assigning the excise revenue of the city to pay for her household and appointing Dr Thomas Fuller as her chaplain. Then he gave the princess his blessing and left her to pursue the war, satisfied that she would be safe, at least for the time being, and well cared for. Their contact had been brief but at least they had met. He hoped, if fortune stayed with him, to be reunited soon with his two children left behind in London at the beginning of 1642. This desire would be granted in due course, though in circumstances far different from those he would have wished. The baby girl in Exeter he never saw again.

CHAPTER SIX

Defeat Without Victory

'Charles, it is very fit for me now to prepare for the worst
. . . wherefore know that my pleasure is, whensoever you find
yourself in apparent danger of falling into the rebels' hands,
that you convey yourself into France, and there to be under
your mother's care; who is to have absolute full power of your
education in all things, except religion.'

Charles I to his eldest son after the Battle of Naseby,
summer 1645

'We are now entering upon a time, the representation and
description whereof must be the most unpleasant and in-
grateful to the reader, in respect of the subject matter of it;
which must consist of no less weakness and folly on the one
side than of malice and wickedness on the other.'

Edward Hyde, earl of Clarendon, in
The History of the Rebellion

ALL THIS TIME, Elizabeth and Henry had remained in London.
The king's pleas that they be allowed to join him in Oxford
fell on deaf ears and the attempts of two of his equerries to
speak to the children were rebuffed. Their official guardian from
October 1642 was Philip Herbert, fourth earl of Pembroke, the
descendant of a family that rose to prominence from humble
Welsh antecedents through marriage to Queen Katherine Parr's

younger sister, Anne. The fourth earl had been in favour at court during the reign of James I, but, despite a passion for hunting and the arts, his relationship with Charles I gradually soured. Henrietta Maria disliked him, perhaps because he was a godly Protestant, and the king never really forgave Herbert's commitment to making terms with the Scots in 1640. Thereafter, the earl's alienation from the court gained pace. He voted for Strafford's attainder and was dismissed from the office of lord chamberlain at the queen's suggestion. It was not surprising that these contretemps, and a long-standing rivalry with the marquess of Hertford, a royalist with a country seat in Wiltshire like himself, drew him into the parliamentary cause. His outlook and lineage made him a suitable choice, in the eyes of both Houses of Parliament, to have official oversight of the king's younger children. But he was much taken up with parliamentary affairs and Elizabeth and Henry's daily routine reverted briefly to the supervision of the countess of Roxburghe when she returned from the Netherlands.

Lady Roxburghe was distressed by what she found. The children's situation during much of 1642, while she was still overseas, was one of straitened circumstances. Parliament had refused to allow the allocation of taxation that had hitherto supported Elizabeth and Henry's household at St James's. Economies imposed on the household were having an impact on everything from dress to diet. When Pembroke took up his appointment, both Houses agreed that Elizabeth and Henry's expenses, temporarily covered out of their father's own privy purse, should be met by the Royal Mint. But it was politics, rather than impoverishment, that spurred Princess Elizabeth into action at the end of 1643. The settlement of their financial affairs had an unwelcome outcome. An inspection of the establishment at St James's was ordered and pictures that might offend Presbyterian sensibilities were removed. More unsettling than these decorative changes was a requirement that the royal children's servants, particularly their chaplain and religious advisers, should reflect the views of the king's opponents.

All persons about them, including their governess, should subscribe to the Solemn League and Covenant. Those who rejected it were to be removed forthwith. The immediate effect of this stricture was the inevitable dismissal of most of the household.

Unwell (as she often was) and deeply upset, Elizabeth, at eight years old, was unable to face the loss of those closest to her. She took matters into her own hands and appealed directly to the House of Lords on 16 December, in a letter she entrusted to Pembroke to present on her behalf:

I account myself most miserable that I must have my servants taken from me, and strangers put to me. You promised me that you would have a care of me, and I hope you will show it, in preventing so great a grief as this would be to me. I pray, my lords, consider of it, and give me cause to thank you.[1]

This simple epistle caused some consternation. The Upper House did not know of the Commons' unilateral action in respect of the royal children and on demanding an explanation invoked privilege, saying that appointments of servants in the household of Elizabeth and Henry could not be made without their approval. A committee of seven lords, including Pembroke himself and the earls of Northumberland and Manchester, was appointed to look into the matter and its recommendations were subsequently implemented. The new household was certainly reasonably generous for two younger members of the royal family. By the time of its inception, Lady Roxburghe was dead and the countess of Dorset, who had known the children from their earliest years, was appointed once again to the role of governess. In addition, Elizabeth was provided with a lady of the bedchamber and four ladies-in-waiting and Henry was given his own staff of attendants. Overall, the household had two physicians, one of whom was Sir Theodore de Mayerne, as well as six chaplains, pages, domestics and tutors.

Elizabeth had won something of a victory though she and her

brother were not free. The gates of St James's were to be locked every evening at sunset and the oath taken by members of the household expressly stated that they were not to foment 'disaffection or misunderstanding between any of the king's children and either House of Parliament'. Attempts at communication between the royal court at Oxford and the children in London were to be reported immediately. Charles I protested at the change in his offspring's conditions and even suggested a prisoner swap but this was refused on the grounds that Elizabeth and Henry were not, in fact, prisoners. The king was roundly told that parliament 'hoped they should take as good care of the souls and bodies of his Majesty's children, as those at Oxford would have done'.[2] Despite this statement of intent, which was no doubt made in good faith, Elizabeth was largely housebound for much of 1643, as the result of a fall while running across a room in St James's, which broke her leg. It healed only very slowly. An examination of her remains in Victorian times showed that she suffered from rickets and she was probably prone, in any case, to the leg problems that had afflicted her father and grandfather.

Immobile she might have been for much of the high tide of royalist success but the recompense in Elizabeth's life was mental activity. Her father's foes did not deprive her of educational opportunities; indeed, they were committed to ensuring that the princess and her brother, when he became old enough, would become learned English Protestant members of the ruling class. Though Henry had two older brothers and there was, at this point, no question of deposing the king himself, still it was thought desirable that the prince be brought up in ways that did not perpetuate Charles I's views of kingship. For the present, while still so young, he had little companionship as a very small boy apart from his sister. Elizabeth, on the other hand, was very fortunate to have her intellect stimulated by a remarkable lady tutor, Bathsua Makin.

Mrs Makin (her first name is a variant of the Hebrew name Bathsheba) was the elder daughter of Henry Reginald, a schoolmaster from Stepney in east London. She was about forty years old when she first began to teach Princess Elizabeth in 1640. Makin was described as 'the greatest scholar, I think, of a woman in England' by the diarist Sir Simonds D'Ewes, who had been a pupil with her at her father's school, and Elizabeth was fortunate to have this exceptionally gifted woman as a teacher. But then Elizabeth herself was an outstanding pupil. Under Bathsua's guidance, she became an impressive linguist for one so young, attaining a high level of ability in Greek, Latin, Hebrew, French, Italian and Spanish. For her age, the princess outshone her Tudor namesake, Elizabeth I. Bathsua also taught her charge mathematics, perhaps inspired by the prowess of her brother-in-law, the noted mathematician John Pell. Nor was the princess the only pupil of this industrious and clever lady. She instructed the countess of Huntingdon and her children, corresponded with continental scholars and was interested in medicine. When she was presented to James I as a young woman of outstanding linguistic skill, the 'Wisest Fool in Christendom' is reported to have asked, with characteristic spite, 'But can she spin?' Her entrée into royal employment was probably based on her reputation and her marriage to Richard Makin, who was a junior member of the king's household. She may well have been a demanding teacher, since Pell described her as a woman of 'no small impatience'. Elizabeth seems, however, to have thrived under her guidance. In the princess's isolation and amid the uncertainties of the first Civil War, Mrs Makin, who had given birth to eight children of her own, provided stability and stimulation.

In March 1645, an important change took place in the lives of Elizabeth and her brother when Algernon Percy, tenth earl of Northumberland, took over Pembroke's role as their guardian. One of the grandees of the parliamentary cause, Northumberland came from a family that had long been the most influential in the north of England and one that had already spawned more than its fair share of over-mighty subjects. Conflict with the Crown was something that ran in the blood of the Percys. Algernon's father

had spent sixteen years in prison for alleged complicity in the
Gunpowder Plot and the two preceding earls, his grandfather and
great-grandfather, were both executed for treason. But the tenth
earl had little direct contact with his northern heritage, having
been born in London in 1602. His relationship with the court
after his father's death was somewhat faltering; it took time for
this descendant of a rebellious house to establish himself in royal
favour. But the queen seems to have approved of him, perhaps
because his views in foreign policy were pro-French and his sister,
Lucy, countess of Carlisle, was one of her ladies. In 1638 Charles
I made him lord admiral. Initially friendly with Strafford, Northumberland believed the second Bishops' War to be a profound
mistake and its outcome disillusioned him at a time when he was
suffering a good deal of ill health. By 1640, he had become an
opponent of royal policy, believing in a balanced constitution and
limitation of the royal prerogative. This scarcely made him a fire-
brand and he was certainly not a religious extremist. Unsettled by
royalist successes in 1643 he had, for a time, favoured peace but
the king's rebuff to such overtures at Oxford hardened his resolve.
After the Scots joined the war he was appointed chairman of the
Committee of Both Kingdoms in 1644 but it was the failure of
further peace negotiations around the so-called Treaty of Uxbridge,
one month before he assumed responsibility for Elizabeth and
Henry, which hardened his attitude.

Caught up with the day-to-day business of parliamentary committees and the management of the war, Northumberland, like
their previous guardians, was too busy to see much of the royal
children or, indeed, his own small son, the child of his second
marriage to Lady Elizabeth Howard. A careful and considered
man whose natural reserve came across sometimes as coldness, his
principles and high sense of duty made him an entirely appropriate choice as the official custodian of the royal children and he
took his responsibilities towards them with all the seriousness of
his nature. Clarendon said of him that his measured demeanour
'got him the reputation of an able and wise man; which he made

evident in the excellent government of his family, where no man was more absolutely obeyed; and no man ever had fewer idle words to answer for'.[3] Another of his sisters, Dorothy Percy, countess of Leicester, spoke more warmly of the 'truth and fidelity in him'. Elizabeth and Henry could have fared much worse, especially as Lady Dorset, who was in receipt of a generous allowance from parliament for her service to the royal children, died within two months of Northumberland's appointment.

*

AT THE SAME TIME that Northumberland was assuming responsibility for his younger brother and sister, Prince Charles's life was also undergoing a major change. With royalist fortunes now much more uncertain, the king decided it was time for his heir to be moved to a safer place and to take command (at least nominally) of his own forces. Bristol was chosen as the Prince of Wales's headquarters because it was a strategic gateway to the vitally important south-west. The project had first been mooted the previous spring but the prince could not be persuaded to go then. Nearly a year later, he did not demur. On 4 March 1645, in pouring rain, he took leave of his father and departed from Oxford. Despite the inclement weather as he headed west, the mood was far from being one of despair, nor was there reason to suppose that father and son would never see each other again.

Charles was well supported in his new environment. The acting governor of the city, in Prince Rupert's absence, was Sir Ralph Hopton, one of the most able of royalist generals. The prince was also accompanied by his governor, the earl of Berkshire, two veteran soldiers, the earl of Brentford and the earl of Capel, and two highly capable civilian advisers, Lord Culpeper, master of the rolls, and Sir Edward Hyde. On paper, it was a reasonably well-balanced group but Hyde had nursed considerable misgivings about the wisdom of dividing royalist command in this way (two other appointees, the earls of Southampton and Richmond, refused to go) and the role of the king's commanders in the

region, Sir John Berkeley, Sir Richard Grenville and Lord George
Goring, *vis-à-vis* the council was never clarified. Thus the capac-
ity for confusion and resentment was present even before the
Prince of Wales arrived in Bristol. It would only get worse.

In part, this was because of a clash of personalities. Whatever
the military skills of his colleagues, Hyde possessed by far the
superior intellect, and he knew it. He was most certainly not a
dashing Cavalier in appearance. Then in his mid-thirties, he
looked rather like a chubby-faced child surprised to find himself
uncomfortably in a man's body. Hyde had been intended for the
Church as a younger son, but when his elder brother died he
changed to the study of law at Oxford, enjoying the intellectual
circles of the Middle Temple in London and getting to know the
playwright Ben Jonson. His first marriage, prematurely cut short
by his wife's death, brought him into the circles of the Villiers
family and the Wiltshire aristocracy. During the 1630s he was
part of the circle that formed around Lucius Cary, Viscount
Falkland, at Great Tew in the Oxfordshire Cotswolds.[4] Hyde was
a man who knew how to take advantage of the opportunities that
came his way, notably a meeting with Archbishop Laud in 1635.
By the time the crisis of 1640 arrived, he had, he felt, managed
to balance his country and court interests well and though he
believed that England was prospering, he was concerned about
royal and judicial abuses of the law, especially the use of ship
money as a form of regular taxation. But, whatever his reservations, a strong allegiance to the Church of England coupled
with outstanding ability in drafting meant that he agreed to stay
on in London to draft statements of royal policy when Charles I
fled the city at the beginning of 1642. Hyde was, by this time,
convinced that parliament's demands for political and religious
reform would overthrow the rule of law and must be resisted. He
was at Nottingham with the king when the royal standard was
raised. Respected by the king, he joined the Privy Council and
was made chancellor of the exchequer after being knighted in

February 1643. He had risen far from his gentry background in Wiltshire.

He had never, though, been an advocate of an aggressive solution to the confrontation with parliament. His strengths were with the written word and in understanding that dividing the king's opponents did not have to be done at the end of a sword. Hyde was no fighting man. Committed as he was to serving Prince Charles, he did not really know the fifteen-year-old, nor did he have the prince's trust. Confident and lawyerly, he was easy to dislike and ill health – he suffered badly from gout – did not help his mood. Although Hyde saw clearly that divided lines of command in the West Country were impeding the royalist cause, his attempts at improving the situation met with resentment. Even if he had been successful in this still-important theatre of the war, it would have, in the end, made little difference. By the midsummer of 1645, parliament had reconstructed its army and cast the doubters, both at Westminster and in the military, adrift. The effects of this sea change would lead to disaster for the royalist cause in the heart of England.

*

IF THERE WAS acrimony in the council of the Prince of Wales in Bristol and divisions among the royalists in Oxford, there were severe recriminations and much soul-searching among the king's opponents as 1644 ended. The earls of Manchester and Essex seemed unwilling to prosecute the war to a successful conclusion and the peace party in parliament, egged on by the Scots on the Committee of Both Kingdoms, sent a set of proposals to Charles, the abortive Treaty of Uxbridge, that were so extreme that they never stood the slightest likelihood of acceptance. These were precisely the sort of divisions that Hyde's well-honed political and legal instincts would have liked to exploit but it was not to be. By the Self-Denying Ordinance, passed in the Commons on 19 December 1644, all peers and members of the Commons who held army commands were stripped of the possibility of doing so for the rest of the war. This legislation was a necessary precursor for the removal of the dilatory aristocrats who seemed increasingly unwilling to pursue an outright victory; its ultimate aim was to create what soon became known as the New Model Army. The necessity for change, and the dangers of not effecting it speedily, were made clear by Cromwell when he rose in the House of Commons in support of the measure: 'If I may speak my conscience without reflection upon any, I do conceive if the army be put not into another method, and the war more vigorously prosecuted, the people can bear the war no longer, and will enforce you to a dishonourable peace.'[5] The measure met more opposition in the House of Lords, but was steered through by Lord Saye and Sele, a mainstay of the original 'noble revolt' against Charles I, and by the earl of Northumberland, custodian of the king's younger children. Sir Thomas Fairfax became commander-in-chief of the army with Cromwell as his second in command.

Royalist critics sneered at the New Model, claiming its officers were lowly born, while Presbyterians feared that it represented the military wing of the rising, if amorphous, religious movement known as the Independents. Neither claim could be substantiated in 1645 but they have powerfully affected the 'Roundhead' image in the popular mind over the centuries. The New Model was slow to get up to strength at the beginning of 1645, allowing the royalists to seize the initiative briefly in the south-west. Here the Prince of Wales was to find that he had little authority in practice when his father unwisely made Goring commander-in-chief of all the forces in the west. Goring was not lacking in personal bravery but he was hot-headed, impossible to get on with and his force was wildly ill disciplined and hated by the local population. His new appointment, one of the king's most serious misjudgements, infuriated Prince Charles's council, Prince Rupert and all the other commanders in the region. Nor was there anything he could do to help the king in Oxford, besieged by parliament and beset by contradictory advice from those around him. Following the ruthless slaughter of parliamentary supporters at Leicester by Prince Rupert's forces at the end of May, the Committee of Both Kingdoms decided to abandon the siege of Oxford and take more decisive action. They ordered a much relieved Fairfax to engage the king's army as soon as possible.

On 5 June he left Oxford, making his way north towards the royalists who occupied a strong position atop Borough Hill outside Daventry in Northamptonshire. His army was in position to make a final advance by the evening of 11 June, despite very wet weather and the late arrival of muskets badly needed by some of his unarmed men. The royalist forces under Prince Rupert were spread out and resting, their patrols apparently relaxed, the horses turned out to feed. King Charles had spent the day hunting in nearby Fawsley Park. It was not until the late afternoon of the following day that contact was made between the two armies when the outriders of Fairfax's cavalry surprised royalist outposts near Daventry. Up till then, Rupert was entirely unaware of how close his enemies were. Very soon, he discovered that it was not just its proximity but the size of the opposing army that posed a very serious threat. He had gravely miscalculated the strength of his foe.

What to do? In conference with his uncle, it was decided that the best option was to retreat northward and try to make a stand at Belvoir Castle. A circuitous route was taken to try to throw off Fairfax's army but, unknown to Rupert, he was being shadowed every step of the way by the New Model's cavalry. And Fairfax was also in possession of a vital piece of intelligence that had been intercepted before it reached Rupert and the king: Goring would not be there if they gave battle. Explaining that he was unable to leave the West Country, Goring exhorted Rupert not to engage the enemy until he arrived. Heartened both by the realization that an important part of the royalist army would not be involved and by the arrival of Cromwell, Fairfax determined to fight.

Aware by now that they had failed to shake off the parliamentarians who dogged their every footstep, the king and his commanders held a council of war at 2 a.m. on Saturday, 14 June.

They had by now reached Naseby in Northamptonshire, seven miles from Market Harborough. As was so often the case with the royalist high command, the king received contradictory advice. Rupert, who has often been criticized for what happened at Naseby, did not, in fact, favour giving battle. Digby and Ashburnham, however, felt that retreat was dangerous and demoralizing and their view prevailed with the king. And so, amid the little valleys and streams of open countryside so typical of the area, the royalist cause was to suffer a defeat from which it never really recovered.

'That dismal Saturday', as the diarist Richard Symonds referred to the Battle of Naseby, began early as scoutmasters on both sides strained in the dawn light of one of the longest days of the year to see the preparations being made by their enemies and the armies moved slowly to take up position. Eventually they lined up only about a thousand yards apart. The king's forces of around 10,000 men were outnumbered by Fairfax's New Model which was around 14,000 strong. The royalist infantry, though composed of professional soldiers (many were Welsh), was significantly smaller and it was they who would suffer the most losses in casualties and prisoners taken. Cavalry numbers were more equal, though even here the advantage lay with the parliamentarians, who had about 6,600 horses to the king's 5,000. And, as at previous battles, the royalist cavalry was ill disciplined, leaving the field at a crucial juncture to attack the parliamentarian baggage train.

The fighting began around ten in the morning when the royalists attacked along the entire length of Fairfax's line. Their infantry and the cavalry of Princes Rupert and Maurice inflicted substantial casualties, severely wounding Cromwell's son-in-law, Henry Ireton, and Philip Skippon, the veteran commander of the parliamentarian foot, who refused to leave the field, despite his injuries. He was 'shot through the right side under the ribs, through armour and coat, but not mortal, yet notwithstanding he kept his horse and discharged his place and would by no means be drawn off until the field was won.'[6] The tide began to turn when royalist cavalry units under Sir Marmaduke Langdale were routed by Cromwell, but, unlike his foes, Cromwell's highly disciplined horsemen were not permitted to ride willy-nilly off the field. Most remained and were turned against the royalist infantry. As the desperation of the situation became apparent, Charles I had to be dissuaded from leading a counter-charge in person. The king was certainly not lacking in personal bravery but it would have made no difference, except for putting his own person in danger. Instead, he left the field by midday as his infantry surrendered in droves. More than 4,500 prisoners were taken by the New Model, who also attacked the royalist baggage train, slaughtering and maiming the female camp followers in an act of singular barbarity. There was nothing romantic about Naseby.

It remains, however, the most important battle in English history since Hastings. Cromwell believed that God had been with parliament's forces and it was to Him and the soldiery that he gave the victory, telling Fairfax: 'He that ventures his life for the liberty of his country, I wish he trust God for the liberty of his conscience, and you for the liberty he fights for.'[7] These themes were ones that the newly appointed lieutenant-general of the New Model Army would return to many times in the years to come, even if the House of Commons, in an early indication of trouble on the horizon, was reticent about too much emphasis on liberty and deleted the entire passage from the published account of his speech. Paradoxically, the Lords allowed it to be printed in full.

But for the present it was the king who had suffered by far the greater public relations disaster. In his baggage train, the victorious parliamentarians found all his secret correspondence with Henrietta Maria. It revealed that he was considering extending toleration to Catholics and using an army from Ireland, as well as European mercenaries, to hold on to his throne. When the collection was printed, under the title *The King's Cabinet Opened*, recriminations were immediate and Charles I's image suffered permanent damage. He could, perhaps, take some comfort from the fact that neither of his two eldest sons was with him at Naseby, though Prince Charles had been obliged to quit Bristol because of a serious outbreak of the plague.

Naseby was a turning point in the Civil Wars. Charles I would never again accompany a large army into the field in defence of his Crown. But the outcome did not necessarily seem quite so clear-cut to contemporaries. The king himself had certainly not given up hope. From Naseby he made his way west into the Midlands and thence over the border into Wales, a country whose men had fought gallantly for him in June 1645. From Cardiff at the end of the following month he wrote to the leading Irish nobleman, the marquess of Ormonde, revealing that he had by no means given up hope of help from that quarter. His letter is tinged with sadness and perhaps a hint of desperation but it is typical of the man: 'It hath pleased God,' he wrote, 'by many successive misfortunes, to reduce my affairs, of late, from a very prosperous condition to so low an ebb as to be a perfect trial of all men's integrity to me, and being a person whom I consider as most entirely and generously resolved to stand and fall with your King, I do principally rely upon you, for your uttermost assistance in my present hazards.'[8] Ormonde was indeed willing to stand and fall with his king, whether Charles I or his eldest son. But he was not able to help the monarchy materially at this point. Much more distressing was the bitterness between the king and his nephew, Prince Rupert, which would soon ensue.

The defeat at Naseby shook Rupert profoundly. He was immediately sent onwards to Bristol, to defend the city against the attack from Fairfax that everyone assumed must be coming. But he believed that his uncle must now treat for peace, as he stated in a letter he wrote to the duke of Richmond:

It is now in everybody's mouth that the King is going for Scotland. I must confess it to be a strange resolution, considering not only in what condition he will leave all behind him, but what probability there is for him to go thither. If I am now desired to deliver my opinion, which your lordship may declare to the King, his Majesty hath no way left to preserve his posterity, kingdom and nobility, but by a treaty. I believe it is a more prudent way to retain something than to lose it all.[9]

Thus spoke the pragmatic politician and supporter of the royal House of Stuart but it was not advice Charles I's conscience wanted to hear. The king was perfectly lucid in his assessment of his situation, as can be seen in a letter he wrote to Rupert:

I confess that speaking as a mere soldier or statesman, I must say there is no probability but of my ruin; yet as a Christian I must tell you, that God will not suffer rebels and traitors to prosper, nor this cause to be overthrown. Whatever personal punishment it shall please Him to inflict on me, must not make me repine, much less make me give over this quarrel; and there is little question that a composition with them [the rebels] at this time is nothing else but a submission, which by the grace of God I am resolved against whatever it costs me; for I know my obligation to be both in conscience and honour, neither to abandon God's cause, injure my successors, nor forsake my friends.

This letter is key to understanding Charles I. He was not deluded about the likelihood of a successful military solution, though he always placed too much confidence in his ability to divide his opponents and exploit their weaknesses. Rebels were, to him, morally deficient and, as such, he saw them as fair game. And he expected complete loyalty from those who served him: 'He that will stay with me at this time must expect and resolve either to die for a good cause or, which is worse, to live as miserable in maintaining it as the violence of insulting Rebels can make him.'[10]

Bristol was the only port city remaining in royalist hands in the south-west of England. It was of paramount importance to Charles I's fading hopes and Rupert had initially assured his uncle

that he could hold the city for four months. This assertion proved
to be over-optimistic. By 23 August 1645, Fairfax's army of 15,000
men encircled the city, outnumbering Rupert's defenders by three
to one. Nor did the prince have the support of Bristol's inhabitants, who had been heavily taxed during its occupation and were
now dropping from the plague. Nevertheless, the attackers met
brave resistance as they stormed the alarmingly high city walls and
the fighting continued for six hours – longer than the battles of
Edgehill, Marston Moor or Naseby. Ultimately, Rupert simply did
not have the manpower to repel Fairfax's troops. He was offered
honourable terms and, after consulting with his council of war,
who supported his decision, surrendered. Carrying their swords,
his men were allowed to leave unhindered on their march to join
the king at Oxford. Rupert, ever-conscious of who he was, cut a
magnificent figure in defeat. 'Clad in scarlet, very richly laid in
silver lace, and mounted upon a very gallant black Barbary horse',
he rode with Cromwell and Fairfax on the first two miles of his
journey.[11] It was the closest he ever came to either of them. Rupert
was a professional soldier and had made a professional soldier's
choice. He knew he could not win and that holding out longer
would have cost more lives. But his relationship with his uncle was
permanently damaged.

Charles I was appalled by Rupert's surrender. From Hereford
on 14 September he wrote that it was '. . . of so much affliction to
me, that it makes me not only forget the considerations of that
place, but is likewise the greatest trial of my constancy that hath
yet befallen me.' Brutally dismissing the charismatic young man
who had risked his life to serve him, he ended: 'My conclusion is,
to desire you to seek your subsistence, until it shall please God to
determine of my condition, somewhere beyond seas; to which end
I send you a pass; and I pray God to make you sensible of your
present condition and give you means to redeem what you have
lost.'[12] A few days later he wrote to Prince Maurice, Rupert's
younger brother, that 'this great error of his (which indeed hath
given me more grief than any misfortune since this damnable

rebellion) hath no ways proceeded from his change of affection to me or my cause, but merely by having his judgement seduced by rotten-hearted villains.' Rupert certainly had long been at odds with several of the king's other commanders, notably Digby, who hoped that his disgrace would be permanent.

Relations between uncle and nephew remained tense; Rupert's temperament was not such that he would take continued insults, like the dismissal of his friend, Will Legge, as governor of Oxford, lying down, and Maurice naturally supported him. Gradually, matters improved, though Rupert was never returned to the command he had previously enjoyed. Both brothers remained in Oxford as Charles I's position grew bleaker, despite his efforts to buy time by appearing willing to treat with parliament and the involvement of the French, at Henrietta Maria's behest, in a scheme which would have seen the Scottish army desert their English allies and fight for the king in return for the establishment of Presbyterianism as the state religion of England. This was a price Charles was not prepared to pay, much to his wife's annoyance. Henrietta Maria thought one heretic was as bad as another and took the view that any promise to them could easily be rescinded in practice. But as the future of the king seemed increasingly uncertain, so, too, did that of his children, scattered in different parts of the country. The Prince of Wales was roaming ever westward trying to elude Fairfax, James remained at Oxford and Elizabeth and Henry moved between St James's Palace and Syon House. Theirs was the most secure existence. But the greatest adventure in 1646 was that which befell the king's youngest daughter, Princess Henrietta, and her intrepid governess, Lady Dalkeith.

*

THE INFANT princess remained in Exeter as her father's fortunes declined. The first year of her life was tranquil and in August 1645 Prince Charles spent a month in the city, during which time he visited his sister. She would only just have been learning to walk and talk, though in speech, as would later become apparent, she seems to have been somewhat advanced for her age. The Stuarts had a strong sense of family and Charles was always fond of his siblings. Henrietta would become his special favourite, despite the gap in age of fourteen years between them. But his father's injunctions that he must not be captured meant that he could not tarry. Shortly after he left, the combined armies of Fairfax and Waller closed in on Exeter and Lady Dalkeith was faced with a difficult decision. If she stayed, her charge would, like the rest of the inhabitants, be subject to the hardships of a siege with an unknown outcome. If she tried to escape and was captured, then Henrietta, like Elizabeth and Henry, would become a ward of parliament. Initially, the governess thought of obtaining a pass to take the little girl to Cornwall, having been ordered by the queen to remove the princess at the first sign of danger. But the letters were intercepted and Henrietta's situation soon became entwined with that of the Prince of Wales. The parliamentarians were determined to prevent his passage out of the country. Hyde put it bluntly to Jermyn that it was not possible to protect both the prince and his sister if they tried to flee and that the priority must be Charles. 'Had it been done,' he wrote of trying to get Henrietta to France at this stage, 'all security for the prince's safety would have passed away.'[13]

In Paris, the queen was beside herself with worry and berated Lady Dalkeith for what she saw as dereliction of duty. This was entirely unjust and Hyde came gallantly to the governess's defence:

> I think it will break her heart when she hears of the queen's displeasure; which pardon me for saying is with much severity conceived against her. I'll be bold to say, let the success be what it will, that the governess is as faultless in the business as you [Jermyn] are and hath been as punctual, as solicitous and as impatient to obey the queen's directions as she could be to save her soul. She could not act her part without assis-

tance; and what assistance could she have? How could she have left Exeter and whither have gone . . .[14]

Whither indeed? Throughout the winter Lady Dalkeith, chaplain Thomas Fuller and the other members of the princess's small household remained in Exeter, as stocks of food dwindled and the besieging army tightened its grip. By spring, Sir John Berkeley, the town's governor, felt that it was impossible to hold out any longer and agreed surrender terms. On 13 April 1646 he escorted Henrietta and her governess as far as Salisbury, having negotiated with Fairfax that the princess, her belongings and household should eventually be located in a residence of the king's choosing but that their maintenance should be paid by parliament. Charles I wanted his daughter to be near the capital. He did not want her to come to him at Oxford, for the simple reason that he was intending to leave there himself, though this was kept secret from even those closest to him. Lady Dalkeith thought Richmond the most appropriate place for Henrietta but parliament disagreed. The order came for the princess and her servants to take up residence at Oatlands, where they remained for three months at Lady Dalkeith's personal expense, since the allowance promised by parliament was not forthcoming.

At the end of May the order came from the House of Commons for Princess Henrietta to join Elizabeth and Henry at St James's, under the supervision of the earl and countess of Northumberland. Lady Dalkeith was determined to resist this development but she did not wish to seem to be defying it outright. Instead, she procrastinated, writing to the House of Lords in late June that she was under injunction from the king not to leave the princess, who was, as far as she was concerned, 'to be disposed of according to His Majesty's directions'. She went on to point out 'that I have preserved Her Highness, not without many cares and fears, from a weak to a very hopeful condition and constitution, that my coming into these parts was voluntary' – this was not true, given the circumstances in which she had left Exeter and the king's own commands for his daughter – 'that I have disbursed a great sum of money for the support of Her Highness and her family' – this meant her household – 'since the treaty at Exeter.' She went on to claim that that she was perfectly willing 'to be subordinate to my lord and lady Northumberland, and, from time to time, receive and follow their directions concerning the Princess . . . all my desire now is to be continued about her person . . . without being any kind of burden to the Parliament, or inconvenience to my lord and lady of Northumberland.' She asked again for reimbursement of her expenses and concluded that she could not, in all honour and honesty, hand over the king's child to parliamentary authority without his express consent.[15]

After waiting another month, in which no reply to this heartfelt but also clever missive was received, Lady Dalkeith decided to take matters into her own hands. She would personally smuggle little Henrietta out of England. Her plot was simple but also required strong nerves and the greatest secrecy. Her designs must be kept from all of the princess's household except the most trusted servants and the French valet who was to pass as her own husband. On 25 July 1646, she set out on foot from Oatlands to walk to Dover, intending to take a boat for France. Princess Henrietta was dressed in rough clothing and disguised as a boy. Although only two years old, the child was accustomed to being treated like royalty and could not be persuaded that this was an enjoyable game, or to keep quiet. When her 'parents' referred to her as Pierre she piped up that she was not Pierre, but a princess and that the clothes she was wearing were not hers. Fortunately for Lady Dalkeith, no one encountered on the road seems to have taken the toddler's indignation seriously. The unlikely trio reached Dover without impediment and crossed to France.

The discovery that the princess and her governess were missing caused great alarm to the rest of the staff left behind at Oatlands but this was alleviated when they received a letter from Lady Dalkeith. She had, she said, awaited parliament's pleasure with patience but had been unable to obtain any justice for

Henrietta or for herself, or, indeed, any of them. She urged them to 'go to the king' if they could (an indication of how little she actually knew about the king's situation) and also to conceal her flight for as long as possible.[16] So parliament did not know that Charles I's youngest child was gone until she had, in fact, arrived in France. The princess's mother was overjoyed by this unexpected development and sent carriages and appropriate clothes to Calais. The reservations felt by Henrietta Maria about Lady Dalkeith's earlier failure to remove her daughter from Exeter were now all gone. The lady herself was so shattered by the stress of the preceding months and the perils of discovery that she fell ill on arriving at the palace of Saint-Germain-en-Laye, where the queen was living. When she recovered, she found herself a royalist heroine; poems were written about her escape with the princess and the English ambassador described the adventure as 'a pretty romance'. It was certainly one that appeared to have a happy ending but the future was uncertain. The little princess, later described by her eldest brother as 'an Exeter woman', never saw the city of her birth again. She would return just once to England, in 1660, by which time she had long become Princess Henriette Anne.

The removal of this youngest member of the royal family was no matter of great regret for parliament. It relieved them of the necessity of finding financial support and its propaganda value to the royalist cause was minimal, given the situation of Charles I. Lady Dalkeith's suggestion to Princess Henrietta's gentlewomen that they should seek assistance from the king was bizarre, since he was no longer free. On 27 April he had slipped out of Oxford in the middle of the night, disguised as a servant, with only his chaplain, Michael Hudson, and Jack Ashburnham, his long-standing confidant, accompanying him. His intentions, as was often the case with Charles I, are unclear. At first, he took a roundabout route to London, getting as close as Harrow, but if he was expecting some kind of message of support, or a safe conduct, anything that would allow him to re-enter his capital on terms that satisfied him, this never materialized. So he rode north into

Norfolk, staying near to the coast, which might have provided him the opportunity of escaping overseas. His preferred option, however, was to stay on English soil and seek armed help from a different source. For some months, the French ambassador to Scotland, Montreuil, had been negotiating with the Scots on his behalf but there was still no written assurance of support. Charles hesitated, sending Hudson into the Scottish camp at Southwell near Newark in Nottinghamshire to see if they could be persuaded before committing his future to them. Verbal assurances, but no more, were given that the Scots would declare for the king if parliament failed to restore him. Apparently accepting that this was the best he could hope for, the king arrived at the Scottish camp at seven in the morning on 5 May 1646. In the words of the great Victorian historian of the Civil War, Samuel Rawson Gardiner: 'He fancied himself to be a guest, but the days of his captivity had in fact begun.'[17]

*

THE FORTUNES of his two eldest sons now took different directions for several years. Prince James, left behind in Oxford with no word of comfort or parting letter from his father, felt understandable anxiety. Later he would use the most clipped and unemotional words he could find to explain this abandonment: 'The king had it once in his thoughts,' he wrote, 'to have carried the Duke along with him, but did not.'[18] His cousins Rupert and Maurice were still with him, as were his servants and tutors, but their situation over the next two months, while Oxford attempted to withstand the parliamentary army, grew increasingly dire. Fairfax had all the weaponry and manpower he needed for a long siege and as the city was already running low on food, James, desirous to show that he would share the hardships of the defenders, declared that he would accept a halving of his rations. This gesture played well with royalist propaganda but Fairfax could trump his enemies in the publicity, as well as the military, stakes. He sent wagon-loads of butter, game and lamb into Oxford as gifts for the young duke of York, thus emphasizing that not only was he unwilling to see the king's second son endure unnecessary hardships but that he also had plenty of supplies for his own army. He reasoned that there could be important advantages in keeping a good relationship with the prince, whose father was now a prisoner of the Scots and whose elder brother, the Prince of Wales, was on the run. James's proximity to the throne and his still (it was hoped) impressionable age meant that he could be viewed as a serious candidate for the Crown in the more moderate monarchy that many wished to see by 1646. The future of the duke of York was a key topic for the discussions that resulted in the surrender of Oxford. Parliament realized he was a prize worth having and were keen that no harm should come to him. James, who stood on his dignity from a very young age, believed that this was out of deference to his rank and it might be argued that such was the case, but not for the reasons that he understood at the time. His days in Oxford were numbered. The city surrendered on 20 June 1646. The palatine Princes left two days later with passes allowing them to go overseas. Rupert had been reconciled with his uncle before Charles fled Oxford but neither he nor Maurice had any future in England. They went their separate ways, Rupert to France to join Henrietta Maria's court and Maurice to Holland. Their thirteen-year-old cousin, however, was to join his younger sister and brother, Elizabeth and Henry, in London by the express order of parliament. So Prince James returned to the palace of his childhood and much happier times, the residence of a sister he had not seen for five years and a little brother he could hardly remember, to be placed, like them, under the guardianship of the earl of Northumberland. For two years he was, at least, to know something resembling a family life, though it was not one he would have chosen and he did not make it easy for himself or his increasingly stressed hosts.

Northumberland was placed in an unenviable position when he assumed the additional responsibility as custodian of the duke of York. He had to balance the need to continue as normal as possible a daily routine of lessons, exercise, religious observance and leisure activities against the need for security and vigilance, while at the same time hoping to avoid giving offence to anyone. Elizabeth and Henry were, by this time, used to their surroundings and the constraints put on them, but James was not. He bitterly resented the removal of all his servants, including a little dwarf who was especially dear to him. The replacement of his household by parliamentary nominees, who all represented a different way of thinking and perhaps displayed less deference than he believed his due, infuriated him. Northumberland discovered that his new charge had a hot temper and was less malleable than his younger siblings. The earl, anxious to make the prince's life as bearable as possible, spent considerable amounts of his own money, above the allowance awarded to him by parliament. He kept detailed monthly records of his expenditure on the royal children in a separate account book. It gives a fascinating picture of the manner in which the children were treated.

While personnel of the household may have changed, the status accorded to the children was still that of royalty. There are bills for buttons, silks, worsted for stockings, caps, garters, ribbons and shoes. There were footmen (James had his own), coachmen, grooms and postilions to convey them from St James's Palace to Northumberland's other residences, notably Syon House in Middlesex, and all these servants were decked out in appropriate livery. Northumberland had to meet the cost for board and lodging for these staff which could amount to more than £200 a year, or about £25,000 today. This is not a minor sum of money for someone whose northern estates had suffered badly during the war, to the tune of £42,500 by 1646, or at least £6 million in modern money. On top of this, he had to pay for horses and their feed and for hounds so that the duke of York could hunt, which he did frequently in the winter of 1647–8. Even the costs of James going by river to Lambeth were noted. These glimpses into the daily lives of the royal children suggest that it was not all the reciting of catechisms and hearing of godly sermons. They were evidently permitted to travel in some style and, in the case of James, to enjoy recreational activities outside St James's Palace, though such journeys must have presented the earl of Northumberland with security concerns.[19] James may have loved the hunt and was never keen on books, though he did acquire a reasonable command of French. While he was with Elizabeth and Henry his education, interrupted by the course of the war and the hardships at Oxford, was resumed under Princess Mary's former tutor, John Durie.

The possibility that his second son was being considered as a replacement for his own occupancy of the English throne reached the king's ears while he was being held by the Scots at Newcastle during the summer of 1646. Charles I was quick to bring it to the attention of Jermyn and Culpeper, who were with the queen in France. Pressure was being brought to bear on Charles, and not just from the Scots but the queen as well, to abandon episcopacy and he was resisting: 'How can I keep that innocency which you (with so much reason) oft and earnestly persuade me to preserve, if I should abandon the Church? Believe it, religion is the only firm foundation of all power.' He went on to add that there was a great desire among the rebel leaders 'to make the Duke of York king'. He wanted pressure brought to bear on France 'to declare for my restoration and set some visible course on foot to order it'.[20] While the young duke himself may have been unaware of the speculation surrounding his name, the consideration being given to his status was genuine, for by that time his elder brother was already in France.

*

THROUGHOUT THAT difficult spring and early summer, when both his father and his younger brother became captives of the different forces threatening the Stuart dynasty, Prince Charles had been on the outermost fringes of the British Isles. Late in the evening of 2 March he left Pendennis Castle near Falmouth in Cornwall aboard a frigate, optimistically named the *Phoenix*, bound for the Scilly Isles. With him went a rag-tag group of supporters, who had seen the royalist strongholds in the south-west fall one after the other to the New Model Army. Despite this, their loyalty was such that they were prepared to share what-ever dangers lay ahead. For some, at least, discomfort and hardship were present almost from the moment they landed on St Mary's, the largest of the scattered island group on the edge of the Atlantic Ocean. Lady Ann Fanshawe, wife of the writer, linguist and diplomat who was the Prince of Wales's secretary for war, described vividly the hardships of this little band:

> The next day, after having been pillaged and [being] ex-tremely sick and big with child, I was set ashore almost dead in the land of Scilly. When we had got to our quarters near the castle where the Prince lay, I went immediately to bed, which was so vile that my footmen ever lay in a better . . . But when I awaked in the morning I was so cold I knew not what to do, but the daylight discovered that our bed was near swimming with the sea, which the owner told us afterwards, it never did so but at spring tides. With this we were destitute of clothes, and meat or fuel . . . and truly we begged our daily bread of God, for we thought every meal our last.[21]

Sensing that the heir to the throne might be slipping from their grasp, the two Houses of parliament politely requested his return. They received a deceptively soothing response, signed by Charles, though probably written by his advisers, saying that the Scillies were poorly provisioned and that he had selected Jersey as his next destination, a part of his father's dominions from which he could correspond with, and receive orders from, parliament. Given the proximity of Jersey to France, this reassurance had a hollow tone. But Charles did not stay long on the Scillies. Less than a month after his arrival a parliamentary fleet surrounded St Mary's. Fortunately for the prince a fierce spring storm dis-persed it. Departure for Jersey was now imperative and Henrietta Maria, in Paris, grew increasingly anxious. 'I shall not sleep in quiet,' she wrote to Sir Edward Hyde, 'until I hear that the Prince of Wales shall be removed from thence.'[22] On 16 April, Prince Charles and about 300 followers, soldiers, courtiers, Cornish officials, clerks and their families, landed safely on Jersey, despite the pilot's nearly wrecking them on the harbour rocks.

The prince was warmly greeted by the island's governor, Sir George Carteret, and proceeded to familiarize himself with the island. He liked what he found and his council were confident that, at least for the foreseeable future, the island offered security, though its neighbour, Guernsey, was held by parliament. Charles set up a little court at his residence, Elizabeth Castle, and from there carried out military inspections and ordered new forts to be constructed. His sixteenth birthday was celebrated with great rejoicing on 29 May and he passed his time pleasantly enough. He learned to sail, a passion which stayed with him for the rest of his life, and engaged in pleasantries with the local ladies – perhaps, in fact, more than that, for there were rumours afterwards that he had sired a child during his stay. Yet though the queen in France wrote to her sister in more positive terms about Charles's safety, saying that he was on 'a small island that is still ours', she was applying more and more pressure for her eldest son to come to her in France.

The prince's council, as was so often the case, was divided on the wisdom of such a move. Hyde, Hopton and Berkshire were opposed to his going, believing that it would sit badly with public opinion. Hyde called it 'a matter of so great importance, on which the fate of three kingdoms might depend'. His great fear was that removing the prince to France would unite the Presbyterians and the Independents, whose quarrels were, by the summer of 1646, becoming obvious. His arguments fell on deaf ears. In late June, Henry Jermyn arrived on the island under instructions from Henrietta Maria to return with the prince. Jermyn would not listen to Hyde's reservations. The queen had earlier written to Charles that she believed that he could not stay longer in Jersey without falling into the hands of the king's enemies and she included a copy of a letter she had received from the king which said that 'his preservation is the greatest hope for my safety, and, in God's name, let him stay with thee, till it is seen what ply my business will take. And, for my sake, let the world see that the queen seeks not to alter his conscience.'[23]

Prince Charles, who had not been keen to go to Paris as a penniless dependent of his young cousin, Louis XIV, now capitulated to parental commands. For more than a year, he had watched his council argue destructively and seen his father's hopes disappear. Jersey had been a pleasant interlude but he felt he could not stay. The dissenters on his council, led by Hyde, refused to accompany him to France and resigned.[24] Bad weather delayed his departure for several days. He left on 25 June, going aboard ship with Digby and Jermyn each taking one of his arms, apparently afraid he might change his mind at the last minute. He landed at Saint-Malo and made his way overland to Saint-Germain, where he was reunited with his mother on 19 July. Not all the wider group of followers who had accompanied him to Jersey went with him to Paris. Ann Fanshawe returned to London while her husband stayed in Caen in Normandy, a city which would be a temporary home to many Protestant royalists. But for Prince Charles, fourteen miserable years of exile lay ahead.

CHAPTER SEVEN

'A foreigner begging your bread'

'I wish the Prince in any place out of France if it were possible.'
Edward Hyde, March 1647

'To a gentleman, any country is his homeland.'
Cardinal Jules Mazarin, 1637

HENRIETTA MARIA WAS elated to be reunited with her eldest and youngest children in the space of a month, the more so because the two years she had already passed in France had been far from easy. Initially, the queen had felt happy to be back in France, a country which she never really left emotionally. Despite the closeness of her marriage to Charles I and the enjoyable life they led together she remained a Bourbon princess. Henrietta divided her time between apartments at the Louvre and Saint-Germain, her childhood home, but the comforting familiarity of Paris and her position as a member of the French royal family were not quite what they seemed at first. Times had changed, not just in England, but in France as well. The queen and her group of courtiers were exiles and no amount of proximity to the French throne could disguise the fact that they were short of financial support. At a court where lavish display was the hallmark of regal magnificence, Henrietta Maria, who had sold most of her jewels in support of the royalist cause, cut an increasingly forlorn figure as the years of her exile went by. She was awarded a pension of thirty thousand livres a month for her household expenses (a rough equivalent today is about £327,500), an amount that had to stretch to support Prince Charles when he arrived, and, in due course, his brother, James. It appears generous but with an increasing number of penniless royalists to support, it was soon swallowed up. And though France had initially rejoiced in the return of its Bourbon princess, Henrietta was not at the centre of events. The thirty rooms she occupied at the Louvre may have been hung with royal tapestries but the king and his mother lived at the Palais Royal, the impressive palace built by Richelieu.[1] She was still indefatigable in her letter-writing and her political machinations, ably supported by Henry Jermyn, a man whose abilities were derided by Hyde and whose reputation has suffered badly until recent work has revealed a more interesting and competent person.[2] In fact, Henrietta was increasingly dependent on Jermyn as the years of separation from her husband grew longer, though their relationship was almost certainly not the secret romance imagined in torrid historical novels. So the queen was not isolated but she was removed from the reality of what was taking place in England. Yet the possibility of complete defeat never seems to have entered her mind. She was convinced that her husband could ride out the storm and successfully divide his enemies, perhaps even return stronger, if only he would compromise on religion. To her, any promises he made to rebels would be meaningless. They were just a means to an end. After more than twenty years of marriage she still did not understand her husband's conscience or appreciate the depth of his belief in his own interpretation of kingship. And the tall, unforthcoming son who now arrived to join her was himself something of a mystery to her.

Prince Charles seems to have passed his early months in France keeping his thoughts well hidden as he tried to analyse what was going on around him. This may have been the result of a mixture of commendable reserve and necessity, since he neither spoke nor appeared to understand very much French. His hosts were quite confounded by how tongue-tied he was and found him rather aloof. That may have suited him, since he had much to learn and very little to give away. For he had come to a land ruled by a child, though governed by a Spanish queen regent of Habsburg descent (and therefore doubly the enemy of France in historical terms) and an Italian cardinal from unremarkable origins in Rome. The country's large and quarrelsome aristocracy could, without careful handling, themselves foment discontent. So it would not have taken a great deal of perspicacity to work out that, whatever the lavish lifestyle of the French court, the throne might not be on the firmest of foundations, as events were to demonstrate only too clearly in the very near future. But for the time being, the prince was dependent on the goodwill of his mother's sister-in-law, the queen known as Anne of Austria, and her closest adviser, Cardinal Jules Mazarin.

*

THE QUEEN REGENT is an interesting and often overlooked figure. Alexandre Dumas did her no favours when he depicted her as a helpless heroine in *The Three Musketeers*. The real Anne was a survivor rather than a beautiful ingénue adrift in the currents of skulduggery of seventeenth-century France. There was, however, much in her long and often unhappy life in France that reads more like fiction than fact. Born in Valladolid in Spain in 1601, she was the eldest daughter of Philip III of Spain and his wife, Margaret of Austria. A portrait of her as a six-year-old shows an attractive and self-possessed child with fair hair.[3] On both sides she was a Habsburg, hence the name which the French gave her. But, whatever their heritage and appearance, the Spanish branch of a house that had roots in Austria had long since adapted to Spanish mores. The infanta Anna was neither dark-eyed nor raven-haired, but she was a true representative of Spain and its interests when she arrived as the fourteen-year-old bride of a reluctant Louis XIII.

It was Anne's misfortune to leave the very strait-laced, protocol-ridden Spanish court for an environment of intrigue and instability in its traditional enemy, France. Her mother-in-law, Marie de Médici, treated her with contempt and her husband, a difficult young man psychologically damaged by his charismatic father and overwrought mother, had only their unhappy union to use as an example of the pitfalls of a diplomatic marriage when he was thrust into one himself. Although she tried, Anne could never win his trust, much less his affection. Initially dependent on her Spanish ladies for companionship and support, she kept out of French politics as much as possible as a very young woman, following the advice her father had given her. But when Louis XIII overthrew his mother's favourites and forced her from the regency in 1617, Anne suffered too. When he asserted himself as Charles I was later to do with Henrietta Maria's French household, Anne learned that her husband was determined to dismiss all but a very few of her Spanish servants. She did not make a scene to match her sister-in-law (who had also behaved badly towards Anne when she first came to France) but the episode was distressing.

Like Henrietta, she learned how to carry on and, again like her sister-in-law, she fell under the influence of self-serving aristocratic women, including the ubiquitous duchess of Chevreuse. Anne's judgement was often suspect. Buckingham's ill-concealed admiration for the French queen threatened her reputation when his pleasantries were reported to have turned into an assault on her virtue. She could not get on with her husband's chief adviser, Cardinal Richelieu, and he was a dangerous enemy. Even more serious was the lack of children. Anne's first four pregnancies ended in miscarriage, the last caused by her slipping on a highly polished wooden floor while playing games with her ladies. Louis XIII, never the most understanding of men, was furious. And he suspected his wife, justifiably, as it turned out, of secret correspondence with her brother, Philip IV of Spain. To be married to a barren and treacherous wife was more than a fragile man like Louis XIII could stand. For years the couple essentially led

Charles I of England and Queen Henrietta Maria by Gonzales Coques.
The first years of their marriage were extremely difficult but they became
a devoted couple.

Charles I, and Henrietta Maria, with their two eldest children,
Prince Charles, and Princess Mary by Sir Anthony Van Dyck.

Henry IV of France.

Louis XIII,
Henrietta Maria's brother.

Anne of Austria,
the Spanish wife of Louis XIII.

Marie de Médici, grandmother of the Stuart royal children.

Louis XIV of France. The monarch would become the Sun King.

From left to right King Charles II, King James II and
Mary, Princess of Orange as children by Cornelius Johnson.

The five eldest children of Charles I (1637)
by Sir Anthony Van Dyck.

Princess Elizabeth by Wenceslaus Hollar. As this portrait shows, Elizabeth was no beauty but she was clever, loyal and loving. She spent the Civil Wars under the control of Parliament with her brother Henry, dying on the Isle of Wight in 1650.

Princess Anne – Anonymous. The tubercular child, who looks so bonny in the Van Dyck portrait, died before her fourth birthday.

Prince Henry, duke of Gloucester by Adriaen Hanneman. Probably aged about fourteen at the time of this portrait, the youngest son of Charles I spent his childhood as a hostage of Parliament. Handsome, spirited and intelligent, his tragic death from smallpox in September 1660 devastated Charles II.

Left Charles I with James. The anxiety that his father might abandon him seems already to be there in James's uncertain gaze.

Right A young princess Henriette-Anne, 'Minette'. Christened at Exeter Cathedral but brought up as a Catholic by her mother in France, the princess had to suffer the condescending attitudes of the French court towards her straitened circumstances.

Left William II, Prince of Orange and Princess Mary Stuart, daughter of Charles I of England. A wedding portrait by Anthony van Dyck. Sadly, the promise of happiness suggested in this picture was never realized. William was a womanizer and his young wife never settled in her husband's country.

Left Algernon Percy, 10th earl of Northumberland and guardian of Elizabeth and Henry from 1645–1649. From a famously rebellious family, the earl did his best to make their day-to-day lives bearable.

Right Sir Thomas Fairfax. The commander-in-chief of the Parliamentary army was charmed by Princess Elizabeth when they met in 1647. He took no part in Charles I's trial.

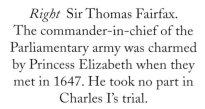

Left Penshurst Place in Kent, where Elizabeth and Henry lived with the family of the earl and countess of Leicester between 1649 and 1650.

James Graham, marquess of Montrose, a disillusioned Covenanter who became an implacable enemy of Argyll and a determined advocate of royalism in Scotland after 1640. His military successes in Highland Scotland in the mid-1640s added to his own conviction that he was a hero in the classical mode and he was driven on by ambition and his relentless dislike of Argyll. Yet his final 'invasion' of Scotland in 1650 was a resounding failure. The courage with which he met his death and his own successful moulding of his image while he was alive have made this handsome, charismatic man a romantic hero.

Oliver Cromwell, lieutenant-general of the New Model Army and later Lord Protector. He met James, Elizabeth and Henry in 1647 and was moved by Charles I's evident affection for them.

separate lives. And then, sixteen years after her last pregnancy, Anne gave birth to a son and heir for the Bourbon dynasty on Sunday, 5 September 1638, at Saint-Germain. She was two weeks short of her thirty-seventh birthday and suddenly there was not just hope, but fulfilment.

The dramatic version of Louis XIV's conception is that his father was forced by December storms and flooding to spend the night at the Louvre, where Anne was staying. This unexpected arrival meant that his rooms were not prepared and he had to sleep in the queen's apartments. It is a good story but probably gained in the telling. There is evidence that Anne and her husband may have been on better terms for a while rather than suddenly discovering a mutual passion on a dark and stormy night.[4] Certainly Anne was overjoyed, and not a little relieved, to find herself pregnant again after so long. She had worried otherwise that she might be exiled or even put in a nunnery. When she gave birth to a healthy nine-pound boy, her position seemed to be transformed. They called him Louis le Dieudonné (the God-given) and his arrival was greeted with great rejoicing. Two years later Anne gave birth to a second son, Philippe, duke of Orléans. The Bourbon dynasty's future was assured but relations between the royal couple went downhill again. Unlike Charles I, Louis XIII could not stand his children. He found their response to him and their obvious affection for their mother profoundly irritating, writing of his two-year-old heir: 'I am most displeased with my son. As soon as he sets eyes on me, he yells as if he were looking at the devil and cries for his mother.'[5]

Perhaps he was also concerned about the scurrilous rumours being spread about his children's paternity, at least one of which originated with his own younger brother, Gaston of Orléans. Displaced as heir to the throne by the new arrival, Gaston took offence at his relegation, remarking crudely that he was convinced that the little prince had emerged from his sister-in-law's belly but that he was not sure how the infant had got there. He would prove to be a notably disloyal and unreliable uncle. Even worse for

Anne was the threat that her husband would take her two boys away from her, which nearly drove her to despair and was only averted when little Louis, no doubt heavily coached, sought his father's forgiveness. His memories of his father were clearly not happy and he seldom spoke of him in later life. The Sun King's model was his dynamic grandfather, Henry IV, not the querulous figure of a tubercular father, who died when he was only five. Although distraught at her husband's passing, despite their dismal relationship, Anne of Austria's moment had arrived. She would soon share it with another, a foreigner like herself.

Jules Mazarin was born Giulio Mazarini in the mountainous central Italian region of Abruzzo and grew up in Rome. His family were not impoverished but were essentially of modest means. His mother came from minor Italian nobility and his father was a client of the powerful Colonna family. It was Giulio's own early educational attainments that enabled him to enter the Jesuit College of Rome at a time of revival in Italian intellectual and cultural life. A good education, coupled with a pleasing personality and refined manners, suggested that he could pursue a promising career. He soon realized that he had an innate capacity to charm people; in the words of a recent biographer, he was 'infinitely seductive'.[6] He was handsome, witty and set to go far. Quite how far perhaps even he did not yet realize. Lacking the connections that gave such easy preferment to the aristocratic class, he knew he would have to make his own way and his self-belief did not waver. When opportunities came he took them. The first of these was as a companion to the second son of the Colonna family, whom he accompanied during the young man's studies in Spain. There he learned to speak Spanish – the native tongue of the queen he would later serve – and to live in another country.

When he returned to Rome his father was in financial difficulties and though Giulio studied at Rome's Sapienza University, where he gained a doctorate in jurisprudence, he did not enter the legal profession. Instead he followed his Colonna patrons into the military during the War of the Mantuan Succession, demon-strating for the first time the diplomatic skills which were to change his life. The Pope, Urban VIII, was impressed by this clever young man who was eventually able to bring about a treaty ending the conflict. Mazarini's career as a papal envoy took off from this point. By 1634 he was papal nuncio at the French court, where he attracted the attention of Cardinal Richelieu. The wily Frenchman had found a kindred spirit in this personable, cunning Italian who was by now an inveterate gambler. Mazarini saw his advantage in becoming Jules Mazarin and devoting his future to France. 'I had attached myself to the Cardinal by instinct,' he later wrote, 'even before understanding from experience his great qualities.'[31] For a man who loved the cards, it was a calculated throw of the dice.

At the beginning of 1640 Mazarin became a naturalized Frenchman and two years later a cardinal. He was impeccably placed to step into Richelieu's shoes but no one could have fore-seen that the first minister and Louis XIII would die within a few months of each other. Louis left his wife as regent but with a carefully selected regency council, including his brother, Gaston, and Mazarin, to make formal decisions. It was now that Anne's Habsburg heritage came to the fore. The women of her dynasty had been accustomed to exercise authority since the time of Charles V. Fiercely protective of her sons and supremely conscious of the fact that Louis XIV was a king as well as a child, she was not content to take a back seat. Acting with a firmness and deter-mination that belied her reputation for laziness, this woman whose only experience of government had been confined to the running of her own household now stepped firmly into the fray. Within days of her husband's death she had persuaded the *parle-ment de Paris*, the highest court of law in France, to change the terms of her husband's will. She was given powers to choose her son's ministers and introduce laws. The man she selected as her chief adviser was Jules Mazarin.

Their relationship was the source of much speculation at the time but it seems to have been one of mentor and pupil rather than of lovers. This does not mean, of course, that there was not a strong emotional bond. Mazarin and Anne communicated in Spanish and for two hours every evening he would brief her in foreign affairs. By the time Henrietta Maria arrived in Paris in 1644, their working partnership was well established. Inevitably, it displeased many, not least Gaston of Orléans, of whom Henrietta was very fond. But she also got on well with her sister-in-law, on whom she was now heavily dependent. When the two women met again, after so many years, they were much changed. Two late pregnancies and the passage of time had considerably increased Anne's girth and given her several chins. Henrietta Maria, though not yet forty, was thin and frail and looked like a tiny old woman. They embraced and the English queen, recognizing her debt to Anne, would add the latter's name to that of her youngest daughter when Princess Henrietta (thereafter known as Henriette Anne) arrived in 1646. Anne was never anything other than kind but her focus was bound to be on her son and on France. Obsessed with the situation of her husband back in England, Henrietta Maria had neither the will nor the influence to play much part in French politics. At the beginning, she believed the charming Cardinal Mazarin would support Charles I. His views of the best course for Charles aligned with hers. But, in the end, he would do nothing at all.

*

HENRIETTA MARIA's hopes were not just for her beleaguered spouse in Newcastle. Prince Charles's arrival in France presented her with other considerations. The royalist cause would be greatly strengthened if she could bring about a prestigious marriage for her eldest son. And there was an obvious candidate for such a match – her own niece, Anne Marie Louise de Montpensier, Gaston's daughter. This young lady was three years older than the Prince of Wales and the richest woman in France – indeed, perhaps in the whole of Europe – having inherited the wealth of her mother, Marie de Montpensier, a princess of the blood, when that lady died just one week after she was born. Gaston d'Orléans had made liberal use of his daughter's fortune for himself, but there was still a great deal remaining. From the English queen's perspective, the princess seemed an ideal choice. But La Grande Mademoiselle, as her contemporaries called her, had other ideas.

She was a tall, well-made blonde, with a large nose and heavy-set features (a typical Bourbon), and she covered herself in jewels and dressed expensively in all the latest fashions, even if these were not always elegantly displayed. One portrait of her depicts her dressed in a costume which looks like a cross between an early version of Britannia and a Roman goddess. She doted on her father but he paid her scant attention, though he could be affectionate on the occasions when they were together. Brought up as a princess of France by Madame de Saint-Georges, the childhood companion of her aunt, Henrietta Maria, her education had been neglected and she was far from cultured. Later attempts to learn Spanish and Italian met with limited success. The epitome of a poor little rich girl, Mademoiselle was vain and shallow, supremely self-confident and, at nineteen, utterly lacking in any understanding of her effect on others. Convinced, with justification, that she was the greatest catch in Europe, Mademoiselle's greatest admirer was herself. This feeling did not moderate with time. She would later write:

> I am incapable of any base action or dark deeds; I am more likely to show mercy than to render justice. I am melancholy and like to read good solid books . . . I enjoy society and the conversation of well-bred persons . . . Above all others, I like soldiers and to hear them talk about their craft . . . I confess that I talk willingly about war; I know that I am brave, with much courage and ambition . . . . I enjoy violins above all other music, and dancing more than I can say . . . No one has ever had any power over me . . . The great sorrows I have known would have killed other people.[8]

Mademoiselle was a force of nature and her life was to be far sadder than she could have ever contemplated when she was thrust into the company of the young Charles Stuart.

Her goal at this point in her life was to marry the Austrian emperor, Ferdinand III. The penurious Prince of Wales, titular head of a principality whose importance could not have figured prominently in Mademoiselle's ambitions, was not the sort of suitor to whom she intended to give her hand. Furthermore, she did not warm to him at a personal level, being unimpressed by his swarthy features and taciturn manners. The realization that he could not speak French was appalling to her. How could any European aristocrat be so uncouth? The lack of attraction was mutual, for Charles knew, instantly, that he could not stand Mademoiselle. Only his mother failed to realize that the two young people were totally incompatible.

While her eccentricity was already well established and her modesty non-existent, history does owe a debt of gratitude to Anne Marie Louise. Her copious memoirs, utterly lacking in irony and therefore all the more entertaining, are an important source for historians of the period, revealing, indirectly, much about the exiled Stuarts at a point where concentration has largely been on the fate of Charles I in England. It is, for example, to Mademoiselle that we owe the description of how the Prince of Wales was introduced to his French relatives in the boiling summer of 1646.

In order to avoid the stifling heat of Paris that year, the French court had moved out of the city to Fontainebleau, the castle in a forested area that had been one of the major architectural projects of Henry VIII's great rival, Francis I, a hundred years before. It was on one of the many roads that criss-crossed the forest that the coach of Henrietta Maria and her son encountered that of the king of France and his immediate French relations: the little duke of Anjou, younger brother of Louis XIV, the queen mother, Gaston of Orléans and his daughter, La Grande Mademoiselle. This apparently chance meeting was, in fact, carefully arranged so as to facilitate introductions without embarrassment. Mindful of the changing events in England and unwilling to risk giving offence by according someone who might be viewed as a renegade the full honours of an official reception, Mazarin and Anne were careful in their handling of a delicate situation. This was to be presented very much as a family affair, a charming coincidence at a rural retreat.

Henrietta Maria's coach stopped and she and Prince Charles got out to meet the waiting French royal party. The prince was presented first of all to the young king. Neither could have known then that Louis XIV's reign would be the longest in French history and that his aspirations for France would engulf Europe in war. In 1646 he was a pleasing-looking child of eight with long curly brown hair, close to his mother and already contemptuous of his little brother. Their difficult relationship started early. Louis never did grow tall, like his English cousin, but he had a well-developed sense of his own majesty, even at this early age. It is unlikely that he was overly impressed with the new arrival from England, who certainly looked like a Bourbon but could not converse like one. It might not have occurred to him to be disappointed – Charles meant little to him – but Mademoiselle remembered her own reservations vividly. The prince was, she recalled, 'only sixteen or seventeen but very tall for his age. His head was noble, his hair black, his complexion brown, his person passably agreeable . . . he neither spoke nor understood French, a most inconvenient thing.'[9] Awkward it may have been, but Charles spent the next three days being entertained at Fontainebleau and calling upon all the French princesses of the extended royal family, of whom there were many.

His mother failed to notice the hauteur of her niece towards her son. Henrietta Maria did not give up easily. She assured Mademoiselle that the prince talked of her incessantly and was alarmed to hear that the wife of the Austrian emperor had recently died. Surely the emperor would not want to lose the opportunity of wooing Charles's imposing cousin. The silent prince, with

Prince Rupert in tow as an interpreter, was forced to act as a companion to Mademoiselle throughout the autumn season, accompanying her to the theatre, dancing with her at balls, handing her from carriages to palaces, even holding a candelabra while Henrietta Maria, who had lent the princess her remaining jewels, arranged Mademoiselle's blonde tresses before an Italian comedy and a *fête* at the Palais Royal.[10] There could be no doubting, on this occasion, that Anne Marie Louise was the belle of the ball:

> My gown shimmered all over with diamonds and was trimmed with tufts of carnation, black and white. I had upon me all the crown jewels, as well as those which the Queen of England still owned then. No one was more magnificently dressed than I that day and I did not fail to find many people to tell me of my splendour and to talk about my beautiful figure, my graceful bearing, the whiteness of my skin and the sheen of my blonde hair. These, they said, adorned me more than all the riches which glittered upon me.

None of this adulation inspired the young lady to think more kindly of her English admirer. Her ambition was to become an empress and she was quite clear-headed about her feelings:

> I realized that the Emperor was neither a young nor a gallant man, but the truth was that I cared more for my establishment than for the person of my suitor . . . I must not forget to say that at this ball of which I have just spoken, the Queen of England noticed that I looked at her son somewhat disdainfully. When she learned the cause of it she reproached me and said that my head was full of nothing but the Emperor. I defended myself as well as I could, but my face disguised my sentiments so poorly that one had only to look at me to discover them.[11]

Mademoiselle's disdain may have owed something to the fact that Prince Charles had spent part of the performance sitting at her feet. This was either a deliciously ironic gesture or the result of weeks of boredom dancing attendance on the vainest woman in Europe.

Charles's time in Paris was not all duty. His childhood companions, the Villiers brothers, passed through the city on a tour of Europe and offered an agreeable alternative to Mademoiselle's posturing and the fractious behaviour of his mother's court, where quarrels and duelling had become a pastime for her hangers-on. The young men followed the eyes of their French hosts and worshipped from afar the beautiful duchess of Châtillon, an object of far greater admiration at the court than Mademoiselle. They visited the shops and strolled the streets of the city, amazed by what it had to offer. The prince may not have been comfortable in the French tongue, but he acquired a permanent admiration for the French aristocratic way of life and the importance of keeping up appearances in an uncertain world. In the coming years, the significance he attached to the perceptions of royalty, to civility and elegance when hardly anything else remained, would serve him well.

Henrietta Maria's matchmaking schemes came to nothing but they did not set her relationship with her adolescent son on a good footing. Charles was mortified by his mother's unsubtle behaviour and the friction would remain. Nor did Mademoiselle get her way. Her father was firmly opposed to any marriage with Ferdinand III, saying it would bring her only unhappiness. It is unclear whether the newly widowed Austrian ruler had ever actually considered offering to share his throne with her.[12] A marriage with the Prince of Wales was never a serious possibility, no matter how much his mother might have wanted it. Still very young, Charles nevertheless knew that he had better keep his options open. His future, and that of his father, might be compromised if he made the wrong choice. Catholic brides were unlikely to appeal to the opponents of royalism at home. And, as the year 1647 dawned, there seemed hope that it might be possible to exploit the growing tensions among the enemies of the Stuarts, despite Charles I's loss of personal freedom.

*

THE SCOTS HAD moved swiftly to ensure the security of their prize. Ten days after he handed himself over to their forces at Newark, the king was in Newcastle. He entered the town in the late afternoon of 13 May 1646, with an escort of 300 horsemen, along a road lined with musketeers and pikemen. Royalist propaganda tried to represent this as a regal entry amid widespread rejoicing but the Scots were not inclined to allow any display of popular support. There were no crowds and not even any local dignitaries. The French ambassador told Mazarin that the mayors of Durham and Newcastle were prevented from coming to see the king. He was lodged at Anderson Place, also known as the New House, under the watchful eye of the Scottish commander Alexander Leslie, first earl of Leven.

Leven was not the kind of man the king would have found stimulating company, even if the elderly earl, then in his mid-sixties, had been minded to entertain his charge. He was an illegitimate son of George Leslie, the captain of Blair Castle in Atholl in the Scottish Islands. His education was neglected and he was nearly illiterate but a military career in Europe and especially in the service of the Swedish king, Gustavus Adolphus, had been highly successful. He felt that the role of the Scots in the victory at Marston Moor in 1644 had not received sufficient recognition, galling for a general who had been honoured by the Swedish king. But if Leven, who had a reputation for keeping out of political intrigue, was disgruntled, so were the local population of Newcastle and Northumberland, who had endured the occupation of his army for more than two years. Though his position in the north of England was somewhat eased by the defeat of Montrose's anti-Covenanter forces at Philiphaugh in September 1645, the king's surrender at Newark had yet to be turned to positive advantage for Scotland. Meanwhile, Charles needed to be fed, housed and guarded very carefully.

This was a dismal period for the king, among the worst of his life. He was utterly disillusioned, badgered by Henrietta Maria and Mazarin to accept a course that his conscience utterly disavowed and increasingly afraid. Misery sat heavily on him when he arrived in Newcastle. He seemed, it was reported by those who saw him, 'melancholy and is very grey with cares . . . his Majesty's face is not shaven but cut round both on the chin and upper lip also. His lock is cut off and his head rounded.'[13] The trim beard and carefully combed hair were replaced by a rough, unkempt appearance. The scales fell from his eyes very quickly in Newcastle. 'It is more than apparent,' he wrote to Henrietta Maria at the end of May, 'that the Scots will absolutely hinder my being any more king in England than they have made me in Scotland.' A few days later he told her that he could not call for any of his old servants nor choose any new ones and that his friends were forbidden by proclamation to see him.[14] He would not subscribe to the Covenant or agree to introduce Presbyterianism into England as the state religion. The price the Scots were trying to extract from him in return for their support was too high.

Early on, within three weeks of his arrival in Newcastle, he had made up his mind, though he kept his decision from his captors. He could see only one way out of his plight and so he told his wife that 'my condition is such that I never expect to see thee, except by the queen's sending to me persons of secrecy and dexterity, [with whom I might] find means to quit for a time this wretched country. Wherefore, I earnestly desire thee to think of this seriously and speedily, for it will not admit of long delay.'[15] It was a refrain he would refer to repeatedly in the coming months, surrounded as he was by 'fools and knaves, all having a tincture of falsehood'. He felt 'barbarously baited', as well he might, since he had to endure lengthy sermons by a Presbyterian preacher with the entirely appropriate name of Mr Cant, who took as one of his texts the seventh verse of Psalm nine: 'O thou enemy, destructions are come to a perpetual end, and thou hast destroyed cities, their memorial is perished with them.'[16] If this were not bad enough, he was compelled to receive deputations of emotional Scottish lords, begging him to submit to the Covenant. After one bruising encounter, he retired, weeping, to his bedchamber. In the middle of May, Jack Ashburnham managed to escape to Holland. Hudson was sent back down to London, leaving the king with only Will Murray as an attendant who he could trust.

Despite the image he portrayed of a forlorn and forsaken king, Charles's mental state was worse than his physical condition. The New House was not a luxurious palace but it had been prepared to receive its royal visitor. Two members of the Scottish nobility, William Hamilton, Lord Lanark, who acted as the king's secretary, and Charles Seton, earl of Dunfermline, were part of his little 'court' in Newcastle and slept in his bedchamber. Both were young men who would be much involved in attempts to balance the interest of the Scots with the interests of the king and Charles, however desperate he sounded to Henrietta Maria, was already beginning to glimpse how he might play various interests off against one another. But the early summer of 1646 in Newcastle passed slowly. It was not exactly house arrest – there were frequent trips out to play golf and to visit Tynemouth – but life was tedious. He ate well enough, on an allowance of £100 a month, but the feeling that he had lost the mastery of his own fate did not go away. Letters from his wife took a long time to arrive and he worried about the Prince of Wales, convinced that Jersey was not a safe place. Paradoxically, the fall of Oxford at the end of June offered him unexpected respite. More of his adherents found their way north, including his barber, Vincent Babington, who, if the earlier description is accurate, was certainly needed.

Then, on 23 July, the English parliamentary commissioners arrived with propositions for peace. The country was weary of civil war, its citizens demoralized by the loss of life, high taxation, the shattered economy and the hardship brought about by bad harvests. The king had been defeated in battle a year ago and now his headquarters at Oxford had surrendered. It was time to bring matters to an end, especially as cracks were beginning to show in the relationship between the victorious army and the parliament in whose name it had spilt blood. So, at Newcastle, Charles I was offered propositions for 'a safe and well-grounded peace, agreed upon by the parliaments of both kingdoms respectively'. This settlement would have restored him to the throne but entirely on parliament's terms. The extent of the defeat that his opponents deemed they had inflicted on him was evident in the stringent terms of the Newcastle propositions. He was to take the oath to the Solemn League and Covenant (and speedily require that it was extended to every one of his subjects in the three kingdoms), give his assent to further acts for the complete abolition of episcopacy and agree to the establishment of Presbyterianism in England. This would, if enacted, have led to a second Reformation in England a little over a century after the first. Swingeing laws were introduced against Catholics, attacking the doctrinal roots of their beliefs and making all who refused the new oath recusants, who would lose control of their children's religious upbringing. In military matters, Charles was to surrender control of the armed forces to parliament for a period of twenty years with the right to resume it subsequently at times if 'the safety of the kingdom be concerned'. Punitive measures were stipulated against the king's supporters, many of whom were excluded from any possibility of pardon or further public employment and were to lose substantial amounts of their lands. The list was headed by Princes Rupert and Maurice and included all the main royalist generals and politicians, in England and Scotland.[17]

If the commissioners who travelled north to present these peace terms to the king seriously believed he would agree to them, they had greatly mistaken their man. There was nothing at all that Charles would even consider in proposals that so humiliated him and struck at the very foundation of his beliefs. His view of kingship could never embrace such a limited monarchy, in which he would, in his own eyes, be nothing more than a figurehead. But he knew better than to reject outright what was put to him. So began his long game of playing for time. It was something he was good at, though over the next two years he was increasingly exposed as untrustworthy. But why, when he had no respect for his enemies, should he trouble his conscience about his duplicity,

even as it became more evident? He was not devoid of intelligence, in both senses of the word. At this point, there was no
question of deposing him. Nowhere in the Newcastle propositions
was there the faintest hint of republicanism. He knew that there
was an increasing rift between the Independents and the Presbyterians and saw that this could be exploited to his advantage.
But this was a tactic, not a strategy, because, at root, he had nothing to offer but the vision of kingship which had sustained him
since he came to the throne more than twenty years before. The
Civil War had hardened, not softened, his commitment to it.
So his first reaction was to contain his contempt in public while
privately assuring his wife and friends in France that he could
never agree to parliament's demands.

On 1 August he wrote to the Speaker of the House of Lords
regarding the propositions he had received for a peace settlement:

> [The proposals] do import so great alterations in government
> both in the Church and kingdom, as it is very difficult to
> return a particular and positive answer . . . to which end His
> Majesty desires and proposeth to come to London . . . where
> by his personal presence he may not only raise a mutual
> confidence between him and his people, but also have these
> doubts cleared and these difficulties explained unto him,
> which he now conceives to be destructive to his regal power,
> if he should give a full consent to these propositions as they
> now stand.

He did not leave any doubt that he was greatly concerned by
what was laid before him but offered room for manoeuvre. His
own demands were, he said, reasonable and 'very much conducible
to that peace which all good men desire and pray for'. At the end,
there was even a carrot in the postscript, in which he promised
that he would immediately send for the Prince of Wales as soon
as 'a happy agreement' was reached.[18] And with Prince Charles
safe in France he could well afford to make such an offer. It had
no more chance of becoming a reality than the quiet boy himself

had of becoming the husband of his condescending cousin, La Grande Mademoiselle.

*

THE ENGLISH commissioners left Newcastle empty-handed and the stalemate continued. Yet as the parliament at Westminster began to bargain with the Scots for return of the king to their custody, Charles grew more and more desperate to escape England altogether. The autumn of 1646 was a wretched period for him. His refusal to accept Presbyterianism and save his throne, while at the same time appearing to give ground on the control of the army, drove such a wedge between him and his wife that their relationship, made all the more difficult by separation, suffered severe strain. The queen was scathing and incredulous at his obduracy. She still felt that Scotland and Ireland, which she had unrealistic hopes of going to herself, offered him better hopes than the English parliament. But the situation in Ireland had been complicated by the interference of both king and queen, which had undermined the peace efforts of one of the royalists' most loyal and able supporters, the marquess of Ormonde. Though splits were beginning to appear in Scotland as well, where the marquess of Argyll and the Hamiltons were about to part company in their policy towards Charles I, these could not yet be turned to the king's advantage. Meanwhile, the queen berated him for the concessions he appeared willing to make in November. She could not believe that he would cede power over the militia to parliament for ten years. This meant, she wrote, that they would never see an end to their troubles: 'For as long as the Parliament lasts, you are not king; and as for me I shall not again set my foot in England. And with the granting the militia, you have cut your own throat; for having given them this power, you can no longer refuse them anything, not even my life, if they demand it.'[19] Charles was distraught at her emotional blackmail; she had, he assured her, been misinformed. At the end of November, he could take no more:

Whatever chiding my willfullness [sic] (as the queen may think), may deserve, for God's sake leave off threatening me with thy desire to meddle no more with business; and albeit I am confident thou dost not really intend, because I know thou canst not in any kind forsake me (of which this were a sort) or leave to love me, as thou lovest me, give me so much comfort (and God knows I have but little, and that little must come from thee), as to assure me that thou will think no more of any such thing . . . [20]

These differences between the king and queen were never fully resolved. She could not understand why he was unable to give way on Presbyterianism and the Covenant, but the king, with considerable justification, saw 'this damned Covenant' as 'the child of rebellion' which 'breathes nothing but treason'.[21] He would have been still more alarmed if he had known that the queen's opinions were shared by Cardinal Mazarin. On 12 November 1646, the cardinal wrote to the French ambassador in Scotland, Bellièvre, claiming that he was passionate about the interests of the English king and felt great tenderness towards his person. 'But,' he went on, 'I despair that none of the efforts that are being made to extract him from the unhappiness in which he finds himself are producing any effect.' He could not understand why Charles would not agree to the establishment of Presbyterianism. He was, he said, equally surprised by the English king's response to the propositions sent to him at Newcastle. If Charles agreed to this change in religion, he would, in a short time, be more powerful than he had ever been. Bellièvre must continue to press him on this point. 'If the king of England could see Mazarin's heart, he would know with what passion he thought continually about his interests, despite all the other great considerations of state that weighed on him.' He would, he claimed, have no difficulty in giving his own blood to extricate Charles from his difficulties. Meanwhile, there were more urgent considerations, such as keeping the Scots onside. The war with Spain pressed on him and he asked the ambassador to see if he could get 1,000 more Scots to join the effort. But his main concern was to deter Charles from coming to France. There would be nothing that would contribute more to his entire ruin (or put a substantial extra demand on French coffers, though Mazarin did not, of course, say this) and though the cardinal might greatly desire to see His Majesty, this was no reason for Charles to abandon the possibility of his restoration to power. And on that note he ended his masterpiece of diplomatic double-speak.[22]

Charles I was not convinced by the exhortations of his wife or the chief minister of France. A Dutch ship had been in Newcastle harbour throughout the autumn, ostensibly having its hull repaired. But the stay had another motive. Charles longed to be with his family again. In Holland, he could count on the goodwill of his daughter, Mary, by then living formally with her husband. The House of Orange might facilitate his eventual arrival in France, to be reunited with his queen. The king's escape was planned for Christmas Day 1646, but it was aborted at the last minute when the behaviour of Will Murray, his servant, attracted attention. This bungled escapade, so typical of the royalists' inability to make the right decision when it came to Charles's security, concentrated the minds of the English parliamentarians in their negotiations with the Scots.

The main sticking point had been money. The Scots demanded reparation for the expenses they had incurred, though there was disagreement between the Hamiltons and Argyll about whether the Scottish army should remain in England or return home and what should happen to the king, as well as concern that no peace be concluded without the agreement of the Scots. After considerable bargaining, the English reduced the agreed sum to £400,000, to be paid in instalments.

On 30 January 1647, the first £100,000 was handed over by English commissioners, headed by the earl of Pembroke, the former guardian of Princess Elizabeth and Prince Henry, who had come up to Newcastle in order to collect the king. Outraged royalists accused the Scots of selling Charles I and comparisons were made with Judas. Four days later, the king began his journey south, to Holdenby (pronounced Holmby) House in Northamptonshire, the residence chosen for him by the House of Commons, who had overruled the preference of the Lords for Newmarket, which was thought to be a hotbed of royalism. Charles travelled slowly, with something of the air of a monarch making a royal progress, despite the fact that he was a prisoner. At Ripon in Yorkshire he touched for the King's Evil – placing his hand on people in an attempt to cure them of the disease which caused an uncomfortable swelling of their lymph nodes – and was greeted by enthusiastic crowds lining the road to Leeds. Outside Nottingham, Fairfax rode out to meet him and kissed his hand. To the parliamentary general – indeed, to all his subjects – he was still their king. Charles told the commissioners accompanying him that the general was a man of honour, a generous but true tribute to someone who had been instrumental in bringing about his own defeat.

As he neared his new residence, the king was heartened by the response he received. The gentry of Northamptonshire came out to meet him in their hundreds; bells were rung and guns fired in Northampton itself and Charles neared Holdenby with cries of 'God bless Your Majesty' ringing in his ears. His mood lifted immensely. He was closer to London, to the seat of power that he began to believe might still be his. There was all to play for.

CHAPTER EIGHT

Vanishing Hopes

'*We will not engage our people in another war.*'
Charles I, Easter 1647

'*No one rises so high as he who knows not whither he is going.*'
Oliver Cromwell, July 1647

THE MAN WHO, PERHAPS more than any other, was to influence
the course of the lives of the royal children met their father for the
first time at the home of Sir John Cutts, Childerley Hall, near
Cambridge, on 7 June 1647. Oliver had come far from the East
Anglian gentleman farmer of limited means who made his parliamentary debut in 1628. The Civil War had transformed him into
a superb soldier and a conviction politician, committed to a concept of liberty fundamentally opposed to the Stuart belief in the
divine right of kings. As such, he would become the nemesis of
Charles I but neither he nor anyone else could have foreseen such
an outcome that summer's day in 1647, when he accompanied his
commander, General Fairfax, to an interview with the king in a
country house not far from where he himself had been born. How
Charles came to be at the home of the Cutts family is a story in
itself.

Charles had found his life and surroundings at Holdenby
much more congenial than his dismal time with the Scots in

Newcastle. In this large house with its splendid chimneys, originally built for Elizabeth I's favourite, Christopher Hatton, he kept
a small court, was waited upon by the parliamentary commissioners and ate well: 'All the tables were as well furnished as they used
to be when his Majesty was in a peaceful and flourishing state.'[1]
The king had always been abstemious when it came to food and
drink and he attributed his own good health to his diet, exercise
and religious devotions. He was not allowed his own Anglican
chaplains, despite a formal request in March, but he seems to have
found the two divines attached to him far more palatable than
the Scottish Presbyterian preachers who harangued him in his
former captivity. His days passed in languid gentility, walking in
the grounds of Holdenby with Pembroke, at a pace the elderly earl
found hard to match, or with Major-General Richard Browne, the
Presbyterian army officer assigned to guard him. During these
perambulations, everyone else kept a respectful distance as the
king engaged in private conversation with his companions. Pembroke fell seriously ill while at Holdenby and his condition was
for a while so bad that his son was summoned to his bedside.
Charles, ever punctilious in such matters, enquired daily for Pembroke's health and visited him twice. The earl was touched by his
kindness and eventually recovered.

The king was very fond of playing bowls and as there was
no bowling green at Holdenby he was allowed to ride over to
Harrowden, the home of the Vaux family, or Althorp, Lord Spen-
cer's house. But the appearance of settled tranquillity in the king's
affairs was misleading. Both he and his captors knew that it was
unlikely to last. There was good reason for his prayers and he
was well aware that nothing was settled. For England was in ferment and the long-simmering hostility between the army and the
Presbyterian members of parliament was threatening to explode.
In Scotland meanwhile, the failure to impose Presbyterianism on
England made some of the king's former adversaries rethink their
strategy. Perhaps his restoration to the throne was the key to
restoring stability in Scotland. Charles saw in these tensions his

own salvation. He could play all sides off against one another, seeming to offer sufficient concessions while biding his time. He hoped the time was soon coming when he could be done with the pleasant emptiness of days in the Northamptonshire countryside and return to his God-given rights as ruler. For the king, nothing had changed. The army in England, however, had other ideas.

It was determined not to be disbanded without arrears of pay and on terms that would allow the soldiery to be reintegrated into civilian life. The men who had fought across the killing fields of civil war were now caught up in the wider struggle for political control of England and liberty of conscience. Their stance infuriated parliamentarians like Denzil Holles, who was committed to the destruction of the New Model Army and became its chief opponent in the uncertain spring of 1647. The death of the earl of Essex from a stroke in September 1646 removed one of the most prominent opponents of the Independents from the national scene and Holles, a sour-faced, intemperate Puritan in his late forties who favoured religious unity between England and Scotland and who had always hoped for peace between the king and parliament, stepped into the limelight.[2] But despite growing disaffection in the ranks, the soldiers still put their faith in parliament, petitioning it respectfully for what they believed was no more than their due. In late March Holles, in a sparsely attended evening session of the House of Commons, pushed through a response to 'the petition of the officers and soldiers of the army', describing its promoters as 'enemies of the state and disturbers of the public peace'. Though there were Presbyterian supporters in the army, this was too much for the majority of Fairfax's men. Holles' Declaration of Dislike, as it became known, united many elements of the army who were offended by their honour being thus impugned and increasingly worried about their future. In May, agitation grew but was firmly resisted by Holles and his supporters in the Commons, who believed they had enough support in the London Trained Bands and the city of London itself to take on the New Model. If it would not back down, they would disband it.

Torn by loyalty to his men and a deep reverence for parliament, Fairfax's health buckled but by late May he recovered and chaired a council of war at Saffron Walden, at which it was decided to hold a general rendezvous of the army near Newmarket on 4 and 5 June. But before that could happen, intelligence was received that parliament intended to move the king from Holdenby closer to London and restore him under favourable terms that would disadvantage the army and might lead to renewed hostilities. Agitation was growing among the junior officers and rank and file, heading in directions that the generals would find increasingly uncomfortable. Suddenly, securing the king became a priority. It fell to an obscure junior officer, Cornet Joyce, of Fairfax's own Lifeguards to ensure that this requirement was swiftly met.

George Joyce was twenty-nine years old and had links to the agitators in the army. Very little is known of his background or even his place of birth but by 1644 he was in Cromwell's horse regiment and in 1647 he was serving Fairfax. The sequence of events which led him to Holdenby is unclear, as is the role of Cromwell in what transpired, even though Joyce was later to claim that he had Cromwell's authority for the actions he took. What happened to the king was only an indirect consequence of quite different concerns. The army agitators were increasingly well organized into committees and one of these appears to have been alarmed that, in those acrimonious and uncertain times, the army artillery train in Oxford might fall into parliamentary hands. Joyce, with a force of about five hundred men, was despatched to secure it. He was in the process of successfully concluding his mission when he received intelligence from an unknown source in London that parliament was about to order the king's removal from Holdenby. Seized with the fear that the army was on the verge of being shut out of a peace deal between the king and its opponents in Westminster, Joyce immediately set off for London, to discuss with Cromwell what should be done. The decision reached was to prevent the king's removal and Joyce sent word to his troops to join him at Holdenby. He got there before them on the afternoon of

2 June, to find the king away at Althorp playing bowls, though Charles returned when told of the cornet's arrival. Joyce's men arrived around midnight in good order and were well received by the king's guards, who fraternized happily with their fellow soldiers, regardless of any religious differences. The next morning, Joyce secured the house. There matters might have rested but circumstances forced George Joyce to take a course that neither he nor Cromwell had foreseen. For in the night the commander of one of the regiments guarding the king, Colonel Graves, who was a supporter of Denzil Holles, had slipped out of Holdenby and was believed to be riding to London to get help. Faced with the possibility of an armed confrontation, Joyce needed to act. It would not be prudent to stay and now he had control of the king, he was resolved to keep it. Probably neither he nor Cromwell had intended to abduct Charles I. With hindsight, it is easy to say that they might have thought through the implications of their actions and seen this as a possible outcome. The army was struggling to remain true to its own conception of the causes for which the Civil War had been fought and did not need further complications. Cromwell claimed passionately afterwards that it was never his intention that the army should assume custody of the king. Yet that is indeed what happened.

Joyce consulted with his men before taking such a momentous step. And they were unanimously of the opinion that the king must be moved. It then became necessary for the cornet to apprise Charles of this necessity. He only gained access to the royal person with some difficulty, having been magnificently patronized by the parliamentary commissioners and the king's servants, who did not consider such a lowly officer an appropriate person to enter his majesty's bedchamber. The news that he must leave early the next morning was not, at first, well received by the king. He had been comfortable at Holdenby and feared for his personal safety. Joyce was polite and reassuring. He assured Charles that no harm would come to him, that he would be treated with respect by the army, not forced to do anything against his conscience, and that he could keep his servants. Thus mollified, the monarch slept.

He still had his doubts, however, as preparations for his departure were made at 6 a.m. on 4 June. Who, he wondered, had given Joyce his orders? Where was his commission? Joyce told him: 'Here is my commission.' Charles was puzzled. 'Where?' he asked, seeing no document. To which George Joyce, pointing to the soldiers, famously replied: 'Behind me.' Charles smiled, appreciating the honesty. 'It is as fair a commission and as well written as I have seen a commission written in my life: a company of handsome proper gentleman as I have seen a great while.'[3] But what, he asked, if he refused to go with them? Would they force him? Joyce, who must, by now, have been getting anxious, replied that they humbly entreated the king to accompany them. Naturally, Charles wanted to know where he was going. The actual destination does not seem to have been given much thought: Joyce suggested Oxford or Cambridge but Charles had spent long enough in the former and Newmarket appealed to him more than the latter because its air agreed with him. Perhaps he thought that it was still full of royalist sympathizers. In fact, it would very shortly be full of disgruntled soldiers, headed by their beloved general Fairfax, who was initially so appalled by the manner in which the king had passed into the army's hands that he threatened to court-martial George Joyce.

Joyce's seizure of the king sent shock waves through the English Presbyterians and their Scottish allies. Overnight, they were put on the back foot. One of their first moves in response was to send a mission to France to try to persuade Henrietta Maria to send Prince Charles to Scotland, where he could lead an invasion into England. But many months were to pass before the Prince of Wales left his mother and then it would not be to command a Scottish army but an English fleet. His father, meanwhile, was surprisingly sanguine. The bitter dispute between parliament and the army merely confirmed Charles I's view that the divisions among his enemies would undo them. Being the army's prisoner was no worse than confinement by Presbyterians; indeed, it might even offer better long-term prospects. He was treated very civilly and by 25 June, when he was residing at Hatfield House, home of the earl of Salisbury, his chaplains were restored to him and he was permitted to use the Anglican prayer book. His spirits rose even more when, in mid-July, he was reunited with James, Elizabeth and Henry, the three of his children who remained in England.

*

THEY HAD BEEN staying at Hampton Court with the earl of Northumberland when their father was taken to Newmarket. Immediately, parliament ordered their return to St James's, fearful that they, too, would fall into the hands of the army. Northumberland protested that the palace was not prepared to receive them but accepted that the order must be obeyed without delay. The king hoped to see his children when he was brought to Windsor, having previously petitioned parliament that they might be allowed to join him there at the end of June, but when he arrived at the castle he found that his request had been denied. Desperately disappointed, he returned to his latest temporary residence, the manor house in Caversham, Berkshire, formerly owned by the royalist earl of Craven. There he enlisted Fairfax's help, and on 4 July he was able to write with some assurance to his second son: 'James, I am in hope that you may be permitted, with your brother and sister, to come to some place betwixt this and London, where I might see you.' He suggested that his son ask parliament for leave to make a journey for a couple of nights' stay but was aware that this could prove problematic:

> But rather than not see you I will be content that you come to some convenient place to dine, and go back again at night. And foreseeing the fear of your being brought within the power of the Army as I am may be objected, to hinder this my desire, I have full assurance from Sir Thomas Fairfax and

the chief officers that there will be no interruption or impediment made by them for your return now and when you
please. So God bless you. Your loving father, Charles R.

He added a postscript: 'Send me word as soon as you can of
the time and place where I shall have the contentment of seeing
you, your brother and sister.'[4]

His confidence in Fairfax was rewarded. The general wrote to
the earl of Manchester, speaker of the House of Lords:

My Lord, I was sent unto by the King on Friday last, to
desire the parliament to give way to him to see his children,
and that they might for that purpose be sent to him. If I may
be so bold to offer my opinion, I think the allowance of such
a thing may be without the least prejudice to the kingdom,
and yet gain more upon His Majesty than denying it. And
if it be the prayer of every good man, that his heart may
be gained, the performance of such civilities to him is very
suitable to those desires and will hear well with all men,
who (if they can imagine it to be their own case) cannot but
be sorry if His Majesty's natural affections to his children in
so small a thing should not be complied with. And if any
question should be concerning the assurance of their return,
I shall engage for their return within what time the parliament shall limit.

This appeal to common humanity could not, however, be
entirely divorced from the power struggle in which the fate of the
entire royal family, and not just the king, was entwined. Fairfax
went on to deny vehemently that he and the officers of the army
were engaged 'upon some underhand contract or bargain with the
King' which, he said, slandered their integrities and was intended
to lead to a 'misunderstanding betwixt the Parliament and their
Army'. After several paragraphs of closely argued justification of
the army and its position, he returned to the treatment of the royal
family itself:

In general, we humbly conceive that to avoid all harshness and afford all kind usage to His Majesty's person, a thing consistent with the peace and safety of the kingdom, is the most Christian, honourable and prudent way ... we think that tender, equitable and moderate dealing, both towards His Majesty, his royal family and his late party (so far as may stand with safety to the kingdom and security to our common rights and liberties) is the most hopeful course to take away the seeds of war, or future feuds amongst us for posterity, and to procure a lasting peace and agreement in this now distracted nation.[5]

The letter was an eloquent mix of common sense and justification of the army's position. Allied with a request from the duke of York that he and his siblings might see their father, it produced the desired effect for the royal family, though the Commons only agreed reluctantly to the request. Sadly Fairfax's wider arguments, pleading for unity in dealing with the problems of the kingdom, were not to be realized. For the present, the king was relieved and delighted that he would, at last, see his younger children again.

The children left St James's Palace early in the morning of 16 July in an atmosphere of high excitement. Their party of three coaches was attended by a guard of city militia, ostensibly for their protection, though the reception as they travelled west into Berkshire was one of general acclamation. The royal children were rarely seen in public and sympathy for them was widespread. As the coach carrying Elizabeth, her two brothers and the earl of Northumberland passed through the small towns and villages of the area there were cries of greeting from the crowds lining the flower-strewn streets. But anticipation had got the better of them and they found when they arrived at the Greyhound Inn at Maidenhead, the appointed meeting place, that they were there an hour too early. Since etiquette would have dictated that the king should not arrive first it was a reasonable delay.

The reunion was a touching one. So much had changed in the

years since Charles I had last seen Elizabeth and Henry that the
king was deeply moved. He found his daughter a serious, pale girl
on the cusp of womanhood, not beautiful but certainly gracious,
with the dignity of bearing that accompanied one raised as a
princess, even in the midst of civil war. Northumberland knew his
obligations to the royal children and, whatever his personal
politics, he had made every effort to ensure that they were treated
as befitted their station in life. In Elizabeth's face the king saw
both the marks of her keen intelligence and the strain of the ill
health that had dogged her from her earliest childhood. James had
grown over the period since his father abandoned him at Oxford
but though he was now a handsome and healthy lad of fourteen
he still clung to his father's side, perhaps wondering how long they
would be together this time. But to the little duke of Gloucester,
Prince Henry, known in the family as Harry, this slightly unkempt
and sad-faced man to whom everyone bent the knee was a complete stranger. 'Do you know me, child?' asked Charles I, to which
Harry, with perhaps more honesty than tact answered, quite
simply, 'No.' The king is said to have replied: 'I am your father,
child; and it is not one of the least of my misfortunes that I have
brought you and your brothers and sisters into the world to share
my miseries.' This sober reflection caused James and Elizabeth to
cry and Charles realized the need for raising their mood. Tradition
has it that he took Henry on his knee. There may be an element
of Victorian whimsy in this account but though Charles never
forgot his regality there can be no doubting his affection for his
family or his pleasure in being with them again.

As the morning progressed, two gentlemen unknown to the
children entered the room in the Greyhound Inn which had been
set aside for the royal family. One was Sir Thomas Fairfax, who
was amused and touched by being singled out by Princess Elizabeth for gratitude, 'for the high happiness she now enjoyed in the
sight of her dear father, which she knew was obtained only by his
industry and management'. She went on to say that she would
always be grateful to him and, that if it were ever in her power (a

sweet but forlorn hope), that she would happily requite the favour. Charmed by her manner, Fairfax asked permission to kiss her hand.[6] She had been a pawn in a complex struggle for the last five years and the manners of this man of high integrity, torn between loyalty to the soldiers he led and obedience to a monarch who still commanded his personal respect, left a profound impression on her.

Similarly impressed by this scene of gentle happiness was another family man. He had lost a son in the Civil War and knew the pain and uncertainty of partings that could be prolonged by fighting and rendered permanent by death. The scene he observed so affected him that he told Sir John Berkeley, with tears in his eyes, that he had witnessed 'the tenderest sight that ever his eyes beheld'. So moved was Oliver Cromwell by the reunion of Charles and his children that his opinion of the king was highly favourable. He called Charles 'the uprightest and most conscientious man of his three kingdoms', saying 'the Independents were under infinite obligations to him for having rejected the Scots' propositions at Newcastle, which his Majesty's interest seemed to invite him to' and he 'concluded . . . by wishing that God would be pleased to look upon him according to the sincerity of his heart towards his Majesty.'[7]

The children were allowed to spend a couple of days with their father at Caversham Manor before being taken back to London. It was a tearful parting but there was optimism that they would soon be in one another's company again. Fairfax, Cromwell and Northumberland all knew that the dispute between the army and the Presbyterians in parliament must soon reach tipping point, with agitation growing in the ranks as the so-called Leveller movement gained publicity and confidence. Tensions in London were running high and the outcome there looked uncertain unless the army moved to contain the situation. Charles I was well aware of these currents which washed around the personal pleasures of his improved family situation. On the very day that he was reunited with Elizabeth, James and Henry, a general council of the army convened at Reading. Its ostensible purpose was to decide whether the army should move immediately against its opponents in parliament and the city but it had a deeper underlying purpose, one that had involved collaboration between leaders of the army and sympathetic members of both Houses of Parliament. Anxious to avoid further war and to close up the dangerous divisions which were appearing in society, the time was believed to be ripe for offering a peace settlement to the king on realistic terms which he could accept comfortably. It was Charles's tragedy, and indeed that of the three kingdoms as a whole, that his corrosive belief that he could always do better by prevaricating and sowing dissension outweighed his ability to compromise. All the time that he was seeing his children at frequent intervals throughout this turbulent summer of 1647, while he rejoiced in their company and their evident happiness in being with him again, he was refusing to engage with the best prospect for peace and protection of his monarchy that he was ever given.

It was an offer that originated not with the dry Presbyterianism of the Scots or the furious Denzil Holles but the more open approach of the army's leaders – Cromwell, his son-in-law, Henry Ireton, and parliamentary grandees like Northumberland and Wharton, who had long looked for a constitutional settlement with the king and hoped, at last, that he would see sense. The king's inability to respond would lead, ultimately, to desperation and to a further parting from the children with whom he had passed a sometimes idyllic interlude in the great houses of Syon and Hampton Court, on the banks of the Thames. In late July the terms of a settlement were drafted under the somewhat prosaic title of The Heads of the Proposals. Essentially, they suggested a period of transition into a more limited monarchy, allowing the king to retain control of the armed forces and appointment of his own advisers for longer than had been proposed in previous discussions, as well as permitting the survival of episcopacy, albeit with restricted powers, and the continued use of the prayer book. The document also called for biennial parliaments (something which might give modern British politicians food for thought) and allowed for the right of religious assembly outside the national Church, an important step towards the extension of religious toleration. The Heads were convincingly argued, clearly presented and combined a workable approach with a reasonable degree of compromise and even generosity towards royalist opponents. Charles I was presented with what many of those who had opposed him believed to be a just and workable solution which would ensure the 'rights and liberties of the kingdom and the settling [of] a just and lasting peace'.[8]

Yet Charles never took The Heads of the Proposals seriously. His refusal to do so is partly explained by the nature of the man and his own, unshakeable interpretation of the duties and responsibilities of kingship, but also reflects the ferment of the times. The king knew very well that there was bitter hostility between the Presbyterians in parliament and the army and that there was a possibility of counter-revolution in London. Though advised by Sir John Berkeley to accept the army's terms, others urged him to prevaricate. This bad counsel chimed with the king's own inclinations. He still believed that he could obtain better terms or even that he might not have to compromise at all. His supporters in Scotland were proffering blandishments that they would fight for the Crown again and from Ireland came hopes that forces loyal to him on the island, where there was resentment of parliament's unsubtle approach, might regroup around Ormonde. Charles never lost sight of the fact that he was a ruler of three kingdoms and he clung still to the belief that this was the key to eventual victory over his enemies in England. When Ireton and other leading army officers came to see him to discuss The Heads of the Proposals they found, despite agreeing to further concessions during the course of intense discussions lasting several hours, that he was unwilling to commit. 'You cannot be without me,' he told them. 'You will fall to ruin if I do not sustain you.'[9] But this was a gross overstatement of his position. Ireton and Cromwell were frustrated and disappointed by the king's attitude but he did not make any genuine moves to change his approach even after the defiance of the London mob fizzled out and the army occupied the capital on 3 August.

During the autumn Charles's belief that the army would not be the means of restoring him to his throne on acceptable terms was hardened by the information he received on further splits between its leading officers and the more junior soldiers. Though the content of the Putney Debates, which took place in late October and November, was not known to him in detail, he was aware from royalists in the Tower, imprisoned with the Leveller agitator John Lilburne, that opinion in the rank and file of the army was hardening against him and that some were referring to him in biblical terms as 'a man of blood'. The fear of assassination returned. It was certainly a factor, though not necessarily the major one, in the conviction gaining on the king daily, even as Cromwell listened with extreme discomfiture to the revolutionary ideas being aired in Putney Church, that he must attempt a further escape from confinement.

There are questions that have never been entirely answered surrounding Charles I's escape from Hampton Court on the night of 11 November 1647 but one thing is certain: it was not a spur-of-the-moment decision. Elizabeth and her brothers had been staying with him, in this great palace which must have brought back memories of the happiness of her early childhood, until just a few days before he fled. The king was carefully, if respectfully, guarded but Elizabeth complained to her father that the sound of the soldiers walking up and down in the long gallery, just outside her bedchamber, disturbed her sleep. Concerned for her delicate health, Charles summoned Colonel Whalley, the officer in charge of the guards at Hampton Court, and asked that the men on duty be quieter. Whalley assured the king that he would give orders for the guards to exercise restraint but the matter did not rest there, since Elizabeth reported that she could still hear the soldiers' footfall. In a second interview, Whalley expressed frustration but he was willing to order that the men be removed to a greater distance 'provided his majesty would be graciously pleased to renew his engagement not to attempt to escape'. The king bridled at the inference that he might use Elizabeth's sleeping difficulties to his own advantage, saying: 'You had my engagement. I will not renew it. Keep your guards.'[10] But whether it had occurred to him, even subconsciously, that a reduction of the guard near his own chamber, which also opened off the long gallery, would help the plans that he was forming we shall never know. The royal children returned to St James's and their official guardian, Northumberland, within a few days of this exchange. The duke of York never saw his father again.

The night of 11 November was wet and windy. The king retired early, as was his custom on a Thursday, to write letters to Henrietta Maria and to Princess Mary in Holland. Just the previous day, parliament had agreed a new set of peace proposals to be put before him, but he did not wait to peruse them. The Scottish commissioners who had seen him earlier that week were already aware of his intention to escape. He talked first of all about going north to Berwick but this may have been mentioned simply because he felt it was a destination that would appeal to his visitors. In fact, when he slipped out of an unguarded rear entrance from his rooms that led to the gardens and a boat waiting to take him across the river, he seems to have had no clear idea of where he was heading. The gentlemen who were waiting for him on the opposite bank of the Thames gave him conflicting advice as the party rode hell for leather to the west of London and into Hampshire. Sir John Berkeley favoured taking a boat to France, though Charles's initial inclination seems to have been to make for Jersey. Jack Ashburnham, who had been involved in the disastrous escape to the Scots eighteen months earlier, pondered the possibility of riding into London to appeal directly to its inhabitants, a gesture as dramatic as it was impractical. His other suggestion, made while Charles rested at Titchfield House, the home of the earl of Southampton, was to make for the Isle of Wight, where the newly appointed governor, Colonel Robert

Hammond, was believed to have royalist sympathies. It proved to be a fatal error of judgement.

Hammond, like many others in the Civil War, came from a family of conflicted loyalties. He had served the earl of Essex with distinction but was not himself a Presbyterian. One of his uncles was a lieutenant-general of artillery in the New Model Army; another was a chaplain to the king. It was through this prominent Anglican that the younger Hammond had been introduced to Charles I. Yet though he was impressed by Charles personally, Hammond was no royalist. His wife was a daughter of John Hampden, cousin to Oliver Cromwell, and a staunch parliamentarian who had died early in the Civil War. The young colonel was committed to the army's resistance to parliament but became troubled by the radicalization of the rank and file. Aware of Hammond's discomfiture, Cromwell suggested to Fairfax that an appointment as governor of the Isle of Wight would be an appropriate solution. He had only been in the post a couple of months when Jack Ashburnham unexpectedly arrived on the island to inform him that the king was at Titchfield.

The news was a thunderbolt to Hammond. Greatly perturbed, he exclaimed: 'You have undone me by bringing the king into the island.' How could he square the obligation of protecting the king on the one hand with the duty he had to the army and parliament? Though Charles was still on the mainland both king and colonel realized that there was no comfortable way out of this dilemma. Writing many years later, Clarendon claimed that the monarch was equally appalled by Ashburnham's initiative in revealing his presence and that his response echoed Hammond's: 'Oh, Jack, thou hast undone me.'[11] But the die was cast and Charles spent the next thirteen months in a new captivity, in the draughty and far from luxurious Carisbrooke Castle, as the consequences of his escape from Hampton Court were played out across his kingdoms and in the wider European sphere. On 26 December he pinned his hopes on a new, secret agreement with the Scots, known as the Engagement. They would invade England to restore him, though he gave little enough away to them in return. As royalist sentiment fed rising discontent in England, the threat of renewed civil war loomed in the spring of 1648. It would have profound implications for the children of Charles I.

*

THE ENGAGEMENT had been signed under the noses of parliamentary commissioners who were trying to agree their own deal with the king over Christmas 1647. This approach he rejected on 28 December, much to the chagrin of the House of Commons. Feeling against him rose and, for the first time, was couched in disrespectful language. Clarendon wrote that 'Every man's mouth was opened against him with the utmost sauciness and licence.' Cromwell was not the only person whose views, so positive back in the summer, underwent a sea change. A few days into the New Year of 1648, the Commons agreed that no further approaches should be made to the king and this vote became official parliamentary policy, as the Vote of No Addresses, on 11 February. Consideration was now being given to forcing the king to abdicate, though not, it should be made clear, to the abolition of monarchy. Two of the king's sons remained in England and while it might be deemed necessary to depose Charles I and disinherit his eldest son, an exile in France, the fourteen-year-old duke of York was seriously proposed as a replacement. During his minority, a limited monarchy would be developed and the young king educated in his new role. James, however, had other ideas.

Though we cannot be certain, he had probably known of his father's plans to escape from Hampton Court. The news of Charles I's flight, when it came, is unlikely to have been a surprise to James, and perhaps not to Elizabeth either. Both had been in secret correspondence with their father and passed a good deal of time in his company. In the first months of 1648, as Charles tried unsuccessfully to get away from the Isle of Wight, leading to the conditions of his stay there becoming a harsher captivity than he had thus far experienced, James also attempted to flee from

Northumberland's custody, as he had been urged by his father. For the earl of Northumberland, increasingly troubled by the responsibility of being governor to James, Elizabeth and Henry and personally disillusioned by divisions among the king's opponents, James was something of a nightmare charge. He was arrogant, hot-tempered and unreliable, even threatening, on one occasion, to fire an arrow from a longbow at a servant who had reprimanded him for an outburst when he learned of Charles I's imprisonment on the Isle of Wight. After he was discovered to be in secret correspondence with the king, James was threatened with a spell in the Tower of London, a prospect which seems to have unnerved him into giving his word of honour that he would not try to get away again. It was an undertaking that he did not keep.

On the chilly spring evening of 20 April, James finally fled the custody of the earl of Northumberland. It was a carefully organized and executed escape, one that had been played out under the eyes of his governor who, though not exactly colluding in what was going on, seems to have deliberately overlooked its implications. He had already told parliament that he could not guarantee the safety of the royal children. The plot involved Princess Elizabeth, who was certainly aware of her brother's intentions, little Prince Harry, who was not, and a pair of lovers who represented both the romance and tawdriness of the royalist cause. For James's liberator, Colonel Joseph Bampfield, was an unprincipled rogue, who became, like others in those turbulent times, a double agent, and his mistress, Anne Murray (later Lady Halkett), a remarkable and highly articulate woman.[12] Anne recorded her dramatic life in an entertaining and revealing autobiography. Together, they engineered the flight of the second in line to the throne.

In her memoirs, Anne Murray states that the king's desire that Bampfield should actively organize his son's escape was communicated to the duke of York by 'a gentleman attending His Highness, who was full of honour and fidelity, by his means he had private access to the duke, to whom he presented the king's letter and order to His Highness for consenting to act what CB [Colonel Bampfield] should contrive for his escape.'[13] Charles I knew and trusted the colonel, who, by his own admission, had been in regular communication with the king since he arrived on the Isle of Wight. 'I had,' Bampfield later wrote, 'found out means of correspondence with him and of giving his majesty constant advertisements of all occurrences which concerned him.'[14] Confident in the colonel's reliability, Charles authorized him to find a means of getting the duke of York away from England: 'I am advertised,' he wrote in January 1648, 'that it has been deliberated by some of the army to possess themselves of the duke of York. Consider if you cannot find ways to convey him out of England.' At the end of the following month, he reiterated this command, saying: 'I approve what you have already done and what you propose for the saving of the duke of York . . . bring him, if possible, to his mother or sister.'[15]

The involvement of someone who had the king's confidence was sufficient recommendation to a suggestible boy, thoroughly indignant at his father's treatment and eager to do anything he could to help the royalist cause. James was very like his parents in refusing to recognize any differences of degree among their opponents. Those who were not unequivocally for them were simply against them. And Bampfield, who was evidently highly plausible, was able to overcome the boy's initial scruples about breaking his word. He assured James that, as a minor, he could not be held to such oaths. His conscience assuaged, the young duke went along with Bampfield's plans wholeheartedly but with commendable caution. They were not to be put into action with any precipitation, but carefully rehearsed for some weeks in advance.

Each evening, for the space of an hour or more, the royal children played hide and seek in the house and grounds of St James's Palace, after the earl of Northumberland had paid them his regular visit. James might have been thought rather old for such pursuits but they could easily be explained by the participation of his brother, who clearly enjoyed the game, and of

Northumberland's own children. Elizabeth, however, knew that the intention was not an innocent one. Often James would secrete himself in such difficult hiding places that it took at least half an hour to find him and sometimes he could not be found at all and came out triumphantly, of his own accord. On the evening of 20–21 April, the game began as usual, after James had spent some time talking to his sister, in the company of her servants. It was important for everything to appear as normal and Elizabeth, who well knew that her brother planned a permanent disappearance that night, seems to have kept her nerve with remarkable aplomb. The endurance of her situation and a gentle nature had earned her the nickname 'Temperance' but she was a girl of steel on this occasion, fighting conflicting emotions. She had greatly enjoyed her elder brother's company during the two years they had spent together after the fall of Oxford and, for this reason alone, she was sorry to see him go. But she was a Stuart princess and she perfectly understood that his escape was vital to her father's cause. It would have crossed her mind, as they chatted, that she might never see him again, yet despite her delicate health, and the uncertainties surrounding the king's future, she was full of hope that the parting would be temporary.

When James bade his sister goodnight, he went back to his room, locking in her little dog, who followed him everywhere. Then he started off down the back stairs, only to return in a hurry to his room and pretend to read, when he caught his foot noisily on the descent. Once he was convinced that his clumsiness had failed to attract attention, he crept down again and went out via the inner garden of St James's Palace into St James's Park itself, triple locking all the doors behind him. He had obtained a key from the gardener, claiming that his own was not working. Bampfield was waiting for James at the garden gate with a cloak and periwig, designed to make him appear like any young nobleman, swiftly whisking him away by coach and then along the river by boat to a safe house near London Bridge, where Anne Murray was ready with the prince's disguise.

The idea was for James to be dressed in women's clothes (in contrast to his little sister Henrietta, who had fled the country in boy's apparel) but Anne had not found procuring something suitable an entirely straightforward task. The tailor to whom she presented the order for a mohair outfit, enough to make a petticoat and waistcoat for a young gentlewoman, was amazed by the measurements he was given: 'He considered it a long time and said he had made many such gowns and suits, but he had never made any to such a person in his life. I thought he was in the right; but his meaning was, he had never seen any woman of so low a stature have so big a waist. However, he made it as exactly fit as if he had taken the measure himself. It was a mixed mohair of a light hair colour and black, and the under petticoat was scarlet.' The measurements of this curious garment suggest that James was not so tall as his elder brother but he was certainly eager to try it on, calling, 'Quickly, quickly, dress me.' Anne Murray, who was greatly relieved by his arrival just as she was starting to think he must have been apprehended, reported that 'He looked very pretty in it.' A barge took the duke of York down-river. It was a slow and difficult journey against the wind and James grew anxious. He was desperate not to return but, in an impulsive action that might be put down to an adolescent not being able to remember his part, but was typical of the injudicious man he became, he gave himself away. The garters on his stockings needed adjustment and his indecorous way of hitching up his hose attracted the attention of the bargemaster. It then became necessary for Bampfield to take this man into their confidence and to persuade him to dim the lights of the barge as it passed the blockhouse at Gravesend. This manoeuvre having been success-fully undertaken, James, duke of York, boarded a Dutch vessel and slipped out of the country. By the morning of 23 April 1648, he was at Flushing and spent the night at Middelburg.

When Princess Mary heard of her brother's arrival she was overjoyed. Tailors were ordered to provide new clothes for James, since he had left England with only Anne Murray's bizarre mohair outfit. From the town of Dort, James was transported in his brother-in-law's own yacht to Hounslerdyke, where William of Orange came to greet him in person. They had not seen each other since the summer of 1641, when Charles I had sought to distract London from Strafford's trial by the marriage of his eldest daughter into the Dutch House of Orange. The little brother Mary remembered had changed into a good-looking young man and she was delighted to see him again. 'So great was Mary's impatience that she ran down to the street door of her palace [in The Hague] and regardless of the presence of bystanders, embraced her brother with passionate tenderness.'[16]

Some hours passed at St James's before there was certainty that James had, indeed, fled. The earl of Northumberland duly informed both Houses of Parliament and a watch was put, much too late, on all roads out of London and on the Cinque Ports. After an inquiry, the earl was cleared of any dereliction of duty and was asked to continue as governor to Henry and Elizabeth, a charge he accepted but with the proviso that he could not be held responsible for their security. The servants of the children were, once again, changed, and Elizabeth and Henry were sent to Syon House, where their education continued, a welcome distraction for Elizabeth from the loneliness brought about by James's absence. Meanwhile, as insurrection broke out in England and the threat of Scottish invasion became a reality during the summer of 1648, the princess's two elder brothers, both now safely out of their father's kingdom, prepared to help fight for his restoration during the confused period of the Second Civil War.

Part Four

'Clean Different Things'
1649–70

CHAPTER NINE

'That man of blood'

*'I had rather you should be Charles le bon, than le grand,
good rather than great.'*

Charles I to the Prince of Wales, January 1649

THE ENGLAND THAT Prince James left behind as his Dutch
vessel slipped out into the North Sea was a disturbed and dismal
country. The unseasonably cold spring turned into a miserably wet
summer with weather more reminiscent of February and sunshine
in short supply. Roads became quagmires and crops were drowned
in the mud, adding to the scarcity of food which a poor harvest
of 1647 had already worsened. It is hardly surprising that, in these
trying circumstances, unrest grew. Many citizens felt aggrieved by
a war that had seemed to be over two years ago but had solved
nothing. There was no structured peace and tensions between the
army and parliament remained, despite a reduction in the overall
number of soldiers. Taxes, particularly excise, were high and much
resented, as were the county committees who were required to
implement Westminster's decisions. Many people did not like the
religious settlement embodied in the Directory of Worship or
the suppression of the celebration of Christmas (something that is
often viewed as a Cromwellian invention but, in fact, was introduced by the Presbyterian majority in parliament) and there were
disturbances in several cities, including London and Canterbury.[1]

The theatres, closed by parliament before the Civil Wars even began, briefly reopened in the New Year only to be faced with a renewed ban and an order that playhouses be demolished. Actors who defied this ordinance were threatened with public flogging. Blasphemy became a capital offence, even before the Westminster Assembly's version of orthodox doctrine was actually published.

Nor was the situation much happier in Scotland. The Engagement split the nobility and the parliament and was denounced by the Kirk. Women in Edinburgh took to the streets declaiming that their husbands would not go to war on behalf of Charles Stuart while many royalists and the so-called 'reformadoes', cashiered officers from the royalist army, went north to Scotland to take up the king's cause. There was even hope of Irish involvement on the king's side.

When news of the duke of York's successful escape was brought to the exiles in Paris, spirits rose. Henrietta Maria's entourage there remained short of money and quarrelsome, its communications with Charles I more difficult since he was incarcerated on the Isle of Wight, but the Scottish situation and James's freedom gave grounds for hope. The French court itself began 1648 with a sigh of relief. Towards the end of the previous year Louis XIV, then aged nine, had contracted smallpox, to the consternation of his mother and his officials. While his younger brother, Philippe, was sent out of Paris for his own safety, Louis, who was a robust child, survived both the disease and the attentions of the medical staff, who bled him and used all sorts of bizarre herbal remedies to get the high fever to break. Anne of Austria seldom left his bedside during the two weeks he was most seriously ill and Mazarin visited daily. As the child improved, he received from the cardinal the gift of an English horse. Louis insisted on seeing the animal as soon as he heard about it, and the horse was actually led upstairs into his bedroom. By 12 January 1648, the young king of France was well enough to attend a service of thanksgiving for his recovery in Notre Dame. The *Gazette de France*, the official news-sheet of the government, echoed the sentiments of the country as a whole

when it wrote: 'Thus we see how well God loves France, content-
ing Himself, as He does, with merely showing her the rods of
punishment with which He beats others.'[2] This could have been an
oblique reference to the untimely death of the heir to the Spanish
throne, a hint of smugness as war between the two countries
dragged on, but it could equally have applied to the disasters that
had befallen the Stuarts across the Channel. Both Anne of Austria
and Henrietta Maria had cause for hope in the spring of 1648 and
both were to be confounded. The last act of the Civil War was not
yet played out in England and a long period of unrest and rebellion
was about to convulse France.

*

As MOMENTUM appeared once again to be swinging back to
Charles I, the king himself was little more than a spectator. The
Engagement had revived his cause, but his own liberty, in contrast
to that of his second son, was more distant than ever. The Isle of
Wight was a tiny domain and Charles was eager to get away from
it. He could not suborn Hammond, but he could and did find
others in Carisbrooke and outside it who were willing to help him.
On the mainland, Ashburnham based himself at Netley House
in Hampshire, which belonged to the Prince of Wales's former
governor, the marquess of Hertford, and continued to work on
schemes for escape. The assistant laundress at Carisbrooke, Mary,
was used for a while as a courier for letters hidden under the
edge of the carpet in the king's rooms but was soon found out
and dismissed. Charles also received visits from the royalist spy and
smuggler Jane Whorwood, the resourceful, red-headed, pock-
marked sister-in-law of the earl of Lanark, who may have briefly
been the king's mistress in the summer of 1648. The precise
nature of their relationship remains open to interpretation because
of the enciphered correspondence that survives. On the face of it,
Charles I is not at all the sort of man one would think of as an
adulterer but his letters to Jane, which refer to smothering her
with kisses and embraces, coupled with the fact that she certainly

seems to have passed two evenings alone in his company, suggest otherwise. He and Henrietta Maria had been apart since 1644 and the king evidently missed female companionship as well, perhaps, as the physical side of his marriage.

Charles tried to get away several times but Hammond was well aware of his intentions. There was an element of farce in the desperation of the king to escape. His first attempt, in March 1648, was foiled because he got stuck in the window from which he was supposed to lower himself. Yet during the spring and summer of 1648, as insurrections broke out in several parts of England, the Scots invaded and the parliamentary fleet mutinied, Charles and his family had reason to believe that his captivity might soon be over.

It was in the west of Wales that discontent first turned to outright insurgency. This part of the principality had a long history, over many centuries, of opposing central authority. Henry Tudor landed here in 1485 to launch his campaign against Richard III so it was perhaps fitting that Pembroke Castle, where the first Tudor monarch was born, should have become the focus of an uprising, led by dissident soldiers, in support of the king and 'the privileges of parliament, the laws of the land and liberties of the people'. The task of subduing the uprising by force fell to Cromwell but not before he had joined a three-day prayer meeting at Windsor at which the leaders of the army wrestled with the notion that God had withdrawn His favour from them because they had sought peace with the king. Such soul-searching provokes incredulity and charges of hypocrisy from our secular age but this is to misunderstand the seventeenth-century mind. For these godly men the withdrawal of divine approval was the most serious check to their consciences that they could imagine and they would not make decisions that involved further bloodshed without a period of sober reflection and prayer. The news that a much-liked officer, Fairfax's adjutant-general, Christopher Fleming, had been killed in Wales, concentrated their minds. They determined that 'if ever the Lord brought us back again in peace, to call Charles Stuart, that man of blood, to an account for the blood he had shed, and mischief he had done to his utmost, against the Lord's cause and people in these poor nations.'[3] It was not the first time that this biblical imagery had been used to describe the king (it had first surfaced in the Putney Debates six months earlier) but the renewed outbreak of fighting in his exhausted kingdoms was now laid squarely on the shoulders of a king who had consistently failed to agree terms. It is highly unlikely, however, that any of the officers present was envisaging a trial that would lead to the king's death. They lived in an uncertain present, aware of what was unfolding around them but without the benefit of hindsight that still colours much of the general perception of historical events. And, despite their concern for the unnecessary shedding of blood, they were not, as time would show, of one mind, faced as they were by the twin challenges of popular unrest and resurgent Leveller activity in the army.

The unrest that disgruntled soldiers had unleashed in South Wales was infectious. The south-east of England also rose in revolt in the spring of 1648. In mid-May a petition from Surrey, calling for a treaty with the king and the disbandment of the army, was presented by 3,000 armed men at Westminster, whose violent fury was only contained by two regiments guarding parliament. A series of uprisings in Kentish towns followed but petered out when Fairfax himself went into the county. Far more serious was the mutiny of the parliamentary fleet in the Downs, the anchorage area for shipping off the east Kent coast between Dover and the Thames estuary, where most of the warships declared for the king. This unexpected turn of fortune, triggered by the appointment of the radical Thomas Rainsborough as vice-admiral, suddenly thrust the queen and the Prince of Wales back into the limelight.[4] Since the king was not in a position to appoint an overall commander who could unite the various groups now growing in size and zeal in support of royalism, it fell to Henrietta Maria and her son at the Louvre in Paris to take the lead. The earl of Holland, a man who had already changed sides twice during the Civil War, was not the most intelligent of choices to command the king's forces in England but as disaffection at county level spread in June to Essex, the West Country and also North Wales and parts of the West Midlands, Fairfax and Cromwell's men faced a series of revolts that threatened to spread their forces uncomfortably thin. For the Prince of Wales and his younger brother, the opportunity to fight for their father after years of uncertainty had finally arrived.

Prince Charles set out from Paris on 25 June 1648, heading first for Calais and thence to the Dutch coast, to take command of the ships that had declared for his father. His aim was to use them as an invasion fleet, to back up the earl of Holland's county forces and the Scottish army of the duke of Hamilton, which was poised to cross into England. His cousin, Prince Rupert, and two long-standing royalist advisers, Culpeper and Hopton's accompanied him on his journey and others of his former council, including Hyde, were ordered to join him. Hyde had a miserable journey. The vessel in which he travelled was taken by Spanish frigates off the coast of Ostend, his jewels and money were plundered and it was some time before the Spanish authorities, who governed what is now Belgium, set him at liberty. Then adverse weather conditions delayed his arrival for more than a month. He was too worn by these adventures to conceal his dismay at the disagreements among Prince Charles's advisers.[5]

The prince himself was in good spirits, full of optimism after two years spent languishing on the sidelines of the French court, enduring his mother's marital schemes, the petty rivalries of those around her and Cardinal Mazarin's polite reluctance to offer any kind of assistance. He hoped that he could count on the support of his brother-in-law, head of the House of Orange as William II following the death of his father, Frederick Henry, at the end of 1647. Charles's sister was now the first lady of the Netherlands, much to the displeasure of her husband's mother, whose attitude towards Mary had hardened over the years. The young

William II, hostile to Spain and sympathetic to the Stuarts, promised Charles four warships but his ability to do much more was hampered by internal politics and the opposition of the States of Holland. The offer from William at least amounted to more than Charles had received from Mazarin, who had refused all financial help when the prince left France, despite Henrietta Maria's pleas. But the prince was considerably aggrieved, when he arrived in the Netherlands, to find the fleet 'in faction and disorder', a situation for which his ill-advised younger brother was, however unintentionally, responsible.

Mary was relieved, as well as pleased, by Charles's arrival at The Hague. She had been concerned about the influence of those around James, notably Bampfield, and was afraid that the duke of York was being encouraged down a dangerous road by the ambition of others. After a family reunion, James having been summoned back from Helvoetsluys for the occasion of a formal dinner, the two brothers set off for the coast. Charles was by now well aware of the situation in respect of the fleet and was keen to exert his authority. For, in truth, James had allowed himself to be led very unwisely. Egged on by Bampfield, who resented the arrival of Sir John Berkeley as James's governor, the boy accepted the role of admiral, to the grave misgivings of those, including his sister, who feared this was a means of Bampfield effectively taking control of the warships and their men. The colonel was a good talker. Clarendon described him as having 'a wonderful address to the disposing men to mutiny', aided by the absence of officers to contradict him. He persuaded them 'to declare for the Duke of York, without any respect to the King or Prince; and when his Highness should be on board, they should not meddle in the quarrel between the King and the Parliament, but entirely join with the Presbyterian party and the city of London.' Bampfield's aim was to get Berkeley dismissed from James's service, 'and then he believed he should be able to govern both his Highness and the fleet'.[6]

James liked the acclaim of the seamen and set about making

appointments. He was, by all accounts, ready to sail without his elder brother's knowledge or permission. Charles's arrival put a stop to this boyish enthusiasm and imposed discipline on what might otherwise have been a foolish and surely ill-fated expedition. He also made sure that Bampfield's influence on James was checked, sending his younger brother back to The Hague and into Mary's care. James was displeased but had to acquiesce. Charles, meanwhile, was joined by William Batten, a senior parliamentary naval commander who felt spurned by the preference shown for Rainsborough. It had taken some time for the realization that Batten was unreliable to dawn on his superiors and he was able to take one of parliament's newest warships with him across to the Netherlands. The Prince of Wales was already at sea when he learned of Batten's defection and ordered the renegade officer to join him, promptly appointing him rear admiral and knighting him. As Batten had been the commander who ordered his men to bombard Bridlington when Henrietta Maria landed there in 1643, Prince Charles's gesture to a man who had caused his mother and her dog to cower in a ditch while under heavy fire was certainly generous, if not misguided. Batten was damaged goods and the royalists with the Prince of Wales, including his cousin, Rupert, were suspicious of him. The new admiral soon lost the trust of the seamen and seemed notably reluctant to fight. He was replaced in October 1648 by Rupert but by that time the royalist revolt in England was well and truly over.

It was the misfortune of the Prince of Wales to get a taste of naval command (something that he relished) without ever being able to engage in serious combat or land in England. Like his father, he was basically an onlooker in the second Civil War. The revolts in Wales, in Kent and in Essex were put down without his setting foot on English soil but the Scots still hoped he might find a way to join them, sending the earl of Lauderdale with their response to the prince's request for help. The reaction of those close to Charles to this unkempt Scot, who lacked their fastidiousness in dress but was, for all his strange appearance, intelligent and able, reeked of English superiority but Charles, somewhat improbably, took to the earl. He agreed, with considerable reluctance, to the demands that Lauderdale carried with him and would have turned the fleet towards Berwick, but the seamen, unpaid, hungry and discontented, were having none of it. They wished to engage the fleet of the earl of Warwick, sent by parliament to challenge the mutinous royalist ships, but a fight at sea was avoided. The Prince of Wales captured several commercial vessels but found that this piracy was losing him the support of alarmed merchants in the city of London, some of whom might have royalist sympathies but who were much more concerned with the threat to their livelihoods. Charles was prevailed upon to return to his sister's court in the early autumn, his brief career as a privateer over. At some point during the summer or autumn of 1648 (the precise date is unclear) he indulged in a brief dalliance with a lady of easy virtue who called herself Mrs Barlow. History knows her as Lucy Walter and she would be the bane of Charles's life in the years to come.

By September, he knew that the Scots had suffered a severe defeat the previous month in the north of England, even if Lauderdale put a brazen face on the catastrophe, claiming it should not divert Charles's purpose of going as soon as possible to Scotland. The prince was not persuaded, and with good reason, for Scotland was, once again, in turmoil. Hamilton's army crossed the border on 8 July. At less than 10,000 men it was only a third of the force that had been authorized by the Scottish parliament and its soldiers were poorly trained and equipped. A divided command and atrocious weather added to the invaders' difficulties, while support from northern royalists failed to materialize and the conduct of the army soon shattered any hopes of further recruitment. Harried by the smaller but much more professional force of Major-General John Lambert, Hamilton was kept at bay in the north-west until Cromwell could come up from Wales. After a series of increasingly debilitating encounters around Preston in Lancashire the Scots made a last stand on 18 August and were conclusively defeated. Hamilton was captured a week later near Stafford, bringing an end to a desperate and doomed Scottish intervention on behalf of Charles I. But even as the west of Scotland broke out in open revolt on hearing of the Engagers' defeat, the English parliament greeted Cromwell's victory by repealing the Vote of No Addresses and opening negotiations with the king on the Isle of Wight for a new treaty. It seemed that, phoenix-like, royalism could still rise from the ashes.

*

THE ARMY REACTED with predictable alarm to the dogged determination of Presbyterians in parliament to reach some sort of accommodation with Charles I. The Levellers once again became more vocal and renewed their agitation for the removal of the king, freedom of religion, equality before the law and regular elections, this time annual. But nothing was said about extending the franchise and the House of Commons, mindful of likely reaction among the army rank and file, as well as more senior officers, sent a surprisingly low-key reply to the Leveller petition. There was probably an element of stalling in its response, since the fifteen commissioners sent by parliament to the Isle of Wight were divided amongst themselves.

Charles was not, at first, keen to negotiate. He could see little point. But he was also tired of being cooped up in Carisbrooke Castle and his carefully attuned ear soon picked up the whisper of underlying discord among the commissioners, who remained divided along Presbyterian and Independent lines. If he could be restored on terms that, from his perspective, safeguarded his royal dignity for a period of twenty years, then he was prepared to listen. Discussions were supposed to be concluded after forty days but dragged on as the king, sitting under his canopy of state in Newport Grammar School, prevaricated with his usual skill, attempting to balance the demands made on him with his conscience and beliefs. After 2 October, when the Commons rejected his counterproposals, he seems to have felt that it would be best to appear to give in on almost everything in order to maximize his chances of escape. On 9 October he opened his heart to his host, William Hopkins, the master of Newport Grammar School. It is one of the frankest letters he ever wrote and its meaning is crystal-clear:

> I pray you rightly to understand my condition, which, I confess, yesternight I did not fully enough explain, through want of time. It is this; notwithstanding my too great concessions already made, I know that, unless I shall make yet others which will directly make me no King, I shall be at best but a perpetual prisoner . . . to deal freely with you, the great concession I made this day – the Church, militia and Ireland – was made merely in order [aid] to my escape, of which if I had not hope, I would not have done; for then I could have returned to my strait prison without reluctancy; but now, I confess, it would break my heart, having done that which only an escape can justify. To be short, if I stay for a demonstration of their further wickedness, it will be too late to seek a remedy; for my only hope is that they now believe I dare deny them nothing, and so be less careful of their guards.[7]

Privately, his mood was increasingly desperate and he acknowledged his unhappiness in a touching letter to Elizabeth. 'I am loath to write to those I love when I am out of humour, as I have been these days by past,' he told her, 'lest my letters should trouble those I desire to please.'[8] So he continued to talk all through October, buoyed by the knowledge that the marquess of Ormonde, who had returned to Ireland at the end of September, seemed on the point of concluding an alliance with the Irish Confederacy following the defection of a prominent Irish supporter of parliament, Lord Inchiquin, to the royalist cause. On 28 October he confirmed the sentiments he had expressed to Hopkins in a letter to Ormonde: 'Do not startle at my great concessions concerning Ireland,' he wrote 'for . . . they will come to nothing.'[9] Neither did his continued hopes of escape. Late at night he confided his hopes to Hopkins on paper, fearful that if he could not get away soon, it would be too late. 'You cannot make ready too soon . . . Where shall I take boat?'[10] He worried about the tides and the wind and other impediments. Yet no further attempt to get away from the island was ever made. The unfortunate Hopkins bankrupted himself entertaining the king and his small band of followers but he was never able to arrange the escape that Charles I so craved.

As the talks dragged on at Newport, concern in the army grew. Fairfax, who had acted firmly in repressing the royalist uprisings of the spring and summer, was now confronting the implications of the bloodshed of those months. He would later seek to distance himself from the eventual complete breakdown of trust between parliament and the army but his own position seems to have been more complex. Ireton, Cromwell's son-in-law, was so troubled by the Newport Treaty discussions that he tendered his resignation. Fairfax refused it and Ireton set about, instead, the drafting of a document which would outline the army's concern and suggest a positive way forward. He may, already, have been contemplating the possibility of bringing Charles I to trial, but it was the continued dithering of parliament that forced his hand. The Remonstrance of the Army, delivered to parliament on 20 November 1648, did not mince words. It demanded 'exemplary justice . . . in capital punishment upon the principal author and some prime instruments of our late wars'. It should be noted, however, that the Remonstrance still did not propose the abolition of monarchy. In keeping with their past inability to judge the mood of the army, the members of the House of Commons decided to postpone consideration of this latest salvo for a full week while they dealt with the most recent responses from the king on the Isle of Wight.

The period from the beginning of December 1648 to the end of January 1649 has fascinated historians down through the centuries and continues to be the source of much debate. What has emerged much more clearly is the hesitancy of the king's opponents to take irrevocable steps and their concern to come to some accommodation with him that might save both his life and the

Stuart monarchy. The popular picture of remorseless Round-heads pursuing a defenceless king to martyrdom has long since been nuanced by scholars who have found not a studied design, the 'rare dissimulation' of which Clarendon was later to accuse Cromwell, but in John Adamson's words, a 'frightened junto' anxious about the implications of the situation in all three kingdoms, particularly fearful that Ireland might be the back door by which the king could ultimately triumph, weary of war and desperate to avoid further bloodshed.[11] The pressure of circumstances, deeply held religious beliefs and the knowledge that there was no precedent for the situation in which they found themselves rested heavily on men who interpreted what was going on around them as evidence of God's design. For no one was this dilemma more grave than Oliver Cromwell, the man who less than eighteen months previously had wept to see the king reunited with his children and who was not even in London when relations between the army and parliament reached their nadir. How much he knew in advance of what took place on 6 December, when soldiers commanded by Colonel Thomas Pride excluded members of parliament who had voted in favour of continuing discussions with the king, is, however, another matter.[12]

Ireton, the prime mover behind these developments, was in correspondence with Cromwell, who had spent the autumn in Scotland and then in the north of England, dealing with fading royalist opposition. Cromwell had opposed the prolonged discussions at Newport, 'this ruining hypocritical agreement' as he called it, and in a letter to Robert Hammond he made clearer the beliefs that had been gaining on him over the last year, perhaps since the king's escape from Hampton Court. He had told the Commons then that 'they should no longer expect safety and government from an obstinate man whose heart God had hardened'. Yet this did not mean that he was a convinced republican, merely that he was sensing that the removal of Charles I was the only road to peace. Indeed, he may well have considered the possibility of replacing Charles with one of his sons but, as the months went by, options in that respect narrowed, following the escape of the duke of York. But Prince Henry still remained in England, a child who had never known his father, well educated and probably amenable, given the right support, to becoming the head of a much more limited monarchy. A long minority in which he was well imbued with principles that sat comfortably with the views of the Independents had considerable appeal. This option would preserve the monarchy but remove the author of the nation's woes. It would be given serious consideration again during the frenetic weeks of December 1648.

The last chapter in the life of Charles I had begun a few days earlier. Colonel Isaac Ewer had replaced the increasingly unhappy and uncertain Robert Hammond as governor of the Isle of Wight. Some of those who knew Hammond best were concerned that he was wavering in his commitment to the army and that he might hand Charles over to parliament if so ordered. Cromwell wrote Hammond, his kinsman by marriage, a remarkable letter in late November, urging the younger man to hold firm to his principles, to seek God's guidance and not to expect 'good from this Man, against whom the Lord hath witnessed; and whom thou knowest'.[13] When Hammond received orders from the army to return the king to close confinement in Carisbrooke Castle, he refused to comply. He was ordered off the island and brought back to the council of officers at Windsor under arrest before the letter from Cromwell actually arrived. He was soon freed but his royal prisoner was not so fortunate.

Awoken by loud knocking in the dark before dawn on 1 December, the king was told that he must make ready to leave Hopkins' house in the little town of Yarmouth. He was irritated at having to rise so early and even more aggrieved to learn that he was being taken across the water to Hurst Castle, a fortress built by Henry VIII to defend the western approaches to Southampton. It occupied a spit of land sticking out into the Solent, surrounded by unhealthy marshland, and was ill equipped to receive a king. But he had no choice other than to acquiesce. All hope of escape was now gone. Lieutenant-Colonel Saunders, then in charge of Portsmouth, reported to Fairfax: 'Our God hath done our work for us, all things are quiet in the island, the king went without any opposition to Hurst Castle, and is there. Your work is now before you.'[14] That much Fairfax, a man with a deeply troubled heart, already knew.

*

CHARLES SPENT two weeks at Hurst Castle, taking chilly walks along the shingle beach while the council of officers considered its next move. Aware of the splits among his opponents, of the thundering denunciations of Presbyterian preachers, and optimistic that Ormonde in Ireland might yet offer him deliverance, the king could also look to Europe for assistance now the continent was at peace. The Treaty of Westphalia finally ended the ruinous European conflict of the Thirty Years' War in October 1648, potentially opening up the possibility of aid from his wife's nephew, Louis XIV, and his son-in-law, William II of Orange. The implications of rising opposition to government in France and the House of Orange in the Netherlands were not yet obvious. Despite the seeming impregnability of Hurst, the king was able to smuggle letters out to Ormonde and to the Prince of Wales. He remained in touch with events beyond the Tudor fortifications that confined him and while the army officers prayed and debated he tried to win popular support by publishing his Declaration Concerning the Treaty, which sought to put a positive spin on the discussions at Newport, emphasizing how close they had come to success and warning of the dangers to his person and the peace of the country from 'the illegal proceedings of them that presume from servants to become masters and labour to bring in democracy and abolish monarchy'. Given Charles's private abjuration of all the main points he had appeared to concede in Newport, there is something unpleasantly hypocritical about the king's posturing in the Declaration, even if it can be justified by opportunism and pragmatism. But Charles was aiming at an

audience that had already lost the main part of the battle, the
Presbyterians who had effectively been sidelined by Pride's Purge.
Power now lay with a coalition of army grandees, led by Fairfax
and Cromwell, and a group of independent peers that included
the present and former governors of Princess Elizabeth and Prince
Henry, Northumberland and Pembroke, as well as the earls of
Salisbury, Denbigh and Warwick. The earls of Nottingham and
Kent also had good relations with the army grandees but none of
this was set in stone. The peers wanted to keep communications
with the king open for as long as possible and to avoid any trial.
They were, in fact, Charles's best hope but he did not realize this
at the time.

In the end it was the pressure of external events that forced
decisions on the 'frightened junto', as the royalist politician Mar-
chamont Needham labelled them.[15] Alarmed by the news that the
Dutch states-general had signed a naval and trade treaty with the
Irish rebels, the grandees believed that England could be dangerously vulnerable not just to an invasion by Ormonde's Irish troops,
now that they had the means of conveyance, but to a full-scale
naval war with the Dutch as well. The peers and the senior army
officers agreed that the best way forward was to make one last
attempt to offer the king a settlement, one that would avoid both
a third civil war and the trial of the king. In preparation for these
negotiations, Charles was moved from his isolated prison at Hurst
to the much more congenial surroundings of Windsor Castle, one
of his great palaces. He arrived there on 23 December, to await
the arrival of the earl of Denbigh, who had been entrusted with
the mission to persuade him to save his kingdoms and himself.

The importance of Denbigh's role and the terms he was offering on behalf of the junto have gone largely unnoticed, subsumed
by the drama of the king's trial and execution.[16] Yet they were the
last attempt by the army and its aristocratic allies to avert a trial
which would lead them down an unprecedented and unpredictable path. Not everyone in the army high command believed
that the king should escape some form of reckoning but the

atmosphere of crisis and an underlying respect for the institution of monarchy itself prevailed. The choice of Basil Feilding, second earl of Denbigh, to approach Charles, was an interesting one. His mother was a Villiers and his uncle had been a favourite of the king's during his early years on the throne, the assassinated duke of Buckingham. Denbigh was also the brother-in-law of the duke of Hamilton, who was now being held prisoner at Windsor. The earl's connections with those close to the king were strong but he had followed a different path during the Civil Wars, whether out of conviction or self-interest is hard to say, and he was currently Speaker of the House of Lords. There is a suggestion that he did not personally like Charles I and had been further disenchanted by his dealings with him on the Isle of Wight in December 1647. Clarendon described him as 'a person very ungracious to the king', who had bridled at Charles's response to the parliamentary commissioners (of whom Denbigh was the chief), saying that they were 'not to be looked upon as common messengers'.[17] This prickliness, combined with the lack of diplomatic skills that Denbigh had demonstrated while ambassador to Venice in the 1630s, suggest that he was far from an ideal choice to make crucial overtures to the king.

The terms that Denbigh was authorized to propose would have been unpalatable to Charles I even if they had come from a person with whom he was much more at ease. There were three major concessions required: the king was to abandon his 'negative voice' (his power of veto over ministerial appointments), consent to the abolition of episcopacy and disown the agreement with the Scots. Presumably he would also have been required to put a halt to Ormonde's endeavours in Ireland. This would have left Charles as a nominal king but no better, in his own eyes and those of his followers, than 'Duke of Venice'. The intention was for Denbigh to put these proposals to Charles on Christmas Day. Whether he did so remains tantalizingly unclear. We do not know whether the king and the earl ever met face to face. The French ambassador, Grignan, who had been watching the situation closely, reported that Denbigh never saw Charles.[18] The other possibility is that Charles did admit Denbigh into his presence but then rejected the proposals outright. He was evidently in good spirits and full of confidence. He saw Ormonde as his saviour. No wonder, then, that he was reported as being 'very pleasant and merry'. Indeed, he was about to rebuff the Denbigh mission publicly with counter-proposals of his own, in His Majesties Last Proposals to the Officers of the Armie. It has been said that, as was so often the case with Charles I, he was offering 'concessions with menaces'. Certainly there was an obvious threat in the declaration that if his offer to come to London and hold talks with the army grandees was turned down, his Irish subjects and his son, the Prince of Wales, would come to rescue him. His assertion that 'no law can judge a king' was certainly something that he believed absolutely. For the officers of the army, the realization that Charles Stuart was unapologetically anticipating another war proved too much. The king had overplayed a hand that was much weaker than he knew.

The decision to go ahead with the king's trial was made by the Council of Officers on 27 December and the next day the House of Commons set about establishing a high court of justice. This was opposed by the House of Lords but they were ignored. On 4 January 1649, the Commons directly contradicted the king by announcing that they were the 'supreme power of this nation'. The future of the Stuart monarchy, however, was by no means decided. For several weeks at the turn of 1648–9 it seemed possible that it might, as had previously been contemplated, rest with Prince Henry.

The details of plans to depose the king and replace him with his youngest son remain as murky as the failure of Denbigh's mission, though the two are closely connected.[19] The king's death was not a foregone conclusion of the trial itself and well into January efforts were still being made to broker a settlement with the king, while Charles seems to have held fast to the notion that there was a growing difference between the more radical and conservative wings of his opponents, a tension that he could exploit to his own benefit. He continued to count on Ormonde, who had threatened Fairfax with retribution if the king was harmed.

Yet in the end, when the trial started on 20 January in the Great Hall at Westminster, Charles must have been conscious of the fact that he was very much alone. Isolated in the Louvre in Paris at the start of 1649, as the civil unrest known as the Fronde raged around her, Henrietta Maria sent letters to parliament and to Fairfax requesting that she be allowed to come to England to see her husband.[20] The letters to the Speakers of both Houses were not even opened and the 'consolation of going to him', which she requested was denied.[21] The Prince of Wales, celebrating Christmas in the Netherlands with James and Mary, also wrote to Fairfax expressing his grave concerns for his father's health and safety and appealing for the restoration of the king to 'his just rights'. According to Clarendon, the letter was read in the Council of Officers 'and laid aside'.[22] Neither was a response forthcoming to similar letters sent, at the behest of Anne of Austria, from the young Louis XIV to Cromwell and Fairfax, saying that he was greatly touched by the plight of his uncle and that Cromwell had it in his power to restore Charles I to his rights and dignity.[23] By the time the letters were written, the king had met his fate.

*

CHARLES I's TRIAL and execution have been the subject of many books and articles and the details do not need repetition here. It was his finest hour and the observation has been made, with much justice, that in the extremity of his life, the king achieved a kind of greatness.[24] His refusal to recognize the authority of the court or to enter a plea gave him a quiet dignity and a confidence that threatened to derail the entire process. There were many who had opposed him who could not quite believe what they were seeing and were profoundly disturbed by the spectacle of a king on trial for his life. Several interruptions of proceedings by a masked

woman in the gallery, later identified as Lady Anne Fairfax, wife
of the army leader, gave voice to these wider misgivings. In her
case, however, they indicated a more personal turmoil. The Fairfax
marriage was far from happy and there were tensions, much
satirized by the royalist press, between the staunchly Presbyterian
Anne Fairfax and the Cromwells. Lady Fairfax's influence over
her husband was widely credited for the general's silence during
the trial (despite his having been appointed as a commissioner
he did not appear) and his lack of public commitment to the
regicide.[25]

Whether Charles I was inwardly as confident as he appeared
at his trial is another matter. His life since 1645 had been one
long series of setbacks, of incoherent plans, raised hopes and
opportunities missed. Ever-stricter confinement was wearisome
and demeaning. The splendid regal attire of van Dyck's portraits
had been replaced by more modest dress and an appearance that
sometimes bordered on the slovenly. The years had wearied him,
adding their weight to a disposition that, deprived of his lively
wife, was always inclined to melancholy. Even in 1646, there was
a part of him that seemed resigned to his fate. From Newcastle,
while in the custody of the Scottish army, he wrote to his supporters with the queen in France: 'I have already cast up what I
am likely to suffer, which I shall meet, by the grace of God, with
that constancy that befits me.'[26] This acceptance was repeated at
intervals thereafter, always in private correspondence with those
whom he trusted or loved. From the Isle of Wight, shortly before
he was brought back to the mainland, he wrote a moving letter to
the Prince of Wales: 'Let us comfort you with that which is our
own comfort, that though affliction may make us pass under the
censures of men, yet we look upon it so, as if it procure not, by
God's mercy to us, a deliverance, it will to you a blessing . . . We
know not but this may be the last time we may speak to you or
the world publicly . . .'[27]

Yet there still existed in Charles, right up to the moment that
the sentence was pronounced, an incredulity that his opponents

would take the irrevocable step of executing him. In his own mind, he had committed no crime. Any accommodation he might have made to save his life (and he was given many chances) would, to him, have undermined the royal prerogative. He would not be a king at all. He requested deferment of sentence so that he could address the Lords and Commons in the Painted Chamber of Westminster Palace. In the speech that he prepared, but was never allowed to give, he expressed himself eloquently as the defender of the ancient laws of the kingdom and the rights of its people: 'Thus you see that I speak not for my own right alone, as I am your King, but also for the true liberty of all my subjects, which consists not in the power of government, but in living under such laws, such a government, as may give themselves the best assurance of their lives, and property of their goods.' He saw no hope of peace or settlement 'so long as power reigns without rule or law, changing the whole frame of that government under which this kingdom hath flourished for many hundred years'. So he challenged their 'pretended authority' and claimed that 'the arms I took up were only to defend the fundamental laws of this kingdom against those who have supposed my power hath totally changed the ancient government.'[28] He ended with a rousing reminder of better times under Queen Elizabeth, his father and the first years of his own reign.

This appeal to the past, so characteristic of Charles I, went unheard. Sentence was passed on 27 January. The court appointed to try him found him 'guilty of levying war against the Parliament and people . . . and that he hath been and is the occasioner, author and continuer of . . . unnatural, cruel and bloody wars, and therein guilty of high treason . . . for which the court doth adjudge that he, the said Charles Stuart, as a tyrant, traitor, murderer and public enemy to the good people of this nation, shall be put to death by the severing of his head from his body.'[29] These grim and inexorable words were, for Cromwell and the fifty-eight others who signed the death warrant, the only just outcome of the trial. Charles I had repulsed all efforts to save his life. If he had hoped, up until the moment that the sentence was pronounced, that he could call their bluff, then he miscalculated. He demanded to speak but was removed from the hall, still protesting, back to St James's Palace, where he had been lodged during the trial. It was the childhood home of Princess Elizabeth and Prince Henry and it was there that they bade him farewell on 29 January.

It was a harrowing and deeply affecting parting. The king had requested that he be allowed to see his younger children before his execution. They were already aware of the sentence, presumably having been told by the earl of Northumberland, a consistent opponent of Charles I but not a supporter of the decision to put him to death. Conveying the news to them must have been the hardest task of Northumberland's time as their guardian. Elizabeth was distraught and her brother bewildered and concerned by his sister's distress. Both seem to have been taken aback by their father's appearance when admitted to his presence. He had aged and an air of vulnerability hung around him that could not be entirely disguised by his own composure. This was in complete contrast to his daughter's discomfiture. She began to weep uncontrollably and Henry also started to cry. Taking them both on his knees, Charles embraced them and tried to soothe them. He had important things to say that he wanted them to hear. These Elizabeth herself recorded, under the heading 'What the king said to me, January 29, 1648–9, being the last time I had the happiness to see him'.

> He told me he was glad I was come, and although he had not time to say much, yet somewhat he had to say to me, which he could not to another, or leave in writing, because he feared their cruelty was such, as that they could not have permitted him to write to me. He wished me not to grieve or torment myself for him, for that would be a glorious death that he should die – it being for the laws and liberties of this land, and for maintaining the true Protestant religion. He bid me read Bishop Andrews's sermons, Hooker's *Ecclesiastical Polity*

and Bishop Laud's book against Fisher, which would ground me against Popery. He told me he had forgiven all his enemies, and hoped God would forgive them also; and commanded us, and all the rest of my brothers and sisters, to forgive them. He bid me tell my mother that his thoughts never strayed from her, and that his love should be the same to the last. Withal, he commanded me and my brother to be obedient to her, and bid me send his blessing to the rest of my brothers and sisters, with commendation to all his friends. So, after he had given me his blessing, I took my leave.

Farther, he commanded us all to forgive those people, but never to trust them; for they had been most false to him and to those that gave them power, and he feared also for their own souls; and he desired me not to grieve for him, for he should die a martyr, and that he doubted not but the Lord would settle his throne upon his son, and that we should all be happier than we could have expected to have been if he had lived; with many other things, which at present I cannot remember.[30]

Desperate to record faithfully her father's injunctions but unable, because of emotion, to recall everything verbatim, Elizabeth's slightly disjointed account of their last meeting reveals the torment of the occasion. The king is said to have told her: 'Sweetheart, you'll forget this,' but there was no likelihood of that. She replied she could not forget, as long as she lived.

Charles then turned his attention to the eight-year-old boy sitting on his knee. For little Henry, his message was direct and uncompromising. 'Sweetheart,' he said, 'now they will cut off thy father's head; mark, child, what I say.' By this time, the king certainly had his youngest son's complete, even fascinated, attention. 'They will cut off my head, and perhaps make thee a king; but mark what I say, you must not be a king, so long as your brothers, Charles and James, do live; for they will cut off thy brothers' heads (when they can catch them), and cut off thy head too at last; and therefore I charge you do not be made a king by them.' To which the child, anguished but unshaken by this gruesome depiction of his family's and his own future, burst out: 'I will be torn in pieces first.' His reply 'made the king rejoice exceedingly'.[31]

But for Elizabeth, as the king divided his few remaining jewels between the two children, there was no solace. Charles took his leave of them and returned to his chamber, but the princess's wracking sobs brought him briefly back out again. A last embrace and blessing, and he was gone. The children returned to Syon House and how they passed the day of their father's execution is not known.

The king spent his last hours in prayer with Bishop Juxon of London, who was permitted to attend him, and writing letters to his family. To the Prince of Wales he had already composed a lengthy homily, in which he clearly still hoped for a reprieve but accepted that death was the likelier outcome. This last testament reveals the depth of his religious convictions and how central they were to his vision of the responsibilities of kingship. 'The true glory of princes,' he wrote, 'consists in advancing God's glory, in the maintenance of true religion and the Church's good; also in the dispensation of civil power, with justice and honour to the public peace.' If his son kept to the true principles of piety, virtue and honour, then 'you shall never want a kingdom'.[32]

Charles received his last letter from his eldest son from the hands of the stalwart royalist Henry Seymour, an experienced and successful courier of messages, on the evening of 28 January. He gave Seymour the final messages to be conveyed to Prince Charles and to Henrietta Maria. The occasion threatened to overwhelm the faithful Seymour, who was desolate to find his sovereign so changed. His response was very similar to that of Princess Elizabeth and he was a grown man: 'Mr Seymour, at his entrance, fell into a passion, having formerly seen His Majesty in a glorious state and now so dolorous; and having kissed the king's hand, clasped about his legs, lamentably mourning.'[33]

On the bitterly cold afternoon of 30 January 1649, with snow threatening, the first Charles Stuart stepped out of the Banqueting House, part of his Whitehall Palace, onto a balcony where a scaffold had been especially constructed. Serene in his faith, he told Bishop Juxon that he was going from a corruptible to an incorruptible Crown, where there would be no more trouble. His small stature never detracted from a regal presence and his nobility of demeanour in those final moments was impressive. The crowd who came to watch, kept back by a strong military presence, were too far away to hear him acknowledge his eternal regret at the part he had played in Strafford's fate, or utter the famous words which epitomized the creed by which he had lived and for which he was about to die. 'A subject and a sovereign,' he told them, 'are clean different things.' He died bravely, his head severed, mercifully, with one stroke of the axe. There is a story that Oliver Cromwell visited the corpse as it lay in its coffin at White-hall and muttered the words 'Cruel necessity' over the fallen king. The tale is not contemporary and did not gain currency until the eighteenth century but, even if apocryphal, it still contains a kind of truth. The king's opponents were as unswerving in their belief in God's justice and providence as Charles I had been. And they had proved the stronger during the Civil Wars.[34]

For the children he left behind, scattered across three countries, their father's death was cruel indeed. In their grief, they would have agreed with the summation, made years afterwards, by Edward Hyde: 'He was the worthiest gentleman, the best master, the best friend, the best husband, the best father and the best Christian that the age in which he lived had produced.'[35] Now his children, like the three kingdoms he had ruled, faced an uncertain future in which they, too, would be 'clean different things'.

CHAPTER TEN

A Quiet Death

'*The sorrowful daughter to our late martyred king.*'
The poet John Quarles, describing Princess Elizabeth, April 1649

THE ENORMITY OF Charles I's execution stunned Europe, causing horror in the monarchies of the continent, but nowhere was it
more keenly felt than in the troubled kingdom of France. News
of her husband's death was broken to Henrietta Maria by Henry
Jermyn in the palace of the Louvre, on 9 February 1649. For
almost two hours she sat motionless, in deep shock, unable to take
in what she had been told. Then she retired for some weeks to a
convent on the rue Saint-Jacques which had happy associations
with her childhood. But those days were long ago and the world
was crumbling around her. Devastated by what had happened to
Charles I, she bent but did not entirely break. Her immediate
thoughts were of her eldest son and how best she could support
his restoration to the English throne. This goal was a more distant
prospect than she was willing to believe. Disagreement and
self-interest predominated among her clique of advisers in Paris
and the European powers continued in their reluctance to involve
themselves on behalf of the Stuarts. The widowed queen's options
were limited. The arrival of the duke of York at her court in
mid-February should have been a comfort, especially as he had
spent some weeks in a Benedictine monastery as part of his travels,

his first exposure to Catholicism independent of his mother. James only learned of his father's death after his arrival in Paris and his immediate reactions are unknown. He does, however, seem to have realized that his foolish enthusiasm for Bampfield's naval schemes must be confined to the past. His first loyalty was to his elder brother. It soon became apparent that he did not get on well with his mother, though he was not unusual in this, as Henrietta Maria's relationships with her children were consistently difficult.

Prince Charles was still in the Netherlands when he learned of his father's death. The baron van Heenvliet, the husband of Katherine Stanhope, the chief lady of Princess Mary's household, reported in mid-January 1649 that the Prince of Wales had returned to The Hague at the request of his sister, because of the very bad news from England, 'which says that the king will be put to death . . . you can imagine how much the Princess Royal is afflicted by this.'[1] Charles I's execution was reported in Dutch news-sheets on 4 February but accounts vary as to whether the new king was informed in a crowded room at court or privately by his chaplain, Dr Goffe, who hesitantly addressed him as 'Your Majesty'. Both sources reported that the initial reaction of this eighteen-year-old so brutally thrust into the role of monarch was to burst into tears.[2] He could, at least, share his grief with his equally heartbroken sister and appreciate the deep mourning ordered by his brother-in-law. Soon his attention turned to the practicalities of politics and how best to regain the three kingdoms that his father had lost, and particularly to the situations in Ireland and in Scotland, either or both of which, he hoped, might aid him in regaining the throne of England.

It is unlikely that he gave much thought to the future of his younger sister and brother, though there is some evidence in an unreliable letter, attributed to Henrietta Maria and perhaps written by a secretary familiar with the queen's preoccupations, that Elizabeth and Henry were not forgotten. Addressed to her 'dearest yet most unfortunate son', apparently in response to a

letter of condolence and encouragement from Charles II himself, she urges him to make the younger children, and particularly
Elizabeth, his priority: 'Yet my afflictions do not make me forget
your brothers and that unfortunate Elizabeth. Oh! If before my
death I could see her out of the hands of the traitors, I could die
content. To this, at least, I will exhort you, to employ every force,
to use every artifice, to withdraw so dear a part of my own heart,
this innocent victim of their fury, your worthy sister, from London.
Do it, I pray, and conjure you, by the spirit of the king, my lord
and your father.'[3] Even if Charles shared his mother's views,
neither of them had seen Elizabeth in more than seven years. The
latest information they would have had about her, how she looked,
what she was like, her disposition and education, must have come
from James. If he had been honest about the time he had spent
under Northumberland's guardianship, he could at least have reassured other family members that there was no 'fury' directed at
his siblings and that they were well cared for. What would happen
to them now, however, remained uncertain.

*

ELIZABETH WAS traumatized by her father's death and the
emotions of their parting. Her spirit had withstood much but her
body, already weak, never really recovered from the strain. Her
slight frame swathed in the plain black dress she habitually wore
now in mourning for Charles I, the princess was a sad figure. Nor
was she to be allowed the reassurance of staying in a place and with
a guardian that she knew. Northumberland was owed considerable
sums of money for the upkeep of Elizabeth and Henry and was
increasingly concerned about problems of security following the
escape of James. But more than either of these considerations, he
simply did not wish to continue with the responsibility that he had
shouldered for four difficult years. By the spring of 1649, after the
abolition of the monarchy in England and the House of Lords, he
wrote to the Council of State from his seat at Syon House, complaining of his situation and asking to be relieved of it:

I have for some months past been put to maintain the Duke of Gloucester and his sister out of my own purse; and for want of those allowances which I should have received by appointment of parliament, have run myself so far out of money that I am altogether destitute of means to provide longer for them, or indeed, for my own poor family unless I may have what is owing to me . . . My apprehension likewise of practices upon the Duke of Gloucester (which probably may not be in my power to prevent) make me think it necessary to acquaint your lordships that I cannot, upon any terms, undertake to be answerable for him. The maintaining and safe-keeping of these children being matters of state, I knew not where to apply myself for directions as unto this council; humbly desiring that you may be pleased to consider how they may otherwise be disposed of.[4]

Chastened by this representation of financial need, the House of Commons did vote to 'pay unto the earl of Northumberland such monies as are due to him'. They also considered an important request from Elizabeth herself, though the outcome for the princess was to be yet another disappointment.

Shortly before Northumberland had expressed his exasperation and perhaps aware that he no longer wished to continue as her guardian, Elizabeth had requested to be allowed to join Mary in the Netherlands. Though this would have meant parting from Henry (whose future she seems to have been willing to leave to others at this point) it was something that she desperately wanted. However, when the request was put to the vote in the Commons, there was a narrow majority against it and so Elizabeth's plea was denied. Instead, the members voted a sum of £3,000 for the two children and consigned their care to Sir Edward Harrington and his wife. The gentleman's son pleaded his parents' age and ill health and so a new solution had to be found. It was better than Elizabeth and Henry might have expected. They were to be removed to Penshurst Place in Kent, to the oversight of Robert

Sidney, third earl of Leicester, and his wife, Dorothy, who was Northumberland's sister. At Penshurst, a house of golden stone set in tranquil countryside, the children were to pass a quiet year away from affairs of state. A new tutor, the elderly Richard Lovell, was appointed for them and he became devoted to his charges.

Elizabeth and Henry came into a family with an illustrious pedigree, including the Elizabethan soldier and poet Philip Sidney. It is unlikely, however, that they were aware of the tensions that beset it. The Leicesters were an interesting couple whose own family were divided by the Civil Wars. The earl was thoroughly disenchanted with the catastrophe that had befallen his country and he had been an early loser in the power struggle between Charles I and parliament. Leicester had been singularly unfortunate to be appointed lord deputy of Ireland in June 1641, just before the outbreak of the rebellion that precipitated civil war in England. Recalled from his position as ambassador to France, events in Ireland prevented him from taking up residence (a blessing in the longer term), though two of his sons, Philip and Algernon, served in the military force sent to crush the uprising. By the summer of 1642, he could not contain his frustration at his situation, writing to his sister-in-law, Henrietta Maria's former confidante, Lucy Hay, countess of Carlisle: 'I am environed by contradictions . . . the Parliament bid me go presently [to Ireland]; the king commands me to stay until he despatch me . . . I am suspected and distrusted of either side.'[5]

The outcome of this dilemma was an uncomfortable one. Charles I preferred to deal with Ormonde on Irish affairs, undermining the official lord deputy, and Ormonde appears to have taken advantage of the situation by accusing Leicester's sons of cowardice on the battlefield. The king's lack of support turned the Sidney family against the royal family, who felt their long-standing loyalty to the monarchy impugned by the king's behaviour towards them. Relations with parliament were scarcely better, especially when the Sidney brothers were arrested as suspected royalists when they returned from Ireland in 1643. Soured by his treatment, Leicester, who was extremely learned and well-read, retired to his country estate at Penshurst and comforted himself from his large library there, determined to stay out of politics as much as possible. He still had a mansion in London which he used on visits to the capital but his naturally reserved disposition found greater solace among his books and gardens. It is not clear what access to her host's collection was afforded to Princess Elizabeth but if she was allowed to peruse it, she would have found much of interest, being a fellow enthusiast in the classics and languages.

Dorothy, countess of Leicester, was of a different disposition – lively, devoted to her large family (she produced fifteen children, eight of whom predeceased her), a keen member of the coterie of Henrietta Maria in the 1630s and an inveterate courtier and letter-writer. The van Dyck portrait of the Percy sisters, Lucy and Dorothy, shows two good-looking young women, full of aristocratic charm and confidence. Yet the Civil Wars took them down separate paths. Lucy used her looks and connections to bed a number of powerful men in pursuit of personal ambition. Buckingham had been her lover in the 1620s; during the 1640s she enjoyed a liaison with the turncoat Henry Rich, earl of Holland, and became a staunch royalist. Holland was executed by the new regime in March 1649 for his part in the second Civil War while Lucy was arrested and held in the Tower of London. At the time that Elizabeth and Henry were put under the care of the countess of Leicester, Lucy was still imprisoned and Dorothy, like so many others, had to deal daily with divided loyalties.[6] Her sister and younger son were royalists (Robert Sidney was with Charles II at The Hague and, like his new sovereign, briefly the lover of Lucy Walter), her two eldest sons were committed to the Commonwealth, the regime that replaced Charles II, and her brother, Northumberland, had just washed his hands of the royal children and passed them on to her. She could expect only limited emotional support from her husband, a distant and rather morose figure trying to steer clear of any political commitment. Small wonder, then, that later in the 1650s their marriage came under considerable strain and they contemplated separation.

Despite the demands of family, Dorothy's attitude to the new arrivals was highly responsible and as warm as could be expected given their unhappy circumstances. They did not lack for kindness while under her roof. The earl himself had a rather more pragmatic, not to say mercenary, approach to his guests, whose financial arrangement he found more than satisfactory:

> In June, 1649, the parliament placed the Duke of Gloucester and the princess Elizabeth with my wife, allowing for them £3,000 a year, which was a great accession of means to my wife in proportion to the charge of these two children and ten or eleven servants; and considering my expenses in fuel, washing and household stuff etc, also that I should have less liberty in my own house than I had, and be obliged in attendance which would be troublesome to me, I thought it very reasonable to abate a great part of that £700 a year, and so from midsummer 1649, I resolved to take off £400 a year – this caused a great storm in the house but I persisted in it.[7]

Clearly Dorothy was not happy with her husband adjusting the household expenses in this way but it was not an argument she won.

Finances aside, there were other considerations relevant to the treatment of Elizabeth and Henry. Instructions had been given that they were no longer to be addressed by their royal titles but merely as Elizabeth and Henry Stuart, though the authorities were inconsistent in this respect, Elizabeth generally being referred to as 'the Lady Elizabeth' and Henry as 'the duke of Gloucester', at least in the *House of Commons Journal*. Nor were they to be served or seated separately from the rest of the family at table – an injunction apparently not followed by the countess of Leicester, who earned the displeasure of the Speaker of the House of Commons, William Lenthall, when he paid a surprise visit and found Elizabeth and Henry still served separately, as they had always been. Dorothy was a woman not easily cowed in such respects and there is no evidence that further action was taken.

During her year in Kent, supported by a small staff of personal servants and under the direction of a well-intentioned guardian, Elizabeth's health seemed to improve. The appearance was deceptive – she was probably suffering from tuberculosis – and it is unlikely she could ever have recovered, even if circumstances had not intervened. The countess of Leicester lost two daughters to consumption – her own Elizabeth, a few years older than the princess, was herself afflicted by the disease at the time – and probably recognized the frailty of her ward. Yet she could not protect Elizabeth from the consequences of her elder brother's attempts to win his English throne. On the evening of 23 June 1650, having abandoned the marquess of Ormonde's Irish initiatives and agreed to sign the Scottish Covenant, Charles II's ships were at anchor in the Moray Firth, off the east coast of Scotland. It is unlikely that, before he set out from his long sojourn in the Netherlands, he had even considered the effect that his coming might have on his younger brother and sister, so long hostages in a war not of their making. His decision was to have fatal consequences for his sister, Elizabeth.

*

IT WAS NOT JUST the threat from Scotland that alarmed the new government in London, nor the realization that former allies had turned against them. The reaction in England itself was unpredictable and members of the House of Commons felt it prudent to consider all eventualities, including the possibility of unrest occasioned by the reappearance of the head of the exiled Stuart dynasty on British soil. It was believed, though without any real evidence, that the younger children of the late king might become the focus for discontent. The danger they represented must be anticipated and contained. Accordingly, there came an order in parliament, based on a report from the Council of State submitted by Sir Henry Mildmay, an assiduous committee worker whose tenure of economically advantageous positions in the republic was all too easily interpreted by royalist opponents of this erstwhile courtier as personal greed. His report, discussed on 24 July, contained ill tidings for Elizabeth and Henry: '. . . in regard of the many designs now on foot, if any insurrections should happen, the public peace would be much the more endangered by occasion of the late King's children, who are remaining here, and may be made use of to the prejudice of the public.' It was therefore recommended 'that Henry Stuart, third son of the late King, and the Lady Elizabeth, his daughter, be removed forthwith beyond seas, and that the Council consider of a fit place whither they may be removed, and the manner of sending them thither, and of a fit maintenance for them there, during the pleasure of Parliament.' Two days later, a firm decision was taken. Lady Leicester would be relieved of her duties and Henry and his sister were to be removed to Carisbrooke Castle on the Isle of Wight.

This outcome horrified Elizabeth. She did not want to leave Penshurst and was cast into despair by the realization that she must go to the place that had been her father's prison for much of the last year of his life. It could hold only gloom and the most distressing of associations for her. The quiet country life in Kent with the genial countess of Leicester and her family had, at least, kept the princess's tuberculosis at bay. She was convinced that the move would damage her already delicate health. Yet once the decision had been made in parliament, Elizabeth was unable to change it, despite writing directly to the Council of State. Her pleas concerning 'her unfitness to remove, in regard of her ill health', and her request that the former royal physician, Sir Theodore de Mayerne, be asked to certify his opinion on her condition, were noted but changed nothing.[8] Instructions were given for Anthony Mildmay, brother of Sir Henry, and his wife to 'take a coach and go to Penshurst and thence attend the Duke and his sister until they are transported [to Carisbrooke Castle].'

The decision of England's republican rulers in respect of Elizabeth and Henry in the summer of 1650 was a product of political nervousness rather than rabid anti-royalism aimed at two innocent children. In terms of Elizabeth's health, it was thoughtless rather than heartless. The younger Stuarts were 'to be furnished with all necessary and fit accommodation' and their expenses would continue to be paid out of the funds assigned to them. But the number of servants to accompany them was further reduced, to a maximum of eight, though they were allowed to make their own choice of who went with them. And there is in the instructions given to Mildmay a proviso that has been largely overlooked: their stay at Carisbrooke was viewed as being only an interim solution. Their future lay beyond England, 'out of the limits of the commonwealth'. Where they should go and the means of getting them out of England were left for further consideration.

Mildmay and his wife arrived at Penshurst at the beginning of August. They left on 9 August with the children, escorted by a military detachment under Major-General Thomas Harrison, a radical and regicide who had organized the funeral of Charles I. How much of his background and views, and of the part he had played in her father's death, was known to Elizabeth is impossible to say, but he was certainly not a tactful choice to accompany the princess on her journey. Harrison, for his part, is unlikely to have been entirely happy with transporting the trappings of royalty which Henry and Elizabeth were still allowed to use, though the hangings, bedding and plate that had once graced palaces were now owned by the state. These included a bedstead of crimson velvet, with a gold and silver lace and fringe, a down bed and pillows, crimson damask window curtains, Turkish carpets, tapestries, velvet stools and chairs, as well as plate and cutlery. Whether Elizabeth and Henry actually used any of these reminders of their royal past at Carisbrooke we do not know but the following year the collection was sold for the modern equivalent of six million pounds.[9]

Before she departed, Elizabeth had expressed her gratitude to the earl and countess of Leicester and entrusted them with the safe-keeping of the only personal items of value she had left, a pearl necklace and a diamond ornament. She told the earl that she would inform him in due course of how she wished to dispose of these items. Little did he know the trouble this would eventually cause.

The Mildmays and the children took a week to reach their new destination, arriving at Carisbrooke on 16 August. The governor of the Isle of Wight, Colonel Sydenham, had earlier received a letter from the Council of State which left him in no doubt that the security of Elizabeth and Henry while on the island was his priority, and that he was to remove any suspect or disaffected persons who might, presumably, have been inclined to stir up trouble or even deliver the prince and princess to royalist sympathizers.

Tragedy soon relieved the governor of one of his responsibilities. Within a week of her arrival on the island, Elizabeth was gravely ill. On 22 August she and Henry, playing at bowls on the green specially laid out for their father at Carisbrooke, were caught out in a torrential shower of rain. They were both soaked by the time they reached shelter and though Henry soon shook off the effects of his dowsing, his sister did not. She began to complain of feeling unwell, with a headache and a rising fever that would not go away. By the first day of September she was too weak to get out of bed and it was obvious that her situation was critical. Mildmay consulted with Sydenham and they decided to summon a doctor. The medical help available on the island was limited and a local physician, Dr Bignall, who practised in Newport, felt that he lacked the expertise to give effective help to Elizabeth. His suggestion was to send for Dr Mayerne, who had known Elizabeth all her life but Mayerne, now nearly eighty and far away in London, could not face the journey. Perhaps he suspected that there was little he could do, even if he came in person. Instead, he sent another doctor with various prescriptions, but these arrived too late.

Attended only by a couple of maids and the faithful Richard Lovell, Elizabeth faced death with an equanimity bordering on relief. While she retained her lucidity, her thoughts were of her little brother, to whom she bequeathed her pearl necklace, and of the countess of Leicester, whose kindness she acknowledged by leaving her the diamond ornament she had entrusted to the earl of Leicester a few weeks earlier.[10] Lovell was with her when she died peacefully, at about three in the afternoon of 8 September. The idea that she was alone at the time and was discovered with her cheek resting on her father's bible, open at the verse 'Come unto me, all ye that travail and are heavy laden and I will give ye peace' is romantic but inaccurate.[11] This is how she was eventually depicted on the marble monument erected two centuries later in her memory.

In a supreme irony, Sir Henry Mildmay reported to parliament on 11 September that the Council of State had, at last, conceded that Elizabeth should be permitted to leave England to live with Mary. She would have received one thousand pounds a year 'so long as she behave herself inoffensively to the Parliament and Commonwealth'. This recommendation was never put to the vote because, as the *House of Commons Journal* notes laconically, 'The House was now informed that the Lady Elizabeth is deceased.' Instead, the revenue committee was asked to consider orders for her interment and to provide mourning for her brother and his servants 'and also for the servants of the said Lady, as they shall think fit'.[12]

Elizabeth received somewhat more honour in death than might have been expected. Her body was embalmed and lay in state for two weeks in the small room where she had died. On 24 September her corpse was put into a lead coffin and taken by coach, with her servants in attendance, to the church of St Thomas in Newport. It is highly unlikely that Henry would have accompanied his sister on her last journey; this was not the custom for members of English royalty. Instead, the coffin was met by the mayor and aldermen of Newport and accompanied to its resting place, in the chancel of the church. It bore a simple inscription, 'Elizabeth, 2nd daughter of the late King CHARLES, deceased 8 September, M.D.C.L.'

Only the letters 'E.S.' cut into the wall marked the grave of a princess born in a snowstorm, most of whose life had been spent in a form of polite captivity during the whirlwind of the Civil Wars. She was gentle, intelligent and gifted and if she viewed herself as a victim, she forbore from saying so; nor does she seem to have harboured any hatred towards those who confined her for so long. An uncomplaining nature helped her through life and a deep Protestant religious faith supported her and helped her face death serenely. Her passing was marked by various royalist poets in verse more adulatory than elegant, but the lines of the Welshman Henry Vaughan are worth repeating:

> Thou seem'st a rosebud born in snow,
> A flower of purpose born to bow
> To heedless tempests, and the rage
> Of an incenséd stormy age.
>
> And yet as Balm-trees gently spend
> Their tears for those that do them rend,
> Thou didst not murmur, nor revile,
> But drank'st thy wormwood with a smile.[13]

Her brothers Charles and James have been criticized for failing to visit her tomb but the seventeenth century did not have our modern preoccupation with public outpourings of grief and much had changed by the time they returned to England. Charles, especially, wished to forget the past. More than two hundred years later Queen Victoria, who loved the Isle of Wight, learned that Elizabeth's remains had been rediscovered when the church of St Thomas was rebuilt in the mid-1850s, so she decided to engage the renowned Italian sculptor, Marochetti, to design and build a suitable monument for this forgotten Stuart princess. It shows Elizabeth on her deathbed, with Charles I's bible and, above her, a shattered portcullis, indicating that death had released her from long imprisonment. The inscription, 'To the memory of Princess Elizabeth, daughter of King Charles I', records that the monument was erected 'as a token of respect for her virtues and of sympathy for her misfortunes, by Victoria R'.

Henrietta Maria noted her daughter's death towards the end of a letter to her sister, Christine, in which she had talked about her niece's marriage and the prospects of Charles II in Scotland before remarking that she had suffered another affliction with Elizabeth's passing. The princess was, she said, well out of the hands of 'those traitors' but the general sense of her words is more of self-pity than sorrow for the loss of a daughter she hardly remembered.[14] Nor did she even mention her youngest son. He had never known life without Elizabeth and now he was left with only the solicitous Mr Lovell and a handful of servants. His was a bitter loss indeed.

CHAPTER ELEVEN

The King of Scotland

'He either fears his fate too much,
Or his deserts are small,
who puts it not unto the touch
To win or lose it all'

James Graham, marquess of Montrose

A SATIRICAL BROADSIDE from 1651 tellingly depicted Charles II's dilemma during his stay in Scotland. It shows 'the Scots holding their young King's nose to the grindstone'. The king, clad in ermine-edged robes, is shown in the full discomfort of his youthful monarchy, a minister of religion pressing his flowing locks down towards the unforgiving instrument which will ensure Charles's commitment to the Covenant. Operating the grindstone is a cheerful worker labelled, patronizingly, as 'Jockie'.[1] Charles might not have appreciated the caricature of his appearance but in every other way he would have identified with the sentiments being expressed. His time in Scotland was an object lesson in humiliation. It began with serious misgivings and ended in disaster. And the overriding lesson that Charles learned from it was that he never wanted to set foot in the country, with its quarrelsome, unreliable nobles and stubborn, dour religious fanatics, ever again.

Yet his reign there had started propitiously, in the dark days following the execution of his father. The parliament of Scotland declared him, on 5 February 1649, 'most unanimously and cheer-fully . . . King of Great Britain, France and Ireland', noting that his father had been 'contrary to the dissent and protestation of this kingdom, now removed by a violent death'. The English, it was asserted, had broken the terms of the Solemn League and Covenant between the two countries, which the Scots themselves intended to uphold, in the person of Charles II. For the tearful teenager in The Hague, shouldering all the misfortunes of his family, this was welcome news but there was a sting in the tail. 'It is hereby declared,' continued the Scottish proclamation, 'that before he be admitted to the exercise of his royal dignity he shall give satisfaction to this kingdom in those things that concern the security of religion, the union between the kingdoms and the good and peace of this kingdom according to the National Covenant and Solemn League and Covenant.'[2] In other words, Charles must take the oath to the Covenant himself before his Scottish subjects could welcome him on the soil of his dynasty. This was a formidable stumbling block, a kind of blackmail that Charles indignantly resisted for as long as he could. But it was by no means the only reason that the Scots did not see their new king for another sixteen months.

Relieved as he was to learn that at least one of his kingdoms recognized his right to rule, Charles was in no position to rush across the North Sea. He stayed in the Netherlands till June 1649, wearing out the hospitality of his brother-in-law and causing embarrassment to the Dutch estates-general, who had made appropriate noises of disapproval when informed of the execution of his father, but whose sympathies were opposed to the interests of the House of Orange and more naturally inclined towards the fledgling republican Commonwealth in England. Like his mother before him, Charles outstayed his welcome in the Netherlands and the murder by royalist agents of the English ambassador to The Hague poisoned the atmosphere even more. There was little alternative but to join Henrietta Maria at Saint-Germain, at least for the time being. Whether the birth of Charles's first illegitimate son, the future duke of Monmouth, was a further impetus to leave is unclear. Though Charles always acknowledged the boy as his, he gave little practical support for mother or child. The ardour of his passion for Lucy Walter, the child's mother, seems to have been short-lived.

Lucy had been born in Wales, in Roch Castle in Pembroke-shire, though her parents were gentry rather than aristocrats. Their marriage did not last and Lucy accompanied her mother to London where her good looks and a personality that certainly was able to attract men, if not to hold on to them, helped her thrive. Soldiers, whether republican or royalist, were her target but the support they could provide was unlikely to be long-term and none of her lovers seems to have entertained the idea of marrying her. Perhaps this was because she was already well on the road to be-coming a professional mistress, the sort of beautiful young woman with no fortune or prospects of her own who would always be dependent on the support of men, and preferably well-connected ones. The diarist John Evelyn, one of the royalist exiles then in France, recalled her as a 'brown, beautiful, bold but insipid crea-ture'. The mystery of how the dark-haired Lucy could be both bold and insipid at the same time is perhaps a reference to her lack of conversational skills. She had not been well educated but she was evidently confident about her looks. Undeterred by the prospect of travelling and aware that a married lady's title would give her a veneer of respectability, Lucy became Mrs Barlow and took herself off to the Netherlands, where she soon ended up in the bed of the Prince of Wales.[3]

The whole affair was handled with considerable discretion among Charles's supporters. The baby, born on 9 April 1649 and named James, went first to a wet nurse near Rotterdam. Lucy was found lodgings in Antwerp. Charles would eventually arrange for her to meet his mother later in the summer in France; no record of this encounter, which must have been awkward, survives. The decision to separate mother and child does not seem to have been one that Lucy found unpalatable at this stage and there is some evidence that she stayed on in France, at the Louvre, when Charles left for Jersey in the autumn. The dowager queen was compelled to seek the assistance of Edward Hyde in removing an unnamed young lady from the Louvre who had found lodgings there without her consent and was being disrespectful. We do not know for sure if this was Lucy but, if so, it was merely a taste of what was to come for the Stuart family in their dealings with her.[4] For now, however, she was left behind.

Wary of Commonwealth fleets patrolling the coast, Charles set off for France overland, enjoying a cordial reception from the Spanish authorities in Belgium as he journeyed south, despite Spain's reluctance to upset the new regime in London. But it was one thing to be treated graciously in Brussels and another to be offered substantive help in Paris, especially by a country as beset by domestic difficulties as France.

The five years of stop-start civil war in France known as the Fronde (the term referred to a catapult or sling used by the Paris mob to shatter the windows of Mazarin's residence in 1648) over-lapped with the second Civil War in England and the republican government of the Commonwealth. Despite periods of relative inactivity, the disorders were not finally over until after Cromwell had removed the Rump Parliament in England in the spring of 1653. For two years, between 1651 and 1653, Mazarin was in exile, his influence over French politics diminished but by no means lost. The Fronde shared some similarities with the Civil Wars in England but these are more superficial than close paral-lels. At its root, it was an attempt by the nobility to regain powers and prestige whittled away by Richelieu's years of dominance. At court and also in the provinces, where respect for the authority of *les Grands* (the Great Ones) was considered the bedrock of social order, there was profound unease at the Crown's encroachment into these traditional areas of civil society. Although the impetus for revolt came from the law courts, the *parlements*, who, despite the name, were not legislative bodies like the English and Scottish parliaments, opposition to royal absolutism soon proved to be widespread and to have reverberations far beyond Paris. There was also deep dislike of the increasing burden of taxation and the fact that the French government had for too long been directed by foreigners, a Spanish queen regent and an Italian cardinal. At various points in the five-year struggle that threatened to wreck the French economy and weaken its position in Europe, everyone from princes of the blood to peasants was caught up in armed conflict, in places as far apart as Normandy and Provence. The royal family were compelled to leave Paris and take refuge in palaces like Fontainebleau and Saint-Germain in the surrounding countryside while the duke of Orléans and his daughter, the indefatigable Grande Mademoiselle, changed sides when it suited them and various noble ladies took up arms on behalf of their husbands or brothers in a period of the Fronde known as the War of the Princesses. Even Marshal Turenne, the country's leading soldier, went over to the rebels for a time.

The first outbreak of unrest, which culminated in an embarrassing invasion by Spanish troops taking advantage of the central government's weakness, was over by the spring of 1649, making it seem safe for Charles II to enter the country for a period of discussion with his mother and her advisers. Henrietta Maria never wrote about the troubles surrounding her family in France in her letters, which seems a curious omission since they were bound to have had an impact on her hopes for her eldest son, not to mention the more immediate danger posed to her safety while she remained at the Louvre. But in June 1649, she was, as she told her sister, Christine, anxiously awaiting the arrival of Charles.[5]

He arrived at Saint-Germain on 12 July, having been warmly received by Louis XIV and Anne of Austria at Compiègne north of the capital but remaining studiedly vague about his plans, despite the gracious offer that he could use Saint-Germain as his home for as long as he needed. At his mother's residence, among the bored and edgy exiles, he found that not much had changed during his absence in the Netherlands. He did not help the situation by announcing that he would not, at that time, name any new privy councillors or officers of state. He declined to settle anything until he was safely established in Ireland. In the summer of 1649, Ireland, thanks to Ormonde's efforts, still seemed the most hopeful source of support and the kingdom from which he could most effectively launch a realistic bid to regain the English throne. Such confidence was, however, misplaced. In early August a force under Colonel Michael Jones surprised Ormonde at Rathmines, just south of Dublin, and routed his forces, nearly capturing the marquess as well. And then, on 13 August, Oliver Cromwell set sail from Milford Haven in south Wales with an expeditionary force of 12,000 men, intending to quell once and for all the rebellion in Ireland that had festered since 1641.

*

IF CROMWELL's arrival in Ireland put the brakes on royalist plans, his military successes there would, during the course of the autumn of 1649, ensure that the prospect of staging a campaign to win back his throne from that country disappeared as a realistic option for Charles II. The emotive descriptions of loss of life in the storming of Drogheda and Wexford have become part of Irish national identity and no amount of returning to contemporary records and producing more balanced accounts (even by some Irish historians), no explanations of the conventions of contemporary warfare in Ireland, nor that the majority of those killed at Drogheda were English, and no establishing fine distinctions of reprisals against the defenders and citizenry of both towns, such as in 'cold blood' or 'hot blood', are likely to change opinions entrenched over the centuries.[6] But it is worth pointing out that, as with so much about Cromwell, simple interpretations miss his complexity. Like the majority of Englishmen at the time, his view of Ireland was coloured by the rebellion of 1641 and the long-standing contempt in which the English had held the people of an island they felt they had never fully conquered. Given these prejudices, Cromwell's comment after the massacre at Drogheda, that it was 'a righteous judgement of God upon these barbarous wretches who have imbrued their hands in so much innocent blood', can be seen in a wider context, even if the savagery of what happened still shocks. Yet he would subsequently declare, before he left Ireland in the spring of 1650, that while he might not 'suffer the exercise of the Mass . . . as for the people, what thoughts they have in the matter of religion in their own breasts I cannot reach; but I shall think it my duty, if they walk honestly and peaceably, not to cause them in the least to suffer for the same.'[7]

Cromwell's determined campaign to lift the threat of attack on the new Commonwealth from across the Irish Sea made it inevitable that the new king and his advisers would have to consider other possibilities. Edward Hyde went to Spain in the autumn of 1649 to seek financial assistance from Philip IV; the king was his normal polite but vague self and nothing was forthcoming from that quarter. Charles himself left France in September. He had always intended to go to Jersey for the winter and it was obvious that nothing would be forthcoming from Mazarin, no matter how much Henrietta Maria pleaded. Besides, the queen had still not given up on the idea of a marriage between La Grande Mademoiselle and her son and the thought of another season of dancing attendance on that young lady was more than Charles could stomach. James came with him to the Channel Islands and they enjoyed a few months of freedom, still hoping that Ormonde might salvage the situation in Ireland.

By the early part of 1650 it was obvious that he could not, though he might yet play his part in supplying men for Charles's new enterprise. Ireland was effectively lost to him but Scotland, as Ormonde acknowledged, remained. Shrewd enough to realize that he should not put all his eggs in one basket, the young king had remained in correspondence with the leading aristocratic Covenanter, the marquess of Argyll, and Argyll suggested to the Scottish parliament in the summer of 1649 that negotiations be re-opened with the king. Once it was accepted that the royalist position in Ireland was irretrievable, Charles summoned his advisers to discuss how matters might be taken forward with the Scots. After much wrangling, it was decided to invite the Scots commissioners to treat at Breda, a southern Dutch town with strong ties to the House of Orange, in mid-March 1650.

Charles, leaving a disappointed James behind in command of the Jersey garrison, arrived at Breda from Beauvais in France, where he had spent three weeks in conference with his mother. Once negotiations got under way, he quickly ascertained that the Scottish commissioners were far from united in their outlook towards him and believed that this could be turned to his advantage. By this time, he was well aware of his ability to charm and confident enough to use this as a weapon to quell even the sober supporters of the Scottish Kirk who deplored the fact that he danced the evenings away. The Commonwealth propaganda sheet, *A Brief Relation*, conveying news from republican observers in Breda, noted: "Tis evident still that he perfectly hates them, and neither of them can so dissemble it . . . and 'tis a matter of pleasant observation, to see how they endeavour to cheat and cozen each other. The king strokes them until he can get into the saddle and then he will make them feel his spurs . . ."[8] Charles's assessment of divisions in Scotland was correct but his own position was weaker than he thought. It soon became apparent that he would be arriving in Scotland much more on the Covenanters' terms than his own and that he would be pressed to sacrifice both Ormonde's treaty with the Irish Catholics and the support he had given to the marquess of Montrose, who had landed on the Scottish mainland from Orkney in early April in an ill-fated attempt to rally the royalist cause in Scotland. On 1 May, still unwilling to abandon the Irish treaty or sign the Covenants, Charles accepted the commissioners' invitation to come to Scotland. Afraid that the negotiations would come to nothing, the Scottish commissioners had exceeded their instructions. This might be viewed as at least a temporary victory for the king, though it soon became apparent that a hurried arrangement, entered into with bad faith on both sides, could not have a happy outcome. For Montrose, however, regardless of his monarch's betrayal, time had run out.

The king and council saw Montrose's arrival on the mainland as a sideshow that might make their own bargaining position with the Covenanters stronger. But the marquess, true to his own character and ambitions, viewed it differently. He had scores to settle with his old enemies, men like Argyll and the earl of Loudoun, and he was weary of years of exile in France and northern Europe. The former Covenanter was passionately royalist and still clung to the belief that one last campaign in Scotland would enable him to bring about the triumph of the royalist cause. It was a heroic aim and one that Montrose, who compared himself to Alexander the Great, saw as worthy of his ideals. Alas, his force of about 1,200 men, mostly German and Danish levies, as well as some Orkney islanders, was not reinforced by local recruits as he marched south through Caithness and Sutherland. At Carbisdale on 27 April 1650 he was surprised by an even smaller unit of around 200 Covenanter cavalry and his men faltered and then ran. Montrose escaped, to wander disguised as a shepherd in the stark beauty of the hills of Sutherland, still one of the wildest places in the British Isles. Seeking food and shelter with the local highlanders, whom he mistakenly believed to be on his side, the marquess found himself confined to a dungeon at Ardvreck and then handed over to General David Leslie.[9] On his long journey south, strapped ignominiously to a small horse before he was put on board a boat at Dundee to sail down the coast to Edinburgh, the marquess passed through many places that had figured in his earlier exploits. He was also briefly reunited with his two youngest children, a boy and a girl, in a parting that has echoes of Charles I's last interview with Elizabeth and Henry. The comparison would have pleased Montrose, who knew that he, too, was going to his death.

He landed at Leith, Edinburgh's port, on 18 May and was put in a cart, his hands tied behind his back and his head bare, led by the common hangman up the Royal Mile. Even those who had hated him were moved by his quiet courage in the face of such humiliation. Two weeks earlier, Charles II had ordered him publicly to lay down his arms, though in a private letter he assured Montrose: 'You cannot reasonably doubt of my real intentions to provide for your interest and restitution.'[10] Well might the marquess have reflected on Strafford's words 'Put not your trust in Princes', for the son, like the father, could do nothing to save one of his staunchest supporters. It was left to Louis XIV to plead in vain for Montrose's life. Brought before the Scottish parliament to hear the charges against him, he told them that his care had always been to walk as a good Christian and a loyal subject. But his was not the stern Christianity of the Covenanters. He was denied the honourable death of beheading that he would, as a nobleman, have expected. Instead, he learned that he was to be hanged on a thirty-foot gallows for three hours, and that his body would subsequently be 'headed and quartered'.

Montrose went to his death supremely conscious that it was a public spectacle that would ensure his place in royalist mythology. If he could not live a hero, he would die one and be remembered down through the ages. Clad in a scarlet cloak, his long hair carefully arranged – 'My head is yet my own. I will arrange it to my taste', he told his captors who questioned his toilette – he played out the last drama of his eventful life to perfection on 21 May. Argyll, who had been up all night while his wife gave birth to a daughter, was not present at what he termed 'the tragic end of James Graham'. He did not, however, think that Montrose was sufficiently prepared to enter the next world.

James Graham would have vehemently disagreed with Argyll's uncharitable judgement. He did not lack faith and was content to die, believing himself, like Charles I, to be a martyr. His military style was more that of a marauder than a responsible general and its violence had made him many enemies but he believed he was above them all. Handsome, poetic, egotistic and brave, he knew that he would become the stuff of legend. Of all the royalist firmament, his star shines the brightest still.

*

IF POLITICS IS the art of the possible, Charles II would learn in Scotland just how limited those possibilities were. His great-grandmother, Mary Queen of Scots, has frequently been criticized for her inability to rule her kingdom effectively on the grounds that she was empty-headed, had poor judgement and was simply not equal to the task because of her sex. One can disagree on all these counts, but, more significantly, it should be said that Charles II, who is not generally considered to have the first two failings and was unhampered by the third, lasted a far shorter time in Scotland than Mary did. Like her, he arrived from overseas with the aim of uniting the various factions in loyalty to his person and, like her, he failed. The underlying weakness of his position was its bad faith and he could never shake off the suspicion of the Scottish Covenanters, whether representative of the nobility or the Kirk, that he would abjure the Covenants as soon as he could.

At anchor in the Moray Firth on the evening of 23 June, Charles knew that he could no longer avoid making an unpalatable decision. At first, he said he would only agree to sign with the proviso that the laws of England took precedence. But the commissioners of the Scottish Kirk were in no mood to make any such concession. They had the king where they wanted him and reacted by inserting a new clause requiring him to impose the terms of the Solemn League and Covenant in any future parliamentary legislation in England. Charles had backed himself into a corner. He fumed but gave way and signed. Yet he had no intention of keeping his word and the men who had all but held a gun to his head suspected this from the moment the ink dried. For both sides, it was a hollow victory. But it bought Charles time and on 4 July 1650 the Scottish parliament voted to allow the king the full exercise of government.

As he journeyed south to Falkland Palace in Fife, a fine French-style residence where Mary Queen of Scots had once played tennis on one of Europe's first purpose-built courts, Charles had time to reflect on how little he knew of the rivalries and animosities that characterized Scottish politics. He was, however, in no doubt about the difficulties he faced, writing to the duke of Hamilton in early August that he had been 'so narrowly watched by the severe Christians that I could not answer your letter before now'.[11] He had already noted that the soldiers of Leslie's army seemed well disposed towards him and that this made 'the severe Christians' uncomfortable. The old general was furious when a purge of the army was suggested, lest the king decide to use it for his own purposes. The cracks in Scotland's body politic were already on display.[12] It remained to be seen whether the king could work with the country's leading noblemen to exploit them to his advantage.

William, second duke of Hamilton, brother of the man who had led the Scottish army south to defeat at Preston in 1649, was at that time banished to the Isle of Arran and in no position to help Charles, despite his loyalty to the Stuart cause. The Hamiltons were Scotland's leading aristocratic family, close to the throne through their descent from James II of Scotland and powerful in their Glasgow heartland. William was granted the title at the age of thirty-three following the elder Hamilton's execution by the Commonwealth. As earl of Lanark he had been instrumental in negotiating the terms of the Engagement with Charles I but he and Lauderdale, a close associate, had taken refuge with Charles II at The Hague when deprived of all their offices by the Scottish parliament at the beginning of 1649. Returning with the new king, he was soon targeted as one of the royalists thought by the Kirk party to exercise a bad influence on Charles, and the king could not protect him. It was not, however, just the Kirk party who wanted him out of the way. He had an implacable opponent in Archibald Campbell, marquess of Argyll, the most formidable aristocrat in Scotland and a man without whose support Charles was never going to make any headway.

The king was well aware of Argyll's importance. Shortly before he left the Netherlands, Charles sent a note to Argyll via Charles Seton, earl of Dunfermline, assuring the marquess of 'the confidence I have of you and [I] shall in all matters that

concern this kingdom desire your advice and counsel, being one
that I very much rely on . . . I hope to see you in a few days.'
Dunfermline, who had been one of the Scottish commissioners at
Breda, came from a family whose loyalty to the Stuarts stretched
back to the fifteenth century, so was a natural choice for such a
mission. He was further entrusted, in a set of private instructions,
to raise with Argyll the delicate question of the king's household
in Scotland. Charles wanted Argyll to 'be thinking about settling
my family as the king my father's was'. Family in this sense did
not mean his brothers and sisters, his kindred as they would have
been known, but rather it retained the Tudor sense of household,
personal advisers and servants. For Charles II, as, indeed, for his
new allies in Scotland, this was a highly sensitive issue. At Breda
the king had been given to understand that precious few of those
who made up his exiled court would be acceptable to the Scots
– their Anglican religion and frivolous lifestyle could find no place
in a Covenanted regime. Charles, however, was not about to give
ground. 'You are to speak to my lord of Argyll,' he ordered Dunfermline, 'that there be no exceptions taken at any persons that
come with me, since they may be both useful to me and to this
kingdom and that if there be any particular exceptions to any of
my servants . . . then I should be advertised privately that I may
send them away before there be any public order against them.'
To David Leslie, the battle-worn commander of the Scottish
army, Charles also sent greeting and an assurance of royal esteem.
He realized that 'because the English are come among the Borders he cannot come where I am, but I hope to be with him in
the Army before it be long.'[13] Showing a mix of tact and firmness,
Charles was evidently convinced that his relationship with Argyll
would be key to his success in Scotland. As things stood at the
end of June 1650, it was a reasonable enough assumption but it
was too simplistic. Much as he would have liked, Argyll did not
run Scotland and Charles II did not know him personally. Their
collaboration would prove difficult for both men.

Archibald Campbell, marquess of Argyll, is one of the least-known but most important British figures of the mid-seventeenth century. He divided opinion among contemporaries and has continued to do so subsequently, though he has more recently found a champion in the Scottish historian Allan Macinnes, who has emphasized Argyll's desire for a British federation (which can scarcely make him a hero to modern proponents of Scottish independence) and the European dimension of the Covenanting movement. Seen through layers of contemporary comment, most of it critical and negative, Argyll has often been viewed as representing the most obdurate and unappealing aspects of how a Scottish nobleman could use religion to further his political ambition. His faith was deeply held, however, and if his hopes for a godly Britain sound self-serving, they were not so readily questioned by the English republicans, even if someone like Oliver Cromwell did not share his Presbyterian commitment to the unifying of Church and state.

Physically, Argyll was unprepossessing, with his sharp nose, squint and reddish hair hidden under the close-fitting cap favoured by Scottish Presbyterians. A severe expression added to the general impression of a man who would prefer a two-hour sermon on an Old Testament text to a good dinner. Short, thin and sometimes accused of cowardice, he was the antithesis of his old enemy, Montrose. No one underestimated his intellect but his appearance, as even those who disliked him as much as Clarendon would acknowledge, was deceptive: Argyll was not devoid of social skills. Clarendon wrote:

> Without doubt he was a person of extraordinary cunning, well bred and though by the ill placing of his eyes, he did not appear with any great advantage at first sight, yet he reconciled even those who had aversion to him very strangely by a little conversation . . . His wit was pregnant and his humour gay and pleasant, except when he liked not the company or the argument . . . When the other faction prevailed, in which there were likewise crafty managers, and that his councils

were commonly rejected, he carried himself so, that they who hated him most were willing to compound with him.[14]

These attributes had been honed during a difficult childhood and adolescence. Argyll's mother died when he was very young. His father married again, to a Catholic, and took himself off to the Spanish Netherlands, leaving his son with responsibility for the extensive Argyll estates but reserving their revenues for himself. This burden and his father's criticism from afar led to a rift that was never repaired. The elder Argyll (appropriately known as Archibald the Grim) told Charles I, when he returned from exile to live in London, to expect nothing from his estranged son. He was 'a man of craft, subtlety and falsehood and can love no man; and if ever he finds it in his power to do you mischief, he will be sure to do it.'[15] The father's vilification of his son's character is deeply unpleasant and certainly turned Charles I against the young Lord Lorne, the title Argyll held until his father's death in 1638, at a time when the king's troubles in Scotland were about to become apparent. The younger Argyll meanwhile had been brought up by his cousin, the earl of Morton, and was generous in his acknowledgement of what he owed to Morton, both in terms of personal affection and advice. So it was perfectly natural that he should marry Morton's daughter, Margaret, and settle down to a happy family life with her.

He and his wife lived graciously and their establishment could stand comparison with any south of the border, according to an unlikely source. Anne Halkett, the lady who had helped Prince James escape from England in the spring of 1648, was herself in Scotland in the summer of 1650. Still in love with Bampfield, whom she resolutely refused to believe was married, she had been supported, at her lover's request, by the earl of Dunfermline and had brought herself to the attention of Charles II when he reached Fife. Her travels also took her to Edinburgh and she recounted the following tale of her encounter with Argyll and his family:

When I had been two or three days in the town I received a
visit from the earl of Argyll, who invited me to his house and
the next day sent his coach for me, which I made use of to
wait upon his lady. When I came upstairs I was met in the
outward room by my Lady Anne Campbell [Argyll's daugh-
ter], a sight that I must confess did so much surprise me that
I could hardly believe I was in Scotland. For she was very
handsome, exceedingly obliging and her behaviour and dress
was equal to any that I had seen in the court of England. This
gave me so good impressions of Scotland that I began to see
that it had been much injured by those who represented it
under another character than what I found it. When I was
brought in to my lady Argyll, I saw then where her daughter
had derived her beauty and civility; one was under some
decay but the other was so evident and so well proportioned
that while she gave to others she reserved what was due to
herself.[16]

Lady Argyll might not have been entirely flattered by Anne's
description but it is likely that she, like other Scottish aristocrats,
was well aware of the condescension of the English towards them.
Nor did Charles II share Anne Halkett's open-mindedness.[17] He
subsequently deplored the lack of sophistication and bigotry of
the Scots, claiming that he saw no women while he was there and
that the people, ignorant and uncultured, even thought it sinful to
play the violin.[18]

Musical interludes were scarcely the king's concern as the
summer progressed in Scotland and he was soon to discover that
Argyll's influence over the Kirk party was not strong enough to
give him any meaningful assistance. There was immediate tension
about Charles's entourage and he exacerbated matters by insisting
on visiting the army under Leslie, encamped near Edinburgh.
The Kirk party and their supporters in parliament had tried to
keep him out of harm's way at Falkland Palace, but Charles grew
restive and decided to interfere in military matters. The common

soldiers, to the consternation of more austere Presbyterians, gave him a rousing welcome. As Charles drew in the Stuart charm to try to win over the ordinary people of Scotland, more extreme Presbyterians feared complete loss of control of this wayward and untrustworthy young man. The determination of the General Assembly of the Kirk to bring Charles to heel was heightened by the arrival of Cromwell's invading army in Scotland. A new declaration of support for the Covenants, with forthright criticism of Charles I and Henrietta Maria and their conduct, was drawn up for him to sign. It was far more unpalatable than the agreement he had made at Breda and it was only after persuasion from an increasingly desperate Argyll, and a mild watering down of the insult to his parents, that he agreed to sign it and, very reluctantly, to be rid of those of his household especially targeted by the Kirk. Humiliated and angry, he left for Perth and seriously considered returning to the Netherlands, abandoning Scotland altogether. His letter to Edward Nicholas requesting that a boat be sent to convey him away was dated 3 September 1650. As he wrote it, he did not know that Oliver Cromwell was annihilating the Scottish army at Dunbar. The defeat left the Kirk party in disarray and the shocked Scottish politicians turned back to their young king as a unifying figure. Charles would, after all, stay.

Cromwell left Ireland at the end of May. He was in London for barely three weeks before being ordered to Scotland by the Council of State, anxious to save the Commonwealth from the threat of invasion. The theatre of war there was new to him. He had spent time in northern England but this was his first venture into Scotland. On a personal level, he had been content to let the Scots retain their independence politically but he opposed the commitment of men like Argyll to turn the whole of the British Isles into a Presbyterian state under a Stuart monarchy, even one with very restricted powers. Both sides accused each other of breaking the Solemn League and Covenant. 'There may be a Covenant made with death and hell,' Cromwell sternly reminded the Scots, adding, 'I will not say yours was so. But judge if such things have a politic aim, to avoid the overflowing scourge, or to accomplish worldly interests.' Piqued, the Scots responded in kind: 'We take not upon us to judge you in anything otherwise than by your carriage and fruits. These we see and know to be bitter as worm-wood and gall.'[19] The uncompromising vocabulary underlined the depths of the betrayal felt by both sides.

The campaign in Scotland gave every indication of being the most difficult Cromwell had yet encountered. He was unwell, the Scots offered fierce resistance and David Leslie, their com-mander, refused to give battle. By the end of August, as desertion, dysentery and supply difficulties weakened the English, his force was twice that of Cromwell's. Unusually for a general who had enjoyed such success throughout the Civil Wars in England and most recently in Ireland, Cromwell had got his strategy wrong. His letter to Arthur Haselrig, governor of Newcastle, quoted at the beginning of this chapter, hints at desperation. It is therefore all the more staggering that at Dunbar, hemmed in by the Scots, his men dropping like flies in the wet, cold weather and entirely dependent on intermittent supplies from the sea, Cromwell won his greatest victory. Ably supported by John Lambert, he launched an attack on the Scots before dawn on 3 September and found, as he had calculated, that his enemy was unprepared for the fero-ciousness of his assault. As with his other notable victories in England, the cavalry played a crucial part but Cromwell, who, despite his confidence, is said to have bitten his lip so badly that it bled before the attack on the Scottish right wing started, knew to whom the victory should be ascribed. The Scots had been made 'by the Lord of Hosts as stubble to their swords'. He and Leslie had fought together at Marston Moor six years earlier. Now Leslie lost 3,000 dead and 10,000 prisoners. Cromwell claimed only a few score dead from the New Model Army, but he probably under-stated his losses.

Leslie retired with the remnants of his army – some 5,000 men – to Stirling, where he was soon joined by an array of fright-ened Scottish politicians, religious ministers and Edinburgh merchants concerned for their safety. Leaving Lambert to secure Scotland's capital, Cromwell pursued them, arriving outside Stirling on 18 September. Leslie refused to surrender, but there was to be no Scottish equivalent of Wexford or Drogheda. Cromwell did not want further loss of life and he still hoped to win round public opinion in Scotland. He preferred to consolidate his gains in southern Scotland rather than attempt one more hammer blow. The scale of their defeat split the Scots and left the policies of the Kirk party in tatters. This should have played into the hands of Charles II but the Committee of Estates, the executive of the Scottish body politic, stubborn to the last, reacted to the defeat at Dunbar and decided to remove a further twenty-four members of the king's household and replace them with their own, more trustworthy Covenanters. Charles was in despair. Argyll, despite the promise of a dukedom, had delivered nothing for him and the west of Scotland, which it was hoped he could control, broke with the authorities in Edinburgh to form a separate military association. It was time for the king to try a different course.

*

CHARLES's disappearance from Stirling on 4 October, in a vain attempt to join up with disaffected royalists from north-eastern Scotland, was ill considered and poorly executed. As a leader, the king had yet to demonstrate maturity. He had dithered so badly about whether to go or stay and talked too freely about the possibility to people he could not trust that he never stood a chance of achieving success. But he had also alarmed the political establishment in Edinburgh, who dealt with him more leniently than he might have expected. Though a force of 6,000 horsemen was sent to recover him, the request for his return was tactfully put and he was not sorry to leave his temporary refuge, a hovel in Glen Clova in Angus, to return to the comparative comforts of Stirling. And thereafter, to his relief, his position appeared to be improving. He presided over the regular meetings of the Committee of Estates and was thus finally able to influence policy. No further assaults were made on the composition of his household. Yet while he could explain away his flight, euphemistically known as 'the Start', to the faltering Kirk party, the men of the west had had enough of his duplicity. Denouncing Charles in a document known as the 'Western Remonstrance', they described the king as ungodly and accepted that the Covenanters should not interfere in English politics – once Cromwell's occupying forces had been removed from Scottish soil. The timing and, indeed, the success of such a goal was less clear than the language in which it was described. Cromwell, ably supported by Lambert and General George Monck, was entrenched in the south of Scotland, waiting out the winter, while the Scots, embroiled in further disputes among themselves and the Scottish army, fragmented.[20] 'It cannot be denied,' wrote one despairing Scottish commentator at the end of 1650, 'that our miseries and dangers of ruin are greater than for many ages have been.'[21] Such gloom was not universal. The main beneficiary of all this wrangling was the twenty-year-old king and, as the New Year dawned in Scotland, his position was further strengthened by his long-awaited coronation.

This took place on 1 January 1651, at Scone just outside Perth, the traditional crowning place of Scottish kings. Not only was it to be the last coronation performed in Scotland, it was also the only ceremony performed using a Presbyterian rite. The church there, on the site of the ancient one destroyed by a mob of supporters of John Knox nearly a century before, dated only from 1624 and was itself pulled down in the late eighteenth century. The 1624 edifice was small for a coronation (a door had to be built to enable Charles to come out onto a platform so that he could be greeted by onlookers) and was probably hung with tapestries for the occasion. But the Covenanters were not men who would have countenanced the richness of an Anglican coronation in Westminster. There was to be no anointing and the sermon, given by Robert Douglas, moderator of the Assembly of the Kirk, emphasized the importance of the Covenants and did not spare Charles II a homily on the misdeeds of his predecessors.

The king may have thought that this and many other scriptural allusions were worth enduring for the theatrical aspects of the ceremony, which he seems to have enjoyed.

He entered the church dressed in crimson velvet, the Honours (regalia) of Scotland borne by the leading peers of the realm. The crown was carried by Argyll, the spurs by the earl of Eglinton and Lord Rothes was the bearer of the sword of state. Argyll had made sure that Charles would not forget the role of the Campbells in his kingdom. The pearl-encrusted crown was offered to the king by his kinsman, John Campbell, the earl of Loudoun, and placed on Charles's head by Argyll himself. The oath he took left no room for creative interpretation. By now enveloped in the purple robe of a monarch, he avowed 'my allowance and approbation of the National Covenant and of the Solemn League and Covenant . . . and faithfully oblige myself, to prosecute the ends thereof . . . and that I for myself and successors shall . . . fully establish Presbyterial government . . . in the kingdom of Scotland . . . enjoining the same in my other dominions. And that I shall observe these in my own practice and family . . .' Having thus sworn, Charles also signed the two Covenants again, 'both being drawn up in a fair parchment'.[22] The ceremony lasted more than three hours and the king, despite all his trappings and the acclamation he received, must have been relieved when it was over and he could return to Perth. He announced subsequently that he had much joy that he was the first Covenanted king of Scotland. It may have been what his listeners wanted to hear but it was far from the truth. For the time being, however, he had got what he wanted – official recognition of his status as king of Scotland. During the remainder of the winter he spent time with the reconstituted Scottish army and was buoyed by the support of Hamilton, who, like a number of other leading Engagers and royalists, had made an uneasy peace with their Presbyterian opponents in the cause of promoting national unity.

Cromwell was ill during the winter of 1650–1 and was content to sit the cold weather out in southern Scotland. By the spring and early summer he was ready to move again and he and his subordinates did so with considerable success, removing the Scots from Fife. By the end of July he was encamped before Perth. The city surrendered to him on 2 August. Two days earlier, the king, the Scottish army and some members of the Committee of Estates had left Stirling, headed south into England. For Charles II, king of Scotland but of England only in name, it was a last throw of the dice. As the duke of Hamilton noted after the royalist retreat from Stirling: 'We must either starve, disband or go with a handful of men into England. This last seems to be the least ill yet it appears very desperate to me.'[23] His words proved to be tragically prophetic.

*

THE CITY OF Worcester sits on two rivers, the Severn and the Teme, in the heart of England. There had been a cathedral on a prominent site above the Severn since the seventh century, though by 1651 it was much rebuilt. It contained the tombs of King John, one of England's most notorious monarchs, and the short-lived Prince Arthur, eldest son of Henry VII. The city's strategic importance meant that its inhabitants were no strangers to the upheavals of the Civil Wars. The first serious engagement of the conflict, in 1642, had taken place at Powick Bridge just outside Worcester, when Prince Rupert's cavalry had routed their parliamentarian opponents. If Charles II recalled this skirmish, he might have hoped that it was a good omen. He had not necessarily intended to make a stand at Worcester but by early September his situation gave him no choice.

The king left Scotland with 12,000 men under his command and with David Leslie as his lieutenant-general. Argyll and Loudoun, believing the invasion to be ill judged, stayed behind, though the earl of Lauderdale rode with him. The king's childhood friend the second duke of Buckingham and Henry Wilmot, later earl of Rochester, were the leading English members of his entourage. The belief was that the north of England would rise to swell his numbers but though there was some residual sympathy for the royalist cause in the north-west, the king was at the head of a Scottish army and the memory of the depredations of Scottish forces earlier in the Civil Wars remained strong. There was no upsurge of support for Charles II, only the fear of a plundering army and doubts about the intentions of a monarch who was still very much an unknown quantity, perfectly content, or so it seemed, to inflict these much detested plunderers on civilians yet again. His claim as rightful king seemed irrelevant to many of the populace who simply wanted peace and stability.

By the time that the king reached Worcester, on 22 August, his men were exhausted after three weeks of marching and illness was spreading amongst them. Neither were they as well equipped as their opponents, generals Lambert and Harrison, who had relentlessly picked off stragglers while marking the king's forces as they made their way down through England. Their numbers were roughly the same as Charles's army but they were about to be joined by a much larger contingent under Cromwell himself, which had come down through Yorkshire. Their combined forces were about 31,000 strong. Charles was still hopeful of royalist sympathizers joining him from the West Country and the Isle of Man but the Commonwealth's highly efficient military intelligence had alerted the Council of State to the danger and Colonel Robert Lilburne was able to deprive Charles of 1,500 reinforcements recruited by the earl of Derby when he confronted and routed them at Wigan. This was a bitter blow but, as Charles's army drew breath and worked on repairing Worcester's defences, the king could not accept that all was lost. And Cromwell, keen to avoid considerable loss of life despite his superior numbers, was well aware that the two rivers, the city's natural defences, would prove a difficult obstacle. So he took his time, using bridges of boats to span both the Teme and the Severn and laying planks for the cavalry to cross. His many victories had made him confident of God's providence, of divine approval for his cause, but he knew that the day would not be easily won.

On 3 September 1651, exactly a year after he had routed the Scots at Dunbar, Oliver Cromwell moved against them again at Worcester. It proved as demanding a battle as any he had fought and it was also the longest. From early afternoon to dusk, the fighting raged in and around the city. Charles, who climbed the tower of the cathedral, had a better vantage point than the combatants on the ground and he could see that his troops were offering fierce resistance. He also spotted that there were weaknesses, particularly in the Commonwealth's centre and right, and decided to lead a hastily assembled force in person to take advantage. This courageous manoeuvre was not ultimately successful, but it forced Cromwell to return to the aid of his right flank. After several hours of fighting the royalists began to give ground. To Charles's amazement, Leslie refused to let his cavalry come to their aid at this crucial point of the battle. The action now raged through the streets of Worcester until nightfall when, despite the king's last-ditch attempts to rally his troops, it was apparent that the day was lost. At around six in the evening, the king was prevailed upon to flee for his life.

Royalist losses were about 2,000 men, but many more, perhaps as many as 7,000, were taken prisoner. Cromwell lost under 200. Leslie and Lauderdale were taken prisoner and the earl of Derby, instrumental in ensuring Charles II's escape, was eventually executed for treason, despite Cromwell's appeal to parliament that he should be shown mercy. The most immediate casualty was the duke of Hamilton, who died of gangrene five days after the battle. He had been wounded in the leg, the decision to amputate, which might have saved his life, made too late after an argument between the king's surgeon and Cromwell's. His last letter to his wife is a moving testament to his love for her and his acceptance of death: 'You know I have been long labouring, though in great weakness to be prepared against this expected change, and I thank my God I find comfort in it, in this my day of trial; for my body is not more weakened by my wounds, than I find my spirit comforted and supported by the infinite mercies and great love of my Blessed redeemer, who will be with me to the end and in the end . . .'[24] He, too, was buried in Worcester Cathedral.

Cromwell called the hard-fought victory at Worcester 'a crowning mercy'. It was his last battle and the end of a remarkable military career, quite unlike any other in British history, for a man who, only nine years previously, had no experience of command. But for the many Scottish prisoners, transported to the colonies of the New World and whose fate is frequently overlooked in the romantic tales of the escape of Charles II after the battle, the outcome of Worcester – the ending of the third Civil War, as it is sometimes known – was not merciful at all.

*

AND WHAT OF CHARLES? 'Of his royal person,' wrote a Scottish officer imprisoned in Chester after the battle, 'I can give no farther account. But certainly a braver prince never lived . . .'[25] The king's personal courage was not, alas, matched by any degree of forward-thinking about how his escape might be managed if the day went against him. By early evening, with fighting raging all around him in the streets of Worcester, it was imperative for him to leave. So he slipped out of the city and headed north, the only way that, at least for the time being, offered him hope of eluding Cromwell's forces. Capture would almost certainly mean death.

By the king's own account dictated years later to Samuel Pepys, there was disagreement among the small knot of royalists, including Buckingham and Wilmot, who managed to get away with Charles. Some thought he should go back to Scotland though Charles preferred London as a destination. Quite what he thought he could do in London, other than hide out among its large population, is not clear. His father's confidence in being able to raise the capital in support was always misplaced. While the group hesitated, got lost in the dark and was nearly taken by a detachment of Cromwellian cavalry, the earl of Derby made a decision. He had hidden at Boscobel House while on his way to join the king at Worcester, recovering from the wounds he sustained at Wigan. It was in a remote location, surrounded by woodland, on the borders of Staffordshire and Shropshire. Its owners, the Giffard family, were Catholics and used to hiding recusant priests. He was confident that they would shelter and protect the king. There, after a false start in the direction of Wales (Charles had, by now, changed his mind as to his destination), the king famously spent a night in the branches of an oak tree, in exhausted slumber, leaning on the numbed arm of a royalist soldier, Colonel William Carlos, who had fought to the end at Worcester before getting away to Boscobel himself. Those searching for him were only feet away, as the king recalled: 'While we were in this tree we see soldiers going up and down, in the thicket of the wood, searching for persons escaped, we seeing them now and then peeping out of the wood.'[26]

Charles was exhausted and often ravenously hungry. Dependent for food on the supplies brought to him by members of the Penderel family, who were tenants of the Giffards, he knew his peril only too well.

The king had little knowledge of the life of Catholic recusants, of their constant experience of discrimination and their need for subterfuge in the exercise of their religious beliefs. He was impressed by their quiet determination to keep him safe but he could not pass many more nights in trees. He must get away. And to do so he needed an effective disguise and to ensure that he did not attract attention. The price of £1,000 on his head might be a temptation even for those who might otherwise be inclined to keep their doubts about his identity quiet. Above all, he needed to travel in the company of someone he could trust. The person found to fulfil this difficult responsibility was a woman, Jane Lane, the sister of Colonel Lane, a royalist officer who was a friend of Wilmot's. Jane already had a pass for herself and a servant to visit a pregnant friend before the battle of Worcester. This could now be used as a means of conveying Charles further away from the danger, into the West Country, where there was hope of finding a ship that could take him to France.

Disguised, not altogether convincingly, as Jane's manservant (he had to be shown how to help a lady to mount a horse) Charles rode with her to Abbots Leigh, near Bristol, the home of the Norton family, where they arrived on 12 September. As England's second largest port it seemed to offer the real possibility of escape, but a boat could not be found. There was danger in staying in any one place too long and soon they removed to Trent Manor in Somerset. There Jane left him on 18 September and returned to her home. Helped by a succession of royalist sympathizers and Catholic families, Charles spent more than a month making his way along the Channel coast. He was recognized several times but nobody gave him away, a testimony to residual loyalty to the royal family and to Charles's own capacity to charm those he met.

The fugitive king eventually took ship with Wilmot from Shoreham-by-Sea in Sussex on 15 October, arriving at Fécamp in Normandy the next day. He always took delight in recounting his adventures so that they acquired an element of Cavalier glamour which remains to this day. In so doing, he turned the disaster of Worcester into a tale of derring-do, a kind of romanticized legend.[27] Of one thing, however, he was certain. When his uncle, the duke of Orléans, asked him if he intended to return to Scotland, his reply was robust: 'I had rather have been hanged first.' He would never set foot in Scotland again, preferring to leave it to its fate as a country unwillingly united with England during the 1650s and pointedly never visiting it during his reign. Oliver Cromwell, his nemesis at Worcester, returned to great popular acclamation in London, a reception that made some in parliament uneasy about his future role and intentions.

Charles II was now faced with the unpalatable realization that his life could be one of permanent exile. The marquess of Ormonde, who had left Ireland for France at the end of 1650, reluctantly accepting that he could play no further part there that would assist his sovereign, remarked on hearing of the defeat at

Worcester: 'His [God] not blessing all our endeavours in so just a cause I would fain understand to be a command to stand still and see the salvation He will work for us.' It was a typically measured comment, an acceptance of the inevitable that did not quite yet discount the possibility of a change of fortune in the future. For Charles II, a king without a country, his pride not yet recovered from the dismal experience of trying to rule in Scotland, it was cold comfort. Ormonde was the leading aristocrat among the exiles and he was entirely committed to Charles II in the 1650s. He could offer much valuable advice but little practical support as his wife negotiated with Cromwell to be allowed to keep her share of their Irish estates. For financial aid, Charles needed to look elsewhere. During the following nine very trying years he and his siblings would be heavily dependent on the loyalty, love and support of their sister Mary, Princess of Orange. Her own life had been far from easy and a recent change in her circumstances threatened to make it more difficult still.

CHAPTER TWELVE

The Protestant Princess

'Her daughter-in-law . . . will spend all his estate upon her
family and party; she and they have undone her son.'

Views attributed to Princess Amalia of Orange on the
treatment of her grandson, the future William III of England

'A nest of malignant vipers. The Princess Royal's and Queen
of Bohemia's court nourishes those creatures.'

Report of Cromwell's spymaster, John Thurloe, 1651

THE FIRST SHOT OF the Civil Wars had not been fired when the
Princess Royal left England with her mother in March 1642 to
join her husband, Prince William of Orange, in The Hague. She
was still a child, bewildered, stubborn and proud. There was nothing endearing about the ten-year-old Mary and, even if there had
been, it is unlikely that her mother-in-law would have acknowledged it, so determined was Princess Amalia not to appear
inferior in any way to the English royal family. The union between
Orange and Stuart, one of the most important dynastic matches
in mid-seventeenth-century Europe, was to play a significant part
in shaping the future of the continent but few recognized this at
the time, least of all the child bride. In the last century, the Dutch
historian Pieter Geyl viewed the Stuart influence on Dutch affairs
as baleful and it is true that few of his compatriots have had much

positive to say about the Princess Royal. Their reservations are understandable and have a good deal to do with the princess's personality as well as her unashamed disdain for her new country. She was not an easy girl to like and the disaster which befell her family put a great strain on an acclimatization that was never going to be easy. This was unfortunate because, as has recently been shown, there was a thread of support for royalism and concern for the plight of the Stuarts among Dutch poets and dramatists.[1] Mary failed to use this effectively. Unlike her elder brother, Charles II, she was not adaptable. But she had good qualities that have been overlooked, the most important of which were an unswerving loyalty to the Stuart cause and devotion to her son.

Mary grew to adulthood without the guidance of her parents but she was not friendless as she matured. The relationship with her mother was always a distant one, made more difficult over the years by Mary's strict adherence to the Protestantism of her father. In the United Provinces of the Netherlands she found a more comfortable maternal figure in Elizabeth of Bohemia, a warm-hearted and supportive aunt who had brought up a large family in exile and understood the difficulties of living in a strange land. The welfare of 'my deare neece', as Elizabeth, using the creative spelling of the time, often referred to Mary in her letters, was close to the heart of Charles I's elder sister. Mary was more fortunate than she realized in having her aunt and a flock of cousins in the same country. They had many interests in common and were able to offer the emotional support that the highly strung Mary needed. If Elizabeth could not change Mary's tendency to depression or moderate her questionable political judgement in dealing with Dutch affairs, she was always a foil to the hyper-critical Amalia, a malignant viper if ever there was one.

The members of the princess's English entourage also provided a sense of connection with the country she had left behind, though it is debatable whether, in the sense of allowing Mary to come to terms with her adopted country, this was necessarily a good thing. The princess was, in fact, the first royalist exile of the

Civil Wars and the sense of dislocation never really left her. However much she might feel comforted by the sermons of her Anglican chaplain, Thomas Browne, who replaced John Durie in the mid-1640s, or flattered by the advice and attentions of Katherine Stanhope and Katherine's Dutch husband, the baron van Heenvliet, the lively court of The Hague and her several beautiful country houses could never compensate for the sorrow she felt at leaving England.

Had she been a few years older, and more open-minded, Mary might have been able to appreciate the more positive aspects of life in the small northern European state that had fought its way, through a prolonged period of rebellion in the previous century, to independence from the Spanish Habsburgs that was finally recognized in 1609. So it was a young nation, made up of seven different provinces, established uneasily on the basis of a truce lasting twelve years which the Spanish, manipulating religious and political tensions, sought to undermine.[2] Mary's father-in-law, Frederick Henry, spent much of his time involved in a series of military confrontations with the Spanish that, paradoxically, strengthened his own position as stadtholder of Holland, the most powerful of the seven provinces, while threatening to undermine the stability of the new republic as a whole.[3] Trade was key to the survival and prosperity of the United Provinces and the constant interruptions of what seemed like a war without end, coupled with the different priorities of the individual provinces, prolonged the uncertainty. War was expensive and while the majority of politicians in the representative bodies, known as 'states', in the individual provinces believed that a negotiated peace was the best way to ensure long-term security, it took until 1648 for the Treaty of Münster to bring about a lasting peace. Even then Zeeland refused to sign but the treaty went ahead.

Against this backdrop of uncertainty it is not surprising that the Stuarts, whose dynasty in Scotland went back to the late fourteenth century, entertained doubts about the viability of the Dutch republic and that Henrietta Maria viewed it primarily as a source of cash to bolster her husband's dispute with his own rebels. Charles I and his wife had married their eldest daughter into a republic, distasteful in itself, and one that might not last. Their need for financial support, and the fact that the Calvinism of the United Provinces would sit well with Puritans in England, made Mary something of a sacrificial victim. Unfortunately, this is how she always saw herself. But republicanism, at least at the court of Frederick Henry and his wife, did not necessarily mean deprivation.

Eager to take his place among European royalty, protocol and hierarchy were strictly observed at court in a manner which would surely have pleased Charles I. Frederick Henry and his wife were also keen patrons of the arts, including drama, painting and sculpture, collectors of books and, in Princess Amalia's case, determined to show that their gardens could match those of other European royal houses. Their interests may have been designed to enhance their own standing, both in the republic and beyond, but they were an indication of the future cultural development of the United Provinces as a whole. Mary could not have known that the Dutch were about to enter into a period of great cultural achievement, a flowering of art that would exceed anything that her father, a collector rather than a connoisseur, had achieved in England. It is worth remembering that, in the year the reluctant little bride arrived at The Hague, Rembrandt painted one of the greatest of his works, *The Night Watch*.[4] Their talent for trade, their inventiveness, their formidable navy and their capacity for hard work would make the Dutch a world power, to the considerable consternation of the English and the French, after the mid-seventeenth century.

This was not yet apparent when Frederick Henry died in 1647, leaving his twenty-one-year-old son, Mary's husband, as head of the House of Orange. Unhappily for William, he was presented with problems that his father never had to face. The most pressing of these was how to exert his authority at a time of peace, when the ill-defined role of stadtholder was not so obviously needed and when his own desire to help his wife's family was likely to be increasingly at odds with the preoccupations of Dutch politicians who expected to exercise more power in the republic. It would have taken a much more experienced leader than the hot-headed, belligerent William to solve this conundrum and his solution was to bring the republic to the brink of civil war.

Yet even before this crisis, Mary did not find much solace in the company of her husband. The fairy-tale boy and girl romance of their marriage in 1641 did not achieve its promise of happiness. This was not because Princess Amalia came between them. Young William did not get on with his mother either, refusing to take her advice in foreign affairs and generally resenting her attempts at interference. Mary and her husband seem simply to have grown apart, or, perhaps, never to have grown together at all. Aside from differences in temperament and age, the fact that Mary was surrounded by an overwhelmingly English household made it difficult for her to acclimatize. She seems never to have bothered to learn more than a few words of Dutch or to try to understand the complex politics of the United Provinces. She spoke in French at official occasions and this was the language she had in common with Prince William. Then there was the delicate question of when the young couple should start to live together as man and wife. Lady Stanhope was under strict instructions from Mary's father that the marriage must not be consummated before the princess reached the age of fourteen. Even then, she would have been a year younger than her own mother when Henrietta Maria married Charles I. A nurse was stationed in Mary's bedroom with the express purpose of guarding the princess's virginity and there was alarm, as well as some very sharp reproaches, when it was discovered at the beginning of 1644 that William had managed to gain access to Mary's chamber 'where he lay with her highness all night'. A furious Katherine Stanhope issued sharp reprimands to the servants who had connived to allow this clandestine visit but could do little more when it was made clear that William had discussed his intentions with both his parents and had their consent. Although Mary had not yet reached the age of puberty, Lady Stanhope watched anxiously for signs of pregnancy, hoping to be able to report these to Henrietta Maria. Amalia van Solms also looked to her daughter-in-law to safeguard the family's position and her tardiness in this respect only added to the friction between the two women.

The lack of a child was perfectly explicable. Mary did not start menstruating until early 1647 and when she did it was not long until she conceived. A miscarriage in October of that year ended her first pregnancy sorrowfully in what was a difficult year for the House of Orange. Not until the beginning of 1650, so far as is known, did Mary become pregnant again. By that time her husband was deeply enmeshed with helping the Stuarts, more out of his own volition that any personal obligation he seems to have felt for Mary. Unfortunately for Charles II, there was a limit to the financial and practical aid he could expect from William, however well intentioned the young Dutch stadtholder might have been. For the Orange family, their link with the Stuarts was a double-edged sword: it had definitely enhanced their authority, both in the Netherlands and beyond, but it also brought them into conflict with the local authorities, especially in the powerful province of Holland, at a time when the country's leading politicians were determined to uphold the ideals of republicanism for which they had struggled so long against Spanish domination. William II of Orange, Mary's husband, saw himself as the leading Dutch noble, a claim that his cousin, William Frederick, count of Nassau-Dietz and stadtholder of Friesland, might have disputed but chose, for the time being, not to challenge. William II, thanks to his father's military successes and political acumen, had influence and access. What he did not have was sovereign power. A Dutch official wrote a letter explaining this to the French ambassador in the 1630s:

The Prince of Orange is in a position different from the King [of France], who has only to express his wishes. Here he [the prince] needs money to put his ideas into effect, and this goes slowly; it can be obtained only from the provinces . . . by a persuasive demonstration of some major advantage . . . in the midst of such a diversity of interests and opinions, His Highness [the prince] must come to a decision and then, gradually clearing the way, bring matters to where they should be. This cannot be done without much controversy and loss of time.[5]

So here was the nub for a young, restless stadtholder like William II. The political system of the United Provinces of the Netherlands required patience and subtlety and a wiser head than he possessed to make it work to his advantage. Such a system was anathema to the Stuart ideals of kingship and authority so it is small wonder that Princess Mary was unsympathetic to it. Absorbed in a personal vendetta against the Spanish, whom he loathed, William II made overtures to the French (who were in no better a position to help him than they were the Stuarts) and was determined to get the monies he needed to support a war from the Dutch states-general. In the two years after the death of his father, he pushed this agenda tirelessly. He might have got his way, despite considerable misgivings about the advisability of abandoning the republic's policy of peace, were it not for the obduracy of the States of Holland, the province's legislature. By the autumn of 1649, William had decided to use the army to break Holland's resistance and to arrest the men whom he considered to be his main opponents.

Despite his nature, the young stadtholder was compelled to bide his time. This was partly because he hoped to act in concert with his cousin, William Frederick, but it was also because he needed time to sway public opinion in his favour. There was strong support at popular level, at least in parts of the United Provinces, for the House of Orange and there was a strain of support for royalism among Dutch poets and dramatists that has been largely overlooked in the emphasis on Dutch republicanism. William intended to milk such sentiments as much as he could.

His use of pamphlet propaganda brought to mind the importance of this tool in the English Civil Wars. But Prince William was playing a dangerous game. Dismayed by his uncompromising attitude and sensing an opportunity to sow discord, the Spanish government considered the option of offering its support to the recalcitrant Hollanders. There appeared to be a similar threat to the Orangists in July 1650, when a forged document purporting to demonstrate a secret pact between the English parliament and Holland was circulated widely. Its offer of a fleet and 10,000 men to overthrow the stadtholder caused considerable alarm. So it was that in the summer of 1650 William's entire attention was focussed on a daring attempt to impose his political will on the republic. His wife's pregnancy, on which the future of his family depended, was not in the forefront of his mind as he laid his plans for what would have amounted to a *coup d'état* against the Hollanders. He arrested six of his leading opponents but had no intention of stopping there. An attempt to use military force to bring about Holland's submission failed dramatically on 30 July 1650, when a substantial army of 12,000 men under William Frederick of Friesland managed to get lost in foggy weather and were spotted by a postal courier who was able to alert the Amsterdam city authorities, who shut their gates just in time.

It was evident that some compromise was needed and one was duly achieved the following month, with the removal of some deputies implacably hostile to William and the stadtholder himself, who had lost more face than he might have liked to admit, agreeing to back down on the requirement for an immediate and all-out military campaign against Spain. He had not, however, given up and continued his discussions with the French while hoping to win round his opponents in Amsterdam in due course. Yet his actions caused widespread unease, even among pro-Orangists in other provinces, and his own mother disapproved of the attempts at rapprochement with France, believing neutrality to be a better option. How this uncomfortable stalemate might have eventually resolved itself is unclear but William did not live to realize his dream of transforming the fortunes of his family and establishing it as the undisputed authority in the Netherlands.

He had been a supportive brother-in-law to Charles II and the duke of York, sheltering them, expending money well beyond his means and encouraging their aims. In this, he was certainly at one with his wife but their personal relationship remained distant. In the last months of her pregnancy, he saw little of her, preferring to hunt with his close friends. William had many enemies and the stories of his drinking and womanizing may be overstated but the rosy picture of his marriage to Mary presented by Victorian writers is some way from the truth. Married so young and with a mother so resentful of his wife, their relationship stood little chance of success from the outset. Had he lived to see his child born perhaps they would have grown closer, but it was not to be. William returned to The Hague from his hunting trip at the end of October 1650 feeling unwell and feverish. Soon it was apparent that he had contracted smallpox and his wife, heavily pregnant and horrified by the danger to her husband's life, was kept well away from him. He died on 6 November, plunging the Netherlands into political uncertainty and Mary into grief and despair. 'My poor neece,' wrote Elizabeth of Bohemia to her son Charles Louis, 'is the most afflicted creature that ever I saw and is changed as she is nothing but skin and bone.'[6] But she went on to say that the pregnancy itself seemed to be proceeding normally and, as the mother of thirteen children herself, noted shrewdly that, although the baby was due in fifteen days, she believed that the birth was imminent.

In an age given to hyperbole and when it was only considered right and proper to heighten the sense of lamentation, the oration preached at William's funeral strikes us today as massively overstated but it did contain some truths about Mary's vulnerability, characterizing it as a further blow to the Stuart cause:

But all words fail us when we come to cast our eyes on the desolate young princess; young a widow, and with child, and sooner a widow than a mother! How many swords have pierced her soul! How many calamities have beaten upon her, like so many crowding waves, one upon the back of another! What deeps has she seen rolling over her and ready to swallow her! She has nothing to direct her eyes to but heaven, for she can never so little cast her eyes down to the earth, but she finds herself obliged to groan for horror and horror of heart; a mother in banishment; a brother in trouble; a father upon the scaffold, and to fill the measure brimful, a husband in a coffin.[7]

Yet all was not quite lost. The young widow had one very important duty to perform before she could begin to adapt to this major change in her life. On 14 November 1650 she gave birth to a healthy son. It was her nineteenth birthday.

*

HER BROTHER the king, then still in Scotland, wrote anxiously to Katherine Stanhope:

> I have been so long and am so well acquainted with you to believe you need to be entreated to take care of my sister, especially at this time when she hath so much need. Yet because there are not many things in my power by which I may make the affection and kindness I have for her appear, and this may be one, I cannot choose but tell you I shall put the service you do her upon my account . . . How my sister does for her health, and with what discretion bears her misfortune; whether my nephew be lusty and strong, whom he is like, and a hundred such questions I desire the answer of under your hand, because a less evidence will not satisfy the curiosity I have for those I am so much concerned in. What care the States take for the young General, and how kind and careful the Princess of Orange is of whom, and what provision is made for my sister's present support I hope I shall hear from your husband.'[8]

The king's concerns were understandable. If Princess Mary had produced a daughter, it is probably fair to say that both she and the child would have become little more than footnotes to history. But the birth of a prince gave the Orangists hope and was also good news for the Stuarts, though the prospects of such a child ever occupying the English throne must have seemed remote. His European credentials, with ancestors who came from the Netherlands and Germany as well as France and Britain, were strong. His situation at birth, however, was much less certain. A royalist then resident at The Hague gave an overview of events which highlighted a number of the uncertainties faced by the infant prince:

> I presume you have before this heard . . . of the death of the prince of Orange, who died about five weeks since of the smallpox . . . About ten days after his death the young prince was born, who is lively and well, but not yet christened, nor the father buried. The Princess Royal is as well as you might imagine a lady in her condition, more cast down with grief and weakness than the joy of a son could revive, but now, with God's blessing, in a clear likelihood of strength. The late prince in his will settled 15,000 sterling per annum for a dowry to the Princess Royal . . . I hear of no guardian to the young prince; but the infant and the estate is yet wholly in the government of the Princess Royal and her officers, but how long it will so continue, or how soon it will alter, those much wiser than I can little imagine. The States General seem to be kind and civil to the prince and the princess but have named no new general of their armies . . . and are most likely to reserve their power in their own hands.[9]

The States-General were never going to name a baby as head of the Dutch army and with the ambitious William Frederick of Friesland harbouring ambitions in that direction, it was hardly surprising that a decision was postponed.

It might have been hoped that the arrival of a male heir would go some way to healing the rift between Princess Mary and Amalia van Solms. In reality, things only got worse. There was an immediate disagreement about the baby's names, with Mary wanting to call her son Charles, after her father and brother, and Amalia favouring William, a more traditional Dutch name as well as the one of her late son, the father that William III of Orange would never know. Mary gave in and the child was christened William Frederick Henry. The manner of his christening, at which an ostentatious display of his claim to royalty was made, did not sit well with Dutch republicans, who disliked the fact that the prince was dressed in ermine. *Mercurius Politicus*, the English pro-Commonwealth newspaper, gave a detailed report of the ceremony, saying that an entourage of at least thirty people had accompanied the child and coaches decked out in mourning, drawn by six horses, carried representatives of the States-General, the states of Holland, Utrecht and Zeeland, as well as the towns of Delft, Leiden and Amsterdam. The baby's godmothers were Princess Amalia and Elizabeth of Bohemia. Given their massive dislike of one another, their joint participation in this ceremony must have added a frisson to the cold January air.

The difficult question of who would be nominated as guardian of the child remained. Within days of his birth, the baron van Heenvliet was writing to Henrietta Maria in Paris to warn her that Princess Amalia was pushing hard for the position of '*tutrice*' to her grandson but that this was being opposed by the state of Holland.[10] Such an outcome would have been equally unacceptable to Mary, though her age and lack of knowledge of the Dutch political and constitutional set-up weakened her influence. Her mother-in-law had acquired a considerable understanding of Dutch politics over the years, realizing that it would strengthen her position when her husband died. Even supposing that Mary had possessed the desire or intelligence to follow such a course herself, it was, in reality, unlikely that, at the age of just nineteen, she would have been considered as sole guardian for her son. Amalia's attitude to the prospect of Mary being left to direct little

William's affairs alone is made clear in the quotation at the head of this chapter, in which Amalia voiced fears that Mary would squander her grandson's inheritance in support of the Stuart cause. Nor did either woman make the slightest attempt to keep their unseemly quarrels out of the public eye. A correspondent writing to William Frederick, not himself a disinterested observer of events, reported that the disagreement between the princesses and their households was becoming daily more bitter, with intemperate language being used on both sides.[11] The dispute over guardianship dragged on for months until, in August 1651, the supreme court settled the matter by appointing three guardians: Mary, who would have one vote, and Princess Amalia and the elector of Brandenburg (the dowager princess's son-in-law, husband of her daughter, Louise Henriette), who would share the other vote. The baby prince's estates were to be administered by the estates council of Nassau. This awkward-sounding compromise was probably the best that Mary could have hoped for, given her age, her fraught relationship with her mother-in-law and the general reservations of a republican administration towards the Stuart royal family.

Although she might not have sensed the opportunity at the time, Mary's widowhood and the arrangements for her son's upbringing freed her to concentrate more on her displaced family. She was resolved to help them whenever she could. Her court and courtiers were always at their disposal for refuge and companionship and though she was frequently short of money herself and often reduced to borrowing, she provided such financial aid as was available to her. This was much appreciated but her increasing reliance on Katherine Stanhope and the baron van Heenvliet was viewed anxiously by Edward Hyde and Edward Nicholas, who believed they had good reason not to trust the ascendancy of this redoubtable Anglo–Dutch pair. Hyde went to Paris, summoned by Charles II, after the defeat at Worcester. His wife and daughters he left in the care of the Princess Royal at The Hague. Anne Hyde became one of Mary's favourite ladies-in-waiting, her future

apparently assured as a courtier. Nicholas, still intensely disliked
by Henrietta Maria, stayed on, furrowed by increasing poverty,
and so fearful that his estates in England would be confiscated
that he seriously considered returning.[12] His problems were far
from unique and, indeed, the Heenvliets themselves had cause
for concern which may go a long way to explaining the accusation made against them that their attitude towards the English
republic was suspiciously equivocal.

Katherine Stanhope believed that she had taken all the necessary steps to safeguard her son Philip's English inheritance when
she married Heenvliet but the execution of Charles I and the
advent of a republican regime jeopardized her careful calculations.
The couple might have made themselves indispensable to Princess
Mary, who is said to have preferred their country home to the
royal palace of the Binnenhof in The Hague, but they could not
afford to overlook the threat to their combined family's prosperity
in England. One has to admire the perspicacity of this husband
and wife team, who deserve to be better known. They took great
care to safeguard the interests of their children. Katherine had left
the eldest daughter of her first marriage in England, in the care
of her grandmother. Philip, the heir to the Chesterfield title,
accompanied his mother to the Netherlands on her marriage to
the baron van Heenvliet, as did her younger daughter, Catherine. They were educated and brought up in the Netherlands,
Catherine serving as a maid of honour to Princess Mary. Heenvliet himself had three daughters from his first marriage and the
middle girl, Walburg, married Thomas Howard, the Princess
Royal's master of the horse. So, on both sides, the couple ensured
as bright a future as they could for their offspring while producing
two more of their own, a boy, born in 1643 and given the impressive names of Charles Henry, to whom Frederick Henry of
Orange and Princess Mary stood as godparents, and a girl,
Amelie, born three years later, when Katherine Stanhope was in
her late thirties. After the execution of Charles I, the Heenvliets
lost no time in trying to ensure the position of the Wotton and

Chesterfield estates in England and their own son's prospects there. In the summer of 1649, Charles II created the three-year-old Charles Henry Kerkhoven (Heenvliet's family name) Baron Wotton of Marley, as well as renewing the warrant which stated that the Crown had no interest in Katherine Stanhope's English property.

This was all well and good but the couple were acutely aware that, unless Charles II could regain his throne (which seemed improbable after Worcester), such assurances were scarcely worth the paper they were written on. They needed to be sure that the republican authorities in England would not move against them. At the end of 1651, things were not looking good and it was clear that action was required, even if the course they needed to take did not sit well with the royalist establishment. Katherine wrote to Henrietta Maria providing further details to amplify the explanation Heenvliet had already given Henry Jermyn as to why his wife needed to go to England. Signing herself Katherine Stanhope, rather than using her husband's title, Katherine explained that her mother had assured her that if she did not come soon, her eldest son's estate would be lost. She assured the queen that she would return to her duties in the Netherlands as soon as possible.[13] Ideally, Philip should have gone himself but he could not be contacted in time and Katherine resolved that she must take on the mantle of compounding for his estates (that is, paying a lump sum to stop the Commonwealth from taking them over) herself.

So the journey was duly made, only for Katherine Stanhope to find herself arrested as soon as she set foot in London and accused of having the intention 'to carry on designs to the prejudice of the peace'. After two weeks she was freed but the process of ensuring Philip's lands was a lengthy and expensive one. She did not return to The Hague until the following June, by which time she had secured her son's Chesterfield estate for £20,000. It is not clear how she obtained such a large sum of money, or why it had taken so long, but the entire business cast suspicion on the activities and motives of the Heenvliets. Sir Edward Nicholas in particular, who disliked the couple intensely and resented their influence on Princess Mary, was not slow in voicing his suspicions. The precise nature of the accusation he levelled at Katherine Stanhope is not known, but the inference is that she had made some kind of accommodation with the English Commonwealth, or passed on information, that was prejudicial to royalist interests. Charles II wrote to Mary expressing his concern but the princess, enraged at this attempt to unseat her favourite and inevitably suspecting her mother-in-law to be behind it, refused to acknowledge that Lady Stanhope was capable of any disloyalty and demanded to know who had accused her.

The affair blew over, and though the Heenvliets' relationship with Nicholas did not improve, they won over Hyde through their attentions to his family and his own friendship with the unhappy secretary suffered as a result. Hyde was well aware of the Heenvliets' support for the Louvre party, as Henrietta Maria and her followers in France were known. In fact, the baron was a most assiduous correspondent, writing frequently to the queen and also to Henry Jermyn. He was well aware of the influence that Jermyn was said to have over the queen and sent him numerous memoranda about the disagreements between Mary and Amalia. In August 1651 he wrote to Charles II at some length about the schemes of the Princess Dowager (Amalia's official title), noting that the Princess Royal was quite open about the fact that her mother-in-law had never liked her. Henrietta Maria's reaction to the unhappy situation of her daughter is not known. The queen's followers in Paris had much to occupy their thoughts and there was, in any case, nothing they could do to improve the situation between the two women at The Hague. Henrietta Maria had been spared the problem of a determined and politically active mother-in-law herself but she understood the importance of her daughter to the royalist cause. When Mary's husband died, the queen wrote to her sister, Christine, that she felt the loss of her son-in-law all the more keenly because 'all the hopes for the re-establishment of my son lay in him'.[14] The birth of her grandson cheered her, however, though she felt she was too old to see him grow to manhood. Little did she know the role he would play in the fate of her husband's dynasty.

*

COULD THERE have been any enjoyment in court life at The Hague when it was dominated by two women who detested one another and a third, Elizabeth of Bohemia, who was chronically short of money? The answer is a resounding yes. Elizabeth may have been penniless (a circumstance of which she complained frequently to her eldest surviving son, Charles Louis, the elector palatine) but at a time when Dutch culture was flowering, one of its most prominent literary figures, Constantijn Huygens, could not wait to get back to The Hague from the provincial pastimes of Maastricht. There was, he advised an English correspondent considering where to settle in the Low Countries, 'no such conversation there, nor such pictures, nor such performances, nor such music as we are able to afford you here'.[15] Huygens' opinion in such matters counted for a lot. He had experienced the English court as a young man and knew Francis Bacon and John Donne. Elizabeth and Mary were both keen supporters of dancing and masques – love of display and theatricals ran in the blood of the Stuarts – and these entertainments, widely reported in the European as well as the English press, reinforced the magnificence of royalism, as well as raising morale among the exiles and perhaps among royalists living quietly in England, who did not share the sneering attitude of the republican press.[16]

Mary spent lavishly on entertainments in her country palace at Honselersdijk and at the Heenvliets' home in Teylingen, as well as in the Dutch capital itself. The style of the costumes and sets would have pleased her mother as a young woman. She even ventured into political satire with the performance of a play in 1654 (by which time the war with England was over and Cromwell was installed as lord protector) which was entitled *A King and No*

King. The play was not universally well received by royalist sup-porters, though it may be instructive to note that one of its most outspoken critics was Sir Edward Nicholas, who, on hearing about the play from his son, wrote to Edward Hyde:

> All good and discreet persons here, as well Dutch as English and Scots, are extremely scandalised that the Princess Royal (who hath so good a cause to mourn even in sackcloth and ashes for the miseries of her family and the malicious practices against her son) should be not only so insensible of them, but so easily misled . . . in preparing and making her servants and dependents to practice and act a play with such a title as if Cromwell himself had made choice of and appointed it on purpose to have thrown scorn on the King . . .[17]

Nicholas's son, however, had interpreted the title as an attack on Cromwell rather than a defence of him but the play was clearly controversial. It was not a new piece (its authors were the Jaco-bean playwrights Beaumont and Fletcher) and it had been performed several times in Charles I's court, where Mary may first have heard of it as a child. For her, its performance harked back to a happier time. The princess seems to have been oblivious to criticism and she was keen to exhibit her understanding of French culture when she introduced a comic ballet in the French mode after visiting her mother in France in 1655.

Mary's avowed support for the royalist cause explains, in part, why her role in supporting exiles from the British Isles in the 1650s is of real significance. To be an exile was to live in a state both precarious and impecunious, without the benefits that came with court life in an established monarchy. The courts of Eliza-beth of Bohemia and Mary Stuart (as well as that of Princess Amalia) dispensed patronage and access as well as acting as con-duits for information about what was going on at home and how Charles II was faring. At The Hague, royalists of English, Irish and Scottish backgrounds hoped to find positions in Mary's court. Many were young (older royalists were more inclined to stay at home and deal directly with the Commonwealth and, later, the Protectorate) and some, like Jane Lane, were already part of royalist legend. While the English Commonwealth was at war with the Dutch, between 1652 and 1654, the political tensions between the Dutch republic and the royal ladies, though not inconsiderable, were subsumed by what was, in reality, a dispute over trade and dominance of the North Sea.[18] When peace came, Mary's determination to help did not change, but her ability to provide financial backing was less certain. It did not stop, however, as Daniel O'Neill, the Irishman who played such a fundamental role as royal servant to Charles II, acknowledged in a letter to Jack Ashburnham in June 1654, saying that 'with infinite industry and trouble I have hitherto, without much incommodating my mistress [Princess Mary], sustained myself and yet hereafter I must live upon her, for there is no other way.'[19]

Equally significant, and only more recently being explored by scholars of the period, is the importance of Mary's religion in keeping alive the Protestant traditions of the Church of England and the patronage she gave to displaced Anglican ministers. Henrietta Maria's court at the Louvre was avowedly Catholic and the Dutch Reformed Church, which Mary was expressly forbidden ever to attend by her chaplain, Browne, too Calvinist for Anglican tastes. The princess and her aunt were determined to keep the Anglican rites, a commitment which earned them the approval of Charles II and caused Cromwell's representative at The Hague in 1658 to refer to the English church there as a 'nursery of cavalierism'.[20]

Certainly Cromwell's government was uneasy about the role of Mary's court in the Netherlands and even her brother, the king, had to accept the fact that, while he was pushed from pillar to post by the vagaries of European politics during the 1650s, seemingly always on the move, living with uncertainty from one month to the next, his sister, though far from popular with Dutch politicians, was firmly established in The Hague and that the survival of royalism depended, to some extent, on her. It seems that the

Charles II
as a young man.

Prince Rupert, nephew of
Charles I and charismatic soldier
for the royalist cause.

Young James II.
The happiest part of his life was as
a soldier of fortune in the armies of France.

Henriette-Anne, 'Minette', as a young woman.

View of the estate of Saint-Cloud, one of the palaces of the duke and duchess of Orléans. The magnificent gardens were much-loved by Minette. The palace was destroyed during the Franco-Prussian war in 1870.

Philippe, duke of Orléans, younger brother of Louis XIV and husband of Minette.

The Palais Royal in central Paris. It was extensively rebuilt by Minette's husband.

Binnenhof Palace in The Hague, one of Mary, Princess of Orange's palaces in the United Provinces of the Netherlands.

Mary, Princess of Orange by Bartholomeus van der Helst (1652). By this time, Mary was a widow with a young son, the future William III of England. Her battles with her mother-in-law continued until Mary's death from smallpox on Christmas Eve, 1660.

La Grande Mademoiselle, cousin to the Stuarts. The richest and most self-absorbed noblewoman in Europe.

Archibald Campbell, marquess of Argyll, the ambitious Scottish politician who supported Charles II in 1650 but subsequently reached an accommodation with the Cromwellian regime, which cost him his life after the Restoration. A committed Presbyterian from one of the leading aristocratic Scottish families, his stern appearance belied a man who could be sociable in company but who was to fall out as badly with his son even as he had, early in life, with his own father.

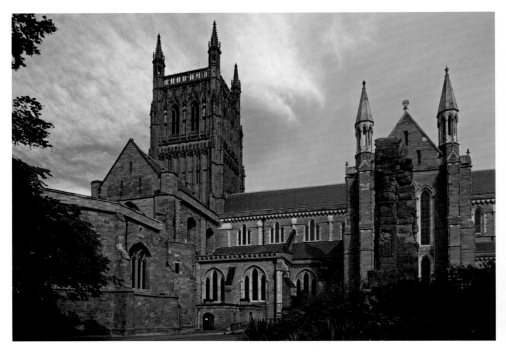

Worcester Cathedral. Charles II climbed its tower to view
Cromwell's forces before the battle on 3 September 1651.

Pendennis Castle, briefly home to the future Charles II
before he escaped to Jersey.

Charles II in exile by Philippe de Champaigne (1653). Despite the seemingly slim possibility of regaining his throne, it was important to keep up a regal appearance.

Charles II sailed from his exile in the Netherlands to his restoration in England in May 1660, accompanied by his brothers, James and Henry.

Charles II coronation portrait by John Michael Wright (1661). The magnificence cannot hide the faint air of disreputability.

James II by Sir Godfrey Kneller, 1684. Still handsome despite the passing of the years.

logic of this situation was not lost on Mary, who sometimes found herself at odds with Charles and was willing to defy him if he piqued her pride or seemed to be interfering in her personal life.

The advent of peace with England strengthened the position of the Dutch republicans *vis-à-vis* the House of Orange and notably that of the grand pensionary of Holland, Johan de Witt. Convinced that the future of the United Provinces lay in commercial supremacy, de Witt was also committed to limiting the powers of the office of stadtholder, which he believed had become too extensive, were ill defined and smacked of an unofficial regality that was contrary to the country's interests. This did not bode well for the young William III of Orange, but the outbreak of war with England brought with it a revival of popular support for the stadtholder's role, deemed by many citizens to be an important unifying force when the republic was faced with aggression. The Princess Royal was well aware of de Witt's sentiments and was gratified by the popular response; there were riots in several cities in Holland and de Witt was threatened with assassination. In July 1653 the province of Zeeland, which then held the chair of the States-General, suggested that William III should be nominated as head of the army and navy as soon as he came of age.

Peace between the two warring republics put paid to such temporary optimism about the prince's future role. Behind the backs of his colleagues, de Witt agreed to a secret clause in the peace treaty with England that barred the Orange family from the stadtholderate in Holland. When the secret clause was revealed, there was much discussion and a great deal of resentment, but it was basically a fait accompli on Cromwell's part. Mary is said to have wept copiously for three hours when informed of this Act of Exclusion. De Witt had tried to exploit the ill feeling between Mary and her mother-in-law by personally informing Amalia that there was no ill will towards her grandson, an assurance that was taken at face value by the dowager princess, who had learned to tread carefully in her relationships with Holland's politicians. A subsequent bout of serious illness, perhaps brought on by nervous strain, suggests that Amalia was not convinced by de Witt's blandishments.

Mary went with her son to Breda in the spring of 1654 to consider her situation. The peace treaty with England also affected her directly in another crucial respect: she was officially forbidden to receive her brothers on Dutch soil again. Distressed but equally determined, Mary decided if they could not come to her, she would go to them. By this time, Charles had been forced out of France by Mazarin's recognition of the Cromwellian regime and was looking for a permanent base. Mary was happy to travel and Charles equally pleased to meet her. The first of these re-unions took place at Spa, in what is now Belgium, a town famed, as its name implies, for the curative effects of its waters. Despite unseasonably bad weather for August, the king, his sister and their entourages (Charles's swollen by an unexpected gift of money from the Austrian emperor) passed the time pleasantly. But when one of Mary's attendants contracted smallpox (she subsequently died) the party left Spa for Aix-la-Chapelle. It was here that Charles was finally joined by the loyal but disenchanted Sir Edward Nicholas, who was officially made secretary to the king. The waters at Aix were thought to be every bit as restorative as those at Spa and the town received the Stuart brother and sister and their followers with due reverence. Like many tourists to this ancient city, they were shown the remains of Charlemagne in the great cathedral. Charles II, happy to be in his sister's company but without any fixed abode, must have envied the success of the great emperor whose skull and right hand were kept as revered relics in Aix's cathedral. Mary dutifully kissed them, while Charles meas-ured Charlemagne's sword against his own. Then they returned to the dancing, drinking and pleasant pastimes that formed the main part of their entertainment in this prolonged summer holi-day. Strapped for money as he had always been, Charles was effectively able to live off Mary for the time being, as her expenses were paid for by the Dutch States-General. Not everyone was convinced by his apparent bonhomie, however. Thurloe's spy, who had infiltrated the royal group and reported their every move, noted: 'For all his dancing, I believe he [the king] has a heavy heart.' It would have been surprising if, beneath the facade that Charles was so well able, by this time, to construct, he was not anxious about his future. Yet in practical terms, he and his advisers were clear on their next move. As autumn drew on, Charles and Mary moved to Cologne.

Here it would be easier to put down roots. The townspeople and the authorities there seemed to like the Stuarts, so why not stay? It was a handsome city but it was also conveniently close to the Imperial Diet, which had promised him a pension. Alas, that money proved as difficult to winkle out of the imperial electors as a French pension had been from Mazarin, much to the dismay of Charles's courtiers, who sometimes did not know where their next meal was coming from. But Mary liked the city of Cologne, deeming it a fit place for her brother's residence, and there she left him, after they had both paid a brief visit to Dusseldorf, to return to her son and spend the winter with him in Holland. The following summer she was again in Cologne but it was her plans for the early part of 1656 that caused a rift between the king and his sister.

*

DURING THE autumn of 1655, Mary resolved to go and visit her mother in Paris. She had not seen Henrietta Maria for twelve years. Never in the strongest health, she convinced herself that she would get better medical advice in France than in Holland. Henrietta Maria was, at first, considerably less keen on receiving her daughter than Mary would have liked, partly because they had been in dispute about a replacement for the unfortunate lady-in-waiting who had died of smallpox at Spa. Mary wanted Edward Hyde's daughter, Anne, to fill the vacancy but there was still much suspicion between Charles II's chancellor and the queen mother, and there was vigorous opposition from the Louvre, not to mention, at first, from Hyde himself, who feared it would make him even more unpopular with Henrietta Maria. In fact, it is a testimony to the enduring influence of the queen mother that her daughter feared her reaction so much that she tried to make it appear that the command for Anne Hyde to join Mary's household came from Charles II. When the appointment was made, Henrietta Maria was highly offended and showed little enthusiasm for a meeting between herself and her daughter. Her opinion changed when, still very much the matriarch, it occurred to her that Mary might not be allowed to see her brother, the duke of York, if the rapprochement between Cromwell and Mazarin forced James to leave France.

The king was unhappy about Mary's trip. A surge in public opinion in favour of the House of Orange at that time should, he thought, be encouraged in order to safeguard his nephew's prospects and Mary's absence in France could undermine the progress being made. So he sent Daniel O'Neill to The Hague to try to dissuade Mary. Perhaps he did not know his sister well enough, since Mary was the sort of woman whose opinions only hardened when faced with opposition. She assured O'Neill that, as everyone believed she was governed by the Heenvliets (who had also been enlisted to dissuade her), the best thing she could do to prove this accusation false was to make the journey to her mother. Faced with this perverse logic, O'Neill confessed himself stumped. 'It is thought here,' he told the king, 'that nothing your majesty can say can persuade her to stay.' But there were other, more important considerations that should be emphasized in any correspondence with Jermyn and Henrietta Maria, concerning the timing of the visit: 'The town of Amsterdam does intend, in March, to invite her highness and the little prince thither; and that if she should be absent, the princess dowager will be invited to go along with the prince, whom, if she once gets the possession of, she will never quit, having now got more interest in Holland than the Princess Royal has.'[21]

Mary was not known for her political sense. She had never bothered to learn more than a few words of Dutch, communicating with politicians and other influential people entirely in French. Given her stubborn nature, something that had been observed in her since childhood, it is hardly surprising that the more she was entreated not to go to France, or at least to postpone the visit until the spring, the more she dug her heels in. Her professed reason for going in the depths of winter – that she wanted to see the carnivals in Paris that heralded the arrival of Lent – seems frivolous, but may be a considerable part of the truth. She was a young woman who enjoyed the company of her siblings and had endured a life where pleasure was in short supply. She may also have been excited to see the French court, having heard of its splendours, and felt that she would be treated in a manner that befitted her position as a royal princess. Much as she and Elizabeth of Bohemia had tried, their courtly entertainments could not come close to what she might experience in Paris. And the thought of seeing her mother again after so long could not easily be put aside.

Nevertheless, her determination to go to France caused friction with the king. Charles II often found it difficult, while in exile, to command the obedience of his family as strictly as he might have hoped. It was not in his easy-going temperament to lay down the law but in this case he feared that if Mary made what amounted to a state visit to France, his own prospects of support from Spain, France's old enemy, might be compromised. He could not count on Cologne as a permanent base and he might need to take refuge in the Spanish Netherlands at some point. O'Neill had pointed out to Charles and to Heenvliet that there might be considerable expense involved in the trip but none of this had any impact on Mary. A belated reproof from her brother only raised Mary's hackles. Why, she asked him, had he not spoken of his concerns, especially those relating to the Spanish, while they were together in Cologne? She pointed out that 'all the world' must think it reasonable that she should desire to see her mother, 'which I have not done since I was a child'. She would, she assured him, speak to the Spanish ambassador at The Hague herself before she set off and she was also more confident about the position of her son in the United Provinces. Once she had settled Prince William's domestic arrangements during her absence, she would be ready to set off.[22] And so she did, on 17 January 1655, escorted out of The Hague by count William Frederick of Friesland and other Dutch noblemen. Following her was a sizeable train of carts and wagons, to accommodate the needs of her household and carrying her all-important wardrobe. Mary had every intention of making an impression when she arrived in France and the French were ready to receive her with appropriate fanfare. 'There is great preparation and disposition to pay her all the honours that she has cause to expect at her arrival, and to divert her during her stay,' wrote Jermyn.[23]

Mary was greeted with great ceremony and respect as she journeyed south. Her brother, the duke of York, met her at Peronne, carrying with him a message from their mother that it would be tactful to decline Mazarin's offer of meeting all her expenses. She arrived in Paris at the beginning of February 1656, where she was reunited with her mother after thirteen long and momentous years. She also met, for the first time, the little sister born in Exeter that she had never seen. Princess Henrietta, now known by the French names of Henriette Anne, was a thin twelve-year-old, brought up in the Catholic faith despite her father's commands, and very much under the thumb of her mother. She was a great favourite of her eldest brother, the king, but led a restrictive and cash-strapped life in her mother's household. The arrival of this sophisticated and rather splendid elder sister was the high point of her year.

Installed at the Palais Royal in a suite of rooms that had once belonged to Cardinal Richelieu, Mary intended to make the most of her stay in France. Received with great civility, the number of her visitors fatigued Henrietta Maria, gratified as she was by the response to her eldest daughter. 'I have to tell you,' she wrote to Charles II, 'that she pleases greatly here, from the greatest to the least. She has been today so overwhelmed with visitors that I am dead with it.'[24] Mary attended a whirlwind of ballets, balls, parties and theatre productions, surrounded by the glittering court of the young Louis XIV, which had, by this time, put behind it the tumults of the Fronde. It was a very different world from The Hague and there was speculation that the Princess of Orange might have intended more than a pleasant visit with her family by coming to France. Was she looking for a husband? Certainly, Mary was a personable young widow, though the fact that she was the only member of the British royal family not in exile did not improve her prospects. Unkind tongues suggested that she would make a play for the king of France himself. Though such a thought might have occurred to her matchmaking mother, it is unlikely that Mary came to France with the underlying motive of becoming its queen consort. Louis XIV showed no romantic interest in her, perhaps because he was attracted to one of Mazarin's nieces at the time.

Mary never showed much interest in a second marriage. During the late 1650s her name was linked to that of Harry Jermyn, nephew of Henrietta Maria's favourite, who had arrived in Holland with the duke of York. When the rumours reached the king, Charles II ordered the younger Jermyn out of the country and back to Brussels. Infuriated, Mary demanded he be allowed back to her court but she was duly reprimanded. Referring to 'this unhappy business', he told Mary:

I am sorry to see you take it as you do and think that my severity is the only thing to be satisfied, when I assure you, what I said and counselled you in the thing was merely out of kindness to you . . . and it appears to me very strange that you should think that the continuing of that which is the cause of the report, should be a means of taking it away. I shall say no more, but refer all to my brother [James]; and only add, that I hope you cannot imagine I am so little careful either of your honour or my own, as to show to the world I know anything of this business, much less to make any public discourse of it.[25]

This was unusually strong and censorious language from the king, who clearly feared for his sister's reputation. It is interesting that she used the same logic to argue for Jermyn's return that she did for her dealings with the Heenvliets in respect of her visit to France. Jermyn himself was known as a womanizer with a penchant for drinking, gambling and bad language. He was far from handsome, being short with a large head and thought generally to be too precious, the sort of gallant whose wit was all learned rather than natural. But he had a formidable reputation as a lover. If Mary was indeed attracted to him, which seems quite possible, since one of his later conquests was Barbara Palmer, the mistress of Charles II, then perhaps her time in France had introduced her to a lifestyle that was much freer than the accepted manners of court life at The Hague.

The Princess Royal stayed in Paris for nearly a year. During this time, she succeeded in improving the uneasy relationship between the king and his mother, charming Cardinal Mazarin (who, with typical political awareness, did not want to burn his bridges entirely with the Stuarts) and resisting her mother's efforts to convert her to Catholicism. Her father would have been pleased with Mary's firmness on this point. She might have stayed on in France for even longer, but her son caught the smallpox and she accelerated plans for her departure in November 1657. The French court news-sheet, *Gazette de France*, was lavish in heaping praises on the princess, recording 'the caresses and sorrows of the queen, her good mother . . . and of her young sister also (a true angel in miniature)' in their sorrow at her leaving.

Prince William recovered from the smallpox, though was left with some scarring. His relieved mother, on her return, continued to support her brothers as best she could, convinced that, without her tireless attention, the Stuarts would never be restored. The relationship with Amalia van Solms was, however, beyond salvation. The nomination of her son to the stadtholderate of Holland seemed a distant prospect, but she was determined to fight Amalia for the regency of Orange itself. The city is now part of France but its independent status was vital for the future of Prince William and his family name. At the time of the death of William II, the city's governor, a protégé of Amalia van Solms, had ignored instructions that Mary should have its governance in the event of her husband's death. The Princess Royal only discovered this later when she opened a sealed chest containing her husband's papers. When the opportunity arose, she asked Louis XIV to intervene during her stay in France and a French army removed Count Dohna, the treacherous governor of Orange. The city's *parlement* named Mary as regent in October 1658. It was a notable victory over Amalia and her clique but one that would be dearly bought. In an early indication of his acquisitiveness, Louis soon decided that he would have Orange for himself. His promises of support to the Princess Royal were soon forgotten and, without the agreement of the Dutch States-General, who did not want to be drawn into conflict with France over an issue that only affected the Orange family, the city capitulated to French troops in March 1660. Its loss was a blow to Mary but by that time her attention was elsewhere, as her family's fortunes were changing again.

CHAPTER THIRTEEN

Soldiering

'The duke . . . was very desirous to improve himself that he might one day be fit to serve in the French king's army as a volunteer.'

James II recalls his eagerness, as an eighteen-year-old exile,
to begin a military career, 1652

'Madame, I cannot forbear renewing my humble suit to your majesty concerning my brother Harry.'

Charles II tries to stop Henrietta Maria's campaign
to convert Prince Henry to Catholicism, 1654

JAMES, DUKE OF YORK, led a restless life in the 1650s. It was often frustrating, even dispiriting, though there were better times when he felt that his existence was not entirely without purpose. He enjoyed being in the United Provinces, in the company of a welcoming and rather indulgent sister. The relationship with his elder brother had its ups and downs; James did not like being told what to do by Charles II, though he did obey. United by their desire for Charles to be restored as king, their views on how this might be achieved were often in disagreement. James had been particularly aggrieved by being left behind on Jersey while his brother effectively sold himself to the Scottish Covenanters. Surrounded by self-interested servants and unreliable advisers,

James was poor in the literal sense (he remembered afterwards, with feeling, that there had been 'nothing so rare as money') and equally impoverished in the quality of the counsel he received. Doggedly loyal to those he trusted, his judgement of men was as lacking as his political sense. Bampfield was a case in point. Never someone to give up easily, he had followed Charles II to Scotland, hoping to retrieve his position as a man indispensable to the Stuart cause. But the king never trusted him and by 1654 the enterprising colonel decided to throw in his lot with the Protectorate in England, working as an agent for John Thurloe.

The duke of York's greatest difficulties, however, lay with his mother. He might have been bored on Jersey, despite the title of lord high admiral bestowed on him by his brother, but the thought of returning to his mother in Paris was depressing. She had been dismissive towards him ever since he joined her shortly after the execution of Charles I. Naturally, James felt belittled and over-looked. When he did go back to Paris, in September 1650, his relationship with his mother took a further turn for the worse. There was no hiding it from the rest of Henrietta Maria's discon-tented court, where this clash of personalities did nothing for the confidence of men like Christopher Hatton, loyal to the Crown but living in concern for the safety of their estates in England, privately wondering how far their devotion could be stretched. Lord Hatton did not mince words in describing the poisonous atmosphere between the duke of York and his mother. He wrote of the queen:

> She omits no opportunity to express her undervalue of him where she thinks she may do it secretly . . . She lately told a lady that the Duke of York had said that the Queen in his and the opinion of all the world loved and valued Lord Jermyn more than she did all her children . . . [the queen added that] the King . . . was of a better nature than the Duke of York, with much more of great bitterness. All of which being reported again to the Duke of York, as it was,

I leave you to consider what impressions these things may make in each of them.[1]

Hatton, who was a great landowner in Northamptonshire and understandably worried about his estates, was always ambivalent towards the Stuarts but he does not seem to have exaggerated the situation between Henrietta Maria and her second son. Given the rumours about the exact nature of the queen's relationship with Jermyn, the comment attributed to James was especially wounding to Henrietta Maria. She had lost all influence over her second son, but those who had gained at her expense were scarcely preferable. While cooped up on Jersey, the prince paid too much attention to the advice of Sir Edward Herbert and Sir George Radcliffe. His head was turned by the schemes cooked up for him by these two royalist exiles looking to increase their own importance through James's gullibility. Why, they suggested, should he not serve his brother by establishing his own army, like the duke of Lorraine? This impractical idea appealed to James but before he could give it serious thought, news came to Paris from Scotland that Charles II had died in battle. James was not the sort of young man to hang around until the report was verified. Against his mother's advice and with his new favourites urging him on, James set off for Brussels, where he proceeded to hand out offices as if his brother were, indeed, dead, though he apparently hesitated to proclaim himself king. This was just as well, for when the embarrassing news came that Charles II was very much alive, James struggled to save face. Negotiations for a marriage to the duke of Lorraine's daughter (which would, at least, have given James access to a ready-made army) stalled. As the young lady's legitimacy was doubtful, this apparent blow to James's prospects was not as serious as it first appeared. Minus an army and a prospective bride, the prince was ordered by his brother to return to Henrietta Maria in Paris. He did not do so immediately, preferring the company of his sister, Mary, after she had recovered from the death of her husband and the birth of her son. He thoroughly enjoyed riding with Mary past the embassy of the English republic at The Hague and hearing the Orangist supporters shouting insults at Cromwell.

This kind of immature behaviour may be explained away by age, but adversity had not matured the duke of York in the way it had his elder brother. His escapades now seemed ridiculous to almost everyone but himself. What to do with James became the bugbear of the queen's court at the Louvre. The wayward young man told his mother and Charles II that he wanted his own household if he was to return to Paris but this was simply unrealistic. The queen could only support her own establishment with difficulty and the French made it clear they would not dip into their pockets to suit the vanity of a junior Stuart exile. This sorry state of affairs was eventually sorted out by Edward Hyde, who had returned from Spain to find Henrietta Maria fretting about the bad behaviour of the duke of York. Though relations between Hyde and the queen were never cordial, she trusted him in this matter, despatching him to Brussels with a letter for James couched in more affectionate terms, inviting him to return to Paris.

Hyde found the duke of York's advisers in Brussels in disarray. They were 'in all the confusion imaginable, in present want of everything and not knowing what was to be done next. They all censured and reproached the counsel by which they had been guided and the counsellors as bitterly inveighed against each other.' But as for his own part in this farce, James remained completely unapologetic. He was 'fortified with a firm resolution never to acknowledge that he had committed an error.'[2] This was certainly the impression he wanted to give Hyde, but it was partly bravado. Thereafter, James did distance himself from the more extreme of his favourites and began to listen to Sir John Berkeley. He had disliked Berkeley intensely when he was first appointed as his governor but during 1651–2, as the other advisers were shed, Sir John saw an opportunity to position himself as the head of James's household. Berkeley had been unwavering in his support of Charles I but the chance to make himself indispensable to an impressionable youth who also happened to be heir to the throne was not an opportunity he could resist. He encouraged James to look for a wealthy French wife and flattered his military pretensions as others had done before. Pursuit of the duchess of Longueville as a spouse came to nothing – Charles II made it clear that his brother was not to marry before he did – and the second Fronde, when Condé and other French nobles rebelled, added to the woes of the royalist exiles at the Louvre. Meanwhile, Berkeley's influence distanced James from the wiser counsels of Edward Hyde and made him less receptive to orders from his brother. And the temporary rapprochement with Henrietta Maria soon disappeared.

On his return to Paris, his mother made him pay for his food out of the allowance she gave him and when his behaviour displeased her, she simply withheld the money. This meant that there were occasions when the duke and his servants went without breakfast and lacked even fuel for heating or candles to light their chilly and sparsely furnished quarters. Henrietta Maria used her son's financial dependence on her as a means of controlling him. James found it unbearable and began to consider alternatives to this dreary and demeaning lifestyle. An obvious mode of escape, via the French court, now seemed like an attractive option. If his mother would not support him, perhaps he could serve the country of her birth, in which he was now so uncomfortably languishing. So James began to polish his French, which was not very good, and make himself pleasant to his aunt, the regent Anne. His new mission was aided by the fact that he was a good-looking young man with excellent equestrian skills. He cut an attractive figure. Yet still the question of how he might join the French army could not easily be resolved. Mazarin did not want to annoy the English republic and Charles II, by now back in Paris after Worcester, could not afford to embarrass his French hosts by putting any pressure on them. Finally, an acceptable way was found for James to become a soldier of France. Hyde put forward the idea that he should offer his services as a gentleman volunteer rather than a commissioned officer, a convenient device for all parties.

The duke of York took leave of his brother under cover of a hunting party in the woods surrounding Saint-Germain in April 1652. This was necessary because the formal responsibility for James lay with Gaston, duke of Orléans, Henrietta Maria's brother, who was, at that time, a supporter of the Fronde. James set off with a very small entourage and his brother's contribution of six puny horses that had proved unable to pull Charles II's own coach. But as two mules struggled along with James's oversized camp bed, the prince himself rode off towards Chartres and the French royal army with a lighter heart. He was keen to serve under the famous French general Marshal Turenne and to learn all about soldiering. It would surely be better than shivering in the gloom of his mother's empty quarters.

*

THE FOUR YEARS that followed were among the most fulfilling of James's life. He had known little happiness since the outbreak of the Civil Wars in England. The privileges of his early childhood had long since given way to uncertainty and hardship. He had received scant genuine affection and chafed under the guardianship of the earl of Northumberland whom he regarded as a traitor to the aristocracy and, more especially, to his father. His mother never bothered to hide that she viewed him as second best, overlooking the fact that James was now his brother's heir. So it was natural for James to want to seek his own path. Service in the French army offered the prospect of adventure and an opportunity to carve out a distinct career. He took to military life immediately, not minding its hardships and privations. He liked the ordered environment, the chance to display bravery and his equestrian prowess. And he soon came to admire his commander more than anyone he had ever met.

Henri de La Tour d'Auvergne, viscount of Turenne, was, at this time, the pre-eminent military commander in Europe. His experience as a soldier, begun in the service of the Dutch republic, was incontestable but his loyalty to the French Crown was less clear. He sided with the Frondeurs in 1649 and was not reconciled to the court party until 1652. But it was not just his support for rebels that made him suspect. Like the Guise family in the sixteenth century, Turenne was viewed with a suspicion bordering on distaste by some at court because his lands were in Sedan in what is now eastern France but was then a separate principality. Turenne was seen as an outsider. His maternal grandfather, William the Silent, led the Dutch revolt against Spanish rule and Henri had been brought up as a Huguenot. The future of Protestantism in France remained a contentious issue and Turenne was bound to be affected by it.

James was himself an outsider at the time he joined Turenne, towards the end of the third Fronde, when the marshal had changed sides and was opposing Condé's final play for power.[3] In his memoirs, the prince described the fighting that raged around the Bastille and the Faubourg Saint-Antoine in July 1652 and the part played by his cousin, La Grande Mademoiselle:

> Monsieur le Duc d'Orléans, believing that all was lost, had shut himself up in his palace and was remaining behind his gardens, his coaches being ready to take him to Orléans. But Mademoiselle, full of courage and resolution, considered that the defeat of Monsieur le Prince [Condé] would involve the whole party in ruin. She went to the *hôtel de ville* and spoke so vigorously to the Magistrates that her reasons, joined to the clamour and threats of the populace who had followed her, wrested . . . an order [to] . . . let Monsieur le Prince's army enter the city. She carried this order herself and saw it executed; she then went into the Bastille and had the cannons fired on the king's troops. In this way her courage saved the Prince de Condé and his army.

Clearly James rather admired his amazon of a cousin. Henrietta Maria's views on the actions of the niece she had tried very hard to encourage her eldest son to woo are not recorded. As it transpired, Mademoiselle's bid for glory, which she recorded with suitable satisfaction in her own memoirs, was dearly bought. Condé surrendered Paris in October 1652 but his revolt continued, with Spanish support, in the south of France well into the next summer. Mademoiselle herself was banished from Paris for five years, to her castle at Saint-Fargeau in Burgundy.

The end of the Fronde brought a greater degree of internal stability to France but it did not bring peace with Spain. James was afforded the opportunity to serve and to learn and he impressed his commander (and his comrades) by his personal bravery under fire. Never afraid to thrust forward into the thick of fighting, it was noted that he 'ventures himself and chargeth gallantly where anything is to be done.'[4] Turenne was even more laudatory, claiming that the young man was 'the greatest prince and like to be the best general of his time'. James was a royal personage (albeit one adrift and penniless at the time) and the childless marshal, who had only married recently, in his early forties, seems to have felt a genuine affection for him. His warm words may be a reflection of the polite conventions of the time and the courtesy he wished to extend to the duke of York but the two men clearly got on well. Whether Turenne's assessment of James's military abilities was accurate is, however, another matter.

It is one thing to show courage and outstanding horsemanship and quite another to be a leader of men. This James never was, as soldier, as duke of York or, in the distant and dangerous future, as king. His memoirs of his life as a soldier shed little light on the wider, more interesting picture of what was going on in France at the time. Instead, they show a young man who hero-worshipped Turenne but was obsessed by recording the detail of military life and obscure manoeuvres. In this respect they are more revealing of the man he was to become than their author might have supposed. James, modelling himself, as he thought, on Turenne, entertained hopes of a lifelong career that might ultimately allow him to occupy the same place in military history. In this he was sadly deluded. For James was never anything other than a diligent aide-de-camp to his general, a reliable lookout for a man whose own eyesight was failing. This physical weakness of Turenne's, in sharp contrast to James's youth and energy, brought the two men closer still. After two years in the service of the French army, James was promoted to the rank of lieutenant-general. His pride in this achievement is evident. He was, he recalled, 'the youngest [general] who served in that Army'.[5] Serve he certainly did but he was never involved in the formation of military strategy and had no actual command of men. In his memoirs, James gives the impression of being at the centre of events because of his indispensability to Turenne. This may well have been true on a personal level but it does not make the duke of York a military genius. In the French campaigns his prime responsibility was that of a carrier of messages and a scout. It would be another thirty-six years before James, an exile once again, led an army into battle (at the Boyne in Northern Ireland, in 1690) with disastrous consequences.

Nevertheless, in the mid-1650s, while his elder brother's reputation for indecision and dissipation was being ruthlessly milked by the republican press in England, news of James's courage on the battlefield restored some lustre to the exiled Stuarts and their followers, who were in sore need of encouragement. The duke of York believed he had found his calling and wanted, above all else, to stay in the French army. The realities of European politics dashed this hope. During the spring of 1654, as one European state after another made peace with Cromwell, who had been made Lord Protector of England in 1653, it became obvious to Charles II that his time in France was running out. Mazarin was about to join the parade of allies of republican England and the king, who had long considered the possibility that he could not count on remaining for an indefinite period in France, now made his move to Cologne.

James's situation was unclear. He did not depart with his

brother and his mother and young sister, Henrietta, were staying in France. A more subtle man than the duke of York might have read the runes differently, in the knowledge that Charles II would inevitably make the final decision on his future and it was highly likely to be one that he would find unpalatable. Instead, James determined to brazen it out. He now commanded, at least nominally, the Irish regiments in the French army. This was all the excuse he needed to stay. Mazarin, ever the diplomat, even if he had just stuck a dagger in the heart of the English royalists, was in no hurry to throw him out. Neither was Cromwell, whose only stipulation was that the duke of York should not be involved in any military action in Flanders. This apparent tolerance on the Protector's part was designed to bring home to the world the irrelevance of the Stuarts while also encouraging disagreements between Charles and his younger brother. It was a clever ploy, the more so since the English government knew that other rifts were opening up in the Stuart family. And these were for the soul of a fourteen-year-old boy who had spent almost all his short life as a hostage.

*

PRINCE HENRY stayed on at Carisbrooke Castle with his tutor, Richard Lovell, and his few servants for two and a half years after the death of Princess Elizabeth. We know very little of his daily life at this time, beyond the fact that Lovell continued to give him his lessons, act as his friend and guide him through the continued uncertainties that faced him. There was talk, from time to time, of his being sent to Heidelberg to the university there, where he would be under the protection of Elizabeth of Bohemia's eldest son, the elector Charles Louis. The Winter Queen herself warmly supported such an outcome. She wrote to her son in October 1650, shortly after Henry had lost his sister: 'they continue the news of sending the Duke of Gloucester to you to be bred. I conjure you as you love me and mine to accept him upon any conditions, £1,500 a year is enough for his present condition, for

God's sake make no scruple in receiving him, so he be out of those devils' hands.'[6] No progress was made with this suggestion, so Henry took matters into his own hands. Saddened as he was by the death of his sister, he knew that he needed to survive and from the middle of 1652 renewed his plea to the Council of State for permission to go abroad. Lovell went in person to London to plead his case. He cited failing health and certainly the ordeal that he had been through at such a young age and his continued semi-imprisonment would have tested the stamina of the most robust child. Finally, permission was given and the *House of Commons Journal* for 7 December 1652 noted that it was resolved 'that Henry Stewart, third son of the late king, be removed from the place where he now is, in the Isle of Wight'. The Commons further ordered 'that it be referred to the Council of State, to send the said Henry Stuart beyond Sea, to such place and with such accommodations, as they shall think fit.'[7] Thus, with such careless inconsistency in the spelling of his surname, did the duke of Gloucester finally learn that his long period as a captive was coming to an end.

Henry did not leave immediately, perhaps because winter was a difficult time for journeys by sea. It was not until 12 February that the young prince and Lovell set sail from Cowes, to go to his sister, Mary, in Holland. He could not possibly have remembered her but the Protestant Mary was the natural choice for his first reception back into the family. He landed at Dunkirk 'with his tutor and two or three servants', as Nicholas reported early in March to the earl of Rochester. He continued:

> . . . being by the rebels sent over, who gave the tutor, one Mr Lovell, £200, to make provision of clothes and other necessaries and to pay the expenses of his exportation and delivered him bills of exchange to several merchants in Antwerp to pay him £500 on sight and £500 more in three months. The Prince is by this at Antwerp, whither the Princess Royal hath sent Mr Thomas Howard, the Gentleman of her Horse, to

wait upon him and to bring him to her . . . intending to have
him here with her till the King shall think to otherwise dispose of His Highness, being now not full thirteen years of
age.[8]

Mary wished fervently to keep her little brother with her
indefinitely. Like most people who met him, she found him
endearing. Elizabeth of Bohemia also wrote warmly of 'my sweet
nephew'. But sadly for the two ladies, and, as events would show,
even more tragically for Henry, he did not stay long at The
Hague. Scarcely a month later, it was made clear by Charles II
that his youngest brother must come to Paris. His mother had not
seen Henry since 1641 and he felt it wrong to deny her request to
have the boy by her side. Nicholas reported that Mary was distraught at the idea of parting so soon from the young duke and
he shared her fears about Henrietta Maria's underlying intentions:

This morning the Princess Royal sent for me and with many
tears told me that she had now received a letter from the
King . . . to send the Duke of Gloucester to Paris . . . she
doth with too much reason apprehend that this may be an
artifice of some papists powerful with the Queen (besides
Her Majesty's intentions and perhaps inclination) who have
further design in it to gain this young Duke (who is full of
spirit and very apt and forward in learning) to turn Roman
Catholic, upon some large promises to make him Cardinal
and to settle on him other great preferments.[9]

Henry duly set out for Paris with Lovell. The boy seems to
have had no inkling of the concerns so clearly laid out by Secretary Nicholas, though it is likely that Lovell was made aware of
them, if they had not already occurred to him independently.
Arriving in the French capital in May 1653, Henry found himself
the object of considerable curiosity. Here was another hapless
Stuart prince come to live off the guarded generosity of Louis
XIV's ministers. Henrietta Maria suddenly found her apartments

full of visitors again, most of whom had come to inspect Charles
I's youngest son, the little prince who had escaped the clutches of
the republican ogres after so many dismal years. The queen herself
was delighted by Henry, or Harry, as the family called him. She
thought he resembled Charles I but his portraits surely attest to
his Bourbon heritage; the very dark hair, full lips and aquiline nose
show that he was, indeed, half-French. He was a good-looking
boy and the queen called him her 'little cavalier'. Perhaps she
thought he was a blank canvas on which she could impose her
own ideals, having lived for so long away from her. If so, her hopes
were to be dashed in a terrible family row far more distressing
than either of them could have imagined.

Although Henry seemed to adapt swiftly to his new role and
surroundings, continuing his lessons, now supplemented by fenc-
ing, dancing and the other polite attributes of a prince, he found
the transition to life in a foreign court, with a domineering
mother, difficult. There may not have been much money, but suddenly there was a station in life he had never really known,
servants, intrigue and a general temptation to behave badly. He
was an adolescent adrift in an alien world. There were criticisms
of how he conducted himself, particularly after Charles II left for
Cologne in the summer of 1654. Lord Hatton confided his concerns to Nicholas, worrying that the duke of Gloucester 'will
contract so great a rudeness (besides other vices) as may be very
troublesome and incorrigible another day'. He regretted that even
Richard Lovell seemed unable to restrain a youngster who was out
of control. The nature of the 'other vices' was not made clear and
many parents of teenagers will recognize the sort of behaviour
apparently alluded to here. His tutor lamented that Henry was a
rather dilatory correspondent. 'I fail not frequently to put the
Duke in mind of writing to his friends, particularly to those princesses of Orange, but beside the natural inaptness he has for that
exercise, sometimes when he yields to be engaged he is otherwise
hindered. This week he writes to nobody at all . . .'[10] At heart,
though, Henry was a good-natured boy who wanted to do what

he could to help his family. The effect of the long years he had spent in the bubble of his restricted life in England could not, however, be suddenly erased. Isolation had bred independence of thought and a resilient nature. He simply did not know his mother and was disconcerted by this small, fierce, French-speaking woman who had once been pretty but was now prematurely aged by sorrow and hardship. He was not of her world and her plans for him caused the greatest crisis and sorrow he had yet faced.

Charles II departed for Cologne without either of his brothers. James, though temporarily back in Paris, was still attached to the French army and the king could not afford to support Henry, so he had to be left behind. The king was uneasy about leaving him, fearing the pressures that might now be brought to bear on him and, frankly, not trusting his mother and her advisers. Although he was both king and head of the family, Charles had long been in a struggle with Henrietta Maria for control of royalist policy. He was well aware that he was leaving Henry exposed on two fronts: to his mother's personal Catholic zeal and to her entrenched belief that, politically and diplomatically, the support of the Catholic powers was vital to any realistic prospects of the Stuarts regaining the throne in England and Ireland. Accordingly, he left specific written instructions for Henry. 'I must give you the same direction my father gave me, that you obey my mother in all things, religion only excepted.' In all matters of religion, Henry was to follow the instructions of his tutor, Mr Lovell, and John Cosin, the dean of Peterborough. Daily Anglican services were, at that time, led by Cosin in the residence of the English royalist ambassador, Sir Richard Browne, and Henry's attendance at these was obligatory. The king had, he said, obtained a promise from Henrietta Maria 'never to endeavour to have you wrought upon towards the change of the Protestant religion in which you have been bred . . . I do charge you never to hearken to anybody who shall endeavour to persuade you to the contrary.' Despite this pledge, Charles clearly was anxious about what his mother might try behind his back. Henry was to report any attempts at conversion to James as well as the king himself.[11] These instructions from a monarch to a younger brother are crystal clear and Henry took them to heart. Yet only three months later a concerted attempt to convert him was the talk of Paris and, even more alarmingly for Charles II, was widely reported in England, too.

Henrietta Maria, in defiance of the king, dismissed Richard Lovell, a man whose influence on Henry she disliked before she had even met him, and sent her son to the abbey of Saint-Martin in the town of Pontoise, about twenty-five miles north of Paris, over which her confessor, Walter Montagu, conveniently happened to preside. There, pressure was applied to change Henry's religion and to point out to him all the personal and material advantages that might ensue. Further plans were afoot to send him to the Jesuit College at Clermont.

Charles was infuriated by these developments. His orders had been deliberately flouted and he remonstrated firmly with his mother. Henrietta Maria chose to interpret her pledge as being only to forego the use of force in Henry's conversion, a semantic distinction which overlooked the fact that Henry was effectively under the control of Montagu, in an unfamiliar place and without the support of anyone he could trust. Only one gentleman attendant had gone with him and he was as much, if not more, of a captive than he had ever been in England, as well as being under far greater duress. James had also been given a clear mandate to intervene if necessary: 'You will take the best care you can to prevent his being wrought upon, since you cannot but know how much you and I are concerned in it.'[12] He applied to his mother for permission to talk to Henry privately but this was denied. James did not push the issue and his failure in this is unlikely to be out of affection for Henrietta Maria. His military career mattered more to him than anything else at this point and he was loath to offend his French hosts, who naturally supported Henry's conversion. Though it was to be some years before he converted to Catholicism himself it is possible that James's private views on religion were already becoming more ambivalent.

Without James's support, Henry, who was always respectful to his mother, felt dangerously exposed. He was only too well aware of his vulnerability and pleaded to be rescued. Anxious royalists in Paris, such as Christopher Hatton, emphasized the dread that the duke of Gloucester's conversion might actually succeed, despite the unfortunate young man's personal disinclination, potentially jeopardizing any prospect of restoring Charles II. While European Catholic states might insist on greater toleration for Catholics in England in return for financial and military support for the Stuarts, the majority of royalist opinion held that the conversion of the duke of Gloucester would be a calamity. Charles II certainly believed that he would never return as king if Henry was suborned in this way.

As Henry struggled to reject all of Montagu's blandishments and their mother cheerfully ignored the king's instructions, Charles resolved to send the marquess of Ormonde, the most senior Protestant aristocrat among the exiled royalists, to remove Henry from Pontoise. The importance that the king attached to this mission was stated in uncompromising language. Ormonde was 'to deliver to the Queen a duplicate of the letter sent to her, and represent the fatal consequence that will ensue from her purpose of changing the Duke's religion, in the loss of the affection of the Protestants and the forcing of the King to withdraw his own kindness from the Catholics of his dominions; if she proceeds in it, he shall believe that her affections and kindness are totally withdrawn from him.' He was disturbed by James's inability to take action to protect Henry and was not afraid to accuse the queen regent of France and Cardinal Mazarin of being involved. If Ormonde's enquiries led him to believe that there was interference from the French court, Charles wanted them to understand his displeasure clearly, 'and the ill blood it may breed between the two crowns and nations'.[13] For Charles, the political implications of his mother's intentions for Henry outweighed any considerations of filial loyalty. He was king and would be obeyed. Hyde wrote to the Princess Royal that the whole business was causing Charles II great stress. He had, he said, 'never in my life seen the King in so great trouble of mind'. Mary herself was thoroughly disheartened by this family crisis, which she had foreseen only too clearly.

Until Ormonde arrived, Henry was obliged to hold out on his own. Assailed from both sides, the fourteen-year-old prince was pushed to the emotional limit. Charles did not mince words in his exhortations to the boy to hold firm. His conversion would, he told Henry, 'be the ruin of a brother that loves you so well, but also of your king and country'. Even more chillingly, he added that, if Henry gave way, 'you'll never hear from me again'.[14]

Henry may have been turning into a spoiled teenage brat in Paris, but he did not deserve to be emotionally blackmailed by his mother and eldest brother. Ormonde arrived in Paris to find the queen mother unrepentant. In their first interview she gave as good as she got, even when the marquess countered her claim that she had not attempted to force any change of religion upon Henry by observing that the course of action she had taken 'could not but be held as a very austere compulsion'. In the end, Henrietta Maria prevaricated, saying she wanted to think more about what he had said but that there was no need for him to go immediately to Pontoise to bring Henry back to the Palais Royal. Ormonde thought differently. The very next day he removed Henry from Pontoise, to the prince's immense relief.

The affair did not end with Henry's rescue from the clutches of Montagu. He was still thought to be under threat and perhaps even not entirely trustworthy by some royalists. Ormonde himself was convinced of the young man's commitment to Protestantism and the ever-loyal Richard Lovell (who had been greatly wounded by Hyde's accusation of weakness in connection with this affair) commented that 'the carriage of his Highness has been incomparable in this business throughout'. There were others who wondered if a penniless prince who had led a restrictive life might not yet be tempted by the comforts, both material and spiritual, of the Catholic Church. Henry proved the doubters wrong. He had endured much in his short life and was more than a match for a mother who believed that her maternal duty to save her son's soul was more important than any undertakings she gave to his dead father or Charles II, her king. Sir George Radcliffe was generous in his praise of Henry's conduct throughout this trying episode. 'I cannot blame them,' he wrote, 'that desired to gain this child to their party: for he has great parts and doubtless by God's blessing will prove an excellent person.'

His mother, though, could not forgive him. Henry remained true to his father and brother, and to his own convictions, at great cost. For Henrietta Maria did not give up easily. She would give this wayward son, who dared to defy her on religion, the most important thing in her life, one last chance. He would have the rest of the day to think about it. Somewhat anxious, Ormonde was relieved to find Henry firm in his decision when he went to talk to him about this latest attempt by the queen. Nevertheless, it was with great agony of mind that the boy presented himself before his mother when she summoned him late at night to her apartments. Nervous and distressed as he was, Henry did not flinch from the course he knew must be taken. He was 'extremely afflicted to find the King and Queen's commands so opposed that he could not obey both.' And then he spoke the words she did not want to hear, that it was his duty as well as his personal inclination to follow the instructions of the king. So Henrietta Maria looked down on him, this disobedient, independent-minded third son of hers, and broke his heart. 'She told him,' reported Ormonde, 'that she would no longer own him as her son, commanded him out of her presence, forbid him any more to set foot into her lodgings, told him she would allow him nothing but his chamber to lie in, till Ormonde should provide for him, to whom he might apply; and when he kneeled for her blessing, refused to give it.'[15]

Henry passed a sleepless night and the next morning Lovell sent a note to Ormonde asking what should be done. In consultation with James and other royalist courtiers, arrangements were made for Henry to go to the residence of Henry Crofts, cousin of the duke of York's secretary, Henry Bennett. When this was vetoed by Henrietta Maria, Lord Hatton stepped in to offer accommodation to the dejected prince and his small household. The queen had lost no time in putting her harsh words into practice. When Henry returned from the usual Anglican morning service, he found furniture being removed from his rooms, his bed stripped and his horses being turned out of their stables. As far as his mother was concerned, he no longer existed.

The prince did not want to leave without saying farewell to the little sister he had got to know and love over the past eighteen months. Princess Henriette Anne was then a thin ten-year-old, pretty in a frail way and entirely dominated by her mother. She had been brought up as a Catholic, against the express wishes of Charles I, but her religion did not stop her from being a family favourite. Her brothers doted on her. She is said to have cried bitterly on hearing that Henry was leaving, suspecting, if she did not already know, that there had been a furious quarrel between him and her mother.[16] They parted in tears, hoping to see one another again in a brighter future. Neither could have suspected that this would be their last meeting.

It had been intended that Henry should join the king in Cologne but he went first to Holland, where his affectionate elder sister and aunt were overjoyed to receive him. As with his first visit, he did not stay long. The treaty between the Dutch and the English republics barred Mary from officially receiving any of her family and Henry moved on to Cologne to join the king.

The eventual conclusion of a treaty between Philip IV of Spain and Charles II, in the spring of 1656, offered a different path for James and Henry, though it was one that the duke of York took reluctantly. Both were to become colonels of Irish regiments in the service of Spain. James now found himself fighting the French who had once been his brothers-in-arms. The parlous position of the royalists in the 1650s and their dependence on foreign powers for help meant that there was no other alternative for the younger Stuart brothers. Charles II had little enough money for himself and could not support them. The king soon found that obtaining any substantial monetary aid from the Spanish was like getting blood out of a stone and he was angered by the renewed suggestion that if he really wanted help from a Catholic country like Spain he should support the conversion of Prince Henry. Charles did not take kindly to a report which suggested that further assistance from Spain and even the papacy might be forthcoming if there were to be 'some visible testimony of your majesty's affections'.[17] Such a gesture might well be the conversion of the duke of Gloucester with the support of both of his brothers. This was a novel approach to an old idea and the king dismissed it with contempt. He would not regain his throne by such an action.

Freed from the oppressive desires of his mother, though distressed by her refusal to receive any of his correspondence, Henry took to soldiering and demonstrated a similar courage in action to that of James. He participated in the Flanders campaigns of 1657 and 1658 against the offensive alliance of France and the Protectorate and fought at the Battle of the Dunes in June 1658, when the Spanish forces were routed in one morning by James's former idol, Turenne. Henry himself narrowly escaped capture near Dunkirk. Not so far away and now residing at Bruges in the Spanish Netherlands, his brother, Charles II, clung to the rituals of kingship in a world which appeared to offer little promise that he would ever return to England.

*

WHILE HIS brothers were compelled by necessity to offer their swords for hire to Spain, Charles II, a pensioner of that great nation, was living in Bruges. As a king in exile, his life was inevitably constrained but he sought, nevertheless, to live it in as regal a way as possible, aware that he was carefully watched, not just by Cromwell's formidable spy network but also, from the comfort and splendour of their own courts, by other European monarchs. It was a curious life, lived out partly in shadow but also in full view of both enemies and supporters. Always strapped for money, dependent on the personal loyalty of men and women who sacrificed much to uphold him, Charles knew the importance of keeping up appearances. If he were not to maintain protocol and the trappings of monarchy, how could he ever hope to regain his throne? Those in power wanted to know how Charles Stuart conducted himself. It was fine that he had courageous and dashing brothers, but the mantle of kingship, even in straitened circumstances, lay on him. How he played to these remote audiences was more important than the way he treated servants and advisers. It underpinned his legitimacy, as well as buying him dinner. 'The king of England,' wrote a Venetian diplomat to a colleague in France, 'passed through Antwerp, staying there two days at the cost of the city. He was lodged in the royal palace and presented in the name of the Catholic king with 25,000 gold crowns.'[18] Charles liked the public theatre of such occasions and was even happier if he could glean some financial advantage for himself and his followers from it.

Lack of funds made it necessary to trim back drastically the scope of the court in exile. It could scarcely be like his father's in Whitehall during the heyday of Charles I's personal rule. His son came to appreciate the sacrifice of courtiers and especially of the lower order of servants much more personally than the dead king could ever have done and this sort of bonhomie, the sharing of hardship and uncertainty, made him a much more approachable person than his father had ever been. Recent scholarship has shown just how difficult life was for the king's followers in exile, deprived of certainty, adrift from home, often cut off for long periods from their families. It is a largely unappreciated tale of sacrifice and endurance lost in the preference that Charles II subsequently showed for remembering only the dramatic and adventurous side of exile and his flight from the battle of Worcester.[19]

As the 1650s wore on, with no sign of an improvement in

Charles's prospects, despite occasional abortive royalist risings in republican England, it is hardly surprising that the king himself seemed to become lazier and more resigned to his fate. Many of the subsequent criticisms of his personal failings, such as his inattention to the business of government or his personal immorality, have taken it as read that the years of exile changed him, exacerbating weaknesses that might otherwise not have surfaced. It can hardly have been the case that Charles was not affected by more than a decade of exile but we cannot know what he would have been like if the throne had come to him by natural descent at the age of eighteen. What is certain, however, is that he was unable to control the petty jealousies and rivalries of those who clung to him, still hoping for patronage and advancement. Keen to keep up the impression of sober regality, his sexual indiscretions and the ill reputation of some of those nearest to him threatened to undermine the image that he needed to project, particularly if he wanted to obtain the support of the strait-laced Spanish court. He had excellent and committed advisers in men like Ormonde and Hyde, but preferred the company of Theobald, second viscount Taaffe, a glib Irishman who had himself fathered a daughter on the ubiquitous Lucy Walter in 1651. Indeed, it was this lady, whose erratic and increasingly hysterical behaviour threatened to cause a public scandal, who came back to haunt Charles II in the 1650s.

Veering between the Low Countries and England in her quest for acceptance and support, Lucy was not the kind to go quietly. For a while in 1656 she was imprisoned in the Tower of London as a royalist spy, having returned with her children to England saying that she was going to claim her mother's legacy. The Protectorate government soon realized that even the royalists were not desperate enough to use such a thoroughly unpredictable woman as a spy. It was not, however, simply the fact that she was the mother of young James Scott, the king's illegitimate son; it was her racy career after her affair with Charles that was causing the most consternation among Charles II's advisers.

A recent lover was Thomas Howard, Princess Mary's master of horse, a married man in a prominent position at the court in The Hague. Salacious reports, emanating from Lucy's maid, claimed that Lucy had aborted two pregnancies and that at least one of the children was Howard's. Daniel O'Neill, despatched to Holland to deal with the situation, feared that there would soon be a major international scandal. Lucy herself had scarcely helped such an eventuality by apparently intending to murder her disloyal servant using the novel expedient of running a needle through her ear while she slept. O'Neill was not impressed by Lucy's methods and even more alarmed by the damage this fiasco could do to the king's chances with Spain and his wider image. He took action quickly, paying for the maid's silence and forcefully suggesting that it was time to stop indulging Lucy's persistent requests for money. There was nothing in her behaviour to indicate that she would stop – she later fell out with Howard and threatened to have him murdered as well – and O'Neill considered that the only way to deal with her was to stop humouring her demands, cut her off completely and ensure that her son was handed over to Charles's custody.

Charles was not quite ready to follow all of this advice, though he soon came to regret his caution. After the acrimonious split between Lucy and Howard, the king decided to cancel Lucy's pension and place his former mistress in the care of Sir Arthur Slingsby in Brussels. Pushed around and without monetary support from the king, Lucy announced that she would 'post up all [Charles's] letters to her' in the public square of Brussels. Charles responded by requiring Sir Arthur to remove her son. Determined to gain public sympathy and cause as much embarrassment as possible, Lucy ran screaming into the street, claiming that her child was being kidnapped, and had to be forcibly restrained by Slingsby. Alonso de Cardenas, the Spanish ambassador to Brussels, was appalled by her rough handling but Charles's own sympathy for someone he had probably never really loved was at an end. He told the Spanish in no uncertain terms that he would be insulted by any help they contemplated giving to someone who had shown such 'mad disobedience to his pleasure.'[20] Cardenas, after a full explanation from Slingsby, agreed to keep Lucy in his house while the king decided what to do next. O'Neill made sure that the correspondence she had intended to reveal was recovered and handed over to the king, bringing a potentially damaging situation to a satisfactory conclusion. Lucy was effectively paid off with money and a pearl necklace. In 1658, she was back in Brussels and James Scott, a pawn in this tug of war, was finally handed over to his father. By then, in any case, Lucy was becoming too ill to look after him. In November of that year she died of venereal disease in Paris, a sordid end to a sordid life. It was rumoured that when she realized she did not have long to live, Lucy Walter confessed to John Cosin that she and Charles had gone through some type of marriage ceremony and gave a document purporting to be proof of this marriage into his keeping. Cosin died in 1671 and no such evidence was ever found. The story, however, proved useful to opponents of James, duke of York, during the Exclusion Crisis of the 1680s because, if Lucy's version of events was correct, her son, by then duke of Monmouth, would have been Charles II's legitimate heir. Few people, then or now, have given much credence to what may have been nothing more than a fantasy in Lucy Walter's troubled mind.

Oliver Cromwell died in September 1658 but his passing did not bring the great change in fortune that Charles II and his supporters had hoped. The twelve months that followed were some of the most desperate and depressing that the king had known. In the autumn of 1659, having seen the small army that, apart from his brothers, was all he could offer to the Spanish almost wiped out by disease in the war in Flanders, Charles went south to Spain, hoping that his presence at peace talks between the French and Spanish would, at least, mean that his hopes for continued support were not entirely dashed. But he derived little comfort from the Treaty of the Pyrenees, which brought peace between France and Spain. Charles returned to Brussels dispirited. Spanish financial support dried up and his personal servants had not been paid for two years. At the very nadir of his exile, the Stuart cause seemed hopeless. Yet before the spring was over, he would be back on the throne of England.

CHAPTER FOURTEEN

The Fall of the English Republic

'Sad days seem to threaten.'
Robert Baynes to his brother Adam, a republican
member of parliament, in February 1660

OLIVER CROMWELL DIED on 3 September 1658, the anniversary of his great victories at Dunbar and Worcester. The previous year he had rejected the offer of the Crown of England made to him in the Humble Petition and Advice, after much deliberation. The power that would accrue to him from kingship he already possessed. It was the title that gave him pause. The opposition of many of his army colleagues, notably John Lambert, who had been the author of the document that underpinned the Protectorate in 1653, the Instrument of Government, was implacable, as was that of the die-hard republicans. He could not square the notion of being 'King Oliver' with his conscience: 'It would savour more to be of the flesh, to proceed from lust, to arise from arguments of self-love . . . it may prove even a curse to these three nations,' he said in April 1657. His entire life since the late 1630s, during all the years of the Civil Wars and the republican experiment, had been based on a belief in God's providence. He never looked to the past and was no political thinker. The arguments and intricacies of political theory wearied him. If God wanted him to have the title, then there would be a sign. When none came, his path seemed clear. He would not, he said, 'build Jericho again'. It was the title of king, as much as the Stuart family, that had been blighted by God.[1] The Instrument had stated that 'the supreme legislative authority of the Commonwealth of England, Scotland and Ireland . . . shall be and reside in one person, and the people assembled in Parliament.' The latter part of the clause had proved problematic – Oliver and parliament seldom got on – but his title of Lord Protector made him, with the advice of a council, chief magistrate and head of the army. He was, as has so often been said, king in all but name and, in one respect, more powerful than Charles I had ever been, since he had the right to nominate his successor.

The Lord Protector had endured bouts of ill health for considerable periods of his adult life, the result, it is generally considered, of his having contracted malaria as a young man, perhaps from the fens of East Anglia, where he was born. During the summer of 1658 the fevers returned and became more frequent. Stress always made them worse and the suffering of his beloved daughter, Elizabeth Claypole, who was dying a painful death from cancer, exacerbated his underlying condition. He had also driven himself relentlessly and achieved more than anyone could possibly have predicted. As the historian John Morrill wrote in his magisterial essay on Oliver in the *Oxford Dictionary of National Biography*: 'No man who rises from a working farmer to head of state in twenty years is other than great.' But the personal cost of serving the righteous God in whom he so emphatically believed was high. His body, at the age of nearly sixty, had been worn by the worry of years of economic uncertainty as a struggling gentleman farmer in his younger days, and by the rigours of campaigning and the frustrations of trying to govern within a parliamentary system that was composed, he sometimes thought, of self-interested men who could not see their duty to the Lord God (or, indeed, the Lord Protector) as clearly as they should. Like him or hate him, he is as hard to ignore now as he was more than three hundred years ago. 'A larger soul, I think,' wrote his steward, 'never dwelt in a house of clay.' His family mourned him deeply and the nation waited.

The royalists, of course, were ecstatic at his death but even they accepted that there would be no sudden return to the past. Elizabeth of Bohemia wrote to her son, the elector palatine, at the end of September:

> Since Cromwell's death there is no change but it is too soon to look for it. Yet he lived with the curse of all good people and is dead to their great joy so as, though he hath gained three kingdoms by undoubted wrong and wickedness, wants that honour to leave a good name behind him in this world, and, I fear, he is not now much at his ease where he now is. All the French court went to congratulate this monster's death with the queen my sister and the Cardinal himself called him _ce vipère_.[2]

It had not troubled Mazarin's conscience too much to ally, when it suited him, with the 'viper', just as it did not bother this devious man, the antithesis of Cromwell, to make the right noises about him to Henrietta Maria after his death. The queen mother knew Mazarin too well by then to take his opinion seriously.

The period that followed Oliver Cromwell's death is one of the least known and most confusing in English history, leading, as it did, to a kind of civil war amongst those who had fought Charles I and were still, in most cases, anxious to prolong the nomadic existence of his sons in continental Europe. What lay at the root of these turmoils was the reality that the differences between the army and parliament, such a key feature of the late 1640s, had never really gone away. And into the dangerous vacuum that developed by the end of 1659 there stepped an ambitious and clever man, General George Monck, whose power base lay in a highly disciplined army that he commanded in Scotland. Monck's role would turn out to be crucial in avoiding what could have been a fourth civil war. On his deathbed, Oliver Cromwell could never have foreseen that one of his most loyal and capable generals would bring the republican experiment to an end.

The title of Lord Protector passed, on Oliver's death, to his eldest surviving son, Richard. There remains dispute among historians about whether the Protector ever actually nominated Richard to the title he had held since 1653. A consensus still holds that, even if there was no written document affording proof of Oliver Cromwell's intentions, he had made his desires known verbally to members of the Council of State as he lay dying in Whitehall Palace. On 7 September 1658, Secretary Thurloe wrote to Henry Cromwell, the lord deputy of Ireland, that 'it hath pleased God hitherto to give his highness your brother a very safe and peaceable entrance upon his government. There is not a dog that wags his tongue, so great calm are we in.' Thurloe may, of course, have been commenting on a fait accompli, without wishing to acquaint the younger Cromwell brother with confusion behind the scenes. It has been suggested, persuasively, that in the hours between Oliver Cromwell's death in the mid-afternoon of 3 September and the mid-evening, when Richard was announced as his chosen successor, there was much activity and soul-searching among members of the council and some nervousness on the part of the civilian Cromwellians as to how their military counterparts might react to Richard's nomination. The reactions of the army grandees, Charles Fleetwood, second husband of Oliver Cromwell's daughter, Bridget, and John Desborough, married to Cromwell's sister, may have given some cause for concern.

Both men, because of their closeness by marriage to the Cromwell family and their own senior positions in the army, could scarcely be overlooked. Desborough had not supported the attempt to persuade Oliver to take the title of king. Indeed, both he and Fleetwood had told Oliver that they believed royalists were behind the Humble Petition and Advice. Now they did not stand in Richard Cromwell's way, perhaps allowing any misgivings they might have had to be balanced by the evident need for a smooth succession of power. Shortly after 8 p.m. on the evening of Oliver

Cromwell's death, the council issued a proclamation declaring Richard Cromwell Lord Protector. Henry Cromwell was assured by his brother-in-law, Thomas Belasyse, Lord Fauconberg, that the missing hours between Oliver's death and Richard's proclamation were 'a time spent only in framing the draught [of the proclamation], not in any doubtful dispute'.[3] Yet the mere mention of such a possibility hints at some degree of uncertainty, at least, as to how to proceed and the need to reconcile potential dissenters. Thurloe had made reference to an undercurrent of concern in his own letter, for though dogs may not have been wagging their tongues he could not pretend that everything was perfect: 'I must needs acquaint your excellency,' he continued to Henry, 'that there are some secret murmurings in the army, as if his highness were not general of the army, as his father was; and would look upon him and the army as divided, and as if the conduct of the army should be elsewhere, and in other hands. But I am not able to say what this may come to. I think the conceit of any such thing is dangerous.'[4] His words proved prophetic.

The first crisis of doubt over, the public proclamation of Richard Cromwell and the ceremony surrounding it promised a swift return to business as usual as far as the government of England was concerned. The aura of magnificence, even the whiff of majesty, underpinned the declaration of the new Lord Protector. Trumpets sounded; heralds, suitably bedecked in official tabards, read aloud the announcement and led the shouts of 'God save His Highness, Richard, Lord Protector'. The army and members of the council were prominent as the procession moved about the city. In the evening, after Richard had taken the oath of Lord Protector in front of the council, the lord mayor of London and senior army officers, guns were fired at the Tower. His son had, apparently without serious opposition, slipped easily into Oliver's place. All seemed set fair. But his tragedy and that of the English republic was, quite simply, that he was not, and never could be, his father. And history would only remember him, if it recalled him at all, by the dismissive label of 'Tumbledown Dick'. In looking back at his brief tenure of office and the dissolving of the republican experiment that ensued, it is easy to read, with hindsight, a royalist script. There was more to the second Lord Protector than old history textbooks have suggested, while the failure of republicanism in England had little to do with the royalists, based, as it was, in the disputes that had divided Charles I's opponents in 1647–8.

Richard was thirty-two years old in 1658. Of his two elder brothers who had survived infancy, Robert Cromwell died while away at school just before the outbreak of the Civil Wars and Oliver, their father's namesake, perished from camp fever while fighting for parliament in 1644. It is not clear whether Richard spent any time in the army at all during the wars, and, if he did, it must only have been for the space of a few months, probably in 1647. His father, anxious to conclude an advantageous marriage for his elder surviving son, does not seem to have intended him for the military or politics. Richard was married to Dorothy Maijor, the daughter of a member of the Hampshire gentry. He settled down with her, had a large family (only four of their nine children lived to adulthood) and enjoyed the life of a county justice of the peace, living so tranquilly that his father became concerned about his perceived 'idleness', both of body and spirit. Oliver Cromwell seems to have thought his son was too soft and exhorted the young man's father-in-law to remind him that while he lived pleasantly and ate too much in the countryside, he was doing so at a time of crisis for England, 'when some precious Saints are bleeding and breathing out their last for the safety of the rest'.[5]

His father's elevation to the position of Lord Protector inevitably changed Richard's life. Having taken no part in politics up to that point, he was returned as a member of the Lower House for both the Protectorate parliaments. But a more prominent role in the life of the nation was played by his determined and capable younger brother, Henry. Richard did not take part in the debates surrounding the Humble Petition and Advice, perhaps finding them distasteful, but after his father's second installation in June 1657 he came much more to the fore. As both member of the new upper chamber and chancellor of Oxford University he was conscientious in carrying out his duties and he behaved responsibly when appointed to the Council of State. Yet he appears to have been unprepared for the death of his father, coming as it did so soon after the loss of his sister. In August 1658, he told Henry, 'We have been a family of much sorrow all this summer, and therefore we deserve not the envy of the world.'[6] It is interesting that he felt the Cromwells were seen in that light.

Perhaps by then he realized that the world was closing in on him, depriving him of the peace and enjoyable repasts of the country squire that his father had once been (though in less comfortable circumstances) and which Richard most probably desired still to be. Yet to suggest that he was never going to be up to the mark is to do him an injustice. He was a good-looking, good-hearted young man of considerable charm, who disliked conflict and wished only to do the right thing. His first two public utterances, to the Council of State and the lord mayor and city of London aldermen, were brief but well considered. He recognized that he was inexperienced in dealing with the massive workload that now fell on him, the demanding business of day-to-day government as well as the foreign policy decisions he would now have to make. He believed that, with the help of more seasoned politicians and the strength God would give him, he could succeed. Certainly there were many, in the countryside and towns, who sent him loyal addresses and congratulations in the first three months he held office, who genuinely wished him well. But affability is seldom a key to political success. In particular, it cut no ice with a quarrelsome and divided council and, even more seriously, with the army. Oliver Cromwell had come to power because of the strength of the army and his years of experience in commanding it. Richard had never commanded men. He knew this, of course, but what could he do about it? The army officers were soon in the habit of referring to him as 'the young gentleman'.

This hardly smacked of confidence in him to make the right decisions in matters that affected them directly. Richard's difficulties in this respect were recognized at the outset by General Monck in Scotland, who proffered sound advice on matters both political and military:

> The calling a parliament will require much consideration, and the house of lords, as a great part thereof, will not take up the least care of his highness . . . the great debts of this nation will oblige his highness to retrench, as much as may be with safety, the charge of the armies and navy . . . and as to the armies in England, Scotland and Ireland, in general a great expense may be saved if they be put two regiments into one, whereby his highness may be free from some insolent spirits, that may not be very safe to be continued, and this action would be most pleasing to the best men in the nation, who were not so free to a hearty conjunction with his highness' father, because they conceived the army in hands they could not trust.[7]

This was sound, and evidently well-intentioned advice from one of his leading generals, a man in charge of the army in Scotland that was, for the most part, well disciplined and whose pay was not so far in arrears as that of its English counterpart. But Monck was far away, in Edinburgh, and the winds of discontent that had swirled round relationships between the army and parliament in the previous decade were already gathering force again. By the time the one and only parliament of Richard's protectorate met at the beginning of 1659 it was evident that they would threaten to blow 'the young gentleman' away.

Richard could not avoid calling a parliament. The country's debt was enormous. The war with Spain, still ongoing, drained funds and the army's pay was in arrears. Government without parliament was not an option. Government with it would raise difficulties that might have been foreseen but were not well handled when the crisis came. The council wrangled over the decision for some time and the army grew nervous, despite a conciliatory and well-delivered address by the Lord Protector to leading officers in mid-October 1658. It had, however, been written by Thurloe and not by Fleetwood, who contrived to leave his wife's brother without any useful advice about how to deal with army malcontents at a time when it was sorely needed. The following month Richard felt it prudent to make his position clear once more. He recognized the danger from the army but was determined to remind its senior officers, with firmness as well as tact, that God's providence, the watchword of his father, had placed him in charge of the civil and military government of the nation. He also reminded the officers of his obligations under the oath of office he had sworn and, acknowledging his own inexperience once more, reiterated that he sought a good relationship and good communications with the army of which he was commander-in-chief. For a while there was quiet as the army turned its attention to the implications of the summoning of parliament.

Given the long-standing difficulties of the relationship between his father and parliament, neither Richard nor his council seem to have grasped fully how problematic the Protector's relationship with the independent-minded republicans of the Commons might be. And these men had striven mightily to get as many of their mind elected as possible. Richard Cromwell's parliament was remarkable for the number of new, and often young members, whose views are largely unknown but to whom the old Rumper republicans could appeal for support. Always suspicious of the army and resentful of the king-like power of the office of Lord Protector, the intransigence of the Commons could not be ignored. By 19 February 1659, after a remarkable piece of filibustering by the republicans' chief spokesman in the Lower House, the incorrigible troublemaker Sir Arthur Haselrig, a motion was passed to limit the Protector's powers in as yet unspecified ways. The recognition of the Other House, as the House of Lords was now known, was eventually conceded by the republicans but by the early spring discontent in the army was widespread and growing. It was feared that Richard favoured parliament over them.

Richard did not go meekly. He was aware that there were elements in the army and in parliament that sought to undermine him but his considerable personal determination was no match for the pamphlet warfare of republican proponents of The Good Old Cause or the growing alliance between Commonwealthsmen in the army and in the Commons. By the end of April his position looked increasingly hopeless. Forced to choose between the army and parliament he sided with the latter, ordering the general council of officers dissolved. Fleetwood and Desborough obeyed at first but the Commons, with characteristic bloody-mindedness and complete disregard for the position of Richard Cromwell, pressed on with the resolution of reorganizing and slimming down the army, replacing it with a militia. At which point, the army felt that it could take no more. Richard refused its request to dissolve parliament and found that the capacity of senior officers to undertake a military coup was as great in 1659 as it had been nearly eleven years earlier. Forced to dissolve parliament on 22 April after what must have been a difficult interview with Desborough, Richard's seven months of rule were effectively at an end. Though he had sought help from his brother in Ireland, Monck in Scotland and the head of the navy, none was forthcoming at the time he needed it. In great agony of mind, he refused help proffered by the French, perhaps because he feared the bloodshed that might follow. His bitterness towards those who had failed to support him is evident in letters to Henry Cromwell. The council, his friends and relations, all had deserted him, he wrote. He called Fleetwood and Desborough 'pitiful creatures' and said his faith was in 'the God of our father'.

He spent the next four weeks powerless and under house arrest in Whitehall, while the parliament destroyed the physical signs of his lost authority, breaking his seal and removing his arms from buildings. They did agree to meet his debts and pay him an annual pension though in practice failed to do either. On 25 May he formally resigned his office. Initially, he hoped he could return to the quiet country life he had enjoyed before his father became Protector but the Restoration put paid to that. Anonymity on the European continent was a safer option. For many years he lived in France, apart from his family, under the name of John Clarke, until he returned to England in the early 1680s. He lived on till 1712, a man whom history, except for scholars of the period, has almost entirely forgotten. He was, said his contemporary, Lucy Hutchinson, in her memoir, 'a meek, temperate and quiet man, but had not a spirit fit to succeed his father, or to manage such a perplexed government'.[8] Yet if Richard was somewhat less meek than she supposed, no one can deny the perplexity of the government that followed his removal from power and that led, however incongruously, to the restoration of the Stuarts.

*

THE FALL OF THE Protectorate did not bring about a sudden resurgence of royalist support in the three kingdoms. Charles II, watching from the Spanish Netherlands, seems to have genuinely believed that a royalist uprising in the summer of 1659 would put him back on the throne. At the beginning of July he wrote to his brother James about how they would communicate with each other when 'you and I are in England' and laid down some ground rules for them both to follow in respect of the key areas of pardons and appointments. Perhaps the king did not entirely trust James's judgement in the glow of their expected victory. He made it clear that he wished 'to draw all persons whatsoever to serve me and to that purpose in my declaration (which will be published at the time I appear) I offer a pardon to all men, except only those who sat upon the murder of our father, and voted for it.'[9] His hopes for a speedy return were soon dashed. Oliver Cromwell had never found English royalists more than a nuisance in practice, despite fears of assassination. England might now be without a head of state yet still the will to organize effectively on the king's behalf was not there. Charles remained in Brussels as his disorganized and cautious supporters failed him yet again. Only the Cheshire knight, Sir George Booth, managed to raise enough men to threaten any real trouble and he soon realized that the possibility of a co-ordinated rising had evaporated. Major-General John Lambert, who had steered clear of politics in recent years, easily crushed Booth's men without great casualties on either side and Booth ended up in the Tower of London. Charles II also contacted, through intermediaries, General Monck in Scotland and he wrote directly to Admiral Sir Edward Montagu, who commanded the republican navy, trying to tempt them to switch their allegiance to him. Neither man replied, though the fact that Montagu, although a staunch supporter of the Cromwell family, had royalist connections made him suspect to parliament and he was relieved of his command, retiring to Cambridgeshire. He and Monck were content, at this point, to watch events quietly from a distance. Their time would come in the early months of 1660.

Meanwhile the king, alarmed by news of peace talks between France and Spain, resolved to attend these discussions in person. He was desperately short of money. 'I am,' he wrote, 'above twelve months in arrear of that small assignation the King of Spain hath made me, so that my wants and debts are great.'[10] At Fuenterrabia in Spain Charles was very courteously received by his hosts but their ceremony was not matched by the depths of their pockets. Mazarin was his usual evasive self and the king, still adrift in the currents of European politics, had no influence on the course of events. A peace was signed between the two great powers, providing Louis XIV with a bride in the person of his cousin, Maria Teresa, a petite lady of whom he was, at least initially, quite fond, but who was no match for the cleverer ladies of the French court who knew their monarch's susceptibilities. That the older Charles II had similar weaknesses was already widely known.

Leaving Spain empty-handed and with no clear way ahead of him to return to England, even the normally sanguine king realized that he was no more than a spectator of events at home. He spent Christmas in Paris with his mother, whom he had not seen for five years. Seldom on the easiest of terms with Henrietta Maria, the king found her little changed in temperament. But he was enchanted by Princess Henriette Anne, now an attractive teenager. The eldest and youngest of Charles I's children developed a rapport and tenderness of affection that lasted throughout the rest of the princess's life.

After Christmas, Charles returned to Flanders, to the hollow life of exile he had known for so long. It is probably fair to say that nobody was more surprised than the king by developments in England that would bring his long period of wandering to an end.

*

AS WE HAVE SEEN, the fall of the Protectorate did not bring about a sudden resurgence of royalist sentiment in England. But the country needed direction and the soldiers who had lost patience with Richard Cromwell soon realized that they could not govern without parliament, despite the profound suspicion between the army and the legislature. Bereft of a leading figure and anxious about their future, the middle and junior officers of the army and the men who served under them were as much worried about indemnity from prosecution for their actions during the Civil Wars by the more vengeful members of the Rump Parliament as they were about arrears of pay. The army had restored the Rump in the first week of May, before Richard Cromwell even left Whitehall Palace, the grandees like Fleetwood and Desborough bowing to a wave of republican sentiment in the lower ranks, particularly in the London area. Anxious for a restoration of order and aware of the danger of royalist uprisings that might occur in such uncertain times, the general council of the officers of the army realized the danger that faced the country. They would acknowledge the role of the Rump because they were 'desirous, like drowning men . . . to lay hold of anything that had the least appearance of Civil Authority'.[11] But this was scarcely a vote of confidence in the Commonwealthsmen of the Rump. The new

Council of State was incapable of acting as an efficient executive and for much of the summer there was a state of emergency. The committee of nominations, on which Haselrig was the dominant figure, was at pains to purge ungodly officers from the army. This damaged morale at regimental level and led to disunity and lack of discipline. In reality, the Rump had never forgiven the army for its role in the events which brought an end to the Commonwealth in 1653. The republicans who believed their cause eviscerated at that time now sought to inflict the same wounds on the army. It would not end well. By October 1659 it was obvious that the army grandees could not work with parliament and the Rump was again dismissed. Buoyed up by the success in putting down Booth's Rising, the army sought to assert itself again as the saviour of the nation. The Rump's dismissal of nine senior officers was the last straw. But in the months that followed, the leadership expected of the grandees, of Fleetwood, Desborough and Lambert, did not materialize. And army unity, the great bond that had underpinned all of the regiments in England, Ireland and Scotland, was torn apart when General George Monck unexpectedly entered the fray from his base in Edinburgh. Making public his support for the expelled Rumpers in a letter to Speaker Lenthall, a man who had somehow managed to hold on to his office throughout the many twists and turns of the preceding years, Monck stated his case clearly. He wrote, he said, 'as a true Englishman' and promised that he would 'stand to and assert the Liberty and Authority of Parliament'.[12]

For a time, this looked like an exceedingly unwise act. Monck barely had control of his cavalry and his officer corps was divided. Desertions grew. He waited in Scotland, repairing the loss of officers from internal promotions. But he was blindsided by the actions of the three commissioners he sent to London to hammer things out with Fleetwood and the other grandees. By agreeing to a plan for a national settlement the commissioners exceeded their brief. Monck was in a quandary, made all the more delicate by the simple truth that he still did not know what the reaction of the expelled Rumpers to his intervention might be. His approaches met with total silence. Six weeks were to pass before Speaker Lenthall's response reached Monck. It not only gave an explanation for the delay but its warmth must have gladdened the general's heart. Lenthall had been unable to return an answer because 'the ways and passages were obstructed. But having now this safe hand I thought it high time to let you know that your seasonable remedy for restoring the present parliament in order to their settling of a glorious commonwealth is not only exceedingly resented [approved] by myself and the rest of the members of parliament in general, but universally appreciated (as far as I can gather), by all sober men of action.'[13] Monck was much relieved. He had not, after all, made a dangerous mistake. It was time to take his next step.

By early December he was sufficiently confident to move his army to Coldstream, on the border with England. During that month, as Lambert took his forces north to meet him, the navy declared for parliament and Desborough and Fleetwood completely lost their fragile grip on power. Lambert's force was larger than Monck's but it had not been paid for some time and there was reluctance on the part of its commander, as well as many of his men, to engage with Monck in a conflict which would lead to the once-united army of republican England killing their own comrades. To add to Lambert's misery, Oliver Cromwell's old commander, Thomas Fairfax, led an assault on the rear of his forces in support of parliament. Humiliated and with his men deserting en masse, Lambert did not offer battle. Bowing to the inevitable, the Committee of Safety, which had replaced the Council of State in these fraught, unpredictable times, restored the Rump for a third time on 26 December. This bid for survival came too late. On the first day of the New Year, Monck's army crossed the Tweed and began its march south to London. The future of the three kingdoms that Charles I had ruled now lay in the hands of a man who had once been a committed supporter of

Oliver Cromwell. But who was he and what were his motives at the beginning of 1660?

Monck was a Devonian by birth, a younger son, who had made his career as a soldier. His father, like many other men from old but impoverished families, married into money. George was partly brought up by his maternal grandfather, a rich Exeter merchant, but he remained close to his relatives, the Grenvilles, a famous Devon family. He seems to have entered the army at the age of about sixteen and was soon serving in Europe. By the time of the Bishops' Wars, he was a lieutenant-general of foot. His experiences, both at home and abroad, were, however, of weak leadership and military failure, something that he never forgot. After the outbreak of the Irish rebellion he spent two years in Ireland under the command of Ormonde but the outbreak of civil war in England strained his loyalty. After refusing to take the oath of loyalty to the king he was sent back across the Irish Sea as a prisoner. Not wishing to lose this physically brave but politically uncertain man, Charles I, in a personal interview at Oxford in 1644, persuaded Monck to continue in his service. It did neither man much good. Captured at the siege of Nantwich, the reluctant royalist was committed to the Tower of London. Confinement bored him and he was embarrassed at having to depend on his elder brother for financial support. Monck wiled away the time by writing a military treatise and perhaps beginning a romance with Anne Radford, a married woman some eleven years his junior whose husband conveniently disappeared several years later. Since her husband was a farrier and she herself was said to have been Monck's seamstress while he was imprisoned, the relationship, which led to marriage in 1653, was certainly not one of social equals. Monck was, however, devoted to his wife, who seems to have had considerable influence over him.

On being released from the Tower, after influential friends had lobbied on his behalf, Monck changed sides. He knew that parliament was winning in the struggle with the king and his own career seemed far more likely to prosper if he took up arms on behalf of Charles I's opponents. Recognition did not come quickly. It was not until 1650 that Oliver Cromwell, whom Monck had taken pains to cultivate, ordered him to join the campaign to subdue the Scots and thwart Charles II's ambition there. Monck acquitted himself well, earning Cromwell's respect. During the war with the Dutch, it was decided to use Monck's prowess as an artillery commander in the field of naval warfare and he served with distinction. Monck's reputation now firmly established, Cromwell entrusted him with the responsibility for the army in Scotland in 1654. His regime there bordered on the dictatorial and his distance from London brought with it considerable in-dependence.

Monck's personal loyalty to Cromwell (and, as he indicated in his letter, to Richard, Cromwell's son) was never in dispute. In Oliver he found the strong, decisive commander that had been a vital missing element for most of his military career. But he did not share Oliver's religious views and was more conservative in outlook than his mentor might have supposed. Monck disliked the sectaries and feared the effect that a plethora of religious ideas could have on central authority. It has been said that one of Monck's primary motives for the course of action he set in train in late 1659 was that he saw in the English army too many fanat-ics who wished to dismantle the Church of England.[14] While this depiction of Monck's opposition to religious extremists is demon-strable, the latter part of the statement is curious. The Church of England was under threat throughout the Civil Wars and only survived in the 1650s in scattered places of worship in various European cities. It could not exist in England while its titular head, Charles II, was in exile and the republicans among the expelled Rumpers were no friends of the Anglican Church. The logical outcome of Monck's desire to preserve the Church of England would surely have been the restoration of the Stuarts. Whether he foresaw this outcome on 1 January 1660 is something that we can never really know.

So he made his move as the New Year dawned, confident by

then that he would be well received by parliament in London and knowing that, in the north of England, he had the support of Fairfax, who would co-ordinate a rising against Lambert's forces there on the same day. Monck was then fifty-one years old, a heavily built and swarthy man, far from prepossessing physically, but a seasoned commander at land and on sea, who knew what it meant to fail. His portraits show a wary man, someone who kept his cards close to his chest. His hand looked stronger as he moved into England but, as to the endgame, he would have to wait on events.

Monck arrived in London on 2 February, having been expressly invited by parliament to guard its members as they strengthened their hold over England as a whole. Initially he followed orders, subduing disorder in the city and occupying it in a supposed gesture of solidarity. Still the Rump did not see the way the wind was setting. Monck, though, was well aware of the general dissatisfaction with parliament in the countryside; it had been brought home to him by numerous petitions demanding a freely elected parliament on his march towards London. By 21 February, encouraged by Presbyterian clergymen in London and their counterparts in parliament, he permitted the re-instatement of members excluded since Pride's Purge, on the ostensible grounds that this would be the most assured way of calling a new election. This concession to the moderates came at a price. He must be recognized as commander-in-chief when he swore to preserve the Commonwealth. A Presbyterian Church that tolerated religious dissent was a further requirement. Like lambs to the slaughter, the MPs did as they were told and, on 16 March 1660, voted to dissolve themselves so that new elections could take place. Whether it had been an ultimate goal or the result of an opportunistic response to developments (Monck could not have been sure of what parliament would do in February), the restoration of King Charles II was now in plain sight.

$\mathcal{N}o$ $\mathcal{M}ore$ $\mathcal{W}andering$

*'His majesty said smilingly that he doubted it had been his
own fault he had been absent for so long, for he saw nobody
that did not protest he had ever wished for his return.'*

Charles II's ironic observations of the response of
Londoners to his return from fourteen years of exile,
29 May 1660

'I confess it is a great miracle to see so sudden a change.'
Elizabeth of Bohemia to her son, the elector palatine, April 1660

MONCK, WITH INFINITE care and secrecy, was in communication with Charles II during March. He would not make the first
move himself but waited for the king to contact him. Nothing,
from Monck's side, was put on paper. He relied, instead, on his
network of West Country relatives, who could pass easily between
himself and Charles. The situation needed very delicate handling,
for what if the elections resulted in a parliament that maintained
a commitment to republicanism? He may have regarded this as
unlikely, given that he had taken great pains to ensure that dis-
senting groups within the English army were kept well apart and,
bereft of leadership, they would be unable to organize themselves
effectively. Monck still had committed opponents. Colonel Valen-
tine Walton, married to another of Oliver Cromwell's sisters and

himself a regicide, was, at the age of nearly seventy, still one of the commissioners of the army. He referred to General Monck as 'General Turd' and asked the pertinent question: 'Could any royalist have done more than the General, for he ties the parliament to break and dissolve?'[1] But the army's leaders had played into Monck's hands and the proud tradition of closeness between officers and their men, such a powerful force in the past, was now neutered.

Not everyone gave in quietly. In early April, John Lambert, Cromwell's 'dear Johnny', once the darling of the army, with his romantic appearance and military prowess, escaped from the Tower of London, where the new regime was holding him under arrest. Although Lambert managed to muster six troops of cavalry at Edgehill, he was a spent force. Perhaps he hoped that revisiting the first battleground of the Civil Wars would inspire a last-ditch rebellion against the Restoration. It was a desperate move, without any clear plan, and it failed miserably when Lambert's forces refused to fight the men sent against them. Lambert was returned to the Tower; he was forty-one years old. Though not a regicide, his reputation, Quaker associations and commitment to republicanism meant that the Restoration government dealt harshly with him. He was found guilty of high treason and spent the rest of his life as a prisoner.[2]

Charles II was at Brussels when the pace of change in England became obvious. He and his advisers were watching with growing amazement and delight the situation at home, daring to hope that this time, at last, their exile might be nearly over. But Monck could not hurry things and all must seem to be done properly. It would be parliament, not an army general, that contrived to end the king's days of wandering. At the end of March, Charles received advice from Monck to move from the Spanish Netherlands to the seaport of Breda in Holland. At about this time, he wrote a heartfelt letter to Monck, realizing that this stolid, rather lugubrious man was close to becoming his saviour:

You cannot but believe that I know too well the power you have to do me good or harm, not to desire that you should be my friend. And I think I have the best ground of confidence that can be that you will be so, in believing you to be a great lover of your country and that you desire to secure the peace and happiness and to advance the honour of it, and knowing very well that my heart is full of no other end, which I am sure you will know yourself as soon as you know me. And whatever you have heard to the contrary, you find to be as false as if you had been told that I have white hair or am crooked.

He went on to mention, not quite in passing, an aspect of their newly discovered close friendship that had also been exercising Monck's mind – that his sense of obligation to the general was great and that he could 'enlarge on that particular, if I did think it would be acceptable to you'.[3] For while Monck's initial concern, as a soldier, may have been to prevent the disintegration of Britain, as the winter moved towards spring he began to give thought to the rewards, financial and social, that the restoration of the Stuarts might offer to him and his family.

When the new parliament met on 25 April it immediately restored the House of Lords. The Upper House was to be composed of Civil War parliamentarians and also peers who had come of age during the Civil Wars, most of whom were strongly royalist. Less than a week later, on 1 May, both houses voted to restore the Stuart monarchy, based on the assurances to the army and to the people of England contained in the document known as the Declaration of Breda, Charles's terms for his restoration, which had been sent to England at the beginning of April 1660. Hyde, Nicholas and Ormonde helped him draw up this masterpiece of evasion, which essentially left all the key questions of government, religion and property ownership to be decided by parliament. Charles had promised 'free and general pardon . . . a liberty to tender consciences, and that no man shall be disquieted or called in question for differences of opinion in matters of religion, which do not disturb the peace of the kingdom'. He was equally bland about the vexed question of property, noting because of 'the distractions of so many years and so many and great revolutions, many grants and purchases of estates have been made to and by many officers, soldiers and others, who are now possessed of the same.' The determination of title was left to be decided by parliament 'who can best provide for the just satisfaction of all men who are concerned'. As for the soldiers, he promised 'full satisfaction of all arrears due to the officers and soldiers of the army under the command of General Monck.'[4] After years of bloodshed and political and religious division, the army went down quietly, as Monck had intended. Nor had the Presbyterians, still committed to the limitation of royal powers, done well in the elections, thus removing the threat they might otherwise have continued to pose. Charles II was returned to the throne on the basis of vague promises made in a brief document that barely runs to a couple of pages. To his amazement, he realized that he could be restored without significant restrictions on his authority, so long as he made the right noises. As Elizabeth of Bohemia wrote wonderingly to her son, 'They present no conditions to the king, but he comes in freely as his father's right heir.'[5]

Royalists, well-wishers and the merely curious now flocked to The Hague to partake of the general atmosphere of rejoicing in the Princess Royal's court. The Dutch republicans who had forbidden Princess Mary to entertain her brothers on Dutch soil found a hitherto entirely unexpected enthusiasm for the king and his family. Charles was gracious and charming to everyone, including the Spanish, who were rather miffed that he would be returning to his throne from a staunchly Protestant country, the Scots, an English parliamentary deputation and even Thomas Fairfax, with whom he spent a considerable time in conversation. For the royalists who had shared his exile, the majority of whom had given up everything to keep the Stuart cause alive, the restoration of their king promised an end to years of suffering and uncertainty. One of the most illustrious of these was Charles's old governor, William Cavendish, marquess of Newcastle, who had continued to write plays and practise his equestrian skills in Brussels, with the support of his feisty second wife, Margaret. Newcastle soon gave Charles further written advice on kingship, pointing out the mistakes his father had made. It was sound counsel but Charles seems to have resented it, since, much to Newcastle's disappointment, he was not given a position in the Restoration government. So the Restoration would prove not to be the return to the promised land for all those who came home after years of absence.

The English commissioners sent by parliament to the king in Holland found him with his brothers, all bearing the marks of the long years living hand to mouth. They were provided with new clothes for their journey to England, so as to make the right impression of royal magnificence when they stood before the crowds again. James went home in a suit trimmed with yellow, while Henry's outfit sported red ribbons. On the afternoon of 23 May 1660, Charles, with James and Henry at his side and his sister, aunt and little nephew following, went aboard the *Royal Charles*, the flagship of the English navy, at anchor in Scheveningen harbour. After they had dined together, Mary left with her son and aunt and the fleet weighed anchor.

Charles entered London to cheering crowds on his thirtieth birthday, 29 May 1660. A combination of favourable winds and tides had brought him comfortably from Holland. The first person to embrace him when he landed at Dover was General Monck, the man who, more than anyone, had been responsible for setting in motion the train of events that had ensured the sudden end of his wandering lifestyle. Perhaps Monck had not set out with the secret intent of being a kingmaker but that was what he had become. Charles made him duke of Albemarle as a reward, as well as giving him a handsome pension and grants of land. Monck continued to serve, both in the army and the navy, but his role in politics was of less importance. From 1661 onwards he had increasing periods of illness and the intolerant attitude of Charles II's parliaments was disturbing for a man who preferred moderation. Personally, he had done well out of the Restoration. There were many others clamouring for position in what was viewed as a new dawn where all kinds of freedoms, especially for the ruling class, would now be possible. This was to prove a delusion in religious matters and the mores of the time did not suffer a sudden sea change. The English republic's reputation for being straight-laced and boring is by no means accurate. The letters of Philip, second earl of Chesterfield and son of Princess Mary's favourite, Lady Stanhope, make it clear that London was still the place to be and be seen in the latter part of the 1650s. During those years he began a relationship with a beautiful teenager called Barbara Villiers, a member of a notorious family. They exchanged passionate letters, even after her marriage to Roger Palmer in 1659.[6] Yet Chesterfield would lose her to a much more powerful rival than a mere husband – the king himself. It is unclear how or where they first met but her position as royal mistress was certainly established within a few weeks of Charles II moving into Whitehall Palace.

*

THE KING HAD, of course, many concerns other than Barbara's voluptuous charms. There was the important question of what to do with his two brothers. The existence of two immediate heirs to the throne was a luxury the English monarchy had not known since the reign of Henry V in the early fifteenth century, though James IV of Scotland had two younger brothers when he stole his father's throne in 1488. Luxury, however, came at a price. Both James and Henry needed to be given an annual income, a household and, if at all possible, a role in government. The latter might need to evolve over time though Charles seems to have decided from the outset that he would not copy the example of France, where Philippe of Orléans, younger brother of Louis XIV, was seldom included in discussion of affairs of state. The duke of York was swiftly made lord high admiral and took his responsibilities in the post seriously. Henry, as duke of Gloucester, seemed destined to play a significant role in the House of Lords until a suitable position could be found for him. After taking his seat on 31 May, just two days after his arrival in London, Henry made various speeches that were well received. The king loved both his brothers but had a particular soft spot for Henry, whose firmness of character and stubborn survival in adversity, allied with a naturally cheerful nature and considerable charm, won him many admirers.

The young man who is said to have thrown up his hat and cried 'God Bless General Monck' on his return to England did not, alas, live to make the contribution to public life that was confidently expected of him. At the beginning of September 1660, Henry contracted smallpox. His health as a youngster had been good and his resilient character gave hope of recovery from what was undoubtedly a very serious disease, though not one that was an automatic death sentence. Henry's condition was thought initially to be relatively mild and his recovery was expected. Yet he succumbed on 13 September, to the great shock of his family. From her mother's home at Colombes near Paris, Princess Henriette Anne, who had been so disturbed by the quarrel between Henry and their mother, wrote a month later to Charles II, explaining that it was hard for her to put into words her feelings: 'So cruel a misfortune has occurred that until this hour I could not make up my mind to speak of it to you, not finding fit terms in which to do so. The sorrow which it has caused you is so just that one can but take one's part in it, and I have the honour to share it equally with you.'[7]

Henriette's rather stiff words concealed a genuine sorrow. Henry's loss devastated the king and the political establishment regretted the passing of a young man (Henry was only just twenty-one) who had shown such promise. Clarendon described him as 'a prince of extraordinary hopes, both from the comeliness and gracefulness of his person and the vivacity and vigour of his wit and understanding.'[8] Independent of outlook, intelligent and with an evident sense of duty, Henry's early death was a great loss to the Restoration court. Although his funeral was private, the order of service, preserved in the College of Arms, shows that he was buried with all the ceremony appropriate for a Stuart prince. His brother, James, duke of York, was the chief mourner and three dukes, Buckingham, Albemarle and Richmond, as well as fourteen earls followed him to his last resting place. He was buried in the same vault as Mary Queen of Scots in Henry VII's chapel in Westminster Abbey where, all too soon, he would be joined by his sister, Mary.

If there was much joy in 1660 among the Stuarts at Charles II's restoration after such a long period of exile, it was tempered by these two tragic deaths. Princess Mary, who had so loved her youngest brother, learned of his death while travelling from the Dutch republic to England in September 1660. She is said to have passed a very rough voyage impervious to her normal seasickness, alone with her grief, until, after several attempts to land, she came ashore at Margate in Kent, returning at last to the country she had not seen for nearly twenty years.

The change in family fortunes had considerably altered her position in the Netherlands and she now felt she could re-open discussions on her son's future from a position of strength. Suddenly, she and Prince William were personages to be courted and treated with respect, at least by some of the Dutch provinces. The city of Amsterdam organized a pageant depicting the triumphs and tragedies of the Stuarts, complete with an insensitive depiction of her father's execution, but despite this lack of tact, Mary was more optimistic than she had been in years. She felt sufficiently confident to petition the Dutch States-General to reinstate her son in his father's title of captain-general of the Dutch army. There was support for her request in a number of the provinces but Holland itself, as ever, was reluctant. The prevarication infuriated Mary, who was not the most patient of persons. Much to her displeasure, Charles II was not prepared to force the point by taking a belligerent stand against Holland so early in his reign. Frustrated and distressed, the princess resolved to press her case in person with the king. She could not, however, arrive in England without his permission.

Mary's situation was complicated by the fact that her mother was also putting pressure on her to visit France on her way to England, a detour that the princess did not altogether welcome. More than anything, she wanted to get away from the United Provinces and Henrietta Maria's request could, she believed, only delay her departure. Appealing to her brother for guidance, she wrote:

> I received a letter from the queen this last post, wherein she says by the next she will send for me into France. I have let her know your resolution of sending for me directly into England, therefore, for God's sake, agree between you what I have to do, which I hope you will not consider as an unreasonable desire, since I have made the same to the queen; and pray do not delay it, for I have great impatience to be gone from hence, and yet rather than displease either of you, I would suffer the greatest punishment of this world (that is to live all my life here) for I know what it is to displease both of you: God keep me from it again.[9]

Finally it was decided that Mary could travel directly to England. These were the king's wishes and, besides, Henrietta Maria had already decided that there were matters in England that needed her urgent presence.

Mary and James went to meet the queen mother and Henriette Anne when they landed at Dover at the end of October 1660. Apart from this occasion, Mary spent much of her time at Whitehall, observing mourning for Henry and giving occasional receptions. Sometimes she rode out on horseback or took a boat on the river Thames, but her public outings were rare. Instead, she devoted her attention to trying to recover at least some of the dowry that had been promised in her marriage treaty, none of which had been paid. When her husband died in 1650, Mary was, theoretically, owed half of the money, but since her father had failed to honour his obligations, and the English republic was never going to step in to help a Stuart princess, Mary had been left with nothing. Charles II was unable to provide such a large sum without due consideration and a commission was set up to examine the princess's request. Then, as now, it was easier to postpone uncomfortable decisions by establishing an official inquiry. Parliament voted the Princess Royal a payment of £10,000 at the beginning of November, which Mary acknowledged in a letter of thanks to the new Speaker of the House of Commons, the colourfully named Sir Harbottle Grimston. As parliament had already agreed to restore her mother's jointure in its entirety Mary must have hoped that she, a Protestant princess, would receive the same consideration as her Catholic mother. While the heavily royalist parliament might have been generous to Charles I's widow, their sentiments were not shared by most of the population. There was no great joy at the queen's return. 'I think her coming,' noted Samuel Pepys, 'doth please very few.'

Financial considerations aside, Mary had not felt well since arriving in London. She claimed that the city's pollution, the smoke of thousands of fires, troubled her chest. As Christmas approached, it became apparent that her condition was much more serious than had at first been supposed. The doctors could not decide whether she was suffering from measles or smallpox but they were determined not to be accused of failing to bleed her sufficiently, a charge which had been levelled at the royal physicians in respect of Henry's treatment. The disease was finally identified as smallpox and though the appearance of the rash gave the patient some temporary relief, the attentions of the doctors, led by Henrietta Maria's own French medical adviser, speeded the queen's eldest daughter out of this life. Zealous bleeding weakened the Princess Royal beyond recovery. She did not seem to be in great pain, nor were her mental faculties impaired, but it was obvious she was dying. Her family, of course, could not come near her for fear of picking up the infection. The queen mother and Princess Henriette Anne were moved from Whitehall to St James's Palace to escape the threat. The queen's maternal concern for her daughter manifested itself in an ardent desire for Mary to convert to Catholicism as she faced death. The princess did not oblige. So she passed her last hours with Katherine Stanhope, and Katherine's son, Philip, in attendance. They watched her sinking as she dictated her will to her secretary, Nicolas Oudaert, striving, to the last, to do the best for her son. She had come to England hoping to improve his future security and now she would leave him an orphan. In her will she stipulated that her mother and Charles II should 'take upon them the care of the Prince of Orange, my son, as the best parents and friends I can commend him unto, and from whom he is, with most reason, to expect all good help, both at home and abroad, praying to God to bless and make him a happy instrument to his glory and to his country's good . . . I entreat his majesty most especially to be a protector and tutor to him . . .'[10]

There was no mention of her hated mother-in-law, Amalia van Solms. Mary, in these final moments, did not want to face the fact that political expediency, as well as practicality, would most likely see her son's upbringing placed in the hands of this woman who had detested her since childhood. The rest of the princess's will was concerned with bequests to her servants, the disposition of her jewels and payment of her debts. Her earthly affairs settled, Mary, who had shown great resolution as she faced death, was bled again. It was too much for her weakened body and those about her noticed that her eyes were becoming dim. She died quietly later that day, on Christmas Eve.

Mary left behind her huge debts, the result of a combination of factors. Her concern with appearances and her royal status meant that she often lived beyond her means. Added to a predilection for overspending, she had borrowed heavily to help keep her brothers afloat during their exile. Charles II asked Oudaert to make an inventory 'of my late gracious mistress's affairs'. It made grim reading. Mary was in debt in the United Provinces to the tune of half a million guilders. Dismayed by the state of her daughter's finances, Henrietta Maria returned the 'great necklace of old pearls' that Mary had bequeathed her.

Oudaert soon discovered that Lady Chesterfield, as Katherine Stanhope was now known, had appropriated much of Mary's furniture and all manner of other possessions, from silver plate to gloves and stockings, while her chaplain, Browne, was holding on to all her chapel items, 'yet did offer to restore them if otherwise ordered'.[11] Such behaviour seems very crass but was commonplace, even expected, at the time. Lady Chesterfield, who was made of stronger stuff than Browne, refused to return anything until Mary's bequest of £400 was paid to her.

The royal funeral Mary was given would have contented this proud princess who had not lived to see her thirtieth birthday. The chief mourner was her brother, James, duke of York, and many of England's leading men, including Hyde and Ormonde, as well as her dashing cousin, Prince Rupert, accompanied Mary to her grave.[12] She was buried, at her request, 'next [to] the duke of Gloucester, my late dear brother'. Elizabeth of Bohemia was distraught when she heard the news. 'I am so sad I fear I write nonsense,' she told her eldest son. In the space of three months, Henrietta Maria had lost two of her children. She had, however, gained a daughter-in-law, much to her displeasure. It was her determination to prevent such an outcome that had brought her to England in the first place.

*

THE LADY WHO caused trouble at this difficult time for the Stuart family was none other than Edward Hyde's daughter, Anne. A maid of honour to Princess Mary, Anne was no great beauty but she had a striking figure and was vivacious, witty and intelligent. These were sufficient attractions for the duke of York to start an affair with her. By the time that James returned with his brothers to England, Anne was pregnant. James's initial reaction was more honourable than his subsequent course of conduct. He begged

Charles for permission to marry Anne Hyde, despite the glaring gap in their social status. The king agreed, only to find that his mother and sister Mary were appalled. So, incidentally, was Hyde himself. Now lord chancellor, one of the greatest offices in the land, he realized that his daughter's behaviour compromised his position. Disowning Anne, Hyde suggested that his daughter be sent to the Tower of London and even executed. This extreme reaction and the criticism that James received caused the duke to change his mind. He did not like being called stupid by his own mother, even if he was used to her dismissive attitude towards him, and the reaction of some of his aristocratic friends was equally troubling. He would not marry Anne after all. Henrietta Maria, who seldom discussed family scandals with her sister, Christine, now wrote claiming that James was not the father of the child and that Anne had tried to end her pregnancy. On 28 October 1660, she told Christine that she was leaving the next day for England, 'to try and marry my son, the king, and unmarry the other'.[13]

Charles II was as yet without a wife, though negotiations were underway with several potential brides. He had recently lost one brother and now the other was proving a liability. But he was not willing for his brother to repudiate Anne Hyde publicly and he insisted, to the consternation of those old enemies, his mother and his chancellor, that the marriage should go ahead. It has been suggested that Charles took a secret delight in the discomfiture of others. If so, he must have been rubbing his hands with glee in this case.[14] There was no way he would agree to 'unmarry' his brother. In fact, Anne and James were married in early September 1660, by James's chaplain, with just one of Anne's attendants and Ormonde's son as witnesses. The new duchess of York gave birth to a son only a month later. Charles could now justify his insistence on the grounds that it had further strengthened the succession. Henrietta Maria was eventually reconciled to her second son's marriage and showed her acceptance of Anne by dining formally with her at the start of 1661. This acceptance of the inevitable may well have been leavened by the plans she was making for an early departure from England. James might have let the family down, but sixteen-year-old Henriette Anne's prospects were brilliant indeed. The queen mother was not at all sorry to leave England at this time. She was taking her youngest child back to France, to be married to Louis XIV's brother, Philippe. It was a match that could scarcely have been dreamt of, for all Henrietta Maria's steadfast optimism, before the restoration of the princess's brother. The youngest child of Charles I would make the greatest marriage of all.

CHAPTER SIXTEEN

Minette

'*To know that you were arrived in England and at the same time you had remembered me gave me the greatest joy imaginable.*'

Princess Henriette Anne to her brother,
Charles II, June 1660

'*I am sure I shall be very impatient till I have the happiness to see ma chère Minette again.*'

Charles II to his sister, December 1661

THE KING DID NOT call her by his pet name often in their letters but it was to this youngest sibling, and now his only surviving sister, that a man who could appear effortlessly to be all things to all men unburdened his most private thoughts. Their openness with each other still has the power to surprise. They exchanged details of their respective wedding nights – both marred by 'the cardinal', a contemporary euphemism for menstruation – and the king gave Princess Henriette Anne more information than she probably needed about his unfortunate wife's miscarriages.[1] And all this to a girl brought up in an obsessively religious atmosphere, who had passed her childhood in the company of nuns, her education directed by her mother's confessor, Father Cyprien de Gamaches. It has been said that she was the only person Charles

II truly loved. Certainly he trusted her implicitly, confident not just in her affection but in her intelligence. Often portrayed as a giddy and empty-headed ingénue, out of her depth in the treacherous French court, the woman whom the French would soon call 'Madame' may have been passionate but she was also no fool.

Her early life was restrictive and her circumstances difficult. As a child she knew penury and cold in her mother's sparsely furnished and sometimes unheated apartments in the Louvre. The kindness of her aunt, the queen regent, whose name her grateful mother had added to the one she received at her christening in Exeter, alleviated some of the worst deprivations of her situation. It did not, though, fully compensate for the condescending attitude of other members of the French royal family and their courtiers. Invited, at Anne of Austria's behest, to take part occasionally in ballets and masques put on by the French court, the little English princess could not have escaped the realization that she was the recipient of an enormous favour. In one particularly embarrassing incident in the winter of 1655, Louis XIV made it quite plain that he would prefer to dance with one of Mazarin's attractive nieces. His resentment at being compelled to lead out Henriette instead was evident. When reproved subsequently he apparently justified his complete disregard for the precedence that should have been accorded his cousin by saying that he did not like little girls. La Grande Mademoiselle soon made it plain, on her return to court in 1657, that she looked down on Henriette Anne as well. After cutting in front of the princess at a ball, Mademoiselle was scolded by the queen mother. The haughty young lady found unexpected support in Louis XIV's younger brother, Philippe, who exclaimed: 'And why should she not? She is quite right. It's a fine thing when these people we give bread to take precedence over us. Why don't they go somewhere else?'[2]

Henrietta Maria, grateful for any support from the court, ignored these insults, still clinging to the vain hope that her daughter might soon become the bride of the king of France. It was a wish she cherished throughout the 1650s and she was disappointed when the Treaty of the Pyrenees brought the dumpy and not very bright Maria Teresa to France as Louis XIV's bride. So Minette grew up in the shadow of her mother, as the unfortunate vessel for Henrietta Maria's dynastic frustrations and sometimes morbid religious devotions. As the queen progressively fell out with the rest of her children, Minette was the one constant in her life, a jewel that had miraculously been returned to her by Lady Dalkeith's daring escape from England. The girl was a living reminder of the Civil Wars in England, the tragedies wrought on her family and a hope of better things to come in France. Yet somehow, Minette's personality survived the queen's attempts to turn her youngest child into a replica of herself. In her own way, the girl rebelled. She became a charming coquette, restless and self-indulgent, prone to impulsive behaviour. She wanted to be her own woman, not an appendage to a prematurely aged, embittered mother. Unfortunately, she was ill equipped for the pitfalls of court life. It is possible that, even if she had heard talk of her future husband's predilections, she did not fully understand what was meant. There would have been little use in consulting either her mother or Father Cyprien on the matter, or the nuns at the Chaillot convent that her mother frequented. When it became clear that her path in life was to be the wife of Louis XIV's younger brother, she accepted it because she had no choice.

At nearly seventeen years of age, the princess was pert and personable, even if, despite the gushing claims of poets, she was not truly beautiful. Madame de Motteville, the confidante of her mother, has left us a detailed description of Henriette Anne:

> The Princess of England was above middle height; she was very graceful and her figure, which was not faultless, did not appear as imperfect as it really was.

This is an elliptical way of saying that Henriette was slightly hunchbacked, a minor deformity which she had carefully learned to conceal by the way that she dressed. Madame de Motteville continued:

Her beauty was not of the most perfect kind, but her charming manners made her very attractive. She had an extremely delicate and very white skin, with a bright natural colour, a complexion, so to speak, of roses and jasmine. Her eyes were small but very soft and sparkling, her nose not bad, her lips were rosy, and her teeth as white and regular as you could wish, but her face was too long, and her great thinness seemed to threaten her beauty with early decay. She dressed her hair and whole person in a most becoming manner and she was so lovable in herself that she could not fail to please. She had not been able to become queen but to make up for this disappointment, she wished to reign in the hearts of all good people, by the charm of her person and the real beauty of her soul. She had already shown much perception and good sense and although her youth had kept her hidden from public gaze, it was easy to see that, when she appeared on the great theatre of the court of France, she would play one of the leading parts there.[3]

This, the balanced judgement of someone who held both the princess and her mother in great esteem and affection, accords with the portraits of Henriette Anne and captures the more elusive aspects of her appeal. Endowed with the charm of her Stuart ancestors, it is possible to detect in her face both her Bourbon heritage and a resemblance to her great-grandmother, Mary Queen of Scots. Her chief attributes were a fine complexion and a dazzling smile (having a good set of teeth was a major asset in those days), as well as graciousness and vivacity. Others were less complimentary than Madame de Motteville. Samuel Pepys, when he saw the princess in London in 1660, pronounced her 'very pretty, but much below my expectation – and her dressing of herself with her hair frizzed up short to her ears did make her seem so much the less to me'. His own wife, he went on, was 'much handsomer'.[4] Louis XIV seems not to have minded Henriette Anne's hairstyle but he did make jokes about her thinness, asking his brother why he was so eager to marry 'the bones of the Holy Innocents'.[5] The princess does seem to have been unhealthily slim but this may indicate tuberculosis, a disease which afflicted her mother, rather than the suggestion made by a modern author that she suffered from anorexia, as a kind of rebellion against the suffocating regime of her upbringing.[6]

Henrietta Maria was delighted when her sister-in-law called on her in August 1660 to request formally the hand of her daughter for her younger son. Marriage to the French heir, the same Philippe of Anjou who had spoken so deprecatingly of the predicament of the Stuarts in exile, was made possible by the restoration of Charles II. Delighted at the sudden end of her family's years of hardship, Princess Henriette Anne could now look forward to a stable future and a leading role in the court of France. She had, of course, been acquainted with her future husband for some years. How much she really knew about him is another matter.

The marriage was not, however, to be concluded immediately. Instead, the princess accompanied her mother to England in the autumn, a trip that proved doubly difficult because of Mary of Orange's death and the queen's reluctance to accept James's marriage to Anne Hyde. Early in the New Year, with Philippe anxious for the wedding to take place, mother and daughter prepared to return to France. They boarded ship at Portsmouth but before they could set sail, the princess fell ill. Measles was diagnosed and she was taken ashore, where she remained extremely unwell for two weeks. Her sickness, coming so soon after the death of her elder sister, caused great consternation and the queen was almost beside herself with worry. Eventually, Henriette Anne recovered, having, it is said, ignored medical advice and absolutely refusing to be bled at all. Aware of what had just happened to Mary, the young woman showed great sense in resisting the treatment which had contributed to her sister's end.

Henriette Anne now prepared for her marriage but the death of Cardinal Mazarin meant that it was further delayed.

Eventually, she and Philippe were married in her mother's chapel in the Palais Royal on 30 March. Though the court was in mourning the bride's attire was still splendid enough to attract the favourable comment of La Grande Mademoiselle. But Henriette Anne would soon discover that her elevation to the position of second lady of France was bought at a terrible price. Her husband was a damaged man.

*

HE HAD BEEN BORN in September 1640 at Saint-Germain, the second son of Louis XIII and Anne of Austria. His arrival, viewed with very nearly as much surprise as that of his elder brother, was greeted with great rejoicing in Paris. The relationship of the king and queen remained tense after the birth of the future Louis XIV but there was no doubting that Anne could produce healthy and attractive infants late in a long and difficult marriage. She was also, by the standards of the time, a much more attentive mother than most royal ladies and seems to have spent longer periods of time with both her sons than Henrietta Maria did with her own children at the same age. Of course, the little prince, given the title of duke of Anjou which was traditional for the second son of French kings, had his own household. His childhood might have been different if his father had lived, but Louis XIII died before Philippe was three years old. The rest of his life would be spent in the shadow of his brother.

The toddler now became known by the official title of Monsieur. As his brother's heir, he accompanied Louis on official functions and they spent much time together. It has been said that Anne of Austria and Mazarin, fearful of the dubious track record of brothers to previous French monarchs, deliberately downplayed Philippe's role and education. But the fact that he was dressed, as a small boy, in women's clothes, though much has been made of it, was normal for the times. So, in van Dyck's portraits of the English royal family, were Charles II and his brother, James. Both were thoroughly heterosexual. Anne of Austria has been accused of encouraging her younger son to develop effeminate tastes so that he would not be a threat to his brother. We shall never know why Philippe developed as he did but the neglect of his education during the Fronde and the constant reinforcement, by Mazarin, who supervised his studies, and by Louis XIV that his role was essentially subservient and empty certainly encouraged Philippe to feel like an outsider. Anne loved both her sons but the untrustworthiness of his uncle, Gaston of Orléans, himself a younger son, intensified her concerns about Philippe. She knew from bitter experience that being close to the throne was no guarantee of loyalty. It could breed ambition and resentment, even rebellion. As regent of France, the greater part of her attention had to be on Louis XIV. Her gregarious and naturally social younger boy must be made to understand his place in the scheme of things. 'Brothers of kings,' wrote Philippe's tutor, 'cannot have too much greatness of soul, nobility of sentiment, or elevation of view, but all of these must be subordinated to what they are duty bound to owe their sovereigns, for even while being their brothers, they do not cease to be their subjects.'[7]

It was a hard lesson to learn and led to many frustrations. As a small boy, Philippe did not always follow these lofty precepts. He and Louis generally got on well but when they quarrelled they did so as children, not as king and subject. The king's valet recalled one particular incident vividly:

The King insisted on sharing a small room with Monsieur. In the morning, when they woke up, the King without thinking what he was doing spat on his brother's bed, when his brother purposely spat back on the King's bed; and the King, rather cross, spat in his brother's face, and then his brother jumped on the King's bed and pissed all over it; the King did likewise over his brother's bed; and then, as they had both run out of spit and piss, they began dragging the bedclothes off each other, and then started to come to blows.

The boys were still fighting when de Villeroy, the king's tutor, arrived and 'read the riot act'. Revealingly, Philippe calmed down quickly, but the king remained furious for some while.[8]

The strange situation of a young man so close to the throne and yet left in no doubt of his distance from it was highlighted in 1658 when Louis XIV fell ill with what was probably typhoid and it was suspected that Philippe, egged on by a dubious group of ladies and his 'friend', the count of Guiche, was preparing to ascend the throne and displace Mazarin. Louis survived, but by then rumours of his brother's intentions were rife. Philippe protested his loyalty but Louis would not let him forget, telling him that 'If you had been king, you would have a terrible time of it.' La Grande Mademoiselle, whose overactive imagination had entertained thoughts of Philippe as a possible husband when she returned to court, was disappointed in his behaviour and his reaction to this unfortunate episode. He might surround himself with women but she suspected his real interests were elsewhere: 'The more I knew him, the more I found him to be a man who thinks more of his clothes and his appearance than of making something of himself . . . So that although I loved him very much as a cousin, I could never have loved him as a husband.' Perhaps Mademoiselle was also hinting at something else. Monsieur was clearly attracted to some women but his preference for men was, several years before his marriage to Henriette Anne Stuart, widely known. His relationship with Armand de Gramont, the count of Guiche, appalled Anne of Austria. In one especially scandalous incident at court, at a fancy dress ball, Philippe had not just allowed, but apparently enjoyed, Guiche pretending not to recognize him, manhandling him and even kicking him in the backside. Mademoiselle was, on a personal level, more tolerant than most people of her cousin's preferences. It was the very public humiliation of the heir to the throne that troubled her. But it did not worry Philippe. His public flaunting of tastes that were regarded as anathema at the time (homosexuality was referred to as '*le goût abominable*') was the ultimate act of rebellion. And yet, pronouncing himself in love with Henriette Anne, he was impatient for their marriage to take place. Later, he would claim that he had indeed loved her – for the first two weeks of their life together. Thereafter, it was a marriage made in hell.

*

THEY BEGAN their life together as the duke and duchess of Orléans. Mazarin and Louis had decided to give Philippe the title on the death of his uncle, Gaston, but not all the enormous wealth that came with it. Louis had been steadfast in his determination to keep Philippe dependent on him and to ensure that while his younger brother remained single he lacked financial security. Nor was he assigned any significant role in national affairs. Marriage to Henriette Anne greatly improved Philippe's prospects and may, indeed, have been one of the principal attractions of allying himself with a young woman of whom he had, not so long ago, been completely dismissive. The Orléans money and estates would come to him on his marriage. And he would be master of his own, very large, household with complete authority there, including over his wife. From now on they would be Monsieur and Madame, the most important couple in the country after the king and queen.

To all outward appearances, they made an attractive pair. Henriette Anne, with her chestnut hair, porcelain complexion and sweetness of personality, balanced Philippe's dark good looks. He was a handsome twenty-year-old, she a delightful young woman three years his junior. They were known to share many tastes. Both loved the theatre and the arts, collecting paintings and beautiful objects (a Stuart taste which was shared by Philippe), dancing and taking part in pageants and masques. Neither was keen on outdoor pursuits such as hunting though both could ride well, as would have been expected of people of their rank. Their milieu was the salon, the ballroom and the stage. Intelligent and outgoing, the wealth and property that now came their way meant that no one, except the king, could rival them, unless, of course, they chose to fight each other. Philippe saw his wife as a decorative appendage rather than an individual in her own right. The adulation she received made him jealous. 'Never has France had a princess as attractive as Henriette d'Angleterre when she became the wife of Monsieur,' wrote the abbé de Choisy. 'Her whole person seemed full of charm. You felt interested in her, you loved her without being able to help yourself.'[9]

Alas, Monsieur soon tired of seeing his wife worshipped by all who met her. He was used to being the centre of attention himself, even if it was for the wrong reasons. But he was not without redeeming qualities, despite his reputation. He may have gloried in his extravagant wardrobe and huge wigs, but Monsieur cannot be written off as a pint-sized, perfumed monster. It is true he was very short, apparently even shorter than his brother, and Louis XIV was only five feet four inches in height. Like Louis, Philippe wore heels to disguise this. But he was not lacking in physical courage and time would show that he was a competent and brave soldier as well as an effective commander of men. He became an affectionate father in later life. Nor was there anything wrong with his intellect and he could, in relaxed circumstances, be witty and interesting. His taste in furnishing and art was exquisite and his support of leading writers of the day, like Molière, and love of music made his houses, especially the Palais Royal, the cultural heart of France. A more secure man might have realized that he could forge a fulfilling role but, for Philippe, it was always exceedingly difficult to be the younger brother of the king. Yet he was the only person who could get away with having a row with Louis XIV. He was much less fortunate in his disagreements with Minette.

Their relationship faltered right from the start. The marriage night proved an embarrassing disaster when Henriette Anne revealed that she was having her period. Monsieur responded to this inconvenience with impatience rather than understanding. When he was able to consummate the marriage it was reported that his wife found sex with him unsatisfying – he could not 'entertain' his bride.[10] Living in an atmosphere where such matters were openly discussed among courtiers would have put a strain on a much more self-confident man than Philippe.

After their marriage they lived briefly at the Tuileries as the king and queen had already removed to Fontainebleau for the summer. This gave the new duchess her first taste of being at the centre of Parisian society and she clearly enjoyed the attention. In May 1661 Philippe took Henriette Anne to Saint-Cloud, the country house that he continued, throughout his life, to furnish with such exquisite taste. The original house was nothing like the magnificent palace that Philippe would develop but he was already involved in schemes for its improvement. The site, above the Seine, was superb but he knew that he wanted to enlarge the structure and work on this continued for years. While married to Henriette, Philippe extended the building, incorporating the original house into what would eventually be the south wing of a much larger edifice. Though she died before the completion of what was really Philippe's life work, Saint-Cloud and its surroundings enchanted his wife, who loved its landscaped gardens, fresher air and sense of peace. Her first visit was, however, short. From Saint-Cloud, the couple moved on to join the court at Fontainebleau. But even before their arrival, Henriette became aware of how she could use her charm and flirtatiousness to devastating effect. Already bored with his naive and unprepossessing wife, whose open adoration of him he found tiresome, Louis XIV's thoughts had turned to his sister-in-law. Even allowing for gallantry, the tone of a letter he sent to Henriette Anne while she was still at Saint-Cloud made it quite clear that he wanted her company: 'If I wish myself at Saint-Cloud it is not because of its grottoes or the freshness of its foliage. Here we have gardens fair enough to console us, but the company which is there now, is so good that I find myself furiously tempted to go there, and if I did not expect to see you here tomorrow, I do not know what I should do, and could not help making a journey to see you.' As an afterthought he added, 'Give my best love to my brother.'[11]

At a time when ladies of the French court fell over each other on their way to the king's bed, his admiration, even if of a platonic kind, was thrilling to the ears of a young woman who had spent long days with her mother visiting convents. But Henriette was playing a dangerous game. The line between coquetry and scandal was one that she seems to have refused to recognize. Her explanation, as Philippe's fury at her behaviour grew, was simple enough. Maria Teresa was completely lacking in social skills, still struggling with the French language and she had engaged her husband's interest for the shortest of times. Louis essentially needed someone who could play the part of queen. Into the void vacated by a Spanish princess who had once asked for permission to kiss her own father stepped the brilliant, hyperactive social butterfly that was Madame.

Soon she was organizing ballets and entertainments, in which she and Louis would take leading roles, and accompanying him on moonlit walks in the forest. Tongues began to wag and Philippe was mortified. His wife rejected his attempts at remonstrating with her and was equally resistant of her mother-in-law's objections. She ignored the rumours that her closeness to the king went beyond the natural affection of family ties, that people were openly saying that she was his mistress. Eventually, she and the king were prevailed upon by Anne of Austria and Philippe to take more care of their behaviour. It was decided that Louis XIV should pretend that his real interest in spending so much time with Madame was because he was pursuing one of her ladies, the seemingly innocent Louise de La Vallière. It was a ploy that worked only too well, when Louis swiftly transferred his feelings for Henriette to the decoy herself. Louise did, indeed, become his mistress while the probability is that his sister-in-law never was. Philippe's relief was brief, however. He soon found out that his wife, who did not take kindly to being supplanted in the king's affections by one of her own household, could easily find new ways to defy him. And who better to do this with than his own lover, the count of Guiche?

The count, like other young aristocrats on the make, was fluid with his sexuality. He liked a pretty face and did not care greatly about whether it was male or female, so long as he could derive advantage from the relationship. It was easy to find occasions to soothe the wounded vanity of Madame and he declared his devotion to her while they were rehearsing for a ballet. An exchange of letters followed and when Henriette Anne became ill – as she often was – her friend Madame de La Fayette reported that Guiche had even been smuggled into her apartments, dressed as a woman.[12] This lady, often referred to as France's first novelist, certainly had a romantic storyteller's eye for the detail of the behaviour of Madame and her new admirer. Philippe was, of course, beside himself with anguish and even went to Queen Henrietta Maria to implore her to reprove her daughter. Somewhat out of her depth amid all the whisperings and scurrilous rumours, the queen mother did her best to help the faltering marriage. But, although Henriette Anne was pregnant, it was already damaged beyond repair.

Madame, the duchess of Orléans, gave birth to her first child in the spring of 1662. With all the stress and ill feeling that now surrounded her marriage, as well as her underlying health problems, it was a difficult time. Charles II was concerned for his sister, writing to her in December 1661 with just the slightest note of reproof: 'I have been in very much pain for your indisposition, not so much that I thought it dangerous, but for fear that you should miscarry. I hope now that you are out of that fear too, and for God's sake, my dearest sister, have a care of yourself.'[13] The baby arrived safely on 27 March 1662 but it was, to the great disappointment of both parents, a girl. Unkind gossip at court claimed that the young mother's reaction, on being informed of the child's sex, was to tell her attendants to throw it in the Seine.[14] Despite her mother's heartless reaction Marie Louise d'Orléans would survive, to become eventually queen of Spain. Madame got over her chagrin quickly. She was soon up and about and eager to get down to the exhilarating business of presiding over *le tout Paris* from the home she and Philippe shared at the Palais Royal.

*

LOUIS XIV GAVE the newlyweds the use of Richelieu's former palace in the heart of the capital. It has often been said that the French king had hated and feared Paris since the Fronde and, as an adult, neglected embellishing his capital. The truth is more complicated. Louis made many improvements in the city. He spent a great deal of money on the Louvre and the new chapel at the Invalides as well as refurbishing the Tuileries. Versailles, with which he is much more closely associated, was not begun in earnest until the late 1660s and only became the official royal residence in 1682. Nevertheless, when Philippe and Henriette moved into the Palais Royal their home lacked the fashionable edge and the elegance of other royal establishments. Madame knew it well, of course, since she and her mother had lived there for the latter years of the 1650s, eking out Henrietta Maria's allowance in apartments that were very far from opulent.

The Palais Royal needed care and repair. After being abandoned by the court in 1652 it was neglected and fell speedily into an alarming state of disrepair. The leaky roof had damaged floors and walls; rooms needed redecoration and remodelling. The challenge to its new master and mistress was daunting. But whatever their differences, Monsieur and Madame were determined to leave their mark on their major residence. During the 1660s they were able to transform it into a centre of culture and social life, though work on the building itself was never-ending.

The couple moved into the Palais Royal with substantial households, though it is revealing that Monsieur's was always much larger than his wife's. In 1663 his servants were numbered at five hundred, covering every office from gentlemen of the bedchamber to stable boys with a hefty complement of doctors, spiritual advisers, chefs and masters of the horse in between. Henriette's staff was only forty-three. Though Madame's household grew by the end of the decade, it was always modest compared to that of her husband. By 1669 Philippe had over one thousand retainers while his wife had two hundred. In theory, Louis XIV would have paid all his brother's expenses because the Palais Royal was still a Crown possession but the huge increase in the household and Monsieur's ambitious renovation programme, probably meant that Philippe was obliged to meet some of the cost from his own finances.[15]

By the early spring of 1662, work was sufficiently advanced at both the Palais Royal and Saint-Cloud for Philippe and Henriette to begin to entertain on a scale that rivalled the king and queen. Parisians were especially glad of Monsieur's affection for their city but, over time, Louis became progressively uneasy about his brother's strong following there. For now, however, he was content to partake of Philippe's hospitality. Monsieur may have already detested his wife but he could not deny that marriage had made him master in his own household. This was a new and empowering experience for a man who had grown up as the little brother. And if his wife was, as it must have seemed to him, a shallow and even spiteful girl whom he could not respect, let alone love, she provided him with an independence that he had never known. Their life together was one long whirl of carnivals, music and entertainments organized and masterminded by Monsieur, as well as sumptuous dinners and parties. Philippe was happy to have the opportunity to compete with the king, to be sought out and feted by people of power and importance. His achievements as a patron of two of the finest playwrights ever produced in France are little known and, in this, he was fully supported by his wife. The encouragement of Monsieur and Madame was crucial to the success of Molière, whose first published play, *L'École des maris*, was dedicated to Philippe in the summer of 1661. Several years later, when the king had become his patron, Molière dedicated a companion piece, *L'École des femmes*, to Madame, who accepted it graciously, despite the fact that the controversial subject matter was about a flirtatious wife. By that time Henriette was also championing Racine at the French court.

Monsieur and Madame loved music and dance, as did Louis XIV. In the winter, several ballets were put on each week at court. These were not just for watching – Louis XIV and his brother were skilled and enthusiastic performers. A contemporary poet praised the dancing of the king and also that of 'Monsieur, his only brother, on whom the just heavens confer all the beautiful virtues which are desired in princedoms'.[16] Sadly, in his relationship with his wife, Philippe was singularly lacking in 'beautiful virtues'. Beneath the glittering facade of their social life, the couple grew more and more unhappy.

Henriette Anne was almost continuously pregnant throughout her marriage. Only her first child, Marie-Louise, whose birth had made her temporarily so wretched, and her last, Anne-Marie (later duchess of Savoy), survived. In between, she had to put up with stillbirths, life-threatening miscarriages and the death of the couple's only son in infancy. Monsieur's jealousy was such that frequently impregnating his wife, despite her increasing ill health, was a way of limiting her supposed amours, as well as allowing him to exercise ultimate control in their relationship. Neither seems to have cared much about their children. Philippe was pleased by the birth of a son, 'a fine, fat boy who appears to be very healthy', as he reported to Charles II in 1664. The appearance was deceptive. In November 1666 the little duke of Valois was taken ill at Saint-Cloud and brought back to the Palais Royal to join his parents. At the beginning of December his condition worsened and he died. Philippe and Henriette have been criticized for their behaviour following his death. Certainly, they did not observe a long period of public mourning, resuming their social engagements in the New Year, but it is hard to know what their private feelings were. The death of children was common at the time and, like other royal parents, they did not spend much time with their offspring.

This loss, as well as Madame's obviously frail health, did not bring the couple any closer. Neither did the death of Anne of Austria, who succumbed to breast cancer after a long and painful illness at the beginning of 1666. Philippe, disobeying his brother's orders, was present at Anne's deathbed and his grief was intense. Her passing deepened the rift between the king and his brother, adding to the strain on relations between Monsieur and Madame. Gossip continued about Henriette's admirers, though stories of lovers hiding behind screens seem impossibly far-fetched. Like all noblewomen of her day, Henriette Anne lived her life surrounded by others. Slinking off for secret trysts was an impossibility and in a court full of innuendo and spies, she would have been aware that the discretion of even the most seemingly devoted lady-in-waiting could not be relied upon. But what was all too real was the relationship that Monsieur had embarked on with a new male lover, the handsome but penniless younger son of the late count of Harcourt. He was also called Philippe, but was generally known as the chevalier de Lorraine.

The man who dominated Monsieur for the rest of his life was extremely handsome in an effeminate way. They had met, probably as a result of deliberate manoeuvring by Lorraine, while Philippe was involved in his first military campaign in Flanders, during the War of Devolution of 1667–8.[17] Monsieur had acquitted himself well and learned a lot, but the obvious attractions of a clever and completely unprincipled young man like the chevalier were such that he could not resist. When they returned from the army, Lorraine was given apartments in the Palais Royal and Saint-Cloud as well as money, jewels and beautiful *objets d'art* from Philippe's extensive collection. He soon became so powerful that much of Monsieur's household depended on his favour. Recognizing Philippe's uncertainties and unhappiness, willing to indulge his most degrading fantasies, Lorraine remained in relationships with women while continuing to dominate his infatuated lover.

Madame prepared to do battle with him but she had to proceed with caution. Her only male ally initially was the bishop of

Valence, Monsieur's chaplain who was now out of favour. Unfortunately he bungled a plot to expose Lorraine through revealing compromising letters the chevalier had written to Philippe. The ascendancy of a corrupt young man who was described by one contemporary as becoming 'more absolute in Monsieur's household than it was allowable to be unless one desired to be taken for the master or mistress of the family' seemed complete.[18] Madame, however, was a resourceful adversary. She had the love and support of her brother, the king of England, and Louis XIV saw her as a weapon to be deployed both in his dealings with Monsieur and, indeed, in the wider sphere of foreign relations. But first, the struggling princess was required to face yet more sorrow when her mother died.

Henrietta Maria, the one person who might have supported Madame through these difficult years, was living in England in the period 1662–5 and then too unwell on her return to France to be of much help to her beloved daughter. The queen mother remained in France till the summer after the birth of Henriette Anne's first child. Satisfied of her daughter's recovery and eager to meet Charles II's new wife, the Portuguese princess, Catherine of Braganza, there were also other reasons for her return to England. There she would be able to live in something of the manner that she had enjoyed as a young wife, a distant and happy time which still tugged at her heart strings. But she also took with her the teenage boy who was the king's eldest illegitimate son, Lucy Walter's child, James Crofts. Belatedly summoned by his father, the boy, as Henrietta Maria must have known, had been badly neglected. At the age of nine he could neither read nor count and although those appalling gaps in his education had been amended, at least superficially, he was urgently in need of being developed into a gentleman, even if he was the king's bastard.

Charles II became fond of his son and, in his desire to repair the damage done to the lad, who was thirteen when he became a regular fixture at the English court, swiftly gave him titles and found him a rich Scottish heiress for a wife. James was just four-

teen when he married the twelve-year-old Anna Scott, countess
of Buccleuch. A knighthood and the dukedom of Monmouth
sealed his position and he received lucrative offices from his father,
which was just as well, as his new mother-in-law had made sure
that he would not immediately fritter away her daughter's fortune
by entailing it out of his reach. Money, titles and influence went
to Monmouth's head and he seemed set fair to become a typical
reprobate of the Restoration court. His father decided that a
military career might harden him and give him skills which his
arrested intellectual development conspicuously lacked. It would
bring him into close association with his uncle, the duke of York,
a relationship that was not always antagonistic but became more
fraught in the 1670s.

Henrietta Maria, relieved of any further responsibility for this
visible reminder of her son's unfortunate past, proceeded to settle
in to Somerset House and live as a dowager queen should. The
next three years would restore to her a good measure of the happiness she had known in the vibrant years of her husband's reign.
Surrounded by the faithful servants who had followed her to
France and shared the long period of hardship, she brought back
her beloved Capuchin friars and was delighted that her home
became a centre of Catholic worship in London again. Once more
there were ballets and masques at her residence and it was commented that London society preferred her court to that of Charles
II's strait-laced queen. Certainly, Henrietta Maria had not forgotten how to entertain, or how to spend money on a grand scale. A
new set of state rooms, with views to the river Thames, was constructed and the queen's private apartments refurbished. Such
additions to the fabric of her home in London required, of course,
the most luxurious of furnishings. Fine carpets, including Persian
rugs, splendid furniture, tapestries and hangings transformed the
interior. The queen mother's collection of paintings was equally
impressive. Works by the great masters Titian, Tintoretto, Cor-
reggio and Gentileschi hung on the walls, as well as van Dyck's
portraits of her family. At night she slept in splendour, in a great

black bed with velvet hangings and matching stools. There were silver candlesticks and mirrors and textiles of scarlet and gold brocade which, according to the English ambassador to France, Ralph Montagu, reporting on Henrietta Maria's inventory after her death, 'will make his Majesty a very fine bed, which I am sure he wants one ... If the King pleases I will have it made up for him here much handsomer and cheaper than it can be in England.'[19] She may have dressed simply in black widow's weeds but she never forgot that she was a queen. Yet though the work she undertook was admired aesthetically by many of her son's subjects, the ostentatious revival of Catholicism, was taken by some to be a concerted attempt to make it not just acceptable but fashionable. Such behaviour offended many. Placards denouncing popery were hung from the gates of Somerset House, a sign of the difficulties to come later in Charles II's reign.

Henrietta Maria did not arrive in England in time for her son's coronation or his marriage. Charles II understood the importance of the image of majesty as much as his mother and he also knew that, despite the example of his parents, romantic love was almost never a feature of royal marriages. His mother got on well with Catherine of Braganza, a buck-toothed, olive-skinned and unfashionably dressed princess who had lived a very sheltered life in the royal palace at Lisbon. Catherine's firm Catholic piety and sweetness of manner pleased Henrietta Maria, but neither woman could have had any illusions about the king's many mistresses. Catherine of Braganza lost an early battle of wills with her husband, who had nominated his mistress, Barbara Palmer, Lady Castlemaine, to be one of the ladies of her bedchamber. Threatening to send all of her entourage home, in an outpouring of anger startlingly reminiscent of his own father's attitude to Henrietta Maria's French servants, the king imposed his mistress on his wife in the most heartless way. Poor Catherine's constant menstrual problems and several miscarriages put paid to the hope of the marriage producing any children by the late 1660s. It is perhaps to Charles's credit that he did not divorce her. As his reign progressed, he came to value her company and her advice as a political sounding board but Catherine knew that his malleable affections would never truly include her. Like his cousin Louis XIV, Charles had married, for reasons of state, a pious and conservative Iberian princess with little knowledge of the real world. Both monarchs cared nothing for the unhappiness that their extra-marital affairs caused their wives. Catherine was well aware that it was the wealth that she brought with her from Portugal's empire that had made her England's queen. Looking back on her life, she would later describe herself, with some bitterness, as having been 'sacrificed' for the interests of her family. It was only too true.

Queen Catherine found an ally in her mother-in-law but not one who could stay with her long. The English climate, so Henrietta Maria thought, disagreed with her health. Since there is not much difference between the weather in London and that in Paris, her desire to return home was probably based on a flare of her tuberculosis combined with concern about Henriette Anne. Charles II was well aware of the warfare between Monsieur and Madame and it is inconceivable that nothing of this had reached the ears of their mother. In the spring of 1665, the year of the Great Plague in London, Henrietta Maria decided to go back to France once and for all. She took up residence in her house at Colombes, just outside Paris, where she lived quietly but in considerable splendour, surrounded by many of the lovely things she had taken with her from Somerset House. The outbreak of war between England and France in 1666 distressed her and it seems that Louis XIV did seek her advice on the peace that was eventually concluded in the middle of the following year. But her health continued to decline and her English revenues dried up as Charles II, trying desperately to manage an exchequer drained by war and the extravagances of his court, cut back his mother's pension. She responded with indignation, saying that Charles's action had 'surprised me to a degree that is very difficult to express to you, it not having entered into my imagination that you would have wished to retrench me, since you know well yourself I had come down as near to economy as I could for my subsistence'.[20] The reality of England's financial problems meant that there was little that could be done, though Lord Arlington, the king's chief minister, who had recently replaced the queen's old enemy, Clarendon, made helpful noises.

During the two years that followed, the queen mother's health continued to decline but her death, on 10 September 1669, came as something of a surprise. In pain and unable to sleep, Henrietta Maria was persuaded by her doctor to take an opiate to help her rest. The dose was too strong for someone in her weakened condition and it killed her. The French bishop Jacques Bossuet preached a famous sermon when her heart was buried at the convent at Chaillot where she had spent so much time. In his lengthy address to Monsieur and Madame, Bossuet referred to 'the memory of a great queen, daughter, wife, mother of a powerful king and sovereign of three kingdoms', but he also remembered 'a fugitive queen, she could find no succour in three kingdoms and for whom her own native land was only a place of sad exile . . .'[21] A state funeral was held a few days later at the cathedral of Saint-Denis, the traditional resting place of French royalty.

Historians remain divided about the role and influence of Henrietta Maria in the English Civil Wars. Her reputation was certainly blackened by parliamentary propaganda but her letters to her husband reveal a strong-willed, opinionated woman who did not really understand the forces unleashed around her. She always saw things in black and white. She was a loyal wife but a difficult mother, although her eldest son had come to appreciate her qualities and resolution of character after he became king. Henriette Anne, trapped in a loveless marriage, at least had the satisfaction of knowing that the husband she detested had been prevented from helping himself to all her mother's belongings at Colombes. Montagu, the English ambassador, immediately obtained Louis XIV's order to seal the house, thus protecting the dowager queen's possessions from both the depredations of Monsieur and Henry

Jermyn, earl of St Albans, who, he claimed, would not have left a silver spoon in the house.[22]

Henriette Anne received Jermyn at Saint-Cloud the day after her mother's death. They both broke down in tears. But Madame yet had a part to play in relations between France, her adopted country, and England, where she had been born. Her leading role in the diplomacy of 1670 infuriated her husband but his determination to thwart her was overruled by Louis XIV.

*

THE FOND, OFTEN frank letters exchanged between Madame and Charles II give no hint of the compulsive flirt whose alleged love affairs remained the talk of the whisperers in French high society. They reveal Henriette Anne in a completely different light; this is no giddy girl but a highly political creature, confident in the world of backstairs diplomacy and deception. She was well informed about European events, intelligent and perceptive, and Charles II for one never doubted his beloved Minette. 'You must see,' she wrote to Lord Arlington, 'that even in the smallest thing, I think of furthering the interests of the king my brother.'[23] And so it was to prove. Her role in the negotiations which culminated in the Secret Treaty of Dover, in which Charles II essentially sold himself and his country to the French, was pivotal. Distressed at the breakdown of Anglo–French relations in 1666 and aware of her brother's desperate need for money, Madame was convinced that she could help broker an agreement between the two countries. With Louis XIV's support she would be able to facilitate a happy outcome. Charles II himself was in no doubt of her influence and abilities. As early as 1665 he told her: 'It must be your part to keep yourself in a state of contributing [to] the events, and having a most principle part therein, which will not be a hard part to your discretion and good talent.'[24]

She did not undertake so delicate a task alone. Charles chose only men he could absolutely trust to assist her from the English side. Arlington was key but the choice of a secretary for the discussions was an odd one. Sir Thomas Clifford, a Devon gentleman who could not speak French and was generally suspicious of foreigners, assisted Arlington. The English king trusted him and may also have believed that involving more obscure but impeccably loyal men like Clifford would lessen the danger of embarrassing public revelations.[25] James, duke of York, was taken into Charles II's confidence as matters progressed. He had been out of favour with the king since he had taken Clarendon's part in the quarrel that led to the earl's dismissal but was undergoing a conversion to Catholicism, with the encouragement of his wife, Duchess Anne, Clarendon's daughter. As the king's conversion to Catholicism was a crucial part of the treaty, Charles may have considered it important to involve his brother and to improve relations with James. Though there was never the animosity between the brothers that existed between Louis XIV and Monsieur, Charles II was always quick to remind James that he was a subject.

Louis XIV's aims in pursuing the Secret Treaty of Dover were to draw England into his wars with the Dutch. He had already conceived the ultimate goal of utterly destroying the Dutch republic. Charles II, mindful of the effect his alliance with France might have on his nephew, William III of Orange, sought to reassure the young man in 1672, noting that 'our interests seem to be a little differing at present' and that he hoped to live 'to be more useful to you'. In truth, the English king's resentment of defeat in the second Dutch war in the mid-1660s was more powerful than any considerations of family. Charles II wanted revenge. But that was not all. In return for his conversion to Catholicism, to be announced to his English subjects at a date of his choosing (a most convenient get-out clause for the king), he would receive a substantial sum of money from Louis XIV. He asked for £200,000 and eventually settled for £160,000. Given how cash-strapped he was, this represented a very handy injection into his depleted coffers.

Discreetly handled, the discussions proceeded well. By February 1670, Charles sought to bring them to a speedy conclusion by requesting that Madame be allowed to make the journey from the Channel coast to Dover during the coming spring. As the French court already had planned a visit to Flanders at the time, Madame would be in a convenient location for what could easily be passed off as a reunion with her brother. The fly in the ointment, as ever, was Monsieur. He knew more than was comfortable about his wife's mission and considered that it should have been entrusted to him. Philippe had courted Charles II throughout the 1660s, hoping that he could be involved in diplomacy between France and Britain. He was coldly and repeatedly rebuffed. Charles knew all about Monsieur's treatment of his sister and did not want him anywhere near negotiations. But the situation was difficult. Henriette Anne, supported by subtle concerns expressed by her brother, had extracted a very important concession from Louis XIV as her assurance that she would not proceed in a manner more favourable to English than French interests. This was the removal of the chevalier of Lorraine from her husband's household. At the end of January 1660, while Philippe and his lover were deep in conversation at the royal palace of Saint-Germain, the captain of Louis's guard entered and arrested Lorraine. He was sent south to Lyon and imprisoned.

It would be an understatement to say that Philippe was infuriated. He removed Henriette Anne from the Palais Royal and took her with him to the chilly and isolated chateau he owned in Villers-Cotterêts, in the countryside north of Paris, from where he wrote a long and impassioned letter to Colbert, Louis XIV's chief minister, complaining of the wrongs done to him and his friend. Lorraine was, he said, 'the best friend I have on earth'. Finally, he accepted the command to return to Paris and was, at least outwardly, reconciled with the king. Lorraine, meanwhile, was freed from prison but forbidden, at that time, to return to Paris. He settled in Rome, to await developments.

At first, Philippe would only agree to let his wife travel to

England if he went with her. Having had it made clear to him that this was simply not on the cards, he grudgingly gave way. Henriette Anne would make the voyage without him. He did accompany the royal party to Flanders but his petulance had not gone away. The royal party, consisting of the king, his mistress, Madame de Montespan, Queen Maria Teresa, the duke and duchess of Orléans and La Grande Mademoiselle, endured a ghastly journey north in the damp spring, huddled together in the royal coach. The queen's humiliation matched Monsieur's but, unlike him, she endured it in silence. Philippe and his wife quarrelled constantly as the coach rumbled along. Henriette seemed exhausted by the trip before she even reached the coast and retired early every night. She complained of stomach pains and was thinner than ever. Mademoiselle, the hardiest of this unhappy little group, finally realized the depth of Philippe's hatred for his wife. It was obvious that they could never be reconciled. 'I have been told that I should have several wives,' she reported him as saying, 'and given the condition Madame is in, I can well believe it.'[26]

Madame and a retinue of 230 people embarked from Dunkirk to England and arrived off the coast of her homeland on 26 May 1670. She was met by Charles II and Monmouth, who had visited her in Paris and got on well with his young aunt. The Secret Treaty of Dover was promptly signed and Madame spent the next three weeks celebrating her brother's birthday, enjoying parties, banquets, ballets and excursions along the coast by boat. She took her leave of Charles and his son James on 12 June and arrived back at Saint-Germain nearly a week later. In her own mind, she had made a major contribution to relations between England and France. Madame's exhilaration was soon dampened by her husband's pettiness and continued determination to oppose everything she wanted to do. He refused to go out to meet her as she neared Saint-Germain and found his brother's almost exaggerated welcome distasteful. Refusing to follow Louis XIV to Versailles, he ordered his wife back to Paris and thence to Saint-Cloud. They arrived on 14 June 1670. Henriette Anne had just over two weeks to live.

*

A DAY TRIP TO Versailles at the express command of the king did not improve Monsieur's humour. His wife was feeling progressively unwell but he seemed not to notice or care, though Louis XIV was alarmed by Henriette Anne's appearance, as were Maria Teresa and Mademoiselle. An insomniac for many years, the princess found the heat oppressive. She took an evening dip in the Seine, against doctor's orders, and strolled in the gardens of Saint-Cloud with her friend Madame de La Fayette till very late. She had never been a person to keep still. On the morning of 29 June, a few days later, she seemed somewhat better and spent some time with her elder daughter, Marie Louise, who was having her portrait painted. At the main meal of the day, which was served at about eleven in the morning, as was the custom in the French court, she ate more heartily than usual and then fell asleep with her head on Madame de La Fayette's lap. But the visible change in her face as she slept greatly alarmed her friend and was even noticed by Monsieur. Still he does not seem to have thought she was in any great danger and in the evening came to take formal leave of his wife in her apartments, as was proper, before going into Paris for the evening.

While he was there Henriette Anne asked for the drink of iced chicory water which she normally took late in the afternoon. This time, it had a catastrophic effect. No sooner had she drunk it than she collapsed in agony, clutching her side and crying out: 'Oh, what a cramp in my side! What pain!' Her immediate thought was that the drink had been poisoned and that she was going to die. Nonplussed and frightened, Philippe called for doctors and stayed by his wife's bedside. He seemed moved when she embraced him, saying: 'Alas, Monsieur, it is long since you have loved me; but that is unjust. I have never been unfaithful to you.'[27] There is no reason to doubt this declaration. Henriette Anne had often behaved with a reckless foolishness in her relentless pursuit of the admiration of male admirers, but it is extremely unlikely that she was an adulteress.

As the evening progressed, Philippe became more and more irritated with the doctors who were hastening his wife's departure from this life. Emetics, purges and bleeding were all tried but Madame grew weaker and weaker. Louis XIV's physician arrived and, in consultation with the two other doctors present, assured Monsieur that his wife would survive. He reminded them that they had said the same about his son, who had died. Their bland assurances of recovery also annoyed the stricken woman, who was in such pain that she felt sure that death was approaching. As the evening wore on, and reports of her worsening condition reached Louis XIV, he called for his coach. Arriving at Saint-Cloud at about 11 p.m., he was deeply distressed by what he saw. Ambassador Montagu joined the growing list of noblemen and dignitaries who had come to watch the woman they called Henriette d'Angleterre die. Wishing to make her confession, Madame had to endure the dire pronouncements of a Jansenist priest who reminded her of her life of sin and frivolity and her distance from God.[28] In the small hours of the morning, the Catholic bishop Bossuet, who had written her mother's funeral oration the previous year, arrived to reassure the dying woman that she had been a good Catholic. She embraced her weeping husband again and at about three in the morning of 30 June, with her crucifix pressed to her lips, she breathed her last. She was twenty-six years old.

Madame's belief that she had been poisoned was a serious one. The king and Montagu wanted to know the truth and Louis ordered an autopsy, which pronounced that the young woman had died of natural causes. The general consensus in modern times is that Henriette Anne died of peritonitis caused by a perforated duodenal ulcer and that she may have been further weakened by tuberculosis. She had not really been healthy since childhood and the rigours of pregnancy and childbirth, added to the dismal relationship with her husband, were too much for her emaciated frame to bear over any length of time.

Philippe's grief did not last long. He went at once to his wife's dressing room and obtained keys to her cabinets. In them he found letters from Charles II to his sister about the Secret Treaty of Dover and also a sizeable sum of money that Charles had given to his sister when she left England. He pocketed the latter and only handed back about half of it when Montagu protested vehemently that Madame had meant it to be distributed among her servants. The majority of her letters from Charles II were returned to the English king at his request. Charles knew that they could be exceedingly disadvantageous to him if they fell into the wrong hands and they were mostly destroyed. Only a copy of the treaty itself remained in the Clifford family in Devon, where it did not see the light of day again for hundreds of years.

In other respects, Monsieur was almost ostentatious in observing the proprieties connected with his wife's death. In a gesture typical of the man, he ordered splendid mourning outfits of purple dresses complete with trains for the three little girls in the nursery at Saint-Cloud, his own two daughters and Madame's niece, Princess Anne Stuart. The five-year-old English princess, the younger daughter of James, duke of York, and Anne Hyde, was receiving medical treatment in France for eye problems. The likelihood of her becoming queen in her own right more than thirty years later could not have occurred to anyone at the time of her aunt's death.

Charles II's sorrow at the death of his sister was immense. For several days he shut himself away from his court, alone with his memories. Now only he and James were left of the six children of Charles I who had survived the English Civil Wars. Troubled times lay ahead for them both.

Epilogue

River Thames, 12 December 1688

He had always been a handsome man, his awareness of his status plain to see in his expression and bearing. Though over fifty, the portrait painted of him in the year of his accession, 1685, attests to the survival of his looks. The contrast with a late portrait of his brother is marked. Charles II, towards the end of his reign, showed the signs of an ageing, raddled roué; a swarthy, heavy-jowled man who was much more Bourbon than Stuart, who had indulged himself freely and yet was wary of revealing too much of his innermost thoughts, the cynic's sneer not quite concealed.

James was not at all like his brother, though he lived much of his life in Charles's shadow. He had soldiered in Europe, been a lord high admiral of the English fleet, gained experience of the city of London and of government in Scotland. Throughout Charles II's twenty-five years as king, James had been the heir. There were those who dreaded the day he would become king and the beginning of the decade of the 1680s had seen a concerted attempt to exclude him from the succession altogether. By then, his conversion to Catholicism was well known and its implications highly controversial. There were rumours for years about his religious affiliations, though he had outwardly conformed to Anglicanism during the first decade of his brother's reign.

His journey towards the old faith was a slow one. As a young man, he resisted the efforts of his mother to make him change his religion but his first wife, Anne Hyde, converted to Catholicism a few years before her death in 1671 and this made a great impact on him. Despite his infidelities, he was fond of his wife and their two daughters, Mary and Anne, the only children who had survived. He kept vigil at his duchess's bedside as she lay dying, deserted by her servants and other family members because she no longer belonged to the Church of England. Her last words, 'Duke, Duke, death is terrible – death is very terrible!' rang in his ears. His own refusal to abjure Catholicism publicly, in 1679, earned him a new, though brief, period of exile, in Brussels. Reports of Charles II being ill brought him home, but the king did not want his brother in London and sent him up to Edinburgh. There he remained till the attempts to exclude him died down. He saw them as an attack on the institution of monarchy. To James, a true Stuart, this was unthinkable. His views had not changed since the Civil Wars.

No one was more surprised than the duke of York when he was woken on the morning of 2 February 1685 to be told that his brother was dying. Charles II had suffered a stroke and was not expected to live. In his confusion and consternation – for Charles's health had previously been considered good – James arrived at the king's bedside with a shoe on one foot and a slipper on the other. Charles lingered for four days, converting to Catholicism on his deathbed, to the joy of his brother and wife. Emotionally drained by Charles's death, James came quietly to the throne. His brother's reign had seen a growth of discrimination against both Protestant dissenters and Catholics. It was hoped that the new king, who personally understood the burden of intolerance, might take steps to remedy the situation of those who had become second-class citizens. The first signs were good. 'Everything is very happy here,' wrote the earl of Peterborough. 'Never king was proclaimed with more applause. He has made a speech to the council that did charm everybody concerning his intentions of maintaining the

Government as it was established in Church and State. I doubt not but to see a happy reign.'[1]

It was not long before such optimism was dashed. James regretted his words almost as soon as he had uttered them. His intention was never to retain the religious arrangement of his brother, but to establish Catholicism on the same footing as the Church of England. This was not quite so sweeping as the aims of the last avowedly Catholic monarch of England, Mary Tudor, who returned the entire country to Rome, but it would have completely changed the religious and social fabric of England that had stood since the days of Queen Elizabeth. The prospect of Catholics being given high office in the government and universities of the country was unacceptable to the majority of the ruling class, who could whip up popular fears of popery if they felt threatened.

The immediate response, of two rebellions, one in Scotland led by the earl of Argyll and one in the west of England led by the king's bastard nephew, Monmouth, was predictable. Both uprisings were doomed. Monmouth managed to attract support among local men in the south-west, but his untrained army stood little chance against the king's forces. He was defeated at the Battle of Sedgemoor in Somerset, the last battle fought on English soil, and was captured a few days later. He behaved abjectly, much to his uncle's disgust, throwing himself at James's feet and also imploring the queen, Mary of Modena, James's second wife, to plead for him. His gruesomely bungled execution on 15 July, which required three swings of the axe, was a miserable end to a life that had started badly and ended worse. For a time, it seemed as if the king would get his way.

A more sensitive and clever man, alert to the undercurrents of anxiety about his intentions, might have weathered the coming storm. But James always saw matters entirely from his own perspective and in the clearest of terms. He began to fill vacant posts at Oxford and Cambridge universities with Catholics and when the fellows of Magdalen College defied him, he stripped them of their fellowships. His untroubled accession and the defeat of rebellion emboldened a man who believed that God was on his side and who held dear his father's conviction that monarchs possessed ultimate authority in the government of their realms. Nowhere did he demonstrate this more clearly than in his ruling of his North American colony in New York. Here James was an absolutist king. Yet it was to be his attempts at introducing wider religious toleration, for Protestant dissenters and Roman Catholics, that led to the greatest opposition. The Declaration of Indulgence and the Declaration for Liberty of Conscience, suspending penal laws against nonconformists of both religions, were introduced in Scotland and England in early 1687. When it became clear that neither parliament nor the Anglican hierarchy would stomach such reforms, he dissolved parliament and began to arrest bishops who would not read the Declaration of Indulgence in their dioceses. The acquittal of these bishops at their trial was a blow but not one that dented his confidence unduly. He would pack parliament through new elections and he would move his country still closer to Rome. And he could now achieve all his aims because he had a son and heir. Little did he realize that the arrival of this prince would be the cause of his downfall.

James's second wife was the Italian noblewoman Mary Beatrice d'Este, or Mary of Modena, as she is generally known. She had married James at the age of fifteen in 1673, when he was forty. The prospect of marrying the heir to the British throne and becoming a duchess at so young an age held no appeal for this long-faced, dark-eyed girl. She had expected to enter the religious life and was sincere and devout in her beliefs. However, in spite of the age gap and their very different backgrounds, she soon adapted to her life at the court of Charles II. James was no more faithful to her than he had been to Anne Hyde, but his affection for Mary was clear.

The new duchess was fertile and constantly pregnant in the first eleven years of her marriage. She either miscarried or produced children who could not survive the first months of life. One had been the much longed-for son. But in recent years there had been no more pregnancies and Mary of Modena, for all her efforts, was childless when she became queen. Then, towards the end of 1687, rumours began to circulate that she was expecting again. This alarmed her two step-daughters, Mary and Anne, and was particularly disconcerting for Mary's husband, William III of Orange. And the one factor that James II had consistently over-looked was the attitude of his nephew, who was also his son-in-law, locked, as William was, in a seemingly endless war with Louis XIV. Thus far James had reigned with the forbearance of subjects who were willing to give him the benefit of the doubt, but who were growing more and more alarmed by his high-handed be-haviour. Unlike him, they did not see the hand of God in the queen's new pregnancy. Across the water in the Netherlands were alternatives to James, his own elder daughter and her husband. And both were Protestant. When the queen's baby was born, on the morning of 10 June 1688, it was a son. The king rejoiced even as stories were put around that the pregnancy had been a fake, or that the child had died at birth and been replaced by a boy smuggled in inside a warming pan. Alas for James, his delight was short-lived. The birth of James Francis Edward Stuart sealed his fate.

*

So NOW, IN the gloom of winter, he sat in a boat on the river Thames, bereft and scared. His queen and baby son had already left for France and it was his intention to join them there. For the moment, there was no other choice. They had all turned against him, the parliament, the people, the Church of England, even the Protestant dissenters he had tried to help. Most bitter of all was the realization, that came late because he simply could not credit it, that his family had betrayed him. He was devastated by the actions of the man he called 'my son, the Prince of Orange', his own sister Mary's child. William had invaded from Holland, land-ing at Torbay on 5 November, the anniversary of the day that Catholics tried to murder his grandfather, James I, by blowing up the Houses of Parliament. Even Anne, the king's younger daughter, had deserted him. Now it was up to Louis XIV to support an English king and his courtiers once again. It did not have to be a permanent exile; he would try, when the time seemed right, to regain his throne.

Yet he was terrified of capture, of facing the same fate as his father. He had completely failed, a few weeks earlier, to mobilize his considerable army against the expected invasion. The building up of these forces was a project dear to his heart but when it came to leadership, Marshal Turenne's dutiful aide-de-camp failed abjectly to command. In this great crisis of his life the soldier who had always taken orders did not know how to give them. His soldiers grew discontented and drifted away on Salisbury Plain. The reign of James II effectively disappeared with them.

He was the last of the children of Charles I but he would not, in the end, give his life for his concept of kingship, as his father had done. He would not go nobly, but petulantly. So he burned the writs for a general election and threw the Great Seal of England in the dark waters of the river. This, he was sure, would cause such administrative chaos that William of Orange's attempt on England would not succeed. But James was neither a great general nor a successful escapee. Off Faversham in Kent his boat was apprehended by fishermen who did not immediately recognize the king and mistook him for a 'hatchet-faced Jesuit'. The seamen had been looking for a prize. They got a much bigger one than anticipated. James never forgot the indignities he suffered at their hands. He was manhandled, his breeches were pulled down as he was searched and he then spent several uncomfortable days in the town until Lord Feversham arrived to rescue him. James returned to London with a cavalry escort. Even then, he might have saved his throne if he had agreed to limit the royal prerogative and name a Protestant as his heir. These terms were too much for James II. On 23 December, he made a second, successful attempt at escape, much to the relief of William of Orange. James landed in France on Christmas Day.

Ten years later he thanked God for the loss of his throne, saying it had allowed him to learn the duties of Christianity. He died in 1701 at Saint-Germain, his mother's childhood home. The Stuart cause, though ultimately unsuccessful, survived till almost the midpoint of the eighteenth century as his son and grandson sought to regain their lost kingdom from the Hanoverians, the descendants of Elizabeth of Bohemia, who now ruled Britain.

Author's Note

The story of Charles I's children and the impact of the Civil Wars on their lives is an overlooked aspect of this momentous period of British history. It has rarely been told and the only two books that have attempted to cover the topic before are Julia Dobson's delightful work for younger readers, *The Children of Charles I* and Patrick Morrah's brief history, *A Royal Family* which, though sympathetic, is now somewhat dated. Otherwise, concentration has inevitably centred on Charles II during his long period of exile and on his subsequent restoration. Yet Charles I and Henrietta Maria had five surviving children, out of the eight born to them since their marriage in 1625, when the king raised his standard in Nottingham that wet and windy day in the summer of 1642. Most people know little about Charles II's siblings or their experiences during the wars and after their father's execution. Nor is it widely appreciated that the king and queen would have one more child, a girl, Henrietta, born in Exeter in 1644, and hers is perhaps the strangest tale of all.

For children born into privilege, who were the recipients of considerable parental affection and interest (though the involvement of Charles I and Henrietta Maria in their upbringing has been overstated) the Civil Wars brought separation, dislocation, interrupted educations and, ultimately, heartbreak. Their experiences were very similar to those of many families in Charles I's realms, who saw their secure lives torn apart. Despite moments of hope and, seemingly, of triumph, it is not a story that has a happy ending but it is full of drama.

That the Wars of the Three Kingdoms, as the Civil Wars should more properly be known, still fail to attract as much interest as the Tudors is something that I, and, no doubt seventeenth-century specialists, find irritating. This is such a rich period of our history and yet, apart from re-enacted battles, it fails to resonate with a wider public. I have tried to do it justice – to introduce some of the extraordinary people, on all sides of the conflict, who played a part in the fate of the royal family, and to emphasize the European context of the children's lives.

Many people have, as always, helped in the writing of this book. I must begin by acknowledging my debt to the late Professor Gerald Aylmer, the head of the history department when I was a student at the University of York, who awakened my fascination with the Civil Wars. Scholarship has, of course, moved on since then and among the young academics now working in the field I should especially like to thank Dr Mark Williams of the University of Cardiff, who valiantly read through nearly all of the draft of this book at a busy time in the academic year. His comments helped enormously. I am also grateful to Dr Sara Wolfson at Canterbury Christ Church University for discussing her ideas. Dr Laura Stewart at Birkbeck College also very kindly provided an early copy of her article on Scotland in the 1640s in the *Oxford Handbook of the English Revolution*. At Pan Macmillan, my thanks, as ever, go to my editor, Georgina Morley, Charlotte Wright, who helped select the pictures, to Tania Wilde and her desk-editing team, Ena Matagic in Production and to my copy-editor, Lorraine Green.

Special thanks to Viscount De L'Isle for letting me look at the De L'Isle and Dudley Manuscript at the Kent History and Library Centre and Lord Egremont for permission to consult the Petworth House Archive in the West Sussex Record Office at Chichester. The archivists and staff at various libraries and private collections have been generous with their time and assistance.

I should particularly like to thank Maria Esain at Chiddingstone Castle, Peter O'Donoghue, York Herald at the College of Arms, the staff at the West Sussex Record Office, Dr Sean Cunningham at The National Archives, and the ever helpful staff at the London Library, the British Library and the Bodleian Library.

Finally, I must mention the constant support of my agent, Andrew Lownie, and my husband, George Porter, who are both key to the completion of any book.

LINDA PORTER
April 2016

Notes

Abbreviations

BL	British Library
ODNB	Oxford Dictionary of National Biography
TNA	The National Archives, Kew

Prologue

1 Quoted in Rosalind Marshall, *Henrietta Maria: The Intrepid Queen* (1990), p. 34
2 Marie de Médici's coronation portrait was painted by Peter Paul Rubens.
3 The incident rankled, however, with Charles I. He referred to it in a letter to Buckingham the following year, when relations between the king and queen had severely deteriorated, blaming 'Madame St George' for putting his wife 'in such a humour of distaste against me'. Sir Charles Petrie, ed., *The Letters, Speeches and Proclamations of King Charles I* (1935), p. 43
4 Simonds D'Ewes, *The Autobiography and Correspondence of Sir Simonds D'Ewes, Bart., during the reigns of James I and Charles I*, ed. J.O. Halliwell, 2 volumes (1845), vol. 1, p. 272

Chapter One

1 See Caroline Hibbard, 'Translating Royalty: Henrietta Maria and the transition from princess to queen', *The Court Historian*, vol. 5, 1 (2000), pp. 15–28

2 Charles I to Buckingham, 26 July 1626, in Sir Charles Petrie, ed., *The Letters, Speeches and Proclamations of King Charles I*, pp. 42–45

3 Charles I to Buckingham, 7 August 1626, Petrie, *Letters*, p. 45

4 Quoted in Katie Whitaker, *A Royal Passion* (2010), p. 85

5 Charles I to Buckingham, Petrie, *Letters*, p. 52

6 See Whitaker, *A Royal Passion*, p. 97

7 M. Houssaye, *Le Cardinal de Bérulle et le Cardinal de Richelieu, 1625–29* (Paris 1875), quoted in Whitaker, *A Royal Passion*, p. 89

8 The major naval embarrassment of Buckingham's career was the siege of Cadiz in October 1626, a disaster in terms of loss of men and morale, though, as has been pointed out, the expedition was seriously under-funded and this was not Buckingham's fault. See Austin Woolrych, *Britain in Revolution* (2002), p. 54

9 The duchess erected a monument to her husband in Westminster Abbey but soon got over her loss. The following year she married the earl of Antrim.

Chapter Two

1 Mary Anne Everett Green, ed., *Letters of Queen Henrietta Maria* (1857), pp. 14–15

2 R. Malcolm Smuts, 'Art and the material culture of majesty', in Smuts, ed., *The Stuart Court and Europe* (1990), p. 93

3 Green, *Letters of Henrietta Maria*, p. 17

4 Mary Anne Everett Green, *Lives of the Princesses of England*, vol. 6, p. 101

5 M.G. Brennan, N.J. Kinammon and M.P. Hannay, eds., *The correspondence (c.1626–1659) of Dorothy Percy Sidney, Countess of Leicester* (2010), p. 117

6 Hester W. Chapman, *The tragedy of Charles II in the years 1630–1660* (1964)

7 Richard Cust, *Charles I and the Aristocracy, 1625–42* (2013), p. 306

8 H. Ferrero, ed., *Lettres de Henriette-Marie de France, reine d'Angleterre, à sa soeur, Christine, Duchesse de Savoie* (1881)

9 *ODNB* entry for Mary Sackville, countess of Dorset

10 British Library (BL) Harleian MSS 6988, f. 95

11 Cust, *Charles I and the Aristocracy*, p. 312

12 BL Add MSS 70499, f. 196, quoted in *ODNB* entry for William Cavendish, first duke of Newcastle-upon-Tyne

13 During the 1650s, Charles II tried to improve his skill in languages and did read, though his favourite material tended to be romances.

14 Margaret Cavendish, duchess of Newcastle, *The Life of William Cavendish, duke of Newcastle*, ed. C.H. Firth (1907), pp. 184–7. Newcastle's apparent antipathy to religion was remarked on by his enemies.

15 *Lettres de Henriette Marie de France*, p. 55

16 Green, *Lives of the Princesses*, vol. 6, pp. 393–4

Chapter Three

1 The term 'Anglican' was not in common usage before the Act of Uniformity in 1662 but I have used it here to denote the established Church of England and its hierarchy of bishops.

2 Quoted in Tim Harris, *Rebellion, Britain's First Stuart Kings* (2014), p. 364

3 Ibid, p. 369

4 The term 'Puritan' is a catch-all to describe the various strands of Protestant belief in England whose primary emphasis was on the understanding of God's word as shown in the Bible, rather than through the liturgy, sacraments and episcopal organization of the Church of England. The term was actually a pejorative and was not how 'Puritans' would have identified themselves. They preferred to think of themselves as 'the godly'.

5 Episcopacy was explicitly attacked in the riots in Edinburgh and elsewhere.

6 Quoted in Richard Cust, *Charles I: a Political Life*, p. 249

7 Petrie, *Letters of King Charles I*, p. 107

8 The statement is curious in that Charles I ruled three kingdoms, not four. Wales was a principality, though perhaps a child in some distress might be forgiven for failing to communicate the difference between kingdoms and countries. The English Crown still claimed titular sovereignty of France but it seems unlikely that this was included in the Prince of Wales's concerns.

9 S.R. Gardiner, *History of England*, vol. 9, p. 76

10 Ship money had traditionally been raised as taxation in coastal counties of England to support the navy. Charles I had extended it to the entire country during his personal rule and it was greatly resented.

11 Quoted in Conrad Russell, *Fall of the British Monarchies, 1637–42*, p. 126, and cited in Cust, *Charles I: a political life*, p. 260

12 See Michelle Anne White, *Henrietta Maria and the English Civil Wars* (2006), pp. 33–4

13 C.V. Wedgewood, *The King's Peace*, p. 317, quoted in White, *Henrietta Maria*, p. 40

14 For a fuller treatment, see John Adamson, *The Noble Revolt* (2007), chapter one

15 *Calendar of State Papers Domestic, Charles I*, vol. 465, 31 August 1640

16 *Calendar of the Cecil Papers in Hatfield House*, vol. 22, 21 August 1640

17 David L. Smith, 'The more posed and wise advice: the fourth earl of Dorset and the English Civil Wars', *The Historical Journal* 34, 4, pp. 797–829, presents an interesting picture of an aristocrat less anti-parliament than has often been supposed but says nothing about his reaction to Henrietta Maria's involvement in the Army Plots of spring 1641.

18 *Calendar of the Cecil Papers in Hatfield House*, vol. 22, November 1640

19 David L. Smith, 'The more posed and wise advice: the fourth earl of Dorset and the English Civil Wars', *The Historical Journal*, p. 804

20 Cust, *Charles I, a political life*, pp. 284–5

21 Quoted in *ODNB* entry for Mary, Princess Royal, by Marika Keblusek. William was referring to a van Dyck portrait of Mary sent to him before the wedding.

Chapter Four

1 J.F.D. Shrewsbury, *A History of Bubonic Plague* (2005), p. 389

2 Marie de Medici died in Cologne in 1642, still estranged from her son, Louis XIII.

3 *Lettres de Henriette-Marie de France*, pp. 57–8

4 *Letters of Queen Henrietta Maria*, p. 354

5 Henry VIII had much of the work on Oatlands done in preparation for his marriage to Anne of Cleves. Instead, he ended up marrying her successor, Katherine Howard, there in the summer of 1540. Oatlands was demolished after the death of Charles I.

6 Father Philip was confined to the Tower of London for a year, accused of attempting to spread popery and influence the Prince of Wales in religious matters.

7 Windebank fled to the continent in 1640.

8 Clarendon, *History of the Rebellion*, vol. 2, pp. 528–9, quoted in *ODNB* entry for William Seymour, marquess of Hertford and second duke of Somerset.

9 Ronald Hutton, *Charles II* (1989), p. 5

10 'Proceedings concerning the Prince', in the *House of Commons Journal*, vol. 2, 2 November 1641

11 Quoted in Cust, *Charles I*, p. 314

12 Quoted in Harris, *Rebellion*, p. 454

13 *House of Commons Journal*, vol. 2, 4 January 1642. For a fuller account of the attempted arrest of the five members, see Adamson, *The Noble Revolt*, pp. 494–9

14 Henrietta Maria's precise involvement remains unknown. S.R. Gardiner in his *History of England*, vol. X, p. 136, quotes her as goading Charles I when he hesitated with the words 'Go you coward, and pull these rogues out by the ears, or never see my face again' but we cannot be sure of what passed between the royal couple on 4 January.

15 Cust, *Charles I*, p. 332

16 Rosalind Marshall, *Henrietta Maria*, p. 90

17 Although oft repeated, this story may have been embroidered over time. The *Gazette de France*, 1642, p. 253, reported that Charles climbed the battlements of Dover Castle to watch the departure of Henrietta and Mary.

18 The role of stadtholder went back as far as the Middle Ages in the Low Countries. It combined elements of magistracy and local leadership that have been likened to the lords-lieutenant of English counties but the House of Orange had tried to invest it with a more national aspect.

19 *Memoirs of Sophia, Electress of Hanover, 1630–1680*, translated by H. Forester (1888)

20 Green, *Lives of the Princesses of England*, vol. 6, p. 127

21 Ibid, p. 130

22 See John Callow, *The Making of King James II* (2000), p. 37

23 The full text is in S.R. Gardiner, *Constitutional Documents of the Puritan Revolution*, pp. 249–53

Chapter Five

1 Eliot Warburton, *Memoirs of Prince Rupert and the Cavaliers* (1849), vol. ii, p. 489

2 Charles Louis left England in the summer of 1642.

3 Cited in Christopher L. Scott, Alan Turton and Dr Eric von Arni, *Edgehill: the battle reinterpreted* (2005), p. 79

4 Scott, Turton and von Arni, *Edgehill*, Appendix D, p. 200

5 Ibid, Appendix E, pp. 201–2

6 This experience forced a change of parliamentary cavalry tactics. Thereafter they met opposing cavalry charges at a trot.

7 J.S. Clarke, ed., *The life of James II, king of England* (1816), vol. 1, p. 15

8 Sir John Hinton, *Memoires* (1679), pp. 10–13

9 Scott, Turton and von Arni, *Edgehill*, p. 151

10 Peter Gaunt, in *The English Civil War: a military history* (2014), p. 78, puts the number as low as a few hundred on each side.

11 'Edgehill Fight', by Rudyard Kipling, first published in C.R.L. Fletcher and Rudyard Kipling, *A School History of England* (1911)

12 Their unease was reinforced by the sending of parliamentary representatives to Holland who claimed that the queen had taken valuables without permission and that the goods were not hers to pledge. White, *Henrietta Maria*, p. 62

13 Green, *Letters of Henrietta Maria*, p. 72

14 Ibid, p. 87

15 It is difficult to determine how much time Henrietta Maria had actually spent in Mary's company since they arrived together in the Netherlands. The queen's focus was on obtaining money and supplies for her husband and her surviving letters make little mention of her daughter.

16 Born Katherine Wotton, Lady Stanhope's first husband was the heir of the first earl of Chesterfield, but died before his father. Relations between the earl and his widowed daughter-in-law became strained over money matters but this did not stop Katherine from having flirtations with several men, including van Dyck. She was initially cautious about marrying Heenvliet, aware that any children of the marriage would have no property rights in England and that, if she died before her new husband, all her English property would revert to the Crown. Charles I's support for the marriage seems to have given her the confidence to proceed.

17 Heenvliet to Lady Roxburghe, 9 October 1642, Bodleian Library MS Clarendon 95, f. 85

18 Cited in Gaunt, *The English Civil War*, p. 170

19 Petrie, *Letters of King Charles I*, pp. 144–5

20 *Memoirs of Prince Rupert and the Cavaliers*, vol. II, pp. 438–9.

21 Parliamentarian losses were estimated at around 300 men.

22 Gaunt, *The English Civil War*, p. 176

23 *Letters of King Charles I*, p. 145

24 Hutton, *Charles II*, p. 7

25 For a description of the difficulties that beset Oxford and its royalist occupiers at this time see Ian Roy, 'The cavalier ideal and the reality',

in Jason McElligot and David L. Smith, eds., *Royalists and Royalism during the Civil Wars* (2007), pp. 89–111

26 *House of Lords Journal*, vol. 6, 29 March 1644. The necessities of childbirth were delicately referred to by Mary Anne Everett Green, in her *Letters of Queen Henrietta Maria*, as her 'trousseau'. See p. 242

27 Mayerne's pass was issued on 17 May 1644. See *House of Lords Journal* for that day.

28 Green, *Letters of Henrietta Maria*, pp. 244–5

29 Minette means 'little pussycat' and has had vulgar associations. Its modern usage is as a reference to a 'cute chick'.

30 Green, *Letters of Henrietta Maria*, pp. 244–5

31 Knowledge had scarcely increased since Mary Tudor was diagnosed with 'hysteria' for what were probably frequent heavy and painful periods over a century before.

32 Philip A. Knachel, ed., *Eikon Basilike: The Portraiture of his sacred majesty in his solitudes and Sufferings* (1966), cited in White, *Henrietta Maria*, p. 152

Chapter Six

1 *House of Lords Journal*, vol. 6, p. 341

2 Quoted, without attribution, in Patrick Morrah, *A royal family: Charles I and his family* (1982), p. 73

3 Clarendon, *History of the Rebellion*, vol. 2, p. 538, quoted in *ODNB* entry on Algernon Percy, 10th earl of Northumberland

4 Falkland's death, at the first battle of Newbury in 1643, shook Hyde to the core.

5 W.H. Abbott, *Writings and Speeches of Oliver Cromwell*, vol. 1, p. 314, quoted in Woolrych, *Britain in Revolution*, p. 302. Cromwell was later exempted from the Self-Denying Ordinance.

6 George Bishop, *A more particular and exact relation of the victory obtained by the Parliament's forces* (1645), quoted in Gaunt, *The English Civil War*, p. 213

7 Abbott, *Writings and Speeches of Oliver Cromwell*, vol. 1, p. 360, quoted in Woolrych, *Britain in Revolution*, p. 319

8 Petrie, *Letters of King Charles I*, p. 154

9 Petrie, *King Charles, Prince Rupert and the Civil War*, p. 9. Rupert was correct that Charles I was considering going north. The king was buoyed by news of the marquess of Montrose's victories against the Covenanters and entertained the idea of joining his remaining forces

with those of supporters of royalism in Scotland. He did not get any farther than Doncaster in Yorkshire before the realization that he could be cut off by a Scottish army allied to parliament and decided to go back to Oxford.

10 Ibid, p. 10
11 Eva Scott, *Rupert, prince palatine* (1899), pp. 182–3, quoted in *ODNB* entry for Rupert
12 Ibid, pp. 14–15
13 Quote in Julia Cartwright, *Madame: a life of Henrietta, daughter of Charles I and Duchess of Orleans* (1901), p. 8
14 Ibid p. 7
15 Ibid p. 12
16 It is possible that Anne Dalkeith meant that they should apply for support from Charles I rather than literally going to join him.
17 S.R. Gardiner, *History of the Great Civil War* (2002 edition), vol. 3, p. 102
18 Quoted in Callow, *The Making of King James II*, p. 44
19 The record book of expenses for the royal children is in the West Sussex Record Office, *PHA 617* (unfolioed). Northumberland's losses in the north are in *Historical Manuscripts Commission 3rd Report, 1872*, 'The Manuscripts of His Grace the Duke of Northumberland' at Alnwick Castle, p. 86
20 Petrie, ed., *Letters of King Charles I*, pp. 204–5
21 J. Loftis, ed., *The Memoirs of Anne, Lady Halkett, and Ann, Lady Fanshawe* (1979), pp. 117–18
22 Green, ed., *Letters of Henrietta Maria*, p. 314
23 Ibid, p. 321
24 Hyde did not see Prince Charles again for two years.

Chapter Seven

1 Karen Britland, 'Exile or Homecoming? Henrietta Maria in France, 1644–69', in *Monarchy and Exile: the politics of legitimacy from Marie de Médicis to Wilhelm II* (2011), p. 124
2 See Anthony Adolph, *Full of Soup and Gold: the life of Henry Jermyn* (2006)
3 Some accounts describe Anne as auburn-haired. Her colouring was evidently a matter of interpretation.
4 See Ruth Kleinman, *Anne of Austria, Queen of France* (1985), pp. 105–6

5 Quoted, without reference, in Richard Wilkinson, *Louis XIV* (2007), p. 13

6 Simone Bertière, *Mazarin: le maître du jeu* (2007), p. 37

7 Quoted in Geoffrey Treasure, *Mazarin: the crisis of absolutism in France* (1995), p. 45

8 Mademoiselle's *Mémoires*, quoted in Vincent J. Pitts, *La Grande Mademoiselle at the court of France, 1627–1693* (2000), p. ix

9 *Mémoires de Mademoiselle de Montpensier* (2006), p. 131

10 Like Prince Charles, Rupert had arrived in Paris in the summer of 1646. He was well received by the French court, where he was made a French field marshal and served with the army against the Spanish. Charles I had written to Henrietta Maria acknowledging his nephew's passionate nature but asking her to receive him cordially.

11 Quoted in Carola Oman, *Henrietta Maria* (1936), p. 184

12 He eventually married his first cousin, the archduchess Maria Leopoldine.

13 C.S. Terry, 'The visits of Charles I to Newcastle in 1633, 39, 41 and 46–7', Society of Antiquaries of Newcastle-upon-Tyne, *Archaeologia Aeliana*, NS vol. 21 (1899), p. 111

14 *Charles I in 1646: Letters of King Charles I to Queen Henrietta Maria* (1856), letters of 20 and 26 May, 1646, pp. 40–3

15 Ibid, p. 42

16 Terry, 'The visits of Charles I to Newcastle', p. 118

17 The Propositions of the Houses sent to the King at Newcastle, Gardiner, *Constitutional Documents of the Puritan Revolution*, pp. 290–306

18 Petrie, *Letters of King Charles I*, pp. 202–3

19 Green, *Letters of Henrietta Maria*, p. 335

20 *Charles I in 1646*, pp. 76–7

21 Ibid, p. 86

22 *Lettres du Cardinal Mazarin pendant son ministère, recueillies et publiées par MA Chéruel*, tome II, July 1644–December 1647 (Paris 1889). My translation.

Chapter Eight

1 Sir Thomas Herbert, *Memoirs* (1702), p. 11

2 Essex's influence was, in any case, minimal by this time and it is worth pointing out that Holles, who had always hoped to avoid civil war, was committed to limiting the king's powers in any peace that was negotiated.

3 Quoted in Woolrych, *Britain in Revolution*, p. 364
4 Petrie, *Letters of King Charles I*, p. 231
5 *House of Lords Journal*, vol. 9, 9 July 1647, pp. 321–4
6 Green, *Lives of the Princesses of England*, p. 356
7 Abbott, *Writings and Speeches of Oliver Cromwell*, vol. I, pp. 473–4
8 *The Heads of the Proposals offered by the Army*, Gardiner, *Constitutional Documents of the Puritan Revolution*, pp. 316–26
9 Gardiner, *History of the Great Civil War*, vol. 3, p. 172
10 Green, *Lives of the Princesses*, p. 363
11 Quoted in Paul Seaward, ed., *Edward Hyde, Earl of Clarendon, History of the Rebellion, a new selection* (2009), p. 297. The assertion that Ashburnham had offered to rush downstairs and kill Hammond when he saw the king's discomfiture is probably false. Hyde was no friend to Ashburnham, though he was close to Sir John Berkeley, whose advice he evidently thought should have been followed when Charles I escaped from Hampton Court.
12 There seems to be some confusion about Anne's mother, Jane Drummond, who is often referred to as the countess of Roxburghe, governess to the royal children, who died in 1643. But Anne's mother, who died in 1647, had married Thomas Murray, Provost of Eton (and tutor to Charles I when he was duke of York), whereas the Jane Drummond who was royal governess married Robert Ker, lord (and later earl) of Roxburghe. William Murray, the king's servant, was Anne's cousin.
13 John Loftis, ed., *The Memoirs of Anne, Lady Halkett and Ann, Lady Fanshawe* (1979), p. 24
14 J. Loftis and P. Hardacre, eds., *Colonel Joseph Bampfield's Apology, 'Written by Himself and Printed at his Desire', 1685* (1993), p. 67
15 *Bampfield's Apology*, pp. 69–70
16 Green, *Lives of the Princesses*, vol. 6, p. 148

Chapter Nine

1 The sabbatarianism of the Presbyterians, which threatened to become ever more restrictive during the spring of 1648, was a further cause of public unrest. See Woolrych, *Britain in Revolution*, p. 406
2 Quoted in Kleinman, *Anne of Austria*, pp. 201–2
3 William Allen, *A faithful memorial of that remarkable meeting . . . at Windsor Castle* (1659), in *Somers Tracts* (1809–15), vol. VI, pp. 498–504
4 Rainsborough had Leveller sympathies and his appointment, which

superseded that of Vice-Admiral William Batten, triggered much ill
feeling amongst the largely Kentish crews of the warships. The men of
his own flagship refused to let him aboard after a visit to the shore and
he suffered the ignominy of being packed off to London in a small boat
with his family. See *ODNB* entry for Thomas Rainsborough and also
Woolrych, *Britain in Revolution*, p. 411

5 'The Prince of Wales's court was full of faction and animosity against
each other, so that the newcomers (Hyde travelled with Lord
Cottington, an elderly peer who was a former chancellor of the
exchequer) were not only very well received by the Prince, but very
welcome to everybody.' Clarendon, *History of the Rebellion*, vol. 3, part I
(1720), p. 165. This happy state of affairs did not last long.

6 Ibid, p. 138

7 Quoted in Gardiner, *History of the Great Civil War*, vol. 4, pp. 220–1

8 BL Sloane MS 3299, f. 147

9 Quoted in Cust, *Charles I: a political life*, p. 445

10 Jack D. Jones, *The Royal Prisoner* (1965), p. 118

11 John Adamson, 'The frightened junto: perceptions of Ireland and the
last attempts at settlement with Charles I', in Jason Peacey, ed., *The
Regicides and the Execution of Charles I* (2001)

12 We do not know precisely how many members were prevented from
taking their seats and the purge went on over nearly a week. The Rump,
as those who were left were called, numbered 200, less than half of the
pre-purge strength. Cromwell later claimed that he did not know
about the plans for Pride's Purge. 'He declared that he had not been
acquainted with this design; but since it was done, he was glad of it and
would endeavour to maintain it.' Ludlow, *Memoirs*, I, pp. 211–12. Fairfax
had already summoned him back from the siege of Pontefract in
Yorkshire and he arrived in London the day after Pride's Purge.

13 Abbott, *Writings and Speeches*, vol. 1, p. 699

14 Jones, *The Royal Prisoner*, p. 158

15 See Adamson, '*The Frightened Junto*', p. 43

16 Ibid, p. 46

17 Clarendon, *History of the Rebellion*, vol. 3, part 1, p. 89

18 TNA, PRO 31/3/89 (Baschet Transcripts), despatch dated 4 January
1649, f. 58

19 The possibility that the Duke of Gloucester might replace his father
was widely known in Europe. It was reported from The Hague in
mid-January that, if Charles I was executed, his youngest son would
be put on the throne under a protectorate headed by Thomas Fairfax.

20 For the Fronde, see below, chapter eleven

21 Green, *Letters of Henrietta Maria*, pp. 348–9
22 Clarendon, *History of the Rebellion*, vol. 3, part 1, p. 252
23 Printed in the appendix of M. Guizot, *History of Oliver Cromwell and the English Commonwealth*, vol. 1 (1854), pp. 369–70
24 By Blair Worden, in *The English Civil Wars, 1640–1660*, p. 101
25 See Hopper, *'Black Tom'*, pp. 195–9
26 Petrie, *Letters of King Charles I*, p. 200
27 Clarendon, *History of the Rebellion*, vol. 3, part 1, pp. 229–30
28 Petrie, *Letters of King Charles I*, pp. 259–61
29 Gardiner, *Constitutional Documents of the Puritan Revolution*, pp. 377–80
30 Quoted in Green, *Lives of the Princesses*, p. 369
31 Ibid, pp. 370–1
32 Petrie, *Letters of King Charles I*, pp. 261–73
33 R. Lockyer, ed., *Sir Thomas Herbert's Narrative* (1959), p. 122
34 See Antonia Fraser, *Cromwell, our chief of men* (1997), pp. 293–4
35 Hyde, *History of the Rebellion, a new selection* (2009), p. 336

Chapter Ten

1 Bodleian Library, MS Clarendon 95, f.249
2 Hutton, *Charles II*, p. 33
3 This letter was translated from French into Italian and then back into English. It contains a number of errors and its provenance is doubtful. The sentiments it contains, however, may well be similar to those of Henrietta Maria. Green, *Letters of Queen Henrietta Maria*, p. 357
4 Henry Cary, ed., *Memorials of the Great Civil War in England, from 1641–1652* (1842), vol. 2, p. 127
5 R.W. Blencowe, ed., *Sydney Papers* (1825), p. xxi
6 The countess of Carlisle was released on bond from the Tower of London in September 1650 but was not allowed greater freedom till 1652.
7 Blencowe, *Sydney Papers*, p. xxxiii
8 It is not clear whether Mayerne was actually asked to give his opinion at this stage. His subsequent comments on Elizabeth's health came after her death. Given the authorities' determination to remove Elizabeth and Henry from the mainland it seems unlikely that Mayerne's views, even if sought, would have made any difference.
9 Green, *Lives of the Princesses*, pp. 382–3
10 This well-intentioned bequest caused the earl and countess of Leicester a great deal of trouble. The government of the Commonwealth viewed

Elizabeth's diamond ornament as the property of the state and accused the Leicesters of purloining it. They were only allowed to keep it after a lengthy lawsuit.

11 Susan Cole, *A flower of purpose: A memoir of Princess Elizabeth Stuart, 1635–50*, Royal Stuart Papers VIII, The Royal Stuart Society (1975), p. 21

12 *House of Commons Journal*, 11 September 1650, vol. 6, p. 465

13 Quoted in Cole, *A flower of purpose*, opposite p. 1

14 *Lettres de Henriette-Marie de France*, pp. 89–90

Chapter Eleven

1 The print is in the British Library.

2 K.M. Brown et al, eds., *Records of the Parliaments of Scotland* (*RPS*), 5 February 1649

3 Antonia Fraser suggests that Lucy may have travelled with her uncle on her mother's side, the earl of Carbery. She also stoutly defends Lucy against the charge that she was little better than a whore. That may be reasonable – Lucy's behaviour was no different from that of some of Charles II's later mistresses, though Nell Gwyn is said to have cheerfully described herself as a whore – but she was certainly unsuccessful in dealing with her situation, or in holding Charles's affection, if, indeed, she had ever really had it. See Antonia Fraser, *Charles II* (1979), pp. 64–6

4 Hutton, *Charles II*, p. 77

5 *Lettres de Henriette-Marie de France*, p. 73

6 See John Morrill's *ODNB* entry for Oliver Cromwell. The traditional view of Cromwell in Ireland is reinforced in Micheál Ó'Siochrú's *God's Executioner* (2008).

7 T. Carlyle and S.C. Lomas, eds., *The Letters and Speeches of Oliver Cromwell* (1904), *The Declaration of the Lord Lieutenant of Ireland for the Undeceiving of Deluded People*, January, 1650, vol. 2, pp. 16–17

8 S.R. Gardiner, ed., *Letters and papers illustrating the relations between Charles II and Scotland in 1650* (1894), p. 74

9 Royalist literature cast Neil Macleod of Assynt as the villain who betrayed Montrose. There had been a price on the marquess's head since the mid-1640s and Neil was in a difficult position in Sutherland, where he could ill afford to displease the Covenanter regime. But it was the wife of one of the Monro clan who first imprisoned Montrose. Cowan, *Montrose*, p. 290

10   Cowan, *Montrose*, p. 284

11   S.R. Gardiner, ed., *The Hamilton Papers* (Camden Society, 1880), p. 255

12   This is discussed at more length in Laura Stewart's article, 'Scotland in the later 1640s: "Down-hill all the way"?' in Michael Braddick, ed., *The Oxford Handbook of the English Revolution* (2015), pp. 114–36. I am grateful to Dr Stewart for letting me see an early draft of this article.

13   Instructions and correspondence in the *Chiddingstone Papers*, Chiddingstone Castle, Kent

14   Quoted in Allan I. Macinnes, *The British Confederate, Archibald Campbell, Marquess of Argyll, 1607–61* (2011)

15   Ibid, p. 27. Although relations were strained between the seventh earl of Argyll and his elder son (especially after he handed over some of his estates to his son by his second marriage), this character assassination, which originates with Clarendon, is a prophecy which came rather too conveniently true and the story is likely to be apocryphal.

16   J.G. Nichols, ed., *The Autobiography of Anne, Lady Halkett* (1875), p. 57

17   Anne stayed in Scotland after the king left, nursing wounded troops and standing up to English soldiers who abused her when they stormed Fyvie Castle, the home of the earl of Dunfermline, in late 1651. She eventually shook off Bampfield and married Sir James Halkett, a Scottish widower with several children.

18   As reported by La Grande Mademoiselle in her *Mémoires*. See Chapman, *The Tragedy of Charles II*, p. 169

19   Quoted in Stewart, 'Scotland in the later 1640s', p. 130

20   The autumn of 1650 in Scotland saw a series of disputes and realignments in politics and the army. It is a confusing period and I have deliberately omitted going into detail about it. Anyone who is interested in Remonstrants and Resolutioners can read about the machinations of these months in David Stevenson's *Revolution and Counter-Revolution in Scotland, 1644–1651* (2003), chapter five.

21   Quoted in John, third marquess of Bute, *Scottish Coronations* (1902), p. 142

22   Ibid, pp. 192–3

23   Quoted in Stevenson, *Revolution and Counter-Revolution in Scotland*, p. 173

24   Letter to Lady Hamilton in the Commandery Museum, Worcester, quoted in Malcolm Atkin, *Cromwell's Crowning Mercy, the battle of Worcester, 1651* (1998), p. 99

25   Ibid, p. 165

26   Quoted in Richard Ollard, *The Escape of Charles II after the battle of Worcester* (2002), p. 38

27 The king's account of his escape was not actually printed until the Exclusion Crisis of the 1680s. See Brian Weiser, 'Owning the king's story: the escape from Worcester', *The Seventeenth Century*, XIV, No. 1, Spring 1999, pp. 43–62

Chapter Twelve

1 A Dutch translation of *Eikon Basilike* appeared within two weeks of the execution of Charles I. See Helmer J. Helmers, *The Royalist Republic: Literature, Politics and Religion in the Anglo-Dutch Sphere, 1639–1660* (2015), pp. 115–48

2 The so-called Generality Lands were added as part of the Treaty of Westphalia in 1648 but they had no local political representation and were directly governed by the States-General, the republic's national representative body.

3 The seven provinces were Holland, Zeeland, Gelderland, Utrecht, Friesland, Overijssel and Gronigen.

4 The painting was little appreciated at the time. Rembrandt was so hard up that he had to dismantle it and sell it.

5 Quoted in Maarten Prak, *The Dutch Republic in the seventeenth century* (2005), p. 182

6 L.M. Baker, ed., *The Letters of Elizabeth, Queen of Bohemia* (1953), p. 179

7 Quoted in Green, *Lives of the Princesses*, vol. 6, p. 164

8 Arthur Bryant, ed., *The Letters, Speeches and Declarations of Charles II* (1935), pp. 21–2.

9 Henry Nash to William Edgeman, 12 December 1650, in S.R. Gardiner, ed., *Letters and Papers Illustrating the relations between Charles II and Scotland in 1650*, pp. 148–9. In fact, William II of Orange was not buried until 8 March 1651.

10 Bodleian Library, MS Clarendon 95, f. 334

11 G. Groen van Printsterer, ed., *Archives ou correspondance inédite de la Maison d'Orange Nassau* (1861), vol. 5, p. 21

12 Both Nicholas and Hyde had their English estates confiscated in 1651, when they were declared traitors.

13 Bodleian Library, MS Clarendon 95, f. 403

14 *Lettres de Henriette-Marie de France*, p. 93

15 Quoted in Ann Hughes and Julie Sanders, 'Gender, Exile and The Hague Courts of Elizabeth, Queen of Bohemia and Mary, Princess of Orange in the 1650s', in Philip Mantel and Torsten Riotte, eds.,

Monarchy and Exile: the politics of legitimacy from Marie de Médicis to Wilhelm II (2011), p. 54

16 Hughes and Sanders, 'Gender, Exile and the Hague Courts,' p. 56

17 Ibid, p. 57

18 The first Anglo–Dutch war followed an overture, resisted by the Dutch, that the two republics of England and the United Provinces should consider uniting as one country.

19 Quoted in Mark R.F. Williams, *The King's Irishmen: the Irish in the exiled court of Charles II, 1649–1660* (2014), p. 216

20 For more on the crisis of the Church of England during the 1650s, see Williams, chapter 3.

21 Thurloe, *State papers*, vol. 1, p. 681

22 Green, *Lives of the Princesses*, vol. 6, p. 238

23 Ibid., p. 246

24 Green, *Letters of Queen Henrietta Maria*, p. 383

25 Bryant, ed., *The Letters of Charles II*, pp. 58–9

Chapter Thirteen

1 Nicholas Papers, vol. 1, pp. 196–7, quoted in John Miller, *James II* (2000), p. 13

2 Clarendon, *History of the Rebellion*, vol. 5, pp. 164–5, quoted in Miller, ibid., p. 14

3 It has been suggested that Turenne's change of heart in respect of the Fronde was partly brought about by envy of Condé's success. See Callow, *The Making of King James II*, p. 65

4 Quoted in Miller, *James II*, p. 16

5 Quoted in Callow, *The Making of King James II*, p. 67

6 Baker, *Letters of Elizabeth of Bohemia*, pp. 178–9. A sum of £3,000 p.a. had, in fact, been under discussion as a grant from the English government to Henry.

7 *House of Commons Journal*, vol. 7, pp. 226–7

8 George F. Warner, ed., *Correspondence of Sir Edward Nicholas (The Nicholas Papers)* (1892), vol. 2, p. 5

9 Ibid., p. 7

10 *Nicholas Papers*, vol. 2, p. 55

11 Bodleian Library, Clarendon MS 48, f. 324.

12 *Letters of King Charles II*, pp. 29–30

13 Rev. W. Macray and Rev. H. Coxe, eds., *Calendar of the Clarendon State Papers*, vol. 2, p. 421

14 Bodleian Library, Clarendon MS 49, f. 137, quoted in Nicole Greenspan, 'Public Scandal, Political Controversy, and Familial Conflict in the Stuart Courts in Exile: The Struggle to Convert the Duke of Gloucester in 1654', *Albion: a quarterly journal concerned with British studies*, October, 2003, vol. 35, pp. 398–427. See also Williams *The King's Irishmen*, pp. 262–70

15 *Calendar of the Clarendon State Papers*, vol. 2, pp. 433–4

16 See Cartwright, *Madame*, pp. 30–1. The dramatic depiction of a wailing Princess Henriette is repeated in Carola Oman's biography of Henrietta Maria.

17 Greenspan, 'Public Scandal', p. 425. Readers of this article should note that Greenspan is mistaken in writing that Henry died six weeks before the Restoration in 1660. See chapter fifteen.

18 Anna Keay, 'The Shadow of a King? Aspects of the Exile of King Charles II' in Mansel and Riotte, eds., *Monarchy and Exile*, p. 107

19 The challenges of exile for one especially important group of Charles II's supporters are explored in Williams's book, *The King's Irishmen*, passim.

20 Ibid., p. 222

Chapter Fourteen

1 Quoted in *ODNB* entry for Oliver Cromwell by John Morrill

2 Elizabeth of Bohemia, *Letters*, p. 278

3 Article by Jonathan Fitzgibbons, 'Not in any doubtful dispute? Reassessing the nomination of Richard Cromwell', *Historical Research*, vol. 83 (May 2010), pp. 281–300, quoted on p. 296

4 T. Birsh, ed., *A collection of the state papers of John Thurloe* (1742), vol. 7, p. 374

5 Abbott, *Writings and Speeches of Oliver Cromwell*, vol. 2, p. 425

6 BL Landsdowne MS 823, fols. 89–90, quoted in *ODNB* entry for Richard Cromwell by Peter Gaunt

7 Thurloe, *State Papers*, vol. 7, pp. 387–8

8 Lucy Hutchinson, *Memoirs of the life of Colonel Hutchinson*, ed. James Sutherland (1973), p. 212

9 *Letters of King Charles II*, pp. 72–3

10 Ibid, p. 70

11 Henry Reece, *The Army in Cromwellian England*, 1649–60 (2013), p. 197. Reece's study, based on a previous doctorate and many years of research, is now a key text on this crucial subject.

12 Quoted in F.M.S. McDonald, 'The timing of General George Monck's

March into England, 1 January 1660', *English Historical Review*, vol. 105, no. 415 (April 1990), pp. 363–76

13 Ibid, p. 370
14 See *ODNB* entry on George Monck by Ronald Hutton.

Chapter Fifteen

1 Frances Henderson, ed., *The Clarke Papers*, Camden Society 5ᵗʰ series, vol. 27 (2005), p. 362
2 Confined on the island of Jersey for many years, he was still regarded as a focus for discontent against Charles II, though his wife was allowed to join him and they lived in a house on the island, under the sympathetic eye of Christopher Hatton. Lambert's wife predeceased him but his family continued to do what they could for him and in the latter years of his life he received distinguished visitors, including the king, the duke of York and Samuel Pepys. He eventually perished during the freezing winter of 1683–4, on Drake's Island in Plymouth Sound, and was buried in St Andrew's parish church in Plymouth.
3 *Letters of King Charles II*, p. 83
4 *Constitutional Documents of the Puritan Revolution*, pp. 465–7
5 *Letters of Elizabeth of Bohemia*, p. 308
6 BL Add MS 19523
7 Quoted in C.H. Hartmann, *The King my Brother* (1954), p. 19
8 Quoted in *ODNB* entry for Prince Henry, duke of Gloucester, by Stuart Handley
9 Green, *Lives of the Princesses*, vol. 6, p. 310
10 Green, *Lives of the Princesses*, p. 326
11 TNA, SP 84/164, ff. 116–24
12 Rupert's companion-in-arms, his younger brother, Maurice, perished in 1652, drowned in a hurricane off the Virgin Islands.
13 *Lettres de Henriette-Marie*, p. 124
14 The reference to Charles enjoying the discomfiture of others is in Callow, *The Making of James II*, p. 91. Callow's account of the chequered background to James's marriage to Anne Hyde does not agree in several points with John Miller's in the *ODNB*, where Miller states that Charles II initially refused James permission to marry Anne.

Chapter Sixteen

1 Hartmann, *The King my Brother*, p. 258
2 Christian Bouyer, *Henriette-Anne d'Angleterre* (2006), p. 63
3 Cartwright, *Madame*, p. 67
4 R.C. Latham and W. Matthews, eds., *The Diary of Samuel Pepys* (1975), vol. 1, p. 299
5 Quoted in N.N. Barker, *Brother to the Sun King* (1989), p. 74
6 Ibid, p. 77
7 Ibid, p. 23
8 Pierre la Porte, *Mémoires* (1839), quoted in Wilkinson, *Louis XIV*, pp. 15–16
9 Quoted in Bryan Bevan, *Charles II's Minette* (1979), p. 54
10 Barker, *Brother to the Sun King*, p. 79
11 Bevan, Charles II's *Minette*, p. 57
12 Madame de La Fayette, *Histoire de Madame Henriette d'Angleterre* (1988), p. 57
13 *Letters of Charles II*, p. 121
14 Cartwright, *Madame*, p. 115
15 Barker, *Brother to the Sun King*, pp. 82–3
16 Ibid, p. 90
17 This, the first of Louis XIV's continental wars, was undertaken in respect of his wife's claim to the Spanish Netherlands on the death of her father, Philip IV of Spain. She had renounced all succession rights on her marriage to Louis, but he ignored this.
18 Quoted in Hartmann, *The King my Brother*, p. 198
19 For details of this and other items of Henrietta Maria's extensive inventory see Erin Griffey and Caroline Hibbard, 'Henrietta Maria's inventory at Colombes: courtly magnificence and hidden politics', *Journal of the History of Collections*, vol. 24, no. 2 (2012), pp. 159–81
20 Green, *Letters of Queen Henrietta Maria*, p. 412
21 Bossuet, Jacques-Bénigne, *Oraisons funèbres*, ed. A. Rébelliau (Paris, 1906), p. 73
22 Historical Manuscripts Commission XVI (1), *Report on the Manuscripts of the Duke of Buccleuch*, p. 438. Montagu did not like Henry Jermyn, as is obvious from this waspish comment.
23 Quoted in Hartmann, *The King my Brother*, p. 283
24 Archives du Ministère des Affaires Etrangères, Paris, MD Angleterre, vol. 26, ff. 99–102, quoted in Barker, *Brother to the Sun King*, p. 110
25 For a detailed discussion of the background to these negotiations see

R. Hutton, 'The Making of the Secret Treaty of Dover, 1668–1670', *Historical Journal*, 29, 2 (1986), pp. 297–318
26 Quoted in Barker, *Brother to the Sun King*, p. 113
27 Hartmann, *The King my Brother*, p. 326
28 Jansenism was an austere form of Catholic theology that took root in France during the seventeenth century. Its emphasis was on man's essential depravity and acceptance of the theology of predestination.

Epilogue

1 *Northants Record Office*, Isham correspondence, 1379, quoted in *ODNB* entry for James II by W.A. Speck

Select Bibliography

Manuscript Sources

BODLEIAN LIBRARY
MS Clarendon 95
MS Rawlinson letters 115

BRITISH LIBRARY
Additional MS 19253, 29869, 46375, 70499
Alnwick Castle MS (papers of the earl of Northumberland),
on microfilm
Harleian MS 6988
Sloane MS 3299

CHIDDINGSTONE CASTLE (KENT)
Chiddingstone Papers (letters of Charles II in the 1650s and 1660s)

COLLEGE OF ARMS (LONDON)
Order of service for the funeral of Henry, duke of Gloucester

NATIONAL ARCHIVES
A 03
E 351/303
PRO 31/3/105–110
PRO 31/3/4
PRO 31/3/87
PRO 31/3/89
PRO 31/3/90
PRO 31/3/91
PRO 31/3/94

SP 25/8
SP 84/158
SP 84/159
SP 84/164

WEST SUSSEX RECORD OFFICE (CHICHESTER)
PHA 617

Primary Sources

(Place of publication for all printed works is London, unless otherwise stated)

A Collection of Original Letters and Papers Concerning the Affairs of England . . . 1641 to 1660, by Thomas Carte, 1739

A Collection of the State Papers of John Thurloe, Esq, ed. T. Birch, 7 vols, 1742

A Faithful Memorial of That Remarkable Meeting . . . at Windsor Castle, 1659, by William Allen, Somers Tracts, vol. VI, 1809–16

A Narrative by John Ashburnham, 1830

Archives Ou Correspondance Inédite de la Maison d'Orange Nassau, ed. G. Groen van Prinsterer, 5 vols, Utrecht, 1857–61

Calendar of State Papers Domestic, Charles I, 1640–49, ed. J. Bruce, W. Hamilton and S. C. Lomas, 1858–97

Calendar of State Papers Relating to English affairs in the Archives of Venice, ed. A. B. Hinds, vols 18–32, 1912–31

Calendar of the Cecil Papers in Hatfield House, vol. 22, ed. G. D. Owen, 1971

Charles I in 1646: Letters of King Charles I to Queen Henrietta Maria, ed. J. Bruce, Camden Society, 1846

Constitutional Documents of the Puritan Revolution, ed. S. R. Gardiner, 1906

Edward Hyde, Earl of Clarendon: The history of the Rebellion and Civil Wars in England Begun in the Year 1641, ed. W. D. Macray, 6 vols, 1958

Edward Hyde, Earl of Clarendon, The History of the Rebellion: A New Selection, ed. P. Seaward, Oxford, 2009

Eikon Basilike, ed. P. A. Knachel, 1966

Historical Manuscripts Commission XVI (1), Report on the Manuscripts of the Duke of Buccleuch

Historical Manuscripts Commission Third Report, the Manuscripts of His Grace the Duke of Northumberland at Alnwick Castle, 1872

Sir John Hinton, *Memoires*, 1679

Journal of the House of Commons, vols 2–7, originally published by HMSO, 1802, accessed through British History Online

Journal of the House of Lords, vols 4–10, originally published by His Majesty's Stationery Office, 1767–1830, accessed through British History Online

King Charles, Prince Rupert and the Civil War, ed. C. Petrie, 1974

La Gazette (later *la Gazette de France*), 1642–70, Paris

Letters and Papers Illustrating the Relations Between Charles II and Scotland in 1650, ed. S. R. Gardiner, Edinburgh, 1894

Letters of Queen Henrietta Maria, ed. M.A.E. Green, 1857

Lettres de Henriette-Marie de France, Reine d'Angleterre á Sa Soeur Christine, Duchesse de Savoie, ed. H. Ferrero, Turin, 1881

Lettres du Cardinal Mazarin Pendant son Ministère, ed. M. A. Cheruel, and G. d'Avenel, 9 vols, Paris, 1872–1906

Mémoires de Mademoiselle de Montpensier, 6 vols, Paris, 1746

Memoirs of Edmund Ludlow, 3 vols, Edinburgh, 1751

Memoirs of Prince Rupert and the Cavaliers, ed. E. Warburton, 3 vols, 1859

Memoirs of Sophia Electress of Hanover, 1630–80, transl. H. Forester, 1888

Memoirs of the Last Two Years of the Reign of that Unparallel'd Prince of Ever Blessed Memory, King Charles I, by Sir Thomas Herbert and others, 1702

Memoirs of the Life of Colonel Hutchinson, by Lucy Hutchinson, ed. J. Sutherland, 1973

Memoirs of the Princess Palatine, Princess of Bohemia, ed. M.P.R. Blaze de Bur, 1853

Memorials of the Great Civil War in England, from 1641–1652, ed. H. Cary, 2 vols 1842

Records of the Parliaments of Scotland, ed. MacIntosh, Mann and Tanner, University of St Andrews online database

Scotland and the Commonwealth, ed. C. H. Firth, Edinburgh, 1895

State Papers Collected by Edward Earl of Clarendon, ed. R. Scrope and T. Monkhouse, 1767

The Clarke Papers, ed. F. Henderson, Camden Society, 2005

The Correspondence (c.1626–1659) of Dorothy Percy Sidney, Countess of Leicester, ed. M. G. Brennan, N. J. Kinnamon and M. P. Hannay, Ashgate, Farnham 2010

The Correspondence of Elizabeth Stuart, Queen of Bohemia, ed. N. Akkerman, 2 vols, Oxford, 2011–15

The Court and Times of Charles I, ed. T. Birch, 2 vols, 1849

The Diary of Samuel Pepys, ed. R.C. Latham and W. Matthews, 11 vols, 1970–83

The Diplomatic Correspondence of Jean de Montereul, ed. J. G. Fotheringham, 2 vols, Edinburgh, 1899

The Hamilton Papers, ed. S. R. Gardiner, Camden Society, 1880

The Letters of Elizabeth, Queen of Bohemia, ed. L. M. Baker, 1953

The Letters of King Charles I, ed. C. Petrie, 1935

The Letters of King Charles II, ed. A. Bryant, 1935

The Life of Edward Earl of Clarendon Written by Himself, Oxford, 1857

The Life of James II, King of England, ed. J. S. Clarke, 2 vols, 1816

The Memoirs of Anne, Lady Halkett and Ann, Lady Fanshawe, ed. J. Loftis, 1979

The Memoirs of James II, ed. A. L. Sells, 1962

The Nicholas Papers, Correspondence of Sir Edward Nicholas, ed. G. Warner, 4 vols, Camden Society, 1886–1920

The Sydney Papers, ed. R. W. Blencowe, 1825

Wishart, G., *The Memoirs of James, Marquis of Montrose*, ed. A. Murdoch and H. Simpson, 1893

Writings and Speeches of Oliver Cromwell, ed. W. H. Abbott, 4 vols, Cambridge, USA, 1939

Secondary Works

Adamson, John, *The Noble Revolt*, 2007

Adolph, Anthony, *Full of Soup and Gold: the Life of Henry Jermyn* (2006)

Allan I. Macinnes, *The British Confederate, Archibald Campbell, Marquis of Argyll, 1607–61*, Edinburgh, 2011

Ashley, Maurice, *General Monck*, 1977

Ashton, R., *Counter-Revolution: The Second Civil War and its Origins, 1646–8*, 1994

Atkin, Malcolm, *Cromwell's Crowning Mercy: the Battle of Worcester 1651*, Stroud, 1998

Barker, N. N., *Brother to the Sun King*, Baltimore, 1989

Beckett, J. C., *The Cavalier Duke*, Belfast, 1990

Bertière, Simone, *Mazarin, Le Maître du Jeu*, Paris, 2007

Bevan, Bryan, *Charles II's Minette*, 1979

Blanchard, J.V., *Éminence: Cardinal Richelieu and the rise of France*, New York, 2011

Bouyer, Christian, *Henriette-Anne d'Angleterre*, Paris 2006

Britland, Karen, 'Exile or Homecoming? Henrietta Maria in France, 1644–69,' in *Monarchy and Exile: The Politics of Legitimacy From Marie de Médicis to Wilhelm II*, ed. P. Mansel and T. Riotte, Basingstoke, 2011

Brotton, Jerry, *The Sale of the Late King's Goods*, 2006

Bute, J., *Scottish Coronations*, 1902

Callow, John, *James II*, 2005

———— *The Making of James II*, 2000

Cartwright, Julia M. C. A., *Madame, a Life of Henrietta, Daughter of Charles I and Duchess of Orleans*, New York, 1901

Celtic Dimensions of the British Civil Wars, ed. J. R. Young, Edinburgh, 1997

Chapman, Hester W., *The Tragedy of Charles II*, 1964

———— *Great Villiers*, 1949

Charles de Baillon, *Henriette-Marie de France*, Paris, 1877

Cole, Susan, *A Flower of Purpose: A Memoir of Princess Elizabeth Stuart*, 1975

Cowan, Edward J., *Montrose: For Covenant and King*, Edinburgh, 1995

Crawford, P., 'Charles Stuart, That Man of Blood', *Journal of British Studies*, vol. 16, 1977

Cust, Richard, *Charles I and the Aristocracy*, Cambridge, 2013

———— *Charles I: A political life*, Harlow, 2007

Dobson, Julia, *The Children of Charles I*, 1975

Dow, Frances, *Cromwellian Scotland*, Edinburgh, 1999

Dubost, Jean François, *Marie de Médicis*, Paris, 2005

Fitzgibbons, J., 'Not in any doubtful dispute'?, *Historical Research*, vol. 83, 2010

Fox, J., *The King's Smuggler: Jane Whorwood, Secret Agent to Charles I*, Stroud, 2010

Fraser, A., *Cromwell, Our Chief of Men*, 1997

———— *King Charles II*, 1979

Gardiner, S. R., *History of England From the Accession of James I to the Outbreak of the Civil War*, 1883–4

———— *History of the Great Civil War*, 4 vols, 1901

Gaunt, Peter, *The English Civil War: A Military History*, 2014

Gentles, Ian, *Oliver Cromwell*, 2011

Geyl, Pieter, *Orange and Stuart* (2001)

Green, M. A. E., *Lives of the Princesses of England*, vol. 6, 1857

Greenspan, N., 'Public Scandal, Political Controversy and Familial Conflict in the Stuart Courts in Exile: The Struggle to Convert the Duke of Glouceser in 1654', *Albion*, 2003

Griffey, E., and C. Hibbard, 'Henrietta Maria's Inventory at Colombes: Courtly Magnificence and Hidden Politics, *Journal of the History of Collections*, vol. 24, 2012

Guizot, M., *History of Oliver Cromwell and the English Commonwealth*, transl. A. R. Scobel, 2 vols, 1854

Harris, Tim, *Rebellion: Britain's First Stuart Kings*, Oxford, 2014

Hartmann, Cyril. H., *The King My Brother*, 1954

Hibbard, Caroline, 'Translating Royalty: Henrietta Maria and the Transition From Princess to Queen', *The Court Historian*, vol. 5, 1, 2000

────── *Charles I and the Popish Plot*, Chapel Hill, 1983

Holmes, C., 'The Trial and Execution of Charles I', *The Historical Journal*, 53, 2010

Holmes, Clive, *Why was Charles I Executed?*, 2007

Hopper, Andrew, '*Black Tom': Sir Thomas Fairfax and the English Revolution*, Manchester, 2007

Hoskins, S. E., *Charles II in the Channel Islands*, 2 vols, 1854

Hughes, A., and J. Sanders, 'Gender, Exile and The Hague Courts of Elizabeth, Queen of Bohemia and Mary, Princess of Orange in the 1650s', in P. Mantel and T. Riotte, eds., *Monarchy and Exile*, Basingstoke, 2011

Hutton, Ronald, *Charles II*, Oxford, 1989

────── 'The Making of the Secret Treaty of Dover, 1668–1670', *Historical Journal* 29, 1986

────── *The Restoration*, Oxford, 1985

Israel, J. I., *The Dutch Republic, its Rise, Greatness and Fall, 1477–1806*, Oxford, 1995

Jones, Jack D., *The Royal Prisoner*, 1978

Keay, A., 'The shadow of a king? Aspects of the exile of King Charles II', in *Monarchy and Exile*

Kelsey, S., 'The trial of Charles I', *The English Historical Review*, June 2003

Kleinman, Ruth, *Anne of Austria, Queen of France*, Columbus, 1985

Lafayette, Madame de, *Histoire de Madame, Henriette d'Angleterre, 1988*

Lockyer, R., *Buckingham: The Life and Political Career of George Villiers, First Duke of Buckingham, 1592–1628*, 1981

Manley, T., *A Short View of the Lives of Those Illustrious Princes Henry, Duke of Gloucester and Mary, Princess of Orange*, 1661

Marshall, Rosalind K., *Henrietta Maria: The Intrepid Queen*, 1990

McDonald, F. M. S., 'The Timing of General Monck's March into England, January 1660', *English Historical Review*, April 1990

Miller, John, *James II*, 2000

Morrah, Patrick, *A Royal Family*, 1982

Ollard, Richard, *The Escape of Charles II After the Battle of Worcester*, 1986

Oman, Carola, *Elizabeth of Bohemia*, 1964

────── *Henrietta Maria*, 1936

Petitfils, Jean-Christian, *Louis XIV*, Paris, 2008

Pitts, V. J., *La Grande Mademoiselle at the Court of France, 1627–1693*, 2000

Prak, M., *The Dutch Republic in the Seventeenth Century*, Cambridge, 2005

Reece, Henry, *The Army in Cromwellian England*, Oxford, 2013

Revolution and Restoration: England in the 1650s, ed. J. Morrill, 1992

Rowen, R. H., *The Princes of Orange*, Cambridge, 1988

Royalist Refugees, William and Margaret Cavendish in the Rubens House, 1648–1660, ed. B. van Beneden and N. de Poorter, Antwerp, 2006

Royalists and Royalism During the English Civil Wars, ed. J. McElligott and D. L. Smith, Cambridge, 2007

Scott, C. L., A. Turton, E. Gruber von Arne, *Edgehill: The Battle Reinterpreted*, Barnsley, 2005

Scott, David, *Politics and War in the Three Stuart Kingdoms, 1637–49*, 2004

Scott, Eva, *The Travels of the King*, 1907

——*The King in Exile: the Wanderings of Charles II*, 1904

Sharpe, Kevin, *Image Wars: Promoting Kings and Commonwealths in England, 1603–1660*, 2010

Shrewsbury, J. F. D., *A History of Bubonic Plague*, 2005

Smith, David L., 'The More Posed and Wise Advice: The Fourth Earl of Dorset and the English Civil Wars, *The Historical Journal* 34, 4, 1991

Smith, G., *The Cavaliers in Exile*, 2003

Stevenson, David, *Revolution and Counter Revolution in Scotland, 1644–51*, Edinburgh, 2003

The Scottish Revolution, 1637–44, Newton Abbott, 1973

Teague, F., *Bathsua Makin, Woman of Learning*

Terry, C. S., 'The Visits of Charles I to Newcastle in 1633, 39, 41 and 46–7', Society of Antiquaries of Newcastle-upon-Tyne, *Archaeologia Aeliana*, NS, vol. 21, 1899

The English Civil War, ed. J. Adamson, 2009

The Library of the Sidneys of Penshurst Place c.1665, ed. G. Warkentin, J. L. Black and W. R. Bowen, Toronto, 2013

The Oxford Handbook of the English Revolution, ed. M. Braddick, 2015

The Politics of Female Households: Ladies-in-waiting Across Early Modern Europe, ed. N. Akkerman and B. Houben, Leiden, 2014

The Regicides and the Execution of Charles I, ed. J. Peacey, Basingstoke, 2001

The Seventeenth Century, ed. J. Wormald, Oxford, 2008

The Stuart Court and Europe, ed. R. M. Smuts, Cambridge, 1996

The Stuart Courts, ed. E. Cruickshanks, Stroud, 2000

Treasure, Geoffrey, *Mazarin, The Crisis of Absolutism in France*, 1995

Van Zuylen Van Nyevelt, Suzette, *Court Life in the Dutch Republic*, 1906

Veevers, Erica, *Images of Love and Religion: Queen Henrietta Maria and Court Entertainments*, Cambridge, 1989

Weiser, B., 'Owning the King's Story: The escape from Worcester', *The Seventeenth Century*, XIV, no. 1, 1999

Whitaker, Katie, *A Royal Passion: The Turbulent Marriage of Charles I and Henrietta Maria*, 2010

White, Michelle Anne, *Henrietta Maria and the English Civil Wars*, Aldershot, 2006
Wilkinson, Richard, *Louis XIV*, 2007
Williams, Mark F. R., *The King's Irishmen*, 2014
Woolrych, Austin, *Britain in Revolution*, Oxford, 2002
Worden, Blair, *The English Civil Wars*, 2009

Picture Acknowledgements

5. Princess Elizabeth Stuart (1635–50) by Wenceslaus Hollar © Mary
   Evans Picture Library.
   Princess Anne of England (1637–40) by Anonymous © Hulton
   Archive / Getty Images.
   Henry, Duke of Gloucester by Adriaen Hanneman (c.1604–71) [Public
   domain], via Wikimedia Commons.
6. Charles I (1600–49) and James, Duke of York (1633–1701), c.1647 by
   Peter Lely © Syon House, Middlesex, UK / Bridgeman Images.
   'Minette', 5th Daughter of Charles I by Charles Beaubrun, Private
   Collection / © Julian Simon Fine Art Ltd / Bridgeman Images.
   William II, Prince of Orange, and his Bride, Mary Stuart, 1641 by
   Anthony van Dyck © Rijksmuseum, Amsterdam, The Netherlands /
   Bridgeman Images.
7. Portrait of Algernon Percy, 10th Earl of Northumberland (1602–68) by
   Anthony van Dyck [Public domain], via Wikimedia Commons.
   Thomas, 3rd Lord Fairfax by Robert Walker © Trustees of Leeds Castle
   Foundation, Maidstone, Kent, UK / Bridgeman Images.
   Penshurst Place © G. Porter.
8. James Graham, 1st Marquess of Montrose, 1612–50, attributed to
   Willem van Honthorst [Public domain], via Wikimedia Commons.
   Portrait of Oliver Cromwell, 1649 by Robert Walker © Leeds Museums
   and Galleries (Leeds Art Gallery) UK / Bridgeman Images.

SECTION TWO

Page
1. Portrait of King Charles II, 1650s by Adriaen Hanneman (1601–71),
   Private Collection / Photo © Philip Mould Ltd, London /
   Bridgeman Images.
   Prince Rupert, c.1666–71 by Peter Lely © Yale Center for British Art,
   Paul Mellon Collection, USA / Bridgeman Images.
   Miniature of James II as the Duke of York, 1661 by Samuel Cooper ©
   Victoria & Albert Museum, London, UK / Bridgeman Images.
2. Princess Henrietta Anne ('Minette') Stuart, Duchess of Orléans by Jan
   de Baen, © Hatchlands Park, Surrey, UK / National Trust
   Photographic Library / Bridgeman Images.
   Perspective view of Royal castle and gardens of Saint Cloud near Paris
   in 1700 by Etienne Allegrain © De Agostini Picture Library / G.
   Dagli Orti / Bridgeman Images.
3. Philippe of France, Duke of Orléans by Pierre Mignard [Public
   domain], via Wikimedia Commons.

Index